THE GREAT MUSEUM
OF THE SEA

THE GREAT MUSEUM OF THE SEA

A HUMAN HISTORY OF SHIPWRECKS

JAMES P. DELGADO

OXFORD
UNIVERSITY PRESS

Oxford University Press is a department of the University of Oxford.
It furthers the University's objective of excellence in research, scholarship,
and education by publishing worldwide. Oxford is a registered trade mark of
Oxford University Press in the UK and in certain other countries.

Published in the United States of America by Oxford University Press
198 Madison Avenue, New York, NY 10016, United States of America.

© Oxford University Press 2025

All rights reserved. No part of this publication may be reproduced, stored in a retrieval system, transmitted, used for text and data mining, or used for training artificial intelligence, in any form or by any means, without the prior permission in writing of Oxford University Press, or as expressly permitted by law, by license or under terms agreed with the appropriate reprographics rights organization. Inquiries concerning reproduction outside the scope of the above should be sent to the Rights Department, Oxford University Press, at the address above.

You must not circulate this work in any other form
and you must impose this same condition on any acquirer.

CIP data is on file at the Library of Congress.

ISBN 9780197780756

DOI: 10.1093/oso/9780197780756.001.0001

Printed by Integrated Books International, United States of America

The manufacturer's authorized representative in the EU for product safety is
Oxford University Press España S.A., Parque Empresarial San Fernando de Henares,
Avenida de Castilla, 2 – 28830 Madrid (www.oup.es/en).

The manufacturer's authorised representative in the EU for product safety is Oxford University Press España S.A. of El Parque Empresarial San Fernando de Henares, Avenida de Castilla, 2 – 28830 Madrid (www.oup.es/en or product.safety@oup.com). OUP España S.A. also acts as importer into Spain of products made by the manufacturer.

This is for Robert "Bob" McNulty and Thomas N. Layton.

Contents

Preface ix
Acknowledgments xix

1. Shipwrecks 1
2. Shipwrecks as Muses 33
3. Shipwrecks as Historical Sites, Graves, and Memorials 61
4. In the Solitude of the Sea 96
5. The Bounty of the Sea 125
6. Shipwreck Salvage 142
7. Shipwreck Archaeology 174
8. Why Do We Care About Shipwrecks? 215
   Conclusion: Shipwrecks in the 21st Century 239

Notes 263
References and Further Reading 269
Index 291

Preface

The scene resonates with emotion. On the deck, a mass of people fight to get to the last lifeboats. Water pours in below decks. The bow dips and the sea washes over it. Boats pull away as screams echo in the night. As the stern rises, the crew struggle to launch one last boat. Furniture slides across decks, people fall, and others gather at the stern as it rises higher into the night sky. A steward comforts a small child, as people slide down the decks or leap off the stern, now high above the sea. *Titanic* glides down, and people continually splash into the cold ocean's waters. The stern disappears, and mist and steam hover over the surface of the water. The end of *Titanic*, as portrayed in both the 1958 film *A Night to Remember* and the 1997 *Titanic*, is perhaps the best-known modern depiction of a shipwreck event.

The hulk of *Titanic*, lying deep in the ocean darkness, is probably the best-known image of a shipwreck at the bottom of the sea. After decades of sea hunting and shipwreck diving, *Titanic* is the one ship everyone asks me about. But there's far more to the subject of shipwrecks than that one wreck. Shipwrecks have different meanings to different people. Those meanings change with the times or the passing of generations. Other meanings seem timeless as they span centuries and even millennia. One thing that does not change is the ongoing debate as to why "we" as people should care or do care about a specific wreck. That's why I wrote this book.

I have been fortunate to have a career that has allowed me to study shipwrecks. My lifelong education began in the 1970s and now extends into the 2020s. I've studied them as cultural phenomena, as historical events, and as the focus of art, music, and literature. I've studied them as physical entities. They are sites that have attracted my attention as an archaeologist, historian, museum director, documentary television host, and government official, but mainly as a human being. Whenever asked what I consider to be important about shipwrecks, the first thing that comes to mind is to explain just what a shipwreck is. What follows is an explanation of how, and thoughts about why we care, as well as a plea to care about shipwrecks. I have studied "wrecks" in the deepest parts of the ocean, in lakes, rivers, bays, sounds, fjords, and bayous, in the shallow ocean, laid out and exposed on sandy beaches and mudflats, and buried beneath urban landfill. Each has a story to tell, and many of the stories I've been privileged to share can only be told through archaeology. But not every wreck could or should be seen as an archaeological site.

To me, though, archaeology is where a shipwreck becomes even more interesting. Archaeology examines who we are as people through that which we leave behind as a physical record of our activities. Archaeology when focused on the maritime world has shown that ships are complex structures, even when they seem "simple" in their construction. "Simple" is the not the word to use. For cultures that did not build massive cities, pyramids, or grand canals, it was their watercraft that represent the apex of their technological advancement. The most successful human seafaring craft ever built is the Polynesian voyaging canoe. That's not overstating the point. Thanks to that type of watercraft, humans learned to adapt to a planet more than 70 percent covered by water and to colonize the Pacific. They used the stars and an understanding of ocean currents to navigate tens of thousands of years ago.

Ships were the means by which humans traded, exchanging goods, ideas, and DNA. Ships enabled the development of a global economy. The rise of European sea power forged a world-spanning economic system through maritime trade. In the 21st century, 90 percent of the world's goods still move by water. The common thread linking humanity across the span of time, language, religion, society, and culture is our relationship with "the water." As a means of transportation, for trade, for waging war, for gathering sustenance from the sea, through successive generations, people knew ships. And so, they also knew of shipwrecks. When ships sank, they carried with them more than the technical details of their construction. They were floating communities, writ large and small. They were filled with the goods and products of each port of call. They carried the personal effects of those who were on board, whether as crew or as passengers. And when they sank, they carried crew and passengers down with them.

For archaeologists, ships are smaller opportunities to study individuals and societies, just as we study neighborhoods, cities, regions, nations, and empires. Shipwrecks as physical entities also attract the attention of divers, salvagers, historians, and governments. Wrecks also attract the interest of many who want to learn more, in our times by clicking on a news story, watching a documentary, or listening to a podcast. Wrecks hold different and at times conflicting meanings. They are the subject of many questions. How and why do ships wreck? What can we correct or take action on to avoid future shipwrecks? What survives after a ship is lost? How many shipwrecks have there been in human history? What survives after decades, centuries, or millennia? What technologies are used to find, study, and recover the remains of lost ships? What are the values of various shipwrecks?

Each shipwreck has a story to tell. In their own time, even if now lost to modern memory, shipwrecks were cultural phenomena, historical events, and the focus of art, music, and literature. It started well before Shakespeare, but Ariel's Song in *The Tempest* remains one of the most quoted shipwreck references in Western culture:

> Full Fathom Five thy father lies;
> of his bones are coral made;
> Those are pearls that were his eyes:
> Nothing of him that doth fade,
> But doth suffer a sea-change,
> Into something rich and strange:
> Sea-nymphs hourly ring his knell.

So, what follows in this book is not just about shipwrecks as archaeological sites. This book is about what I have learned in five decades of interacting with shipwrecks, in various capacities, and all things associated with them.

As a historian, I've read about them, studied records in archives, stared long hours at imagery, some of it haunting. I will never forget the experience of assessing the morgue photographs of *Titanic*'s recovered dead, or the personal effects found on some of those bodies that were never claimed by families or friends, which now reside in the archives and collections of the Maritime Museum of the Atlantic. Through personal accounts from those who were there, including one-on-one interviews, especially with Pearl Harbor survivors from both sides of that attack, I have vicariously been "there." Whether it was a ship pounded on rocks or sand, as decks were washed by waves that swept people away, or as flames roared up from below, or as a collision in the dark sent water rushing in, I remember those tales. I've interviewed men who felt their ship shudder as shells or torpedoes tore into steel hulls, as bombs fell and bullets plowed through decks and men, and as mighty vessels exploded into fireballs. These forces have a direct and indirect impact on human lives that can transcend generations.

As an archaeologist, the span of time the wrecks I've been privileged to explore, document, and study ranges from antiquity to the dawn of the nuclear age and the Cold War. Those explorations includes scuba, diving in submersibles, and with "dives" beyond human reach with robotic, remotely operated vehicles (ROVs). The lost ships that first sparked my passion were vessels that sailed to California in 1849, in response to the discovery of gold, and were then buried in the mud and sand that shrouds the former harbor of San Francisco, or in the mud of the Sacramento River. Since then, most of my work has been focused on the 19th century, when the modern world we live in now began to emerge as a global, technological, contentious society. That has included the wrecks of early to late 19th-century immigrant ships, cargo carriers, fishing craft, whaling ships, coastal schooners, and wooden-hulled and iron-built steamers that were lost to fire, fog, storms, collisions with rocks, reefs, and other vessels, or were crushed in Arctic ice.

That work has included studying unknown and unidentified fragments as if we were doing "Shipwreck Crime Scene Investigation." It's also been studying complete hulks and broken wrecks of ships of wood, iron, and steel, either on beaches, in shallow waters, or in the depths. They include vessels lost in less than glamorous but important trades such as lumber schooners, the tea clipper *Ambassador*, the copper ore carrier *Vicar of Bray*, the lead ingot carrier *Frances*, a four-masted cargo schooner, *La Merced*, and another four-master that is likely the lumber schooner *Else*. It has included early steamships, from the massive wooden sidewheeler *Great Republic* to early iron paddle wheelers like the 1840s *Robert J. Walker*, late 19th-century propeller driven craft, and *Titanic* and *Carpathia*, the ship that rescued the survivors of that disaster.

I have been on expeditions to ships lost or abandoned during the Klondike Gold Rush at the end of the 19th century, including the lake steamer *A.J. Goddard*, and mid-19th century submarines built of iron. One was a craft lost to history, and one of my favorites, Julius Kroehl's amazing *Sub Marine Explorer*, which rusts away on an isolated beach in Panama. Another is the Peruvian wooden steamship *Apurímac* off Callao, a warship known only to Peruvian naval cadets and historians. Another fascinating and frightening wreck, discovered by Estonian colleagues, is the 19th-century Russian monitor *Russalka*, which rests in the darkness of the Baltic with most of its crew still inside. I will always remember that long, cold descent into darkness and seeing the massive hull emerge as we neared the seabed.

Wrecks from the U.S. Civil War that I have been able to study include the ironclad USS *Monitor*, the blockading steamer USS *Hatteras*, sunk off Galveston, Texas, and the transport USS *Oriental* off Cape Hatteras. I led the excavation of the blockade runner *Mary Celestia* lying off the reef it hit in Bermuda. I also was part of the team who identified the cursed naval training brig *Somers*, which sank in 1846 off Veracruz, Mexico. I have investigated ships of Arctic exploration, notably Roald Amundsen's polar ship *Maud* and the steam yacht *Fox*, which famously searched for the lost Franklin expedition in the Arctic. I've sailed the South Atlantic and walked on beaches strewn with the abandoned hulks of whalers that once hunted in those sub-Antarctic seas.

My adventures with shipwrecks include expeditions into the mountains and in inland forests far from any large body of water, to examine late 19th- and early 20th-century floating gold dredges. Other projects include studying 19th- and 20th-century ship graveyards of the Falkland Islands. Closer to home, I've led the survey of a forgotten ship's graveyard on the Mobile River in Alabama. There, we identified one of those wrecks as *Clotilda*, the last known slave ship to arrive in the United States. At the tip of South America, we explored the wrecks of the Straits of Magellan. The focus of that project was HMS *Doterel*, a British warship that exploded with a tragic loss of life. The cause of that explosion? Not an enemy shell, but a leaking jar of highly volatile chemicals used to dry the paint in notoriously humid early metal-hulled warships and a dropped lantern that set it off. At the time of its loss, the explosion was blamed on terrorism. It was simply an accident.

Lost warships of the late 19th century that I've been fortunate to dive and study include the Spanish-American War–era USS *Baltimore*, scuttled after partial scrapping in 1944, and now resting over a thousand feet deep off Pearl Harbor. I dived the Spanish fleet lost in Cuba in the Battle of Santiago during the Spanish-American War. These hulks, some shallow, others deep, are rarely dived in a country where diving is illegal. The cruisers *Vizcaya*, *Oquendo*, and *Cristobal Colon*, sent to Cuba to confront and lose to superior American gun-power, died heroically and in vain with many of their crews. We swam out from the beach to the large guns that stuck above the surface that mark their graves. The coal carrier USS *Merrimac* lies exactly where it was scuttled at the narrow mouth of Santiago harbor in a failed attempt to block that Spanish fleet from fleeing. It sits in the main shipping channel, and as we dived, large freighters passed over us unseen as we felt the pull of their propellers and heard their rumbles as they spun slowly in the dark silty water 30 feet above us.

The 20th-century sunken warships I've been able to explore and study include the World War I British battleships HMS *Triumph* and HMS *Goliath*, lost off the shores of Gallipoli. The wrecks took on an even more emotional meaning to me as I toured battlefields ashore that are now plowed fields. In the furrows are fragments of human bones and spent bullets. If the ships had been able to force the fortified straits at Gallipoli, those lives would not have been lost, nor lost in vain. I have dived and studied World War I submarines and the German raider *Cormoran*, in Guam, as well as the German cruiser *Dresden*, which lies deep off Robinson Crusoe Island far from the coast of Chile. It was sunk in one of the most controversial naval engagements of World War I, when British ships opened fire to sink it in violation of the laws of war. As we climbed the cliffs that ring the bay below where *Dresden* lies, the pock marks of shell hits and unexploded shells embedded in the soft stone tell a forensic story, along with the sunken wreckage of *Dresden*, torn open by the shells from British ships that entered the bay to shoot at *Dresden* point blank.

The lost warships of World War II—some of them dived and studied by my colleagues and me while survivors were alive to share their stories and feelings, made them among the most profound dives of my career. They include USS *Arizona*, USS *Utah*, and the Japanese midget submarines sunk in the Pearl Harbor attack. The extremely deep wrecks of the carriers *Akagi*, *Kaga*, and USS *Yorktown* from the Battle of Midway are another project that was both a technological challenge and an emotional experience. No less haunting were dives on the wrecks of D-Day in Normandy, or Battle of the Atlantic wrecks in Canadian and American waters. Those wrecks include the tragically lost HMCS *Clayaquot*, the submarine U-215, and the torpedoed Liberty Ship *Alexander Macomb*. In the Pacific, robotic dives on the torpedoed merchant ship *Coast Trader* off the coast of British Columbia recalled a little known (except to historians) reminder of Japanese submarine warfare off the U.S. and Canadian west coasts.

Dives off Hawaii in submersibles allowed me to join the teams exploring and documenting the Japanese World War II submarine aircraft carriers I-400 and I-401, and the humble but hard-worked cable and net-layer USS *Kailua*. A more recent find in 2024 was the former USS *Stewart*, the only seagoing U.S. warship captured by the Japanese Navy and used as a warship by its captors during World War II. *Stewart*, badly damaged and scuttled in the early months of the war in the Pacific, became a patrol boat hunting American submarines. Captured at the end of the war, it was recommissioned by the U.S. Navy. Towed home to the United States, it was scuttled with gunfire off the California coast and buried at sea. A high-tech AUV (autonomous underwater vehicle) found it 3,500 feet deep, upright and buried in mud to its former waterline. With friends and partners, we were able to dive and document it.

The wrecks of the Cold War I've been able to explore, document, and share in books and on television include the sunken test fleet at Bikini Atoll, notably the carrier *Saratoga*, the battleships *Nagato* and *Arkansas*, the destroyer USS *Anderson*, the attack transports *Gilliam* and *Carlisle*, and the submarines *Pilotfish* and *Apogon*. We also dived and documented the landing craft that lie scattered in and around the subsea crater from that 1946 atomic blast. I have been part of missions to explore the ships that "survived" Bikini only to be sunk or be scuttled as contaminated vessels after the tests—the German cruiser *Prinz Eugen* at Kwajalein, the battleship *Nevada*, sunk miles deep off Hawaii, and the carrier *Independence*, scuttled off the central California coast.

One consequential find was the bow of HMS *Volage*, the first naval casualty of the Cold War, which lies in the Corfu Strait off Albania. That mission also provided an opportunity to make a risky investigation of a Soviet submarine base buried in an Albanian coastal mountain. Those dives were all the more amazing as diving under Albania's Communist dictatorship had been illegal. Post-dictatorship, dives like the ones I was fortunate to participate in revealed wrecks un-impacted by any diving or collecting. A Roman wreck of the third century AD, for example, was still loaded with amphorae and dishes. I've also been privileged to rediscover and document wrecks of World War II submarines that lasted into the Cold War. Both *Bugara* and the Brazilian *Humaitá* (formerly USS *Muskallunge*) lie deep, and were remembered only by their former crews and historians until rediscovered; it was again a privilege to be one of the first to see these lost subs, decades after they sank. Sorry for the list, but it's these wrecks and so many more that define a career spent touring the great museum of the sea. Those experiences, those stories, and the people met on the five-decade journey, alive and dead, compel me to write this book.

I've been fortunate to be part of teams that created museum exhibits to share that maritime past with the public, as well as sharing wrecks and their stories with hundreds of millions of television viewers through the National Geographic Series *The Sea Hunters* and *Drain the Oceans*. I've written other books for fellow scholars, the public, and children. It is always a pleasure to hear back from the many who have shared their personal connection to ships, shipwrecks, and our maritime past. It's also special when the young—and by that, grade schoolers—reach out with their parents to talk about wrecks and history.

Not yet ready or willing to retire, but with five decades behind and with the full expectation of more adventures and opportunities to learn, nonetheless I felt it was time to merge all of these experiences, approaches, and global travel into a book. It's subjective, but I've worked hard to be comprehensive, inclusive, and above all else, as passionate about the subject as when my curiosity and desire to learn about the world we live in and its past took hold of me as a young student. Why should we care? What is important to know? What can shipwrecks tell us? What do wrecks tell us about ourselves? This book summarizes a lifetime of varying experiences with diverse, famous, unknown, and yet all of them powerful sites, and to explain how and why society interacts with shipwrecks.

JAMES P. DELGADO

Washington, D.C.
November 2024

Acknowledgments

I am grateful for the many colleagues with whom I have had the privilege and pleasure to interact over the past five decades as we have worked on projects, discussed, debated, and worked to share the story of shipwrecks. I also am forever in the debt of family members, descendants, veterans, and all who have been powerful witnesses to the human stories that come with shipwrecks, be they from the wrecking event, the rediscovery of a lost vessel, or the generational traumas that result from such a loss.

I want to thank those whose have significantly influenced my thinking on the subject:

Robert D. Ballard, Daniel J. Basta, Michael L. Brennan, Pete Capelotti, Vince Capone, Art Cohn, David L. Conlin, Annalise Corbin, Clive Cussler, John B. Davis, Ben Ford, John William Foster, Jay Haigler, Daniel J. Lenihan, Colin Martin, Mack McCarthy, Innes McCartney, Michael McCaughan, Robert McNulty, Larry Murphy, Steve Nagiewicz, Larry Nordby, Kamau Sadiki, Crispin Sadler, William N. Still, Jr., Thomas N. Layton, Ole Varmer, and Gordon P. Watts.

I am thankful to Michael Brennan, Ann Goodhart, and Ole Varmer for reading earlier versions of the manuscript.

I very much appreciate the steady hand and helpful guidance of my editor, Stefan Vranka, and the exceptional team at Oxford University Press.

Any errors and omissions are my responsibility.

I

Shipwrecks

When I reached the cabin, the scene that presented itself to my view, can never be erased from my memory. Mothers screaming, and children clinging to them in terror and in dread; the furniture… all upturned; the ship was lying on her beam ends; the starboard side of her opening, and the waves were washing in and out of the cabin, when we were informed that a rope had been conveyed to the reef by a sailor, who had fastened one end of it to a rock.…I considered to remain on the ship was sure death, and I might save my life by trying to reach the reef by means of the rope.

—B. F. Pond, *Narrative of the Wreck of the Barque "Julia Ann" in the South Pacific Ocean*, 1858

The American barque *Julia Ann*, bound from Sydney, Australia, to San Francisco with 56 immigrants and a cargo of coal, went ashore on a reef in the Society Islands in the South Pacific on October 4, 1855. *Julia Ann* perfectly speaks to what the word "shipwreck" represents. The ship hit a reef, where the power of the sea tore it apart. In 1995, Australian, Tahitian, and American maritime archaeologists rediscovered the remains of *Julia Ann* on that same reef, and conducted a detailed archaeological study of those remains. While the wooden form of *Julia Ann* was no longer present as an intact vessel, the wrecking event and the passage of a century and a half had left scattered bronze fasteners used to build the ship, some of the copper that protected the bottom of the hull from wood-eating marine organisms, an iron anchor, and other artifacts scattered in the shallows of the reef. The archaeologists mapped the site and recovered artifacts that were preserved, studied, and displayed at the Australian National Maritime Museum in Sydney. Both the loss of *Julia Ann* and *Julia Ann* as a ship that wrecked and was then transformed into an underwater site encompass and embody the term "shipwreck."

What's in a Name?

The case of *Julia Ann* underscores that, as a word, "shipwreck" is a noun and a verb, and so there actually isn't anything simple about the word or the concept. Merriam-Webster defines it as "a wrecked ship or its parts," "the destruction or loss of a ship," or more widely, an "irretrievable loss or failure." As a verb, it is a process; "to destroy (a ship) by grounding or foundering," to cause "to experience shipwreck," or simply stated, "to ruin." Dictionary definitions aside, "shipwreck" is a powerful word that speaks to one of the most prevalent themes in human history: namely, our often-perilous relationship to the waters of the world. Shipwrecks as events are probably humanity's most common form of disaster. As such, shipwrecks—aside from epidemics, warfare on land, or great natural disasters—have been the cause of the greatest number of human deaths throughout history. Thanks to ships and other watercraft, humanity did not just walk across the globe from its ancestral home in Africa. We made use of the ocean as a source of food and as a means of travel on our global journey.

Humanity's relationship with the water has also been shaped by the reality that for as much as is taken from the sea, something is lost. Those losses are ships, the goods on them, and people. Shipwrecks as events therefore have inspired one of the oldest genres of human reflection on the nature of life. "Shipwreck" and ships' wrecks have been and remain a muse for religious thought, literature, music, and art. In that context, and for this book, a shipwreck is examined as an event that has had an impact on people—individually, as a group or family, and as a society.[1] The nature of a shipwreck as an entity is that of a lost or abandoned structure, whether it rests intact or in pieces. It is at this point that a shipwreck becomes scientifically as well as socially interesting. Ships were—and to an extent still are—complex structures that for some cultures represent the apex of their technological ability. It follows, therefore, that when ships sank, they carried with them more than the technical details of their construction. They were floating communities. They were filled with the goods and products of each port of call. They carried the personal effects of those who were on board, whether as crew or as passengers.

Ships provide opportunities for archaeologists to study individuals and societies, just as they study neighborhoods, cities, regions, nations, and empires. Archaeologists and other scientists and professionals study shipwrecks as detectives study a crime scene. What caused a wreck, especially when the cause of a loss was not obvious, leads to efforts to learn more. From accident investigations, one of the most famous being the U.S. and British governments' inquiries into the sinking of *Titanic*, to courtroom cases, finding cause has been key to resolving insurance cases, as well as passing new regulations and laws. It has also been key in determining fatal flaws in a ship's construction, fitting out, or operation. From these investigations came remedies through legislation, regulation, or practice. One key area where these remedies are still in use includes the introduction of scientifically determined practical limits to which a ship could be loaded.

As new technologies came into use on the water, many were unregulated. The introduction of steam power and the rise of steamboats on rivers and lakes soon gave rise to ocean steamships. Governments were wary of regulations, fearing that restrictions would stifle innovation and investment. A spate of early accidents, including boiler explosions that engulfed passengers in scalding steam and literally cooked people alive, led to the first "Steamboat Act" in the United States in 1838—requiring licenses and inspections—but that law proved inadequate. Charles Dickens famously noted, in 1842, after touring the United States and taking a steamboat from Pittsburgh to Cincinnati, that "western steamboats usually blow up one or two a week in the season." It was a fair observation. The Commissioner of Patents noted in an 1848 report to Congress that between 1816 and 1848, 233 steamboats had suffered explosions, more than half of them from the boiler bursting or the flue collapsing. These incidents killed a reported 1,805 people, and caused nearly a million dollars in damages, or nearly four billion dollars in today's currency.

Compounding public outrage was the fact that in a number of cases, rival steamboats and captains had pushed their craft too far in races that Mark Twain later reminisced on, in *Life on the Mississippi*, as a "sport that makes a body's very liver curl with enjoyment" with "two red-hot steamboats raging along, neck-and-neck, straining every nerve—that is to say, every rivet in the boilers—quaking and shaking and groaning from stem to stern, spouting white steam from the pipes, pouring black smoke from the chimneys, raining down sparks, parting the river into long breaks of hissing foam."[2] The loss of lives, steamboats, and a massive amount of money notwithstanding, it still took Congress four years to pass a new act in 1852. Nonetheless, disasters still happened, as the 1852 law omitted regulations for working craft such as tugs, towboats, and ferryboats.

More disasters followed, including three steamers that I know well, having worked on the wreck of one and extensively researched the others. In a two-month span, in the first four months of 1853, all four wrecked, and were events noted in a then popular lithograph as "Disasters of 60 Days." The steamship *Independence* caught fire and burned off the coast of Baja California, killing 150 passengers; the steamship *Tennessee* went ashore and was a total loss north of San Francisco's Golden Gate, as was the steamship *Samuel S. Lewis*, north of the Golden Gate and wedged into the rocks of Duxbury Reef; and the steamboat *Jenny Lind*'s flue collapsed on San Francisco Bay, scalding 50 people to death. A contemporary account in the national news spared no details; "all were killed instantly or have since died. Many of them had their clothes torn from them and the skin entirely burned off their faces and bodies. The sight presented was horrible beyond description, not simply the scalded, but all were more or less mangled by the fragments of the boiler and bulk head, and streams of blood flowed from the mutilated bodies."

There was no change to the laws, even after the worst maritime disaster in U.S. history, when the overloaded steamboat *Sultana* exploded and burned on the Mississippi River in April 1865, killing as many people

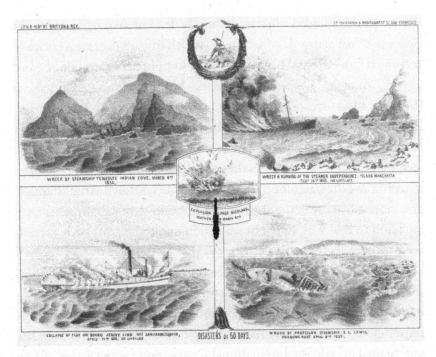

Image 1.1. "Disasters of 60 Days," published by lithographers Britton & Rey of San Francisco, depicts the loss of four steamers to fire, explosion, and running aground on the Pacific Coast that spanned the brief period of February–April 1853. Library of Congress, LC-DIG-ppsca-32191.

as lived in a small town. The Customs Service reported more than 1,500 dead, and the total count remains unknown. It was not until 1871 that a new, tighter law was passed when Congress created the Steamboat Inspection Service, which in time became part of the Department of Commerce. The Steamboat Inspection Service was renamed the Bureau of Marine Inspection and Navigation in 1936. That Bureau was shifted to the U.S. Coast Guard's control during World War II, a change made permanent in 1946. The 1871 law remains the active statute.

The overloading of merchant ships, as well as the practice of sending worn-out, damaged, and overworked ships on "just one more voyage," was a common cause of shipwrecks. Advocates for seamen's rights coined the phrase "death ships" and "coffin ships" to highlight the practice. *The Death Ship*, a novel first published in Germany in 1926 as *Das Totenschiff* and subsequently in English in 1934, helped popularize the phrase, an attribution likely aided when its author, B. Traven, went on to write *The Treasure of the Sierra Madre* in 1927, which in 1948 became a critically acclaimed film by John Huston, starring Humphrey Bogart. Long before Traven, though, a British politician, Samuel Plimsoll, elected to Parliament in 1867, sought to end the practice. His book *Our Seamen: An Appeal*, published in 1873, reached a wide audience, but efforts to pass legislation faltered. The "Unseaworthy Ships Bill," introduced in 1876 by Plimsoll, led to the marking of ships with a line that needed to remain above the waterline of a ship once loaded. Known as the "Plimsoll line," it is still in use in the 21st century, but now with various other lines on a hull to deal with different sea conditions and factors such as fresh versus saltwater, salt being more buoyant.

After the loss of *Titanic* in 1912, hearings in both the United Kingdom and the United States resulted in the first international agreement setting standards for the construction, equipping, and operation of merchant ships following an international meeting held in London in November 1913. Signed in 1914, the International Convention for the Safety of Life at Sea (SOLAS) came in response to *Titanic*'s not having adequate watertight bulkheads, lifeboats, or 24-hour radio watches. Another key result of the loss of *Titanic* was the creation of the International Ice Patrol in 1914. There was also the matter—with a strong recommendation—of the insufficient number of lifeboats, with new rules stemming from the recommendation of the British Wreck Commissioner that "the provision of lifeboat and raft accommodation on board such ships should be based on the number of persons intended to be carried in the ship and not upon tonnage." The United States passed the Radio Act of 1912, later amended, and strengthened in 1927. The latest version of the SOLAS came into effect in 1974.

What Causes Shipwrecks?

Human error was and is the most common cause of shipwreck. Human error can lead to pushing a ship, its crew, or its machinery beyond practical limits. It can include errors in loading, or in maintaining a vessel properly. It can be an error in navigation, which usually meant hitting something, such as an uncharted or poorly charted rock, shoal, sandbar, reef, island, or the mainland shore. Going ashore or stranding is the most common cause of shipwreck. The frequency of wrecks in these circumstances is dramatically illustrated in areas where ships by necessity must pass in and out of a narrow or confined space. An example of this is a strait, such as the Straits of Messina, feared by the ancients as the home of Scylla and Charybdis, depicted in the *Odyssey* as ship-eating, immortal monsters.

Thucydides, in the *History of the Peloponnesian War*, notes that "the strait in question consists of the sea between Rhegium and Messina, at the point where Sicily approaches nearest the continent, and is the Charybdis through which the story makes Odysseus sail,"[3] while Virgil, in the *Aeneid*, wrote, "The right side Scylla keeps; the left is given to pitiless Charybdis, who draws down to the wild whirling of her steep abyss/ the monster waves, and ever and anon flings them at heaven, to lash the tranquil stars. But Scylla, prisoned in her eyeless cave, thrusts forth her face, and pulls upon the rocks, ship after ship."[4] Strabo, in *Geography*, wrote that "Homer has described to us the phenomena of the ocean under the form of a myth."[5] There are many straits, essential for effective or faster navigation, in the world's oceans, and many of them are graveyards of lost ships. "Threading the needle" by navigating a narrow strait was inherently dangerous in the age of sail—and to a certain extent, in the centuries that have followed.

In the days of sail, any mistake could be fatal if the dual forces of wind and current were in opposition. One error, taking the wrong tack (bad steering) for example, placed a ship "in irons," which meant the bow was pointed directly into the wind. The sails would "luff," or fall off, no longer filled with the wind that drives a ship. It was then helpless, and unless action was taken to shift the ship and catch the wind, currents could drive it into another vessel or onto the rocks unless the crew quickly dropped anchor. In a narrow channel, or in a chain of islands and shoals, that was not always possible. For example, during the age of sail the French port of Saint-Malo was heavily used, but it also was dangerous, with submerged rocks and reefs that formed a natural barrier known as La Natière, with strong currents and a tidal range that led to many wrecks.[6] In the Atlantic, the islands of Bermuda, strategically important as a British naval base and a center of active maritime trade, are surrounded by reefs and are another ship graveyard as a result, with over 400 known wrecks. In the United States, the mouth of the Columbia River in Oregon, known as the "Graveyard of the Pacific," the Outer Banks of North Carolina, known as the "Graveyard of the Atlantic," the shores of Cape Cod, Massachusetts, and the Dry Tortugas (the islands, shoals, and reefs at the edge of the Florida Keys) are places where large numbers of ships wrecked. At just one small part of the Dry Tortugas, Pulaski Reef, at least 21 ships are known to have wrecked. The earliest recorded loss there was in 1839, but archaeologists found three wrecks from different times wrecked atop one another, the oldest an 18th-century ship, and the other two 19th-century vessels. At another part of the Dry Tortugas, Loggerhead Reef, at least 55 ships were wrecked. Archaeologists call such places "ship traps."[7]

Another factor in wrecking in such places is the simple truth that a congregation of ships, over time, coming in and out of a port, enter a river mouth or bay, navigate past an offshore cape or barrier islands, or come into a harbor protected by seawalls. The largest concentrations of wrecks are always found off the mouths of the great ports—London, New York, Boston, San Francisco, Astoria, Oregon, Sydney, and Hong Kong are prominent examples. It is off these and other ports, with little room to maneuver, or with the lack of attention that can come at the start or end of a voyage, that accidents happen. This phenomenon is not confined to ships. Studies of automobile accidents found that most occur close to home, while changing lanes, in congested traffic, and when going in and out of a parking lot. In a busy parking lot (or a harbor), distractions, heavy traffic, and jockeying for a spot to park (or dock) means that many wrecks, especially collisions, can and do happen. In the maritime world, shipwrecks in harbors were more often not fatal to the ship or those on board and were the equivalent of an automobile fender-bender. But they could be worse.

Shipwrecks caused by a collision with another vessel were common in congested waterways, especially entering or leaving port. The most famous modern example of a ship collision shipwreck is the liner *Andrea Doria*, which when off the Massachusetts coast, bound from Italy for New York, sank after being rammed by the freighter *Stockholm* on July 26, 1956, killing 46 people. Another example is just off San Francisco. On August 22, 1888, the inbound immigrant steamer *Oceanic* rammed and sank the small coastal steamship *City of Chester*, which was heading out the Golden Gate after departing the San Francisco waterfront. *City of Chester* sank quickly, taking sixteen passengers and three of the crew down with it. There was plenty of room for the two steamers to pass. Some blame was attached to the strong tidal current close to the Gate, which is a mile-and-half narrow gap that connects San Francisco Bay to the Pacific Ocean. The wreck was never raised, and its remains were only rediscovered in 2013 by hydrographers working with archaeologists in 216 feet of water just 400 feet from where the collision had taken place. The force of the collision tore so deeply into the iron hull of the ship that the bow is now severed from the rest of the hull. These are just two of thousands of examples—but two that I have seen as an archaeologist.

Wrecked by the Ice

Shipwrecks were and are also caused by collisions with ice. While *Titanic* famously went too fast and hit an iceberg, it was not the only ship to do so. On June 22, 1802, the ship *Lady Hobart* struck an iceberg at full speed at night after leaving Halifax, Nova Scotia. The captain ordered the lifeboats loaded, and unlike *Titanic* 110 years later, *Lady Hobart* fortunately carried enough to save everyone. As soon as the last member of the crew and their passengers were off, the ship sank rapidly by the bow. The men and women in the boats then sailed over a rough, ice-dotted sea 350 miles to reach the safety of St. John's, Newfoundland. The last ship known to have been sunk by an iceberg, the steel-hulled Danish steamer *Hans Hedtoft*, sank with all hands off the tip of Greenland on January 30, 1959.

None of the 95 people aboard survived. More recently, the ship *Explorer*, a pioneer in the adventure cruise industry, sank off Antarctica on November 23, 2007. All 154 people on board were rescued. A subsequent investigation found that the captain did not have sufficient experience in navigating through Antarctic ice, but praised his actions and those of the crew in saving all on board.

Shipwrecks have also been lost to ice when they have become trapped. Sea ice, such as that encountered in the polar regions, is made up of masses of ice that move with the current and sea swell. Sea ice cracks, pushes up, and fractures, forming ridges and dense sheets of ice that are thrust up at steep angles into the air. Ships trapped in ice can be squeezed and crushed, even when specially designed and built to withstand pressure. The most famous example is *Endurance*, the expedition ship of Antarctic explorer Ernest Shackleton. After setting off for Antarctica in late 1914, the ship was trapped by thick ice in early January 1915. Drifting with the ice for months, *Endurance* sank after being steadily crushed on November 21, 1915. The ordeal by ice twisted, wracked, and finally broke the hull, flooding it. Shackleton described the damage to the stern as having been crushed "concertina fashion." The crew were stranded beyond hope of rescue on a small island.

What followed made the ship and its commander famous as Shackleton undertook an epic journey in a small boat named *James Caird*, with a handful of men, to seek rescue for his crew. After incredible hardship, he succeeded, and the crew of *Endurance* were rescued in the summer of 1916. Shackleton's feat is considered one of the greatest small boat voyages in known human history and an exemplar of heroic leadership. *Endurance*'s story, and the dramatic photographs taken by the expedition's photographer, Frank Hurley, which became iconic images, ensured the stories' continued relevance and inspired quests to rediscover it. The rediscovery of the wreck, at 3,038 meters (9,869 feet) at the bottom of the Weddell Sea, less than five miles from where *Endurance* had finally sunk after the ice released it, produced "ghost ship" images of the easily identifiable ship, with its name still visible on the stern, that made it the major shipwreck story of the year.

There are other examples, especially in the Arctic, where the centuries-long quest for the Northwest Passage cost both ships and lives as vessels were either crushed or trapped beyond hope of escape. The most famous example of Arctic ships lost to the ice are the British ships HMS *Erebus* and HMS *Terror*, which, under the command of Captain Sir John Franklin, left England in 1845 to navigate the "last link" of the Northwest Passage and disappeared. A series of expeditions sent north to find them subsequently met with disaster and the loss of more ships. The perseverance of searching, however, discovered that trapped by ice for years, the crews of *Erebus* and *Terror* had abandoned their vessels and attempted to walk out of the Arctic. None of them made it. The "fate of Franklin" inspired more than the quests to find and rescue—or learn what had happened. It also inspired a legend that entered into public discourse, popular culture, and Inuit memory.[8]

Despite a number of surveys and efforts to discover the wrecks, it was not until modern times that the lost ships were discovered, damaged but essentially intact, preserved by the environmental conditions of the Arctic: *Erebus* in 2014 and *Terror* in 2016. Found close to shore, they may have been reboarded by surviving crew who sailed them a relatively short distance in a failed attempt to escape the ice. Like *Endurance*, the "ghost ship" qualities of the wrecks are the same as those of two other 19th-century, high Arctic shipwrecks of British explorers—HMS *Investigator* and HMS *Breadalbane*. These four lost ships of exploration, lost at the top of the world and "frozen in time," captured public attention when they were found. They are amazing archaeological sites because of the lack of marine organisms that consume wood in the near-freezing water, which enables exceptionally high levels of preservation.

These wrecks, like *Endurance*, are recognizable, as they still look as they did when afloat and captured in period imagery, with well-preserved interior spaces. The Franklin ships, *Erebus* and *Terror*, have been the focus of years of archaeological documentation and limited recovery by Parks Canada. The images of their work show dark, spooky interiors of the ships, with intact cabins with bunks, desks with drawers, and individual, personal items such as a leather-bound folio with a quill pen stuck between the pages, an officer's drafting tools—likely used in chart making—a hairbrush with strands of hair, and epaulettes from a uniform. Like *Endurance*, these Arctic wrecks are time capsules cracked open by ice, but now facing loss through warming seas brought on by climate change, the colonization of Arctic waters by wood-eating worms, and storm surges and wave action in increasingly less icy conditions. I'll return to this theme later in the book.

The Power of the Sea

The power of ice notwithstanding, the power of the sea is the second most common factor in the loss of ships after human error. Powerful wind has snapped masts, leaving a sailing ship helpless in heavy seas, unable to maneuver, and battered until it sinks. Masts can be strong enough to withstand the wind; nonetheless, a ship hit by a sudden squall or gust can capsize and sink. There are many examples in recorded history. For example, an 1878 treatise on "Great Shipwrecks" provides the example of the French schooner *Doris*, heading into the port of Brest on September 19, 1845, when a sudden "southwesterly hurricane came up, accompanied by a storm of hail." There was no time for the crew to act by taking down sails; hit "abreast by the squall," the wind filled the sails and capsized *Doris*. The sea poured in through the hatches, and the schooner went down within seconds.

Seeing the signal lights of the schooner go out, a sailor on another ship called out for help. Boats quickly launched saved nearly half of the crew of *Doris*, who were found in the dark, clinging to pieces of wreckage and "struggling with the courage of despair." The commonness of wrecks like this is underscored by the fact that the account notes that the rescuers sent out to *Doris* discovered four men clinging to the side of their capsized but not yet sunk fishing boat.[9] Loss to weather was not, nor is even now, confined to sailing vessels. More modern vessels, whether steam-powered or metal-hulled, have been overtaken by the power of a storm.

Famous examples include the Great Lakes freighter *Edmund Fitzgerald*, lost to the wintery "gales of November" in 1975 on Lake Superior, with all 29 of its crew. Another is the nearly 800-foot-long cargo ship *El Faro*, which was battered and sunk by Hurricane Joaquin on October 1, 2015, while steaming from Jacksonville, Florida, to San Juan, Puerto Rico. None of the 33 crew on board survived as the ship was battered and sank in high winds that were gusting to more than 150 miles per hour. Heavy seas progressively flooded the ship, killed the engines, and then hammered *El Faro* down, 15,000 feet deep, in a matter of minutes. In one of the most heartbreaking stories I've heard of many about shipwrecks, one of the crew, Second Mate Danielle Randolph, sent her mother an email from *El Faro* telling her they were heading into the hurricane, "straight into it, Category 3, last we checked. Winds are super bad. Love to everyone." The last message from the captain, as he called the shore by satellite phone for help, reported that the ship's hull had breached, a scuttle had blown open, there was water in the number three hold, "with a heavy list," the main propulsion unit was down, and the engineers could not fix it.[10] It's stories like that, and those of other families, that make shipwrecks more than a subject that I study as an archaeologist. When I lived in Jacksonville, Florida, where *El Faro* had sailed from, I made it a point to go, more than once, to the *El Faro* memorial at Dames Point Park. It is a very personal memorial, not often visited, I suspect, other than by the families of the crew. Personal items, and what I suspect were favorite things of the lost crew, were often left next to the memorial markers.

The story of *El Faro* highlights another common cause, which is when the inevitable power of the sea overwhelms the ability of ships to survive. This happens because of old age. It happens due to cost-cutting, a lack of maintenance, crew error, or incompetence. It also happens when a captain and crew are pressured to go to sea because an owner or employer demands it, or because they simply need a paycheck. That was clearly the premise of the "Perfect Storm." The official inquiry into the loss of *El Faro* faulted the owners for putting an older ship to sea. But go one must, if that is their job and the rent needs to be paid and food needs to be put on the table. The famous loss of the fishing boat *Andrea Gail*, as chronicled in the "The Perfect Storm," depicted a crew that simply had to sail, despite warnings, in order to make a living. Instead, in their gamble, they all died when the boat sank. This is a very common occurrence, especially among the working boats of any port, namely fishing craft, tugs, and short- and long-haul barges. The U.S. Coast Guard investigation into the loss of *El Faro* faulted the captain, the company, and the actions taken, while the National Safety Transportation Board's investigation into the loss criticized the Coast Guard's decision to "grandfather," or allow older vessels to operate, despite the fact they did not meet modern standards, as well as the company for operating an outdated, deteriorating vessel. Samuel Plimsoll would have been disgusted, but not surprised.

Fire at Sea

Cooking and heating on ship, whether by open hearth, or in later times, stoves, always posed a threat. Some of the more tragic shipboard fires were those on board ships carrying immigrants, where crowded ships and insufficient boats meant large losses of life as blazes swept through a wooden vessel that few could escape from. One tragic example is that of the immigrant steamer *Austria*. On September 13, 1858, heading from Hamburg to New York with 542 passengers, the steamer burned and sank. It happened due to a simple and stupid accident. The ship's hold was infested with lice and fleas. Fumigating with a thick smoke was the answer, or so the captain and crew thought. They heated an iron chain to a red-hot state and dipped it into tar. Then the crew member holding it dropped the red-hot chain. The heat set the spilled tar on fire, and flames raced across the wooden deck. The fire spread to the varnished bunks, tables, and cabins in the hold, and the interior of the ship quickly filled with dense, thick smoke.

The smoke quickly killed many below decks, including the engine room crew. That left the steamer running at half speed and unable to stop. The onward progress and inrushing air stoked the fire, which burst out onto the open deck. The man at the wheel abandoned his post as the flames headed for him, and the steamer swung into the wind. Attempts to lower the ship's boats failed as people rushed them, and the boats were swamped. To avoid burning, a number of passengers and crew jumped into the sea, preferring drowning to burning. The smoke drew the attention of the French barque *Maurice*, which rescued 67 people; the next day, another ship picked up 22 more.

The possibility of fire on ships as a result of boiler explosions, or fuel leaks in the motor age, was another common cause. As noted previously, the worst maritime disaster in the United States was the burning of the riverboat *Sultana* after its boilers exploded north of Memphis on the Mississippi River on April 27, 1865. A hasty repair of a boiler, an overcrowded boat filled with Civil War prisoners of war returning home, and engineers probably pushing the faulty boiler too hard led to first one and then all three boilers exploding. The blasts ripped up through the decks, killing many, and set *Sultana* afire. As it drifted in the river current, men leaped into the river and drowned. The final death toll was calculated to be 1,547 of the 2,137 people estimated to have been on board.[11]

In the past, some cargoes were dangerously prone to combustion, notably coal. When wet, coal will heat and then begin to burn without an open flame, posing a hidden danger. In the age of wooden ships, a coal fire was inevitably fatal, and even iron and later steel ships also succumbed. How many wrecks happened because of coal fires? Historians have argued that many ships sailing with coal simply went "missing" after leaving port, and coal shippers could conveniently continue to ship a dangerous but lucrative cargo around the world. A British Royal Commission on "Spontaneous Combustion of Coal on Ships" in 1876 and subsequent recommendations for safer stowage notwithstanding, at least 50 coal-carrying ships were lost on the Pacific alone between 1876 and 1896.[12]

The frequency of coal fires is perhaps best illustrated by the mid-19th-century account of Mrs. D. B. Bates, whose husband was a ship's captain. Their ship *Nonantum* was sailing from Baltimore to San Francisco in 1850 when the cargo of coal combusted, throwing off tremendous heat and noxious gases. *Nonantum* was 800 miles to sea, and so the crew worked to smother the coal to keep it from blazing into open flame. Captain Bates headed for the closest land, the Falkland Islands. After five days of fighting to keep the ship afloat by sealing the hatches and caulking seams to keep air from the smoldering coal, the Bates scuttled their ship in the Falklands, sinking it to extinguish the fire. From there, they took passage on the ship *Humayoon*, bound for Valparaiso with a cargo that contained coal. It, too, caught fire, but burst into open flame. That forced the crew to abandon ship. A passing ship rescued them, but unable to feed two crews, transferred the Bates to the ship *Fanchon*, bound to San Francisco with a cargo of coal. *Fanchon* also combusted, but the crew managed to keep it from flaring into fire, and after a three-week harrowing voyage, reached Peru, where *Fanchon* burned.[13]

Another, more modern ship loss is a reminder that even with regulations for fire safety, steel ships also burn with tragic results. The Ward Line steamer *Morro Castle*, a relatively new, four-year-old ship, caught fire while steaming from Havana, Cuba, to New York on September 8, 1934. The captain had died that evening of an apparent heart attack after dinner, and his mate was in command. A small fire in a storage locker quickly spread, burning the electrical cables that provided light to the ship, and cutting off the radio after only one distress signal had been broadcast. As the fire spread and *Morro Castle* raced toward the New Jersey coast, not every lifeboat could be launched, as some of them were already burning, and some of the 549 passengers and crew were trapped by flames. Passengers on deck began to jump overboard, where some of them died of broken necks or drowning. Others were burned alive in their cabins.

Rescuers from other ships arrived, but 135 passengers and crew died. Bodies began washing up on New Jersey's beaches, and the still smoldering hulk came ashore next to the Asbury Park Convention Hall. *Morro Castle*'s much-photographed hulk, featured in a Fox Movietone Newsreel as a "flaming hulk on a raging sea," became a grim tourist draw and an icon for the next six months until it was towed away to be scrapped, an event also featured in a Fox Movietone Newsreel. Inquiries into the disaster faulted the acting captain and crew. The captain, chief engineer, and the company's vice president were convicted of willful negligence and jailed (until released on appeal). The saga of *Morro Castle* continues to be a modern controversy, with unproved allegations that a member of the crew set the ship on fire.[14]

Scuttling

Scuttling is the deliberate sinking of a ship. A ship may be scuttled because it is a dangerous derelict, afloat without a crew, and poses a greater danger to other ships if afloat. Captain Bates's scuttling of *Nonantum* to stop the combustion of the coal in his ship's hold is a perfect example. Ships can also be scuttled to help fulfill a mission. During the Civil War, the Union Navy scuttled a fleet of old wooden whaling ships off Charleston, South Carolina, to close the channels used by Confederate ships running the blockade of the port. The first scuttling of 16 ships was followed by a second operation that sank an additional 13 ships. Despite their numbers, they had a limited effect, as archaeologist James Spirek has noted in his study of them. Known as the "Stone Fleet," these wrecks are still being studied by archaeologists, all part of a massive, submerged battlefield from one of the more protracted naval sieges of the U.S. Civil War. Archaeologists have also studied the wrecks of blockade runners lost while seeking to avoid the obstructing stone fleet, but hitting them and sinking.

During World War II, a group of ships were scuttled off the beaches of Normandy to create a breakwater for the artificial harbor brought in to support the D-Day invasion in June 1944. Known by the code name "Gooseberry," it largely consisted of older ships and more modern American Liberty ships that had been ballasted with concrete and scuttled bow to stern in rows to form the offshore breakwaters at five different locations off Utah, Omaha, Gold, Juno, and Sword beaches. Gooseberry 2, just off Omaha Beach, consisted of 55 ships, gathered from the merchant fleets of Great Britain, the United States, and other allies.

The code name for the ships themselves? "Corncobs." Sunk with just enough clearance for the decks to remain dry, they were outfitted with antiaircraft guns, and supplies for the gun crews were shifted to the unflooded upper levels.

Ships have also been deliberately sunk as targets to test new weapons by various navies around the world. Robert Fulton, best known as the American "inventor" of the steamboat, was also a key figure in the development of the submarine and sub-marine explosives. Fulton named his explosives "torpedoes" after the electric eel (*Torpedo nobiliana*). Today they are known as sea mines. Fulton successfully tested his device on October 5, 1805, off Deal, England. Two tow boats with "torpedoes" attached to cables running behind them made a run at the anchored brig *Dorothea*, which was blown in two and sank. It was the first use of a mine to wreck a ship. Another naval "first" was testing newly developed explosive shells developed by French naval officer Henri-Joseph Paixhans. The retired wooden ship-of-the-line *Pacificateur*, moored off Brest, was maimed and then sunk in 1824 in a test of Paixhans's new shell. It marked the beginning of the end of the use of solid-shot cannon balls in naval warfare.

Larger-scale scuttling as part of tests include those the famous demonstration of Brigadier General William L. "Billy" Mitchell off the Capes of Virginia in June and July 1921. Mitchell, an advocate of air power, used aircraft to successfully sink surrendered German warships to demonstrate the effectiveness of aircraft in naval warfare. Mitchell repeated the results in tests that sank three decommissioned American battleships in September 1921 and September 1923. Archaeologist Rod Mather, working with the National Oceanographic and Atmospheric Administration (NOAA), has located, mapped, and documented the German battleship *Ostfriesland*, the cruiser *Frankfurt*, and other vessels. Together, on the seabed, they represent more than individual ships—these shipwrecks are an early archaeological "signature" and a historical site that graphically speaks to the coming domination of aerial warfare at sea.

Another large-scale sinking came with the post–World War II atomic bomb tests "Operation Crossroads" at Bikini Atoll in the Pacific. A fleet of 95 target ships, deployed in formations for two tests of the atomic bomb, were subjected to an aerial detonation on July 1, 1946, and an undersea detonation on July 25. The first test sank five ships. The second test sank eight ships. Due to blast damage and residual radioactivity, most of the surviving target ships were then sunk as targets between 1946 and 1951. The ultimate legacy, post-tests, are 61 shipwrecks that lie at or near Bikini, off the Marshall Islands' atoll of Kwajalein, the California coast, Oahu, and the coast of Washington State.[15] The nuclear "ghost fleet" is one of the largest—in numbers and in the scale of the "site"—collections of scuttled warships through naval testing, although some have argued, including myself, that the ships were also sunk by the newly developed bomb as a global demonstration of American power.[16]

Image 1.2. The battleship USS *Nevada* under fire and struck by torpedoes while being sunk in a naval exercise, 1948.
Naval History and Heritage Command, 80-G-4981.

Yet another "ghost fleet" is the German fleet that surrendered to the British Royal Navy at the end of World War I that rests at Scapa Flow. Surrendered and interned at the Royal Navy's Scottish fleet anchorage during the armistice that ended the war, the fleet of 74 ships was moored with skeleton crews on board starting in November 1918. Fearing that the treaty of Versailles, then being negotiated, would result in the seizure of every German ship, the commanding officer of the interned fleet ordered his crews to prepare to scuttle them all. On June 21, 1919, the date the treaty had been scheduled to be signed, the Germans scuttled 52 of the ships. While a number of the ships were subsequently raised and scrapped, not all were, and three battleships, four cruisers, and one partially scrapped destroyer remain. A popular site for wreck divers, and occasional scrappers, the fleet has also been studied by maritime archaeologist Innes McCartney.[17]

Scuttling also involves deliberate sinking of ships to dispose of them through a "burial at sea," including derelicts found adrift at sea that cannot be salvaged and pose a threat to navigation, as well as circumstances where they are sunk deliberately to perpetrate insurance fraud. That act is a maritime crime known as "barratry." Barratry is one theory for what happened with the famous *Mary Celeste* when it was found adrift without its crew off the Azores in early December 1872. Multiple theories abound, and the ship remains one of the favorite subjects of wild speculation as to why no one was found aboard the drifting vessel, with some of its sails still set and making its way "erratically." The crew of the brigantine *Dei Gratia*, which encountered the empty *Mary Celeste* on the high seas, found the logbook open with the last entry nine days before they boarded the derelict. Insurance fraud was just one of multiple theories as to what had happened. Many wild stories circulated, some of them published, and *Mary Celeste* became one of the great 19th-century stories of the sea.

Its history after the derelict was sailed into port, sold for salvage, and returned to commerce was one of its unprofitable voyages as a "cursed" ship. The end of the saga came in December 1885, when then master Captain Gilman C. Parker, inbound to Haiti, deliberately plowed *Mary Celeste* onto the rocks of Rochelois Reef off the Ile de Gonâve while approaching Haiti's mainland. Parker's insurance claim for the ship and a "valuable" cargo was found to be false; the cargo was old junk, and an inspection of the wreck found that it had also been burned. A trial on conspiracy to commit insurance fraud ended in a mistrial before Parker was set to go on trial for barratry, which carried the death sentence had he been convicted. The mistrial led to a plea bargain. Parker and his crew repaid the insurance company. Parker never returned to sea, and the remains of *Mary Celeste*, stuck on Rochelois Reef, became the setting for a colony of Haitians who gradually built a shell-fishing settlement alongside its coral-shrouded bones, which is where Clive Cussler and the Sea Hunters found the wreck in 2001, and detailed analysis indicated that this was indeed the pitiful remains of the famous, if not notorious, vessel. It is also one of the few known archaeological examples of a shipwreck definitively known to have been lost to barratry.

Another aspect of scuttling is the environmental impact of some of these vessels, especially those sunk loaded with chemical and biological warfare bombs as part of post–World War II disposal of unwanted ordnance, and post–Cold War disposal of some of the deadliest non-nuclear weapons on the planet. An unknown but vast poisonous legacy rests on the seabed inside and alongside scuttled ships. There are hundreds of deliberately sunk ships lying on the seabed off the U.S. coast that were discarded by the U.S. government. Some of these were the results of weapons tests. Obsolete warships made perfect targets for new types of torpedoes, coordinated aerial attacks, and missiles. They also provide near-wartime experience for naval crews as a live-fire training exercise. The name for these is a SINKEX.

I've seen a number of ships that were sunk during SINKEXs; one was the former USS *Peterson*, a 1970s *Spruance*-class guided missile destroyer that had an active career in the Persian Gulf and the Mediterranean, and saw combat during Operation Desert Storm. After being decommissioned in 2002, the Navy sank it in 2004. The location was known to the Navy but was not general knowledge; however, when the E/V (Exploration Vessel) *Nautilus* of the Ocean Exploration Trust was working off the west coast of Florida in the Gulf of Mexico in July 2014, a dive with a remotely operated vehicle on a 500-foot-long sonar target revealed that the target was the hull of *Peterson*. It had been stripped of equipment and emptied of fuel, and was found still painted and slowly decaying in 7,800 feet of water. That level of clean-up prior to sinking was not always done in the past, especially after World War II and well into the Cold War.

One of those ships with a poisonous legacy—of which I have firsthand, eyes-on knowledge—is in the Gulf of the Farallones, which lies off San Francisco on the California coast. After World War II, the Hunters Point Naval Shipyard in San Francisco became the focal point of the U.S. Navy's study of the effects of atomic weapons. Ships used as targets for the atomic bomb tests at Bikini Atoll in 1946 were brought to Hunters Point for study. They included the aircraft carrier USS *Independence* (CVL-28). Burned, battered, and irradiated, *Independence* remained at Hunters Point until 1951. Hunters Point was the location of the newly established Naval Radiological Defense Laboratory. In addition to the research done on the ship, the University of California Radiation Laboratory, across San Francisco Bay, also worked with radioactive material. In late 1950, Navy officials decided to dispose of USS *Independence*. The easiest decision, after stripping the engines and boilers, was to load it with radioactive waste, contaminated equipment and gear, and sink the carrier. Navy tugs towed *Independence* out to sea, reportedly over a hundred miles, and sank it with explosive charges on January 26, 1951. The wreck's location was not disclosed, nor was it ever charted.

A sonar image from seabed made by the NOAA in 1990 revealed the wreck's position while mapping the Gulf of the Farallones National Marine Sanctuary. It lay in nearly 3,000 feet of water, a dozen miles off the coast. I was part of the team that used robotic vehicles to confirm that it was *Independence* in 2015, and we returned in 2016 with Dr. Robert Ballard and his team from the Ocean Exploration Trust with remotely operated vehicles (ROVs) to more fully explore the wreck. Our dives, broadcast live over the Internet, revealed that the battered carrier was upright, with a badly damaged aircraft inside its forward elevator on the hanger deck. There was no measurable radiation, but we did see a steel barrel lying alongside the aircraft. It was a 50-gallon oil drum that had been sealed with concrete. This meant that it was one of the many barrels full of "atomic waste" placed on *Independence* before it was scuttled.

The concrete proved to be a thin "cap" or plug, and it had fallen free. Inside the barrel, as the cameras on the ROV zoomed in, they revealed wads of latex gloves. The thought of those gloves as "atomic waste" struck me two ways as an archaeologist and a historian; the first was that as innocuous as the gloves appeared, they didn't fit what I'd thought of as atomic waste. But they were. The other was that a thin layer of latex for workers dealing with radioactive material was no protection at all. What we were seeing inside the wreck was a telling artifact of the dawn of the atomic age and of not only ignorance but also a seeming lack of care for both the workers and the environment. The Cold War meant it was time to move full speed ahead, to beat the Russians in developing new and more powerful weapons, and damn the consequences. *Independence* and its contents, however, are not the only artifacts of the attitudes and actions of that time and place.

The seabed of the Gulf of the Farallones is also an approximately 250-square-mile disposal site for some 47,800 containers of what has been described as "low-level" radioactive waste from the nearby laboratories. These containers—barrels and equipment encased inside concrete blocks—were dumped offshore from 1946 to 1970. The military also disposed of unwanted bombs and chemical weapons in the same waters. Several surplus World War II cargo ships were also loaded with weapons and sunk, reportedly in very deep water. The first was the Liberty Ship *William C. Ralston*, sunk in April 1958 with 8,000 pounds of what the local press described as "deteriorating" mustard gas bombs and containers of lewisite, a chemical agent that blisters the skin, eyes, mouth, and sinuses; it also contains arsenic.

The environmental consequences of uncontrolled ocean dumping of weapons, waste, and entire ships, whether loaded with deadly cargoes or not, are a global problem. That includes the large number of ships lost in both world wars that remain loaded with their fuel, many of which continue to leak. Known as "slicking time bombs," they are one of the lesser known global pollution problems. However, in the past decade, increased attention and actions taken by governments and nonprofit foundations are starting to address the problem. The U.S. Congress funded a study by the NOAA, working with the U.S. Coast Guard. That study assessed over 20,000 wrecks and ultimately identified 87 of those shipwrecks as the highest risks for potentially catastrophic release of their trapped oil when their hulls failed decades after they sank. That's just in the United States. The International Union for the Conservation of Nature (IUCN) estimates that 8,569 wrecks worldwide pose a high risk of releasing as much as 6 billion gallons of oil within the next decade. That is, as they noted, 545 times as much oil as the *Exxon Valdez* spill and 30 times more than the Deepwater Horizon disaster spilled. Those figures all point to a global environmental disaster that *will* happen.

Slowly, but with an increasing pace, governments and nongovernmental organizations are taking action. Some are reactive responses to leaks; the U.S. Navy has removed oil trapped in the World War II wreck of the tanker USS *Mississinewa*, lost in Ulithi Lagoon in the Pacific, as well as the German cruiser *Prinz Eugen*, which sank at Kwajalein atoll in the Pacific after being damaged in the Bikini atomic bomb tests. In the United States, working with funds set aside and managed by the U.S. Coast Guard, Resolve Marine, a private company, has removed the oil trapped in the ships *Coimbra* and *Munger T. Ball*, both sunk by German U-boats off the coasts of New York and Florida. I've been part of teams that have sought out some of the ships on NOAA's list of 87 high-risk potentially polluting wrecks. We've assessed the steamer *Coast Trader* and the freighter *Fernstream*. *Coast Trader* lies off a marine reserve on the west coast of Canada's Vancouver Island; *Fernstream* sits in the mud near San Francisco's Golden Gate Bridge. Both vessels were found broken, which means much of that oil was released decades ago. We've also been part of an international team that has conducted detailed surveys to determine how much oil remains trapped from the leaking hulks of the target ships sunk during the atomic tests at Bikini Atoll in 1946. These are just a few of the efforts I've been involved in that are part of a growing global response to the terrible environmental legacy of those thousands of 20th-century shipwrecks.

Do other scuttled or sunken ships pose environmental threats? Yes, some do, including those loaded with outlawed weapons. Others contain other pollutants. Concerns over the legacy of shipwrecks like these mean that fewer ships are now deliberately sunk. In the United States, the passage of environmental laws and the establishment of the Environmental Protection Agency led to rules and regulations, as well as the Marine Protection, Research and Sanctuaries Act (MPRSA) of 1972, which now regulates the deliberate scuttling of ships in American waters. These disposals require a permit, and must be sunk in specially designated zones only after any other alternative for disposal (such as scrapping) has been exhausted. Fuel tanks need to be emptied, as well as fuel lines flushed with water; any other possible pollutants, including polychlorinated biphenyls (PCBs), asbestos, and any debris that might float, such as insulation, have to be stripped. Vessels disposed of by permits need to be sunk at least 12 miles offshore and no less than 300 feet deep.

A focused look at more recent non-military SINKEX ship disposals off the Hawaiian island of Oahu indicates a range of older working vessels and large barges that include a 161-ton long-line fishing vessel and two passenger vessels, one of them a 1946-built former dinner cruiser that did dinner cruises on the Potomac before being sold, remodeled to vaguely resemble a historic sailing ship, and motored to Hawaii in 1980. After years of sitting idle at Honolulu's Pier, the former *Delaware Belle*, then known as *Kulamanu*, was towed offshore and scuttled in several thousand feet of water. I'm sure future generations of archaeologists will be completely baffled by the strangeness of that shipwreck.

Fifty miles off the coast of the Hawaiian island of Kauai, the Pacific Missile Range Facility is a thousand square miles that non-military ships are warned to stay away from. Statistics vary, as not all tests were announced, but as of 2015, 52 decommissioned Navy ships had been sunk in SINKEXs. A typical shipwreck in that range usually lies miles deep; the depth helps mask for now classified results from weapons tests.

One example is the live-fire exercise that sank the former guided missile frigate *Ingraham* in August 2021. In that exercise, F-35C Super Hornets, the first and for now the only long-range stealth strike fighters built for carrier operations, fired laser-guided missiles. At the same time, a P-8 Poseidon maritime patrol and reconnaissance aircraft fired an over-the-horizon, anti-ship Harpoon missile. The third "combatant," the fast-attack submarine USS *Chicago*, fired both a Harpoon and an advanced capability torpedo to demonstrate how a joint task force, using what the Navy called an advanced "kill-web," could take out enemy vessels. Just as future generations may ponder the strangeness of the odd-looking dinner cruise vessel *Kulamanu* off Oahu, the damage wrought by the most advanced weapons of the early 21st century may also provide fascinating material to future archaeologists and historians.

In modern times, ships are also deliberately sunk as diving attractions and to become "artificial reefs" following a rigorous program of environmental clean-up, which includes cutting away hatches and making openings in a hull so that divers can safely go in and out of a wreck. I was introduced to this aspect of wrecks in 1991 when I arrived in Vancouver, British Columbia, as director of the Maritime Museum. The newly formed Artificial Reef Society of British Columbia had acquired the 1943-built freighter *G.B. Church* in 1989, and was busy stripping it of any contaminants, including flushing fuel lines and tanks of oil, as well as the bilges. The group included more than one lawyer, all of them divers, and so what struck me as an incredible amount of diligence took place as they went through the ship looking, with a diver's perspective, at anything that would snag, fall, or slam shut and trap a diver. In August 1991, it was towed to a marine park off Vancouver Island and readied for sinking, with holes cut to not only flood it, but strategically placed to sink it upright and to land on the bottom when explosive charges were set off. An ugly, non-descript and rusty hulk quickly became a habitat for anemones, wolf eels, octopi, and a range of fish—and a ship that, while no one would bother to tour it dock side if asked to pay admission, by dint of becoming a wreck, attracted divers who paid well for dive gear, air fills, and a boat ride to the site.

In my time at the museum, they went on to sink three retired Canadian destroyer escorts between 1992 and 2006. They subsequently sank the destroyer HMC *Annapolis* in 2015 and a former U.S. Navy vessel, the 375-foot-long ship-shaped concrete barge YOGN-82. I'm a fan of concrete ships not only because they were a unique and ultimately fated type of craft, but also because as a child, when I went camping with my family on the coast near Capitola, California, one of my first wrecks was the former concrete ship SS *Palo Alto*, converted into a beach fishing pier that was breaking apart. The ocean had breached the concrete hull, and through the open deck hatches, my brothers and I could hear the booming echo of the waves as they washed inside the cavernous hold, and look down and see fish swimming. So with that confession of one of my first shipwrecks, to sail past the old concrete hulk was a delightful discovery for me when I saw it for the first time afloat as part of a floating breakwater for a log pond in Powell River, British Columbia. Built of reinforced concrete in 1943, it served in the Pacific until 1959, and was sold to the Powell River Company two years later. After surveys showed that the hull was deteriorating past the point of safety, the owners transferred it to the Artificial Reef Society, and they sank it in June 2018. While I see it as a historic craft, and a deliberately sunk one with no dramatic story, but nonetheless an impressive shipwreck for what it was—a rare type of craft—divers see it differently. Beauty truly is in the eye of the beholder.

There are impressive wrecks that are recreational dive sites. One of the largest of them is the *Essex*-class aircraft carrier USS *Oriskany*. At 888 feet in length, it's the largest ship to be turned into an artificial reef. Sold for scrap in 1995, *Oriskany* ended up as a reef when the Navy repossessed it, had it towed to Texas, and then gave it to the State of Florida. It was scuttled off Pensacola in May 2006, and came to rest upright in 200 feet of water. It is a popular dive site, but like other ships sunk as "reefs," questions over the long-term effects of corroding iron, heavy metals, paint, and especially PCBs have led to scientific studies and lawsuits. According to studies done by the State of Florida, PCBs from electrical insulation left on board *Oriskany* have been found in the tissues of fish living in and around the wreck.

Lost in Battle

Throughout the past 500 years of history, war at sea has likely resulted in the largest number of shipwrecks. These include not only warships but also merchant vessels involved in naval activities, as well as merchant ships engaged in regular maritime commerce which were attacked and sunk by hostile powers at sea or in harbor. The largest number of such losses came with the era of modern warfare beginning in the mid-19th century and culminating in huge losses in World Wars I and II, especially as a result of unrestricted submarine warfare. Given humanity's penchant for violence, I believe that most shipwrecks happened because of battles. There are numerous references to lost warships in this book, and so I'm not going to launch into a series of examples at this point in the narrative. I'll leave it at the fact that, as I've said before, the sea is our greatest battlefield, spanning millennia. Every type of weapon invented has been brought to sea and used. When I think of the single greatest period in history that resulted in shipwrecks, it has to be the six-year span of World War II. The millions of deaths in World War II included 36,950 combat deaths of naval officers and enlisted sailors. Many of their bodies were never recovered, and monuments in the various national cemeteries include cenotaphs with the names of those missing, who in many cases lie entombed in their sunken vessels.

Unusual Losses

Shipwrecks were as commonly "accepted" as automobile accidents are in modern society. They were frequent, more often than not caused by factors that everyone understood, especially those who had more regular contact with or an understanding of the nature of working on the water. Over the course of the 19th and 20th centuries, newspapers had regular columns that reported "marine news," noting vessel arrivals, departures, and notable events, such as the launch of a new ship, an exceptional voyage, and wrecks. What made shipwrecks jump from the back to the front page were wrecks with a loss of life, especially those with large numbers of dead. Shipwrecks that averted mass tragedy through rescue also inspired major stories. In that way, coverage of notable shipwrecks was the same as 21st-century coverage of airplane crashes. The coverage and response to the Tenerife disaster of March 27, 1977, when two aircraft collided on the foggy runway of that Canary Islands airport, killing 583 people, echoed earlier accounts of shipwreck deaths. The disappearance of Malaysia Airlines Flight 370 on March 8, 2014, was another modern example of how society responded to major maritime disasters a century ago. It reminded me of the many tales of ships that disappeared without a trace. In contrast, the story of US Airways Flight 1549, which, with its engines stalled after a midair bird strike, was glided safely down into New York's Hudson River by Captain Chesley "Sully" Sullenberger on January 15, 2009, echoes amazing rescues at sea by skilled mariners two centuries ago.

Unusual shipwrecks also captured attention. One of the more famous examples is that of the ships overwhelmed by volcanic gasses and heat in the harbor of Saint-Pierre, on the isle of Martinique on May 8, 1902, when the island's volcano, Mount Pelée, erupted. The volcanic cloud traveled down the slopes of the mountain at 420 miles per hour, engulfing the town in ash and gas heated to nearly 1,830°F, killing some 28,000 people. Eighteen ships in the harbor were set afire and sank, among them the Canadian freighter *Roraima*. *Roraima* remained afloat, but with most on board killed by the heat and a thick ash that covered the decks and set *Roraima* on fire. A nearby ship took off 15 survivors before *Roraima* sank. News of the volcanic destruction of the town made international headlines, and *Roraima* remains one of the most unique and famous shipwrecks of the past century. However, the volcano-sunk shipwrecks of Saint-Pierre harbor are unusual but not unique. The Japanese oceanographic research ship *Kaiyo Maru No. 5* was lost with its 31-person crew on September 24, 1952, at Myōjin-shō, a volcano that formed a new island in Japan's Izu island chain. As the research ship monitored the volcanic activity, a subsea eruption apparently sank the ship without time for it to broadcast a distress call. All that searchers found of *Kaiyo Maru No. 5* were pieces of floating wreckage with lava and pumice fragments adhering to them.

Ultimately, perhaps the best-known unusual shipwreck is the whale ship *Essex* of Nantucket. While whaling in the South Pacific, *Essex* sank after being rammed twice by an unusually large sperm whale on November 20, 1820. The partially submerged hulk remained sufficiently afloat for two days. That gave the crew time to salvage supplies and load three small whaleboats in an attempt to reach land thousands of miles away. The voyage of the whaleboats was hellish. The boats were separated, and many men died of thirst and starvation. In desperation, the crews turned to cannibalism; on the captain's boat, after drawing straws, they killed and ate Owen Coffin, the captain's 17-year-old first cousin. Two of the boats were rescued by other ships, one 89 days and the other 93 days after they abandoned *Essex*. The circumstances of the story commanded international attention. Being "stove" (broken open) by an angry whale was unusual. The prolonged voyage, marked by misery, death, and cannibalism, was not unusual in tales of loss and survival on the open sea, but this was a shocking case. The eeriness of the tale included the fact that *Essex*'s captain, George Pollard, almost immediately took command of the ship that had rescued him and his fellow survivors, *Two Brothers*. On its next voyage, with Pollard in command, *Two Brothers* wrecked in the northwestern Hawaiian Islands. Pollard never returned to sea, remaining ashore in Nantucket as a cursed "Jonah."

The loss of *Essex* and the ordeal of its survivors would go down in history as the famous whaling shipwreck of the 19th century because it inspired a very famous book, *Moby-Dick*, which drew on the circumstances of its loss. *Essex*'s tale is a reminder of how strongly the maritime world and shipwrecks had an impact on society. That impact was not immediately felt by a global audience, however. Fame would only come when Herman Melville, learning of the incident while at sea himself, would later turn to the subject. The impact of the book, and its connection to a real shipwreck, emerged as an internationally known and important cultural phenomenon only in the 20th century. Today the book is known more from its movie adaptations, including *In the Heart of the Sea*, adapted from Nathaniel Philbrick's book about the *Essex*.

In the 19th century, the notoriety of *Essex* was briefly noted in national news. The impact of shipwrecks like *Essex* and others was not that they reached a large audience—it was that they impacted families and communities, and in a world and time when the sea and ships were the backbone of commerce, communication, travel, and for coastal communities, sustenance. Communities like Nantucket, closely related and insular on their island, would more intimately and privately react to a shipwreck; this was before the era of instant news and global news coverage, with panels of experts and commentators opining on what happened and what it all means. For thousands of years, shipwrecks were a profound and common aspect of life and labor at sea, and hence of the frailty of human endeavors and dreams. The realities of what author Nicholas Monserrat aptly called "the cruel sea" are that the global ocean promises nothing. The multiple reasons and realities of why shipwrecks happen meant little to a grieving family; what mattered was that their loved ones and their livelihood were lost.

Perhaps some found comfort in the reminder from the Bible that the "Lord giveth and the Lord taketh away" (Job 1:21). Death at sea was a fact of life, and shipwrecks, as they occurred, were a consistent reminder that many ships and sailors lay, as Melville wrote, beneath "the great shroud of the sea" as it rolled on, as it had done, for millennia of human experience. How grief was processed was and is an individual, family, and at times a community response. As communication of events spread first by news carried on ships, then by undersea cables transmitting telegraph signals, to radio, and now by satellites and fiber-optic cable-conveyed electronic messages, the result was the emergence of a global community and worldwide response. The impact of the telegraphed messages from and about *Titanic* in 1912 was a powerful example of this. This was the advent of "breaking news" that persists, often to excess, in the 21st century.

It's very important to be reminded that the nature of tragedy is intensely personal. It is also an absolute certainty that people respond differently to tragedies, whether their own or those of another. Those responses may have profound results in society and culture. "Tragedy" as defined by Aristotle was an opportunity to vicariously experience sympathy and fear from the unfortunate circumstances of another—in his time, the "pain" of actors on a stage. Through that play, an audience would also have release, or catharsis. The truth of Aristotle's view of how society responded to tragedy, however, began to shift in the modern era. Because of global news networks broadcasting "breaking" news on mobile devices, modern society is awash in tragedy. Bad news sells, but I believe it also numbs us. We are inured to disaster unless it is an epic event; the loss of a fishing boat, or a bulk carrier that fails to arrive in port, does not often get noticed in the media. Between 2013 and 2022, 807 vessels were lost at sea, worldwide. Most were cargo ships; 311 in total, followed by 117 fishing boats, 53 bulk carriers, tugs, tankers, Ro-Ros (car carriers), container ships, offshore and supply ships, dredgers, and barges.[18] But these stories rarely make global headlines. Ships remain the means by which global commerce thrives and the majority of the world is fed, and how nations project power and protect their own shores. Unless you live in a port city, take a cruise, or have a family member who works at sea, this aspect of life is not front of mind. But if the failure to install bolts on a door plug explosively decompresses an aircraft, that's a headline. That is understandable, because for many, that is how most of us travel, and it is that aspect of human experience—when common, shared experience goes terribly wrong—that Aristotle was writing about thousands of years ago.

2

Shipwrecks as Muses

The ship brought up suddenly and violently as if she had struck a rock, and trembled for a few seconds like a leaf.... I perceived the head of the ship to be gradually settling down in the water.... We were more than a thousand miles from the nearest land, and with nothing but a light open boat, as the resource of safety for myself and companions.

—Owen Chase, *Narrative of the Most Extraordinary and Distressing Shipwreck of the Whale-Ship Essex*, 1821

[T]he solid white buttress of his forehead smote the ship's starboard bow, till men and timbers reeled.... Through the breach, they heard the waters pour, as mountain torrent down a flume.... And now concentric circles...spinning, animate and inanimate, all round and round in one vortex, carried the smallest chip of the *Pequod* out of sight...then all collapsed, and the great shroud of the sea rolled on as it rolled five thousand years ago.

—Herman Melville, *Moby-Dick, or The White Whale*, 1851

The failed endeavors of humans on the waters, relayed through tales of shipwrecks, have inspired cultural responses for millennia. Some of our oldest and long-standing stories are those of shipwrecks. The power of the sea to destroy the best that humans can build and to defeat the most skilled sailor is a well-known and oft-told tale. That basic tale has been passed down to modern times through scripture, music, poetry, art, personal narratives, and more recently, through photography and film.

The oldest known surviving work of literature, the *Epic of Gilgamesh*, written on clay tablets in ancient Mesopotamia more than 5,000 years ago, tells of a great flood and the instructions of the gods to a man named Utnapishtim to build a boat by which he could save both people and "all the animals of the field." He did so, just before a great storm killed all humanity, sparing only those on Utnapishtim's great boat. Like the story of Noah in the Bible, the *Epic of Gilgamesh* speaks to humanity's understanding of the power of the sea to destroy, and the importance of a vessel that does not sink. Biblical scholar Ronald Hendel argued in 1995 that this may be because the shape of Utnapishtim's great boat was that of a ziggurat. Nautical archaeologist Ralph K. Pederson makes a more compelling argument for seemingly arcane statements in the epic suggesting that the vessel being described was a traditional sewn-boat of the era.[1]

As I noted in the previous chapter, shipwrecks were a common and well-known form of disaster and great loss of life for much of human history. In the face of such disasters, people saw the hand of God (or in antiquity, the gods—as in Poseidon) as both causing a shipwreck and as the means by which some or all of the passengers were saved. No matter the faith, the act of a ship's wrecking became a religious metaphor: the shipwreck as an act of God, as either a test of faith, a trial that only faith can overcome, a lesson of comparative human hopelessness in the face of an overwhelming power unless rescued by an even greater power, a punishment for the faithless, or the means by which the faithful go to heaven.[2]

The shipwreck as a punishment for human hubris, or other sins, was a common religious theme for centuries. In the King James Version of the Bible, the prophet Ezekiel prophesied the end of the Phoenician port of Tyre and equated the fate of that proud, godless city to that of a lost ship:

> When thy wares went forth out of the seas, thou filledst many people; thou didst enrich the kings of the earth with the multitude of thy riches and of thy merchandise. In the time *when* thou shalt be broken by the seas in the depths of the waters thy merchandise and all thy company in the midst of thee shall fall. (Ezekiel 27:34)

Among biblical references to punishments endured is the lament that "[t]hrice times I was beaten with rods, once I was stoned, thrice I suffered shipwreck, a night and a day I have been in the deep" (2 Corinthians 11:25). The Bible also relates the best-known shipwreck account known to Christians, the story of Saint Paul's shipwreck on Malta (Acts 27:27–88). Paul's faith and the intervention of the Lord save him and his companions. The same is true in various Buddhist texts that speak of divine intervention and protection from shipwrecks. In the Talmud, Rabbi Akiva nearly drowned in a shipwreck until a plank from the wreck gave him a platform on which he could float and survive (Yevamoth 121a). This is an ancient story from antiquity, and one that served as an allegorical debate on what constitutes moral behavior, generally assessed against the question of taking a plank or other means of floating from another person, or casting others into the sea in order to save one's own life.[3] That aspect of shipwreck, both religious and philosophical, is a universal point of conjecture.

Edmund Burke, in his *Philosophical Enquiry into Our Ideas of the Sublime and Beautiful* (1757), summed up the sublime as terror—and with that, the ocean as the means for humanity to be tested:

> No passion so effectually robs the mind of all its powers of acting and reasoning as fear. For fear being an apprehension of pain and death, it operates in a manner that resembles actual pain. Whatever therefore is terrible, with regard to sight, is sublime too, whether this cause of terror, be endured with greatness of dimensions or not.... And to things of great dimension, if we annex an adventitious idea of terror, they become without comparison greater. A level plain of a vast land, is certainly no mean idea; the prospect of such a plain may be as extensive as a prospect of the ocean; but can it ever fill the mind with any thing so great as the ocean itself? This is owing to several causes, but it is owing to none more than this, that the ocean is an object of no small terror. Indeed terror is in all cases whatsoever, either openly or latently the ruling principle of the sublime.[4]

The sublime nature of shipwrecks—and indeed, disaster—is a recurrent theme in culture, and while in more modern times global cataclysms, comet strikes, pandemics, and zombie apocalypses reign in print and at the box office, for much of human history, shipwreck—singular and plural—was the muse.

Shipwreck Tales

Tales of shipwrecks speak to those seeking allegorical meaning. They are symbols of fate, being "one of those brief instants in time when the primal isolation and helplessness of the human condition are revealed."[5] Narratives of voyages, of ocean-based exploration and discovery, tales of shipwrecks, piracy, and other calamities were eagerly listened to or read. The appeal was suspense, adventure, drawing the reader closer, but not too close, to violence, danger, and certain death without the risk of going to sea. As one editor of an 1834 compendium, *The Mariner's Chronicle*, noted, readers "have the enjoyment of his adventures without their dangers. It is pleasant to listen to perils we do not share—to feel our hearts beat, not from fear, but from interest and excitement."[6] The Roman poet Lucretius said it earlier, and it was paraphrased by Robert Southey in 1805: "It is sweet, when the winds disturb the waters on the vast deep, to behold from the land the great distress of another; not because it is a joyous pleasure that any one should be made to suffer, but because it is agreeable to see from what evils thou thyself are free."[7] It is perhaps because of this that the most popular form of firsthand accounts and adventure tales were "true life" stories of shipwrecks in the 18th, 19th, and early 20th centuries.

The popularity of "true" shipwreck tales is demonstrated in one of my favorite books, *Narratives of Shipwrecks and Disasters, 1588–1860*. Edited and introduced by Keith Huntress and published in 1974, it is far more than a catalog. Huntress (1913–1990), then a Professor of English and Distinguished Professor in Sciences and Humanities at Iowa State University, was described by a colleague as "the most literate man I've ever known." It shows in Huntress's compilation and discussion in *Narratives of Shipwrecks and Disasters*. Huntress particularly focused on the period between 1650 and 1860, "the peak period for the wooden sailing ship in commerce and in war."[8] With the ship as the world's sole means of far-flung trade, projection of power, immigration, and even the delivery of goods to market, ships commanded attention in a way that modern readers could not comprehend. Huntress listed 189 separate tomes, the first dating back to 1550, followed by more books and broadsides, published with increasing frequency as the world opened to global maritime trade. With more ships at sea, more disasters were an inevitable consequence. What readers found compelling was the human drama. Shipwreck stories focused on the human experience as defined by behavior as much as fate—or acts of God. Bravery, cowardice, stupidity, hubris, humility, and more played out across the pages as readers sat at home and shivered with horror, or vicarious delight.

Looking at the published tales of shipwrecks of the era, the ones that stand out are those in which the circumstance of loss were horrific; a simple stranding on a beach where no one died was not about to make headlines, let alone be remembered years later. Accidents like those were as common back then as automobile and semi-truck wrecks on the highway are today. An 1873 chart of shipwrecks in and around the hundred miles of coast that surrounded San Francisco's Golden Gate, collated by the U.S. Coast and Geodetic Survey, documents hundreds of incidents. The Golden Gate, at the center of that chart, was the point where ships engaged in trade with the great American port of the Pacific, San Francisco. Some of those wrecks were strandings where a vessel went up onto the rocks or a beach and was later pulled off. Others were total losses when a ship foundered, was overtaken by storms or waves, collided with another, or hit the rocks and broke up. The sheer volume of the "wrecks" would not surprise a modern automobile insurance agent who knows the bad spots on a road—a certain interchange, or freeway on- and off-ramps, if you will. Most car accidents happen going in and out of parking lots. The port of San Francisco in the 19th century was that parking lot. The majority of the wrecks on the 1873 chart, therefore, were a common occurrence that merited only a brief mention in the shipping news section of the local paper, and perhaps were relegated to commentary among the waterfront community of ship owners, pilots, tugboat masters, and underwriters. However, if the wreck had a terrible back story—a tragic loss, a major loss of life, or a spectacular rescue, then it hit the headlines, and might go from local to regional to national, if not international, news.

Shipwrecks in Literature

In the hands of the right author, poet, musician, or artist, even a mundane shipwreck could become something more. Henry Wadsworth Longfellow was inspired, as he explained in a letter to a friend, by "working upon *people's feelings*."[9] Thus he wrote "The Wreck of the *Hesperus*" in 1842. It tells the story of a ship's captain who, while sailing home with his young daughter, is caught in a freezing, offshore storm. As he struggles to bring the schooner *Hesperus* to port, he ties his child to the mast so she will not be washed overboard, even as he continues to reassure her. But he freezes to death at the wheel; the schooner crashes into the reef called Norman's Woe and is lost, as Longfellow wrote, "in the midnight and the snow!"

> At daybreak, on the bleak sea-beach,
> A fisherman stood aghast,
> To see the form of a maiden fair,
> Lashed close to a drifting mast.

The poem closes with the prayer that "Christ save us all from a death like this, On the reef of Norman's Woe!"[10]

"The Wreck of the *Hesperus*" was a success for Longfellow. The schooner *Hesperus*, in real life, was wrecked at anchor in a storm in Boston Harbor, moored off Rowe's Wharf with no one on board on the evening of December 15, 1839. The storm, which was the first of three powerful gales "that took a heavy toll in shipping across the New England coast" that winter, inspired Longfellow to write his poem, perhaps drawing from other accounts of disaster where the dead had washed ashore, lashed to a mast, as well as from reading newspaper accounts of the many wrecks caused by the 1839 storms. The mundane shipwreck of *Hesperus*, as Longfellow's muse, became famous. Norman's Woe is a real reef, near

Gloucester, Massachusetts, and a modern street on the land above it is now named for the schooner *Hesperus*, which never actually wrecked there.[11]

However, as Longfellow himself noted, it does not "matter to the legend lover that the ill-fated schooner was not 'gored' by the 'cruel rocks' just at this point."[12] The introduction to an 1888 illustrated small edition of the poem praised "this ballad in the quaint, old-time style, with its nervous energy and sonorous rhythm, wherein one hears the trampling of waves and crashing of timbers." "Love, the usual ballad motif, is absent and not missed," with the poem focusing on the "almost human struggles and sufferings of the vessel," and the conduct of the "daring, scornful skipper" and his "gentle, devout" daughter. The poem with its "abundant emotion and imagery," with "lines packed with color, movement and meaning," were what made famous a mundane schooner wrecked while at anchor with nary a soul on board.

While nearly all the wrecks of that time are not known to a modern reader, they were publicized in the headlines of the day. Other famous authors of the past wrote about shipwrecks, either reporting the event as fact or using the event as a muse. Henry David Thoreau, in his walks along Cape Cod, was inspired by what he saw: "The sea, vast and wild as it is, bears thus the waste and wrecks of human art to its remotest shore. There is no telling what it may not vomit up; it lets nothing lie....It is still heaving up the tow-cloth of the *Franklin*, and perhaps a piece of some old pirates ship, wrecked more than a hundred years ago, comes ashore to-day."[13]

What Thoreau did not see, Charles Dickens did. The iron-hulled steam clipper *Royal Charter* blew ashore on the Welsh coast near Anglesey in late October 1859, killing over 400 on board, and with only 39 survivors, all lost within sight of shore as the stranded hull was torn apart by the surf. Dickens visited the wreck site, and recounted the tale of the loss, as well as his on-the-scene observations, two months after the disaster, in *The Uncommercial Traveler*:

> Even as I stood on the beach with the words "Here she went down!" in my ears, a diver in his grotesque dress, dipped heavily over the side of the boat alongside the Lighter, and dropped to the bottom. On the

shore by the water's edge, was a rough tent, made of fragments of wreck, where other divers and workmen sheltered themselves, and where they had kept Christmas-day with rum and roast beef, to the destruction of their frail chimney. Cast up among the stones and boulders of the beach, were great spars of the lost vessel, and masses of iron twisted by the fury of the sea into the strangest forms. The timber was already bleached and iron rusted, and even these objects did no violence to the prevailing air the whole scene wore, of having been exactly the same for years and years.[14]

Dickens employed shipwrecks and shipwreck imagery in other works—it was a favorite source of inspiration for him, in fiction, notably literally and as a metaphor in works that include *David Copperfield*, *Dombey and Son*, *Bleak House*, *Barnaby Rudge*, and *Martin Chuzzlewit*. He also did so in his 1856 collaboration with Wilkie Collins, "The Wreck of the Golden Mary," and in factual accounts. Victorians were fascinated by the concept of shipwreck—and the consistent reality of shipwreck loss in that island nation. It's no surprise that Dickens, as the quintessential Victorian author, also loved a shipwreck tale and published several of them.[15]

Another author inspired, not by what he saw, but by what he heard, was Mark Twain; his widely reproduced articles about the loss of the clipper ship *Hornet* and the ordeal of its few survivors first brought him to national and then international attention. Samuel Clemens, going by his *nom de plume*, was residing in Honolulu in the early summer of 1866 as a correspondent for the Sacramento *Daily Union* when he heard that a lifeboat with 14 men, starving and nearly dead, had washed ashore on the north shore of Hawai'i. With a nose for a story, Clemens interviewed the survivors in the hospital in Honolulu, where several of the survivors had been taken to recover. The story they told was harrowing.

The clipper ship *Hornet*, a veteran of the California trade, left New York for San Francisco on January 15 with a dangerous cargo of 20,000 gallons of kerosene and 67 boxes of paraffin candles, as well as iron rails and three locomotives for the transcontinental railroad then being built. On May 3, 1866, in the middle of the open Pacific, a hundred miles north of the Equator, the ship caught fire when the mate and two men dropped a can of varnish they were filling in the hold while holding a lit candle.

In a few seconds, "the fiery torrent had run in every direction, under bales of rope, cases of candles, barrels of kerosene, and all sorts of freight, and tongues of flame were shooting upward through every aperture and crevice toward the deck."[16] There was nothing to be done to save the ship, as the fire spread to the masts and sails within minutes. Captain Josiah Mitchell ordered passengers and crew into three boats, which were hastily loaded with provisions. They stood by as *Hornet* burned to the waterline and sank the following morning.[17]

After 18 days at the sea, the three boats "parted company," as "there were three chances for the saving of some of the party where there could be but one chance if they kept together."[18] After 38 days at sea, the boat with the captain was down to their last rations. In desperate condition, 43 days after the loss of *Hornet*, they finally reached the shores of the Big Island, where they were rescued by the local islanders as they came toward the surf breaking on the reef. The other two boats and the men in them were never seen again. Twain, after his interview, "took no dinner" as he realized he had a major scoop on his hands. He wrote through the night and had a major story ready the next day. Racing to the dock where the "now-and-then" (intermittent) schooner was casting off for San Francisco, Twain nearly missed putting it on board, but "my fat envelope was thrown by a strong hand, and fell on board all right, and my victory was a safe thing."[19] Twain's story broke, with its exclusive interviews, in the July 19 edition of the Sacramento *Daily Union*. From there, carried by telegraph, it was a major story and launched Twain's career as a great American author.[20] A century and a half later, *Hornet* remains a well-known shipwreck, at least to maritime-minded folks and Twain aficionados.

The power of a good shipwreck story, authors discovered, lay in more than a simple recitation of the facts—usually tragic—inherent in the disaster, regardless of whether death came quickly, or slowly. If death did not come, the ordeal itself was transcendent, offering life-changing transformation.[21] The "cruel sea," as author Nicholas Monsarrat called it, was an ideal metaphor to test a human being, strip away pretense, and reveal human nature in the struggle for survival. American writer Stephen Crane, best known for *The Red Badge of Courage*, drew upon his own ordeal to relay that helpless, life in the balance, sense of a shipwreck. One of his most-read tales, "The Open Boat," is a short classic of shipwreck literature. Crane, as a newspaper correspondent, took passage on the steamship *Commodore*, bound from Jacksonville, Florida, to Cuba, carrying guns and ammunition to support a rebellion against Spanish rule of the island. *Commodore* sank off the Florida coast after hitting a sandbar on January 1, 1897.

Crane, the captain, and two other men were cast adrift in a small dinghy. They rowed for 30 hours, heading for the shore. Crane's initial writing on the wreck, published in newspapers throughout the United States, powerfully conveyed in a few meaningful words the reality of the wreck; "there were no shrieks, no groans, but silence, silence and silent, and the *Commodore* sank. She lurched to windward, then swung back, righted and dove into the sea." The wreck is in the past in the short story; Crane focused on the ordeal in the dinghy, and in doing so, created a shipwreck tale that powerfully puts the reader in that overcrowded, 10-foot boat. The story opens abruptly, in the boat:

> NONE OF THEM KNEW THE COLOR OF THE SKY. Their eyes glanced level and remained upon the waves that swept toward them. These waves were gray, except for the tops, which were white, and all the men knew the colors of the sea. The line between sky and water narrowed and widened and fell and rose.[22]

The power of Crane's story is his personal, natural expression of the ordeal, of struggling to reach shore, of finally swimming in rough water to reach the beach, and finding one of his companions dead, washed up on the sand. Stephen Crane published his account in *Scribner's Magazine*, and then in his collection of stories *The Open Boat and Other Tales of Adventure*. Men battling the sea for their lives, survival, and the death of the one crew member all play prominent roles in "The Open Boat." It is an amazing use of personal experience, fictionalized, and as such, a compelling account of people in *extremis*, an ordeal that for some scholars demonstrated how the power of a shipwreck event points out the fragility of our existence, and how we fail when we try to protect ourselves from the power of the sea.[23] What makes this all the more powerful to me as a shipwreck tale is that the wreck of *Commodore* has been located and mapped by archaeologists. A mundane ship, and a common wreck experience, albeit harrowing, were made famous by an author, and that context has inspired discovery and study.

Even the act of encountering a wreck, adrift and lifeless, and perhaps full of the silent dead as another ship passed by it on the open ocean, could be a frightening, if not transcendent, experience. H. M. Tomlinson recounted in his 1920 story, "The Derelict," a steamer's encounter with a half-sunk schooner, "mastless and awash...a lifeless and saddened hulk." The tale ended as they steamed past the wreck with the narrator turning to find a fellow passenger "who had wanted to find the sea. She was gazing at the place where the wreck was last seen, her eyes fixed, her mouth a little open in awe and horror."[24] Tomlinson, as the narrator, assumes the role of a savvy, if not jaded "man of the sea." The poor woman who had wanted to find the sea offered a vicarious opportunity for the reader ashore to shiver in horror while seated, perhaps, by a warm fire, far from the sea.

Shipwrecks in Cultural Expression

Historians note that epic Greek stories like the *Iliad* and *Odyssey* started as songs, and so Odysseus's shipwreck, as laid out by Homer, is one of the earliest known shipwreck songs. As a song, presented in a public performance, the verse, as sung, was not a historical or journalistic account, but rather was intended to evoke an emotional response. That tradition continued in pre-literate as well as non-literate societies. Now, in the early 21st century, the medium of music and song has conveyed the image, emotion, and social messages of shipwrecks to the public more than any other creative medium except the modern motion picture. As the ancient Greeks knew, music conveys emotion. Ballads also tell stories, and they, like ditties, can be effective social protest.[25]

One of the oldest English sea songs, *Neptune's Raging Fury*, dates to around 1650 and lasted for centuries, exhorting the sailor to not be faint-hearted "when the stormy winds do blow."[26] Songs like this celebrated the seaman as a figure of skill and courage, battling a cold, indifferent ocean, as well as disasters brought on by cruel masters and incompetent companies and naval bureaucracies that had led to shipwreck. So, too, did songs about specific shipwrecks. A forgotten example, "The Loss of the *Central America*," was penned in response to the sinking of the U.S. Mail steamer *Central America* off the South Carolina coast on September 12, 1857, in a wild storm, taking 423 people. As news of the disaster reached San Francisco, where most of the dead had sailed from, indignation turned to rage when it was discovered that the steamer was in bad shape and the owners had sent it to sea rather than incur the cost of repair. The song pulled no punches, noting that the steamer, "painted so fine, went down like a thousand of brick," and that the owners had "murdered and swindled the people for years," ending with:

> 'Twould be very fine were the owners aboard,
> And sink where they never would rise;
> 'Twould any amount of amusement afford,
> And cancel a million of lies…
> Their bones should be left in the ocean to rot,
> And their souls be at Satan's commands.

This was no standard parlor song, but rather a rousing protest against corporate malfeasance. It was not a complacent acceptance of disaster. It was a resolution to protect innocent humanity from human error, and a vivid reflection of San Francisco's reaction to a disaster that should not have happened.[27]

Shipwreck songs have been narrative in their nature, telling a story, while at the same time stressing themes also found in shipwreck literature, such as fate, pathos, unnecessary loss, heroic death, and the lack of closure when there is nothing to bury. In reading the sheet music for 19th-century parlor pieces, the emotion and sentiment, perhaps melodramatic to modern eyes and ears, still resonate as voices from that time:

> Sad at heart and resign'd, yet undaunted and brave, They lower'd the boat a mere speck on the wave. First enter'd the mother enfolding her child, It knew she caress'd it look'd up and smiled, Cold was the night as they drifted away.[28]

Or, in addition to pathos, there are frustration and anguish for those who watch from the beach as a near shore wreck is revealed to be one from which nobody can be saved:

> No human power in such an hour, the gallant bark can save;
> Her mainmast gone and hurrying on, she seeks her watery grave.
> Man the life boat, man the life boat, See the dreaded signal flies;
> Ha! She's struck, and from the rock despairing shouts arise.[29]

Shipwrecks and religion, previously mentioned, also brought about a number of hymns.[30] A late 19th-century Baptist hymn, "Throw Out the Lifeline," by Edward S. Ufford, asked the faithful to throw out a line, across "the dark wave," to save a brother who "winds of temptation and billow of woe" were imperiling unless the faithful acted. The Reverend Ufford wrote his song, he later noted, as a religious man who lived near the sea, and knew of shipwrecks and rescues from them via a Lyle Gun "throwing out" a lifeline to rig a breeches buoy and ferry people over the surf, and who one day while preaching saw that his congregation, in his words, "seemed to be in the breakers and needed a life line."[31]

Songs about shipwrecks include some of the most famous wrecks; in all, hundreds of pieces of music were written about the wreck of *Titanic*. The sinking of *Titanic*, with 1,517 dead, was a great loss of life in peacetime. It was shocking that a newly built ship said to be a technological marvel of the age, with an experienced master and crew, could hit an iceberg and sink so quickly in a "modern age." The prevalent cultural response was not confined to outrage, but also pathos, and turning to religion for solace in the face of God's punishment for human folly. Contemporary images strongly made that point, including imagined images of the last moments for *Titanic* victims. Many accounts stressed heroism, citing the men who stood by to allow women and children to fill the lifeboats; others blamed the loss on arrogance and corporate mismanagement, but many invoked religious themes. While the last song played on the deck of *Titanic* was likely not "Nearer, My God to Thee," but perhaps a lively ragtime tune, the song remains powerfully associated with the disaster. Miss E. J. Thibault's song, "Our Sea Heroes," combined both heroism and faith, noting, "Calm and brave our men

Image 2.1. The acceptance of their fate by *Titanic* passengers and the enduring story of the music "Nearer, My God to Thee," a *Toledo News-Bee* cartoon published in Marshall Everett's contemporary book, *The Story of the Wreck of the Titanic* (1912). Wikimedia Commons.

stood upon the *Titanic*, Amid the horror they never forgot honor," and went on to plead "God place our heroes, of the sea, Nearer to Thee, Nearer to Thee."[32]

Titanic's loss, noted by *Titanic* scholar Wyn Craig Wade as a "watershed between the nineteenth and twentieth centuries," proved so powerful a muse that it inspired the greatest cultural response to a shipwreck in the 20th century.[33] The sinking was an international headline, and news coverage of *Titanic*, a century later, still commands banner headlines.

A vast number of songs and ballads, including the folk favorite "When That Great Ship Went Down," were penned. The song was covered by a number of folk musicians, including Leadbelly, Woodie Guthrie, and Pete Seeger; "Yes, it was sad when that great ship went down." The late Harry Chapin, another master of the ballad, sang of shipwreck in his "Dance Band on the *Titanic*." In more recent times, "My Heart Will Go On," Celine Dion's theme song for James Cameron's *Titanic*, a best-selling single that sold in the millions, became the best-known musical link to the wreck for late 20th- and early 21st-century audiences.

The same can be said of another song, which, in its way, made an all-too common shipwreck a legend. The Great Lakes freighter *Edmund Fitzgerald*, bound from Superior, Wisconsin, to Detroit, sank in a powerful winter storm now made famous as the "Gales of November." Caught in heavy freshwater sea, *Edmund Fitzgerald* foundered, taking all of the 29-man crew to the bottom of Lake Superior on November 10, 1975. While known to the Great Lakes community, and a regular occurrence on these inland seas, the wreck gained international fame when Canadian songwriter/singer Gordon Lightfoot hit the charts with his 1976 "The Wreck of the *Edmund Fitzgerald*." Like other bards, poets, and songsters, Lightfoot read of the wreck and penned his ballad. Like Longfellow and the wreck of *Hesperus*, Lightfoot took artistic liberties; nevertheless, the power of the song, telling the tale of a doomed ship and crew, and the closing lines of "does anyone know where the love of God goes, when the waves turn the minutes to hours?," as well as the church bell chiming 29 times "for each man on the Edmund Fitzgerald," made it a 20th-century hit and a cultural landmark.

Canadian folk singer and cultural icon Stan Rogers (1949–1983), who grew up on the shores of Lake Ontario, was no stranger to maritime stories. His first song, the salvage of the fictional shipwreck *Mary Ellen Carter*, told the story of the ship sinking after hitting a rock in a "pouring driving rain," and what it took to bring it back from the sea: patching the hull, sealing the vents, closing the hatches and portholes, rigged cables, and after using a compressor to fill the hull with air, and haul on the cables, to "make the *Mary Ellen Carter* rise again."[34]

While the written and sung word is a millennia-old human response to shipwrecks, the other is artistic depiction. There is a considerable body of art that, with artistic license, nonetheless offer a straightforward depiction of the event: a ship hitting the rocks, a ship on fire, a ship sinking on a violent sea. The late 18th century's Romantic era was a time when marine painting flourished, including shipwreck art; Claude-Joseph Vernet's *The Shipwreck* (1772) and his powerful image of two vessels driving ashore onto the rocks, *A Shipwreck in Stormy Seas* (*Têmpete*) (1773), are two of the better-known examples. However, shipwrecks also inspired metaphorical depictions, especially in the Romantic age of the 19th century; one stand-out among the more famous is Théodore Géricault's *Le Radeau de la Méduse* (*Raft of the Medusa*), painted in 1818–1819. The painting depicts the horrific aftermath to the loss of the French naval frigate *Méduse*. The frigate wrecked off the West African coast as part of a naval convoy on July 2, 1816. The wreck, stranded off a desolate, uninhabited coast, was abandoned three days later, except for a handful of those who opted to remain. Little more than half of the people on board fit into the ship's boats. A huge, makeshift raft, rigged from loose wood and spars, and crowded with 146 people, was towed behind the boats.

The going was rough, and soon the boats cast off the raft, leaving the 146 on board without sufficient food or water. Thirteen days after the raft was cast off, a passing French naval ship discovered the raft, adrift with only 15 survivors. The tale they told when they reached France of madness, murder, cannibalism, and suicide was a national scandal because the disaster was the result of the incompetence of the captain of *Méduse*. The scandal soon became international.[35] A reviewer of Géricault's painting noted after an 1820 showing in London, the disaster, "with its attendant horrors" was well known, but as art historian Christine Riding points out, "there was no significant visual response to the shipwreck in the form of a painting" before Géricault.[36]

Géricault's painting shocked Paris when he unveiled it, after a lengthy period of study, and then putting brush to a very large canvas measuring 338 square feet. A disturbed sea, with clouds on the horizon, a tilted, jury-rigged mast with a small sail, billowing with wind, and the surface of the raft covered with the dead, dying, and desperate, two of them wildly waving to attract attention, dominate the viewer's gaze. Darkness, death, and despair and a glimmer of hope, too late for some, command the scene. The painting is not a historical document. It is a calculated artistic rendition that "discarded journalistic verisimilitude" as Géricault "dared to depart from the literal truth in his expression of a more powerful meaning."[37]

J. M. W. Turner's *A Disaster at Sea*, or *The Wreck of the Amphritite* (1833–1835), is a powerful and horrible scene reminiscent of Gericault's *Raft of the Medusa*.[38] Turner never completed the painting, which depicted the September 1, 1833, wreck of the British convict ship *Amphritite*, which ran aground off the coast of France in a storm after leaving for Australia. The "passengers," 125 convict women and their children, all drowned when the captain refused to allow them to be rescued out of fear for his own liability. The wreck sparked a wave of outrage in Great Britain. In the painting, Turner depicts women in the process of watching the sea take and kill their children.[39]

An Armenian Crimean painter of the 19th century, Ivan Aivzovsky, in *Moonlit Seascape with Shipwreck* (1863), created a moody, dimly lit shipwreck scene depicting the power of the sea, despair and hope, and the tragedy of a shipwreck; his *The Ninth Wave* (1850), where the sea is about to overtake survivors clinging to a broken mast, is yet more powerful. This theme of broken masts and the loss of hope was also depicted in the aftermath of the wave that kills by Virginie Demont-Breton in *Stella Maris* (1894) as a wave-tossed broken mast rises out of the swell with the limp bodies of two drowned sailors. Alfred Guillou captured a heartbreaking image of a man, possibly the father of a drowned boy, holding the corpse as he clings to an overturned boat in tossing waves and broken masts in *Adieu* (1892).

As Dickens, Thoreau, and others were inspired by encountering wreckage strewn on beaches or coastal rocks, so too was artist Ary Renan, whose *Jeune fille contemplate un crâne près d'un bateau naufragé au bord de la mer* (*Young Woman Contemplating a Skull by a Shipwreck on the*

Beach) (1892) has a classically inspired figure of a young woman looking at a human skull lying next to a rusted, seaweed-draped anchor inside a broken, weathered hull on a beach at low tide. It graphically reveals the consequences of shipwrecks, but in this case, that of an unknown ship and an unidentified victim.

The perils of Arctic exploration and the loss of ships to polar ice served as inspiration for visual depictions of these disasters that were rarely drawn from reality, but rather from the popular imagination, or as allegorical lessons. Edwin Landseer, in *Man Proposes, God Disposes*, and Frederick Church, in *Iceberg*, depicted broken masts and shattered hulls on icy shores, while Caspar David Friedrich's *Die Gescheiterte Hoffnung* (*The Polar Sea*, sometimes referred to as *The Sea of Ice*) captured the masses of impenetrable ice in a land that eats ships. Friedrich's *Schiff im Eismeer* (*Ship in the Sea of Ice*) and his *Das Wrack der Hoffnung, das Eismeer des Polarmeres* (*The Wreck of Hope, The Sea of Ice Polar Sea*) are better-known images of the human costs of Arctic voyages.

Shipwreck and fate dominate Winslow Homer's 1899 painting, *The Gulf Stream*, as a dismasted, derelict vessel drifts with a seaman lying on the deck while sharks circle. Scholars also see the painting as one that "probes the dialectic of inclusion versus exclusion" as the Black sailor on the derelict "has broken the mold of the servant role to become an individual actor on the historical stage."[40] There are two versions of the painting—another shows it empty and awash as sharks thrash about the drifting hulk—perhaps a nod to the seeming inevitability of shipwreck—and yet in Homer's painting *After the Hurricane* (1899), a Black man lies on a beach, next to boat wreckage, seemingly asleep and not dead. While some viewers may feel that the man in the boat is doomed, scholar Peter Erickson argues that the painting raises a "more open-ended question" as the man in the boat may be struggling to survive. Scholar Peter Wood, however, sees the painting as an allegory speaking to the reality of Black life in America from colonial times, through slavery, and beyond in the face of "seemingly insurmountable odds." It is important to remember that *The Gulf Stream* was painted during the Jim Crow era.[41]

Photography as art also relied on shipwrecks as a powerful subject. These included *carte d'visite* views, postcards, many of them of shipwrecks stranded and broken on the shore once the storm subsided, majestic ships speared and hanging off coastal rocks, or other images that are artistic and also stark and powerful. Iconic examples include photographer W. K. Case's image of the Canadian Pacific Railway steamer *Princess May* stranded at low tide on the rocks at Sentinel Island in Alaska's Inside Passage in 1910; Frank Hurley's images of the trapped barkentine *Endurance* crushed and taken by the ice off Antarctica in 1915 during the doomed Trans-Antarctic Expedition of Sir Ernest Shackleton; Leslie Jones's compelling images of the listing steamer *Vestris* sinking off the coast of Virginia on November 14, 1928, as men struggle in the image to get across a heavily listing deck and launch the lifeboats; and photographer Harry Trask's Pulitzer-winning series of photographs of the liner *Andrea Doria* sinking off Nantucket on July 26, 1956. The power of

Image 2.2. The Canadian Pacific Railroad steamship *Princess May*, stranded on the rocks of Sentinel Island in Alaska's Inside Passage.
Photograph by W. H. Case, 1910. Wikimedia Commons.

photographs remains potent in a digital world; Remo Casilli's images of a migrant shipwreck's wreckage and personal items, including a child's clothing, backpacks, and shoes, strewn on the beach amid pieces of the wooden hull at Steccato di Cutro near Crotone, Italy, on February 26, 2023, are stark reminders that deadly shipwrecks are not confined to the past.

In the 21st century, the power of shipwreck imagery has now transcended images taken at the time of loss before the wreck "disappeared" into the sea or sand. Underwater photography and film that provide a glimpse of ships at various depths allow the world to reconnect with lost vessels—including those that most people have never heard of—through the power of the image. There are a number of amazing photographs of shipwrecks that date back to the earliest underwater photos by the Cousteau team of piles of amphorae on the Mediterranean seabed, or the photographs of ancient wreck sites off the Turkish coast taken by Institute of Nautical Archaeology's Don Frey—the types of images that once defined the covers and pages of *National Geographic Magazine*. The advent of underwater photography began to share more images, especially as the digital age began, of "iconic" collections of wrecks at Truk (Chuuk) Lagoon, and in the Great Lakes, where the fresh cold water preserved vessels so intact that they earned the name "ghost ships."

The eeriness of a diver swimming through a flooded dining saloon, or pushing open the door of a passenger cabin, or hovering over the helm in the ship's wheelhouse, were captured and shared, first in print, and then online as publication evolved. A recent book by Jonas Dahm and Carl Douglas is a personal favorite. *Ghost Ships of the Baltic Sea* is an apt title, for the Baltic, with its lack of wood-eating marine life, preserves vessels centuries old. Dahm and Douglas, explorers dedicated to a "look, don't touch" ethos, capture images in the green-tinged sea of intact or nearly intact vessels of centuries past, noting that "each shipwreck is a time capsule with its own journey and its own story."[42]

The images in the book hint at those stories—cannon still protruding from the gunports of wooden warships, anchors still slung and caught on the edge of a 300-year-old ship, masts and rigging blocks lying on the seabed alongside an intact hull, a wooden door on the seabed next to the wrecked ship it came from, with the iron key still in the lock—or the intact iron hull of the steamship *Elise Podeus*, which vanished at sea without a trace in 1900, never seen again until now. A passenger saloon with tables and chairs in position and the gimballed fixture for an oil light hanging from the overhead; a wooden box with its top off and filled with gold pocket watches of the 18th century in one wreck, bottles of champagne in a straw-filled crate on another; a captain's cabin with his uniform jacket and his bowler hat, reminders that "[h]istory has stood still in this room. Phrases like 'time capsule' and 'frozen in time' seem somehow inadequate. This is a highly personal time capsule. Unusual even for the Baltic, it gives us an exclusive insight into the people's lives on board."[43] But the eeriest—and evoking the iconic power of shipwreck imagery—is the unsmiling face of the figurehead of an iron barque of the 19th century that now rests 260 feet (80 meters) below the Baltic.

Recent scholarship by Sara A. Rich focuses on the images of and derivative imagery drawn from shipwrecks as *memento mori*. I find her approach fascinating.[44] The draw of ruins is an old and favorite human pastime, be they in deserts, jungles, atop mountains, or under the sea. They offer the viewer an opportunity to confront human vanity, failure, and entropy, as well as to reflect on fortitude, perseverance, and hope. These all come to the forefront with the opportunity to gaze at the Sphinx, the Forum of Rome, Delphi, Copan, the Great Wall, Stonehenge, and many other sites. For me, that moment happens often, given my travels as an archaeologist who remains as eager to see the remnants of the past as I was 50 years ago as a teenager. One of those opportunities arose at the edge of the desert, outside Luxor, Egypt. The Colossi of Memnon, two massive funerary monuments to Pharaoh Amenhotep III, towered before me, 10 times taller than I was. I stood in awe on that first visit, thinking of not only the archaeological meaning of these monuments, but also the opportunity to recite Shelley's "Ozymandias," invoking the poem's sense of how the two colossi, damaged but still standing, now mark an empty space where once a great building stood that spoke to the power of the Pharaoh. "Look on My Works, Ye Mighty, and Despair!" Yes, indeed—that is the power of ruins. They can compel inspiration, or a reflection on the impermanence of human endeavor and achievement.

Add into this mix, then, the concept of the shipwreck, a liminal body that rests in the oceans, lakes, and rivers of the world, especially those which rest nearly intact in the deep ocean, as Dahm and Douglas powerfully present in *Ghost Ships*, or the underwater images of Shackleton's recently found *Endurance*, seemingly caught between life and death, past and present, and once home to humans, now habitat for marine organisms. In *Shipwreck Hauntography*, Rich delves into the nature and meaning of various wrecks, in a variety of settings, that span the modern era of the past 500 years, from *Santa María*, a wreck not yet "discovered" and yet well-known and replicated, to *Costa Concordia*, with famous examples that include *Mary Rose, Batavia, La Belle*, HMS *Erebus*, and HMS *Terror*.

The interface with art and archaeology is powerful, and Rich's work points to and strengthens that interface with archaeology underwater and especially with shipwrecks. With this focus, Rich includes, and magnificently so, her own art along with the text, to drive home the book's essential point: that wrecks are not dead, nor do they need us to "save" them or resurrect them; rather, we should see them as enduring artifacts that speak beyond their own space and time as post-human and in their marine environment as habitats, as nonhuman spaces. The artworks, or "Hauntographs," are, like portraits of long-dead people, a means by which we in the modern seek to bridge the gaps between life and death. They also help us cope with bereavement. These images, haunting and yet compelling, come back to how we confront that which was not truly lost, but for most remains beyond the veil—or at least until a diver, submersible, or robotic vehicle encounters it.

Another medium now graphically sharing shipwrecks is two- and three-dimensional digital imagery using photogrammetry and Light Detection and Ranging (LIDAR), as well as high-resolution sonar. These products range from orthomosaics, which have replaced two-dimensional photomosaics, to practically "virtual" dives. The bright colors of high-resolution sonar and LIDAR offer surreal virtual tours of shipwrecks, particularly those that are more intact, especially when rendered as 3D point clouds. This technology is used in navigating robotic vehicles that inspect and document the submerged environment (such as infrastructure) as well as wrecks. Through photomosaics and the use of smaller remotely operated vehicles to go into deep wrecks where divers cannot reach—or do not dare to enter for safety reasons—the realm of shipwreck exploration can now be a desktop exercise in the 21st century.

The same technologies have been used to make increasingly accurate and detailed models of seabeds, and as machine learning and artificial intelligence (AI) have emerged, have aided in locating and documenting wrecks.[45] Color satellite imagery in turbid waters is also now being used to locate shipwrecks in shallow coastal waters by tracking the movement of silt around the hidden forms of ship hulls.[46] Just a decade ago, technologies such as BlueView® became available, providing brightly colored models of the intact Klondike Gold Rush steamboat *A.J. Goddard*, and the Civil War gunboat USS *Hatteras*'s machinery as it emerged from the sandy seabed of the Gulf of Mexico. The imagery makes a powerful point. What was once the realm of artists working with oil paint to convey what a shipwreck looked like is now a digital product. One example of this again focuses on *Titanic*. The only way to convey all of the wreck to the public at the time of its discovery 40 years ago was through the art of Ken Marschall. His paintings—on the cover of *National Geographic* and in books, are iconic art. Decades later, in 2024, robotic vehicles captured high-resolution images of *Titanic*. These images replaced earlier photos, taken in 2010, that were created by merging hundreds of individual images of focused portions of the wreck into a unified whole. The leaders of the 2024 expedition include two of the leaders of the 2010 mission, Dave Gallo and Evan Kovacs. What returned from the seabed are stunning, high-resolution, three-dimensional images of the wreck. *Titanic*'s wreck has at last been raised "virtually."

Another recent example is the work done by Falko Kuester and Dominique Rissolo of the University of California, San Diego's Qualcomm Institute's Cultural Heritage Engineering Initiative (CHEI), and the University's Center of Interdisciplinary Science for Art, Architecture and Archaeology (CISA3) with Philippe Rouja, Bermuda's Custodian of Historic Wrecks in the Bermuda 100 Project. A series of shipwrecks, scanned and rendered, are available online for virtual dives, drawing on LIDAR data that captured point clouds, high-resolution photography, and photogrammetry, as well as structure-from-motion that converted two-dimensional images into the three-dimensional computer models that are now online. Other examples include the same approach taken to document the wreck of Shackleton's *Endurance* when it was discovered.

Where this new technology may prove beneficial, as well as disruptive, is film. Shipwrecks on film, both newsreel footage and as cinematic art, have followed the traditional narratives of a cruel sea and humanity's ineptness, cowardice, fate, noble sacrifice, salvation, and redemption. Shipwrecks, real and fictional, both as part of a larger story or as a standalone in a disaster film, have been frequent players on the screen. I've previously mentioned the saga of the wreck of the whaleship *Essex*, and how it was fictionalized by Herman Melville in 1851. That book was the basis of the 1926 silent film *The Sea Beast*, starring John Barrymore, followed by the better-known *Moby Dick* (1956), starring Richard Basehart and Gregory Peck. The film may be dated, but Peck's powerful performance and, even without modern graphics, the ramming of *Pequod* and the slow spin of the battered hulk in the vortex as it sinks are still moving to viewers. The 2015 film *In the Heart of the Sea*, based on Nathaniel Philbrick's bestselling book, focused on the real-life *Essex* and its tale of shipwreck and harrowing survival. Whether the events as shown in the ramming of the ship, or its burning and sinking, are accurate or fictional, the result and the soundtrack convey both despair and hope. The dramatic moment where Mr. Chase is nearly lost is shipwreck drama at modern Hollywood's graphic best.

The wreck of *Titanic* has inspired the largest number of films, with the standouts being *Titanic* (1953), the 1958 classic *A Night to Remember*, and James Cameron's epic *Titanic* (1997). Cameron's subsequent *Ghosts of the Abyss* (2003) not only provided a powerful sense of the site and the technology and effort required to reach it, the trailer tagged it as "the adventure is real—the experience is real, and the boundaries between you and a legend will disappear." *Ghosts of the Abyss* brilliantly merged imagery of the actual wreck with computer graphics and superimposed "ghosts" from *Titanic* to give viewers an evocative sense of the disaster at a human scale. I'll talk more about this amazing film later.

Other standout famous shipwreck films include Alfred Hitchcock's *Lifeboat* (1944), *The Poseidon Adventure* (1972), and its 2006 remake, *Poseidon*, by Wolfgang Peterson. *The Perfect Storm* (2000), another Peterson film, based on the bestseller by Sebastian Junger, recounts the real-life loss of the fishing boat *Andrea Gail* and offers a heartbreaking portrayal of the ship and crew's last moments. Hope raised when the storm seems to pass gives way to terror as *Andrea Gail* climbs a massive wave, and then falls and capsizes. The captain stays in his sinking vessel as it goes down. The last survivor rides the waves until he surrenders to the sea. Another evocative scene is fictional. In *The Life of Pi* (2012), Pi hangs suspended below the ocean surface as the ship, lights still on, glides down into the darkness.

Into the Depths

The thought of shipwrecks at rest below the water has inspired a variety of cultural responses. As with music and art, they have ranged from *memento mori* to metaphor. One of the best-known examples is Thomas Hardy's 1912 poem, "The Convergence of the Twain," that starts with *Titanic*, lying "In a solitude of the sea, Deep from human vanity," cold, silent, dead, with

> Dim moon-eyed fishes near
> The daintly gilded gear
> Gaze querying, "What means this sumptuousness down here?"[47]

Engravings drawn from divers' impressions in the 19th and early 20th centuries gave readers of illustrated magazines of the era an impression of the "terrors of the deep," ranging from "monstrous" sea creatures inhabiting what once had been a human space, and encounters with the floating dead trapped in sunken hulls. Other images of the era showed divers in "sub marine armor" at work exploring and salvaging shipwrecks.

The accounts of undersea explorers and their adventures included 19th- and early 20th-century accounts from the "Heroic Age of Diving."[48] Pioneer divers like John Green and William Taylor in the mid-19th century, or early 20th-century U.S. Navy diver Tom Eadie, thrilled readers with true-life tales of discovering shipwrecks below, what they found, and their close escapes. Those pioneers wore thick canvas suits, with lead or bronze weighted boots, and helmets, usually made of bronze, with air fed by hose into the helmet or "hardhat." Known in diving circles as "standard dress," this gear was the means by which underwater exploration took place in the 19th and 20th centuries, and modern versions of standard dress, including helmets, or "hats," are used in the 21st century.

The reminiscences of divers, be they explorers, archaeologists, or treasure hunters, remain a frequent subject of publication, as well as the basis for recurrent television series and specials that first gained an audience with the undersea adventures of Jacques Cousteau. Cousteau's *The Undersea World of Jacques Cousteau*, which aired from 1968 to 1976, remained a staple of reruns globally for years after. Shipwrecks featured on the show include an unsuccessful search for a Spanish galleon supposedly laden with treasure, and Truk (Chuuk) Lagoon and its lost fleet from World War II.

The wreck, as an entity in the deep, has also inspired fiction writers, among them Peter Benchley, whose book *The Deep* (1976) told of a Spanish wreck, overlain and hidden beneath the later wreck of a freighter, *Goliath*, lost in World War II with a cargo that includes morphine, and of a young couple's dives and misadventures. As a bestseller, *The Deep* was the basis for the 1977 film by the same name, and it has been remade in later years as *Into the Blue* (2005) and *Fools Gold* (2008). Benchley's *Jaws* does not feature a shipwreck, but as has been noted, the shark ends up sinking the boat *Orca*, sent to hunt it, in a dramatic ending sequence not unlike the end of *Moby Dick*. The actual *Orca*—a movie prop "boat"—is now itself an archaeological "shipwreck" that has been investigated by archaeologist Pete Capelotti, who has noted how fans of the movie have taken something fictional, treated it as real, and looted the "wreck" for souvenirs. Art imitates life.[49]

At the same time, Clive Cussler, in *Raise the Titanic* (1976), introduced the world to the quest for and the discovery of shipwrecks in the submarine world through his protagonist, Dirk Pitt. Derring-do, high tech, shipwrecks, and lost treasure were persistent themes, but always with ties to historical ships and shipwrecks. For more than four decades, Cussler and his co-authors built a vast library of over 80 books, two of which were made into motion pictures, and also inspired a six-season National Geographic series modeled on Cussler's real-life shipwreck hunting adventures, *The Sea Hunters*. Cussler sponsored a series of expeditions in search of famous shipwrecks; his book *The Sea Hunters* chronicled the stories behind the ships and the adventures he and his team underwent in quest of these lost ships. *The Sea Hunters* (2000–2006), thanks to shipwrecks and Cussler, was watched by some 400 million viewers in 196 international jurisdictions.[50]

At roughly the same time, shipwreck divers John Chatterton and Richie Kohler, made famous in the book *The Shadow Divers*, starred in *Deep Sea Detectives*, produced by Lone Wolf, a U.S.-based company, for four seasons as it followed the two as they worked as "underwater detectives" to "solve the mysteries behind the dark underwater graves of ships, planes and submarines."[51] It was also highly popular and drew an international audience. Since then, a number of documentaries have been made, including stand-alone specials on specific wrecks or locales, as well as a number of series. One longer-lasting series was *Drain the Oceans*, by Mallinson-Sadler Productions. I had the privilege of serving as the series advisor. Starting over a decade ago as a one-off special for National Geographic, it grew over several years into a regular series. The premise, using accurate data to create computer graphics that present the viewer with what lies below in broad daylight, proved popular, and six seasons ensued until 2023. *Drain the Oceans* viewers powerfully responded to *Titanic*, 19th-century wrecks in the Gulf of Mexico, Kublai Khan's lost fleet off Japan's Takashima Island, wrecks from the D-Day landings, battleships lost in both world wars,

Baltic wrecks, American Civil War shipwrecks, U-boats, the atomic test fleet at Bikini, pirate wrecks, the slave ship *Clotilda*, and a number of other sites. The series reached people around the world, of all ages and of different backgrounds. It was a reminder that shipwrecks and the work that I and my colleagues do as archaeologists have appeal beyond the academy. Proof of that are the times when people recognize me from my appearances on such television shows as *Drain the Oceans*. Individual documentaries, including James Cameron and Robert Ballard in "Back to the Titanic," were highly popular and award-winning; these "visual narratives" reached a global audience, as did *Drain the Oceans*, *The Sea Hunters*, and *Deep Sea Detectives*.

Ultimately, shipwrecks appeal to us because they speak to resilience, survival, heroism as well as sacrifice, loss, helplessness, and some of the worst as well as the best aspects of human behavior. They speak to adventure, to discovery, to the quest into the deep for that which was once lost and is now found. That includes stories lost or forgotten, or at one time suppressed. Shipwrecks feature in popular culture because they intrigue, horrify, and compel us. The rapid spread of news stories of new finds of shipwrecks, even the humblest, like winter storm-exposed broken wooden bones of a ship on a beach, reminds us of how shipwrecks compel us to stop and take notice, even if for a moment, in a fast-paced world. Shipwrecks, however, are more than just the subject of curiosity and fascination. As physical entities, they also have value to society.

3

Shipwrecks as Historical Sites, Graves, and Memorials

When we left that sad spot unmarked in the waters of Lake Erie, we knew and felt no less robbed of hope than if it were an earthly grave.
—John B. Green, 1861[1]

There are many famous ships in history, celebrated for their roles in exploration, immigration, and naval battles, or recognized as exemplars of a type of ship, or known because of their nefarious role in slavery or piracy or for the tragic circumstances of their loss. If a poll was taken a century ago on America's most famous or most important ships, the answers would likely have been what generations past viewed as icons—ships of colonial exploration or expansion, sea power, engineering, or shipbuilding prowess. Among the famous ships that likely would have been named then would be Columbus's *Nina*, *Pinta*, and *Santa Maria*, Francis Drake's *Golden Hinde*, the Pilgrim ship *Mayflower*, USS *Constitution*, the clipper ship *Flying Cloud*, the battlecruiser USS *Maine*, the battleship USS *Arizona*, the aircraft carrier USS *Enterprise*, and the nuclear submarine USS *Nautilus*. Those were seen as iconic ships that became symbols.

In the cases where these ships were lost or sank, the ruins of these famous ships also were seen as "iconic." One example is the late 19th-century discovery and excavation of Viking-era ships in Denmark, Norway, and

Sweden. Those finds and digs coincided with a Victorian-era revival of interest in Nordic heritage and "Scandinavism," the term for a new sense of nationalism in those countries as they celebrated a common ancestry. The discoveries and exhumations of the hulks of the thousand-year-old Viking ships made them symbols of national and pan-Scandinavian pride.

The construction of a sailing replica for the 1893 Columbian Exposition in Chicago, a replica of the Gokstad ship, excavated just 13 years earlier, was funded by public subscriptions. Sailing that replica, named *Viking*, to the United States to appear at a fair honoring Christopher Columbus was a stroke of marketing genius, especially as long forgotten sagas of a Norse presence in America before Columbus were retold. In Sweden, the 20th-century raising and lengthy restoration of *Vasa* made that ship, once forgotten, a symbol once again of Swedish pride. The same happened with the lengthy decade-long excavation and raising of Henry VIII's *Mary Rose*. Its connection to a famous British monarch made even a warship plagued by design flaws into a modern distraction and a source of British pride as the country was wracked by a counterculturalrevolution, social unrest, and riots.

The concept of a ship embodying the ethos of a nation or people, or being "heroic" through the actions of its crew in an epic voyage or great sea battles, is nothing new. When Francis Drake completed his circumnavigation of the world in 1580, his ship *Golden Hinde* was preserved and displayed on the Thames until it rotted decades later and was broken up. The Royal Navy ship of the line *Victory*, flagship at the British victory at Trafalgar, was saved by the Royal Navy after public outcry over plans to demolish it in 1831. In 1922, after a new campaign to save and restore *Victory*, it became a museum ship and monument to Horatio, Lord Nelson, the victor of Trafalgar, who died on its deck in the heat of battle. It remains on display at Portsmouth as the world's oldest naval vessel that is still in commission after nearly three centuries.

In the United States, a wide range of battleships, aircraft carriers, destroyers, submarines, and other warships, many of them National Historic Landmarks, are preserved and displayed as symbols of American might, service, and sacrifice. The first ship to go through the Northwest

Passage, the Norwegian sloop *Gjoa*, is displayed after a near-complete rebuilding at the Norwegian National Maritime Museum. The wooden-hulled motor schooner *St. Roch*, built in the 1920s for the Royal Canadian Mounted Police, and the second vessel to go all the way, as well as the first vessel to completely circumnavigate North America, is a Canadian icon and is displayed at the Vancouver Maritime Museum in British Columbia. In Havana, the yacht *Granma*, on which Fidel Castro returned to Cuba in 1956 to resume his revolution against Fulgencio Batista, has been displayed in a glass building next to Havana's *Museo de la Revolución* as an iconic symbol of Castro and his revolution.

I've seen all of these historic ships, as well as over a hundred other famous preserved ships. That includes raised and restored vessels, and the world's oldest, the exhumed and reassembled cedar hull of Pharaoh Khufu's solar ship. Interred with other craft in pits cut into the rock of the Giza Plateau next to the Great Pyramid, it is nearly 5,000 years old and the world's oldest intact ship. Other ancient Egyptian craft exist only as fragments. These ships were interred with Pharaoh, along with other items, for his use in the afterlife, but the boat had special meaning, as it would carry him across the sky with Ra, the Sun God. Made of the fabled cedar wood of Lebanon, the 143-foot-long ship is long, sleek, and beautifully modeled from hundreds of pieces of wood, with the hull mimicking the appearance of more ancient Egyptian craft built of bundled papyrus reeds. Egyptian archaeologist Kamal el-Mallakh, whose excavation at Giza revealed the pit in 1954, oversaw its reconstruction and display in its own special museum next to the pit where it had been found. While not a shipwreck, the sun boat shares the same status of other maritime relics brought back "from the dead" as a symbol of ancient glory and a modern connection to those fabled pasts.[2] It was moved from its original museum to the new Grand Egyptian Museum in August 2021.

While visiting many museums, historic ships, and shipwreck exhibitions internationally in the later decades of my career, my love of ships, fascination with shipwrecks, and initial education came from an intensive and focused decade at home in the United States. In my 13-year-career with the National Park Service, I helped establish and led the national maritime preservation program from the mid-1980s into the early 1990s. One of our major tasks was to inventory, document, and study America's large preserved historic vessels to determine which should be specially designated as National Historic Landmarks. I personally conducted many of the surveys, traveling the country to steam, motor, and sail, or visit restoration work in progress.

Out of more than 300 of these "Great American Ships," as our inventory was ultimately titled when published, we prepared the paperwork for nearly half of them to be considered as landmarks. While some reflected turning points in history, revolutionary changes in design, or were the setting for major events, others were exceptionally well-preserved examples of vanishing types of vessels, among them fireboats, schooners, presidential yachts, tug boats, snag boats, riverboats, and lightships. Given the focus of the landmark program, though, only three shipwrecks that I studied were designated as National Historic Landmarks. They were all warships—USS *Monitor*, USS *Arizona*, and USS *Utah*. They were all made landmarks because of their mythic status as symbols of bravery and sacrifice.

Engineering achievements were also a key part of the decision to designate USS *Monitor*, because it embodied and incorporated changes in propulsion, armament, and construction. It featured a hull kept low below the water, a thick armored belt of iron and wood, a flat iron deck, and a rotating turret with two powerful cannons, and it was propelled by a steam engine that drove a single propeller. The impact of its signature battle in changing the face of naval warfare was another. In their famous clash at Hampton Roads in March 1861, *Monitor* and *Virginia* forever changed war at sea in the first battle between two ships of iron. The age of wooden warships had come to an end. But that was not the only reason it was designated as a landmark.

The Civil War–era view that *Monitor* had stopped *Virginia*'s destruction of the wooden U.S. Navy fleet, as opposed to what really happened—a stalemate—made it a national "hero." In essence, that is what I, as the author of the landmark study, ended up arguing. *Monitor*, thanks to the

Image 3.1. A research diver hovers over the bow of the wreck of USS *Monitor*. Monitor National Marine Sanctuary, National Oceanic and Atmospheric Administration.

sense in the North that it had won the fight with CSS *Virginia* and had staved off a Union disaster, was transformed into a near-sacred symbol of American valor and victory. The low-freeboard, "cheesebox on a raft," built quickly and to a hitherto untried design, ultimately proved a technological dead end. But in 1862, only a few engineers and naval officers knew that or the battle's inconclusive ending. Instead, the myth of USS *Monitor* inspired the cult of the ironclad, with souvenirs, songs, poems, and the phrase "that's an ironclad guarantee" as part of American culture. That it was designed by John Ericsson, an immigrant who had made America his home, embodying one of the defining aspects of the American dream, was also key in its designation as a National Historic Landmark in 1986.[3]

Historical significance also comes through a vessel's participation in local, regional, national, and international areas of trade. These included global whaling, fishing, the shipment of grain from California to Great Britain in the 19th century, the international copper trade, dominated by

Britain but important to the economies of Cuba, Chile, and Australia, and the opium and tea trades, with their significance to India, China, Great Britain, and the United States. The passage of time has left few examples of ships engaged in these trades afloat or in a museum. Only one American whaler, *Charles W. Morgan*, survives afloat. British tea clippers were sleek 19th-century sailing ships, built to make what were in their time incredibly fast global voyages to deliver tea from India to the British and American markets in an age when tea was an expensive luxury item. These vessels raced each other across the South China Sea, the Indian Ocean, around the Cape of Good Hope, and then up the Atlantic to Britain. The first to arrive home would command the highest prices. Newspapers regularly followed the tea races, bets were made, and the tea clippers dominated the trade until the emergence of faster, larger ocean steamers and the opening of the Suez Canal in 1869, which became the shortcut used by the steamers. These factors made the tea clippers obsolete by the early 1870s.

The demise of the tea clippers has left only two vessels that survived into the 21st century that are not sunken wrecks. One has been preserved and restored. That is *Cutty Sark*, preserved and displayed in its dry dock in Greenwich, England. Built in 1869, at the end of the era of clipper dominance in the tea trade, *Cutty Sark* did not last long as tea trader, shifting to carrying bales of wool from Australia to Britain before becoming a general cargo ship. After being sold to Portuguese owners in 1895, the 53-year-old clipper returned to Britain as a training ship for sea cadets. Retired in its 85th year, *Cutty Sark* was placed in a dry dock, restored, and put on public display in Greenwich. The century-and-half-old ship remains on display today as one of the world's best-known historic ships. The only other tea clipper above the water is the iron skeleton of the tea clipper *Ambassador*, which lies ashore on a beach in the Straits of Magellan. I've made the pilgrimage to those bones twice. In addition to being a tea clipper, it is also one of only three composite-built ships that survive ashore or afloat. Composite-built ships of the 19th century were wooden-clad iron-framed vessels. The use of the iron allowed ship builders to launch sleek, sharp-lined clippers that, while not able to carry much cargo, could sail fast—the seemingly winning formula that worked for the few decades that the tea clippers survived as viable ocean traders.

The various British ships lost in Canada's Arctic Archipelago during the 19th-century quest for a Northwest Passage are also historic sites. England's interest in contesting Spain and Portugal's increasing global domination followed Spanish voyages and conquests in the Americas and the Pacific. The idea of an oceanic passage across the top of the world, essentially bypassing the tip of South America, spurred a series of voyages starting with the reign of Queen Elizabeth I. Voyages by Martin Frobisher in 1576 and 1578, John Davis in 1587, and Henry Hudson, who instead sailed into the great bay that bears his name, were followed by Robert Bylot and William Baffin in 1616.

Their instructions were to sail to the 80th parallel and thence head west to Japan. Instead, they mapped the edges of the great bay that bears Baffin's name. Thick ice blocked the Arctic Archipelago that trended west, and ice soon closed Baffin Bay. It was two centuries before warming temperatures and the entry of whalers into those newly thawed waters that expeditions headed north with the hope of thence going west. The early 19th-century voyage of William Edward Parry almost sailed all the way through in 1818–1819, but his ships *Hecla* and *Griper* were stopped by ice. After a long Arctic winter, they were able to retreat in 1820 and return home. Despite difficult conditions, no one died. Hope in Britain was high for the "conquest" of the Northwest Passage.

What followed were expeditions by land and canoe, led by traders from the Hudson's Bay Company, and a disastrous trek led by Lieutenant John Franklin of the Royal Navy in 1819–1821. Parry returned in 1821, but the expedition quickly ended after the shipwreck of one of his ships, HMS *Fury*, and a close escape from ice that threatened to trap his surviving ships in 1823. Subsequent voyages by Parry, Captain John Ross, and Captain George Back all concluded without success and as near-disasters. Ross lost his ship *Victory*, but escaped in small boats after wintering and surviving from provisions left by Parry at Fury Beach, where that ship had been lost years earlier. Four years after entering the Arctic Archipelago, Ross and his men were rescued in 1833. Back's expedition ended in near-shipwreck in 1837. His crew constantly manned the pumps to get their ice-wracked ship home.

The Northwest Passage's bad reputation did not deter a major push by the Royal Navy to send John Franklin, then a captain, into the Arctic with two ships, *Erebus* and *Terror*, and 134 men. They sailed from the Thames in May 1845, rendezvoused with a supply ship in Greenland's Disko Bay, and sailed west, never to be seen again by anyone but the Inuit people they encountered in the archipelago. Trapped by ice, suffering from bad provisions and a variety of ailments, they all died. The failure of *Erebus* and *Terror* to make the passage became apparent by 1848, sparking the first of what would be multiple missions that found abandoned camps, personal items, and a few graves dug into the frozen ground with the frozen corpses of some of Franklin's crew.

Then came a shocking report from Dr. John Rae, who searched for Franklin on land for his employers, the Hudson's Bay Company. Encountering nomadic Inuit, whose language he spoke, Rae learned that the ships had been trapped by ice, abandoned by their crews, and that none of them had survived. The last desperate survivors, he was told, had turned to cannibalism to survive, and then died. Rae purchased a number of relics of the expedition from the Inuit. His account shocked Britain, and led to more expeditions to seek more evidence and hopefully find survivors. Those expeditions ended disastrously. The ship *Investigator*, trapped by ice, was abandoned and its crew barely escaped. A major expedition with several ships, led by Captain Edward Belcher, was also trapped.

Belcher abandoned many of his ships to the ice and fled in 1854. That left more shipwrecks in the "land that eats ships," as the Arctic came to be called. A private expedition sponsored by Franklin's widow in 1858 found more relics, skeletons face down on the tundra, and a note sealed in a metal cylinder tucked into a rock cairn. Dated April 25, 1848, it had been left by the surviving officers of Franklin's ships. They wrote that Franklin had died in 1847, and they had just abandoned their ships and were marching south. While other traces of lost men and relics persisted well into the 20th century, no survivors, nor the wrecks of *Erebus* or

Terror, were discovered by subsequent explorers in the century and a half that followed.

The centuries-long quest for the Northwest Passage, therefore, is seen by historians and the public as one of the great endeavors in the history of exploration, much like the quests for the North and South Poles. These polar enterprises were the subject of fierce international rivalry, epic human achievement, the advancement of geographical and scientific knowledge, and at times incredible suffering and tragedies that captured the world's attention. It follows, then, that the ships associated with those quests, individual voyages, and personalities, and as the settings for various expeditions and their work, are historically significant. Four of those ships survive ashore in museums or afloat as national landmarks; *Gjoa*, the first vessel to navigate the Northwest Passage, restored and displayed at the Norwegian National Maritime Museum in Oslo; *Fram*, another Norwegian ship used in polar exploration, which now rests inside a specially built structure at the museum; *St. Roch*, a Canadian-built wooden-hulled motor schooner of the Royal Canadian Mounted Police, and the second ship to navigate through the Northwest Passage, now housed ashore at the Vancouver Maritime Museum; and *Effie M. Morrissey*, a former fishing schooner used extensively in Arctic exploration and science from 1926 to 1945, and preserved afloat at New Bedford Whaling National Historical Park.

The need for closure, or for additional clues to the disaster, as noted, spurred a number of searches for Franklin's ships. So, too, did other searches that found other Arctic wrecks; in 1980, an expedition led by explorer Dr. Joe McGinnis discovered the wreck of one of Belcher's ships, *Breadalbane*, ice damaged but remarkably intact, 320 feet below the surface of the water and seasonal winter ice. Parks Canada's scientists and archaeologists discovered the wreck of HMS *Investigator* in 2010, just 26 feet below the surface of a remote island. Meanwhile, others of us conducted numerous surveys: of the wreck of the ship chartered by Lady Franklin that found the "last note," the steam yacht *Fox*, which ended its career in Disko Bay on the Greenland coast; of polar explorer Roald Amundsen's *Maud*, wrecked and partially visible in Cambridge Bay, both projects of mine in the Canadian Arctic; and archaeologists working with the Inuit recovered pieces of John Ross's *Victory*'s steam engine but did not find the ship itself. Archaeologists also mapped the polar bear–mauled wreckage of supplies and gear left on Fury Beach by its crew when Parry abandoned it to the ice, but the wreck itself remains elusive.

But the "celebrity" wrecks of the Arctic were Franklin's ships. That is what led to decades of searching and multiple expeditions. I co-directed one of them in 2000; we surveyed over 100 square miles of seabed from a shallow-draft Royal Canadian Mounted Police vessel in shallows and next to outcrops of rocks and islets in a section of the Northwest Passage where the charts were literally blank—it was terra incognita. I understand that to this day the only depths marked on the charts are the ones we recorded in that summer of 2000. There were several aspects that were driving the ongoing search at that time, a century and half after the end of Franklin's expedition. Increased attention was finally coming back to the Inuit accounts, as they had observed the entire tragedy, and Inuit traditional knowledge and oral histories would ultimately play a key role in finding the wrecks.

In 2014, Canadian researchers working with Parks Canada finally found *Erebus* off the Adelaide Peninsula and in waters known today as Wilmot and Crampton Bay—but, I am told, the site was known and still is to the Inuit, long before the modern discovery, as "Shipwreck Bay" in Inuktitut. A separate expedition discovered the wreck of HMS *Terror* in the appropriately named Terror Bay off King William Island. As is the case with Arctic exploration vessels that are preserved ashore and afloat, the wrecks of the Arctic exploration ships that rest beneath the water and ice of the north are valued as historic sites. All four wrecks in Canada's Arctic waters are designated as National Historic Sites. But there is more to the wrecks than their status as historic sites; *Erebus* and *Terror*'s finds became matters of national importance, diplomacy, and ongoing archaeology by Parks Canada, which works closely with the Inuit. These wrecks are archaeological time capsules; also, as British ships of exploration that irrefutably had sailed into the Northwest Passage, they were seized on by the Canadian government to lay claim to the waters of the Northwest Passage as an internal waterway, not an international strait. That assertion is a subject of diplomatic disagreement, especially between the United States, Russia, and Canada.

The iconic nature of polar ships also led to the expedition that recently discovered the wreck of *Endurance*, lost in 1915 during the Antarctic expedition of Ernest Shackleton. It had been sought by wreck hunters and historians as the "holy grail" of Antarctic shipwrecks and was found in March 2022 after two lengthy and expensive expeditions. That discovery, by a ship itself wedged in ice for the survey and ROV dives, made international headlines, and was followed by an assertion of international significance, a management plan to protect it (with no recovery of artifacts), bestselling books, and a major feature documentary. That is an important step for the most southerly shipwreck yet found. It stands in sharp contrast to the history of Roald Amundsen's *Maud*, which I surveyed with colleagues in 1997.[4] A strong desire by Norwegians to return the wreck home led to a multi-year project that in 2016 raised *Maud* from its half-sunk Arctic grave in the Northwest Passage. After raising it and placing the wreck on a salvage barge, they slowly towed it back to Norway, arriving in the port of Vollen, its new home, in August 2018. Now there, *Maud*'s restoration is reportedly taking place.

The raising of the wreck harkens back to early wreck projects of the 1960s, like *Vasa*, to raise iconic wrecks and restore them as symbols of national pride. I'm torn on this question; there was something about *Maud* as a wreck, lying in the Northwest Passage, which made it a compelling site. I'm also not sure of the status of the restoration, as the project website's last news was posted in February 2019. But climate change in the Arctic would have ultimately doomed the wreck, as waters warmed and the wood-borers arrived to eat its hull. Some colleagues have criticized the recovery as insensitive to the Canadian and especially the Inuit connections to *Maud* from its long sojourn at Cambridge Bay. We will see what happens next to *Maud*; for now, it is a reminder of how "iconic" shipwrecks take hold of the imagination and spur quests to find them, and for some, to possess them. While I do not dispute *Maud*'s emotional pull for some Norwegians, I would also argue that the significance of *Maud* is more than the sum of its Norwegian connections. It is also tied to the history of Russia, and to Canada through its Arctic voyages through the Northeast Passage, attempts to reach the North Pole, and the science conducted on it during those early 20th-century voyages, making it an internationally significant shipwreck that transitioned in the span of a century from ship to shipwreck to relic. It is now safe from climate change, marine borers, and ongoing decay; will it instead face the fate of other historic shipwrecks brought up and placed in museums only to decay, fall apart, and be discarded? Money and time will tell.

The iconic nature of shipwrecks that leads to projects to find them, and then for some to raise them, has been one aspect of human responses to wreck finds that fascinates me. These "resurrections" often have multiple motives; where that gets difficult is when the wreck in question has a complex and disturbing past. For the past several years, the project I have been heavily involved in is the archaeological identification and study of the schooner *Clotilda*. I was also the lead author of the government study that placed the wreck in the National Register of Historic Places, the official means by which the nation's most significant historic properties and archaeological sites are recognized. It is the last known vessel to arrive in the United States with captives from Africa for the purposes of enslaving them. While archaeologists have identified and studied other wrecked slave ships, *Clotilda* is unique. It is not only the last known American slave ship in the four-century history of the transatlantic slave trade. It is a near-intact example, which means that as we dived on this wreck, we were able to enter the actual hold and see the physical evidence that helped prove that this was a slave ship. That evidence included the remains of the platforms where the captives were confined on narrow shelves, naked, probably chained, for the voyage, in a space that totals no more than several hundred square feet. The horror of the setting remains preserved in that loose mud of the Mobile River. While damaged by the fire that burned off decking and charred the interior of the main cargo hold, *Clotilda*'s hull had held together, encased in mud in the shallow fresh water of the Mobile River.

Image 3.2. SONAR image of the wreckage of the schooner *Clotilda* in the Mobile River, Alabama.
Image by SEARCH, Inc./Alabama Historical Commission.

When we excavated inside that hold, we exposed the upright posts that supported the platforms on which the captives were stacked as human cargo. A bulkhead built specifically to confine the captives in about half of the hold was still in place, and behind it, another indicates that the crew of *Clotilda* locked away the food and water and rationed it to maintain control of their captives. But the most damning evidence was the physical proof of crowding of those people. Historical accounts and documentary evidence of people lying chained, closely packed on narrow shelves, exist; the dives on *Clotilda* are for now the only known physical survival of a slave hold. *Clotilda*'s hold occupies 500 square feet, and in that space, 110 men, women, and children were held for over a month's voyage from Africa to Alabama.

Archaeology of this shipwreck reveals the brutality of the slave trade, indifference to human suffering, and crimes against humanity. The wreck of *Clotilda* sits exactly where its illegal voyage ended. Of the 110, not all survived the voyage; recent scholarship drawing on survivor narratives documents the deaths of some captives, including three children.[5]

When landed in Alabama under cover of darkness, the captives were separated into groups, enslaved, and for some, shipped far away to other towns and likely other states. For a number of them, the *Clotilda* captives never saw their fellow "shipmates," as they referred to themselves, again. The story of *Clotilda* also includes the resilience of the captives; they retained their culture, their beliefs, and their religion. They forged new lives when, after the abolition of slavery at the end of the Civil War, they were unable to return home to Africa.[6] They married other captives or other formerly enslaved African Americans. One group of captives, living in the Mobile area, purchased land from their former enslavers and created a community, which today still carries the name of Africatown. That community, ringed by factories and rail lines, and with a state highway cutting through its heart, has survived as a symbol of resilience. It is one of America's most consequential historic Black communities. While only one descendant is known to still reside in Africatown, captives and their families are buried at the nearby cemetery, and the church they founded when they embraced Christianity is one of the more powerful, visible reminders of not only their ordeal, but their survival.

The story of *Clotilda* was at first denied, as it took place in 1860, 52 years after the United States passed a law making American participation in the transatlantic slave trade illegal. Slavery remained the law of the land, however. As the cotton economy of the Deep South blossomed after the Louisiana Purchase, and following the creation of Texas as a new country and then as a state in the American Union, massive plantations funded by investors both in the North and South arose. They needed cheap labor, and chattel slavery was the answer to that need. Enslaved families in the Northern states were sold, and others were kidnapped and sent "down the river" to work on those plantations. But the need was such that the illegal slave trade boomed, with ships sneaking in under cover of night in open defiance of the law, even when the crime was made a capital offense akin to piracy. No American slave ship captain was hanged for his crime until the Civil War. Government officials looked the other way; some were complicit co-conspirators. News of *Clotilda*'s arrival nonetheless made international news in 1860, but the

Mobile newspapers mocked the story as false news. It was not until decades after the voyage and the end of the war that the conspirators confessed, but they faced no punishment.

Meanwhile, some of the captives told their story. Kossola, known in America as Cudjo Lewis, told the story of his life, capture, sale, the voyage on *Clotilda*, and his life after arriving in Alabama to local historian Emma Roche after the turn of the twentieth century. He also told his story to anthropologist, ethnographer, and author Zora Neale Hurston.[7] Others told their stories to their families, and many of those stories are now emerging into the wider community as a result of the identification of the wreck. It lies just up the river from Africatown, off the property of one of the enslavers, and was "hidden in plain sight," with its identity known to many in the community but denied by local officials. Emma Roche published a photograph of its outline at low water in 1912. The wreck was actually charted by the U.S. Coast and Geodetic Survey, as were other nearby wrecks from later use of that portion of the river as ships' graveyard.

Detailed forensic and archaeological work conclusively identified the wreck after a second attempt to locate it was made by a local reporter and the University of Southern Mississippi in 2018. After additional survey work with archaeologically focused sensors, and assessing every other wreck in that graveyard, the archaeological team turned to "target five," and in 2019, with the results double-checked and peer-reviewed, the wreck's identity was confirmed. Additional work followed to better understand its condition, what had survived, and in 2024, the results of those studies were shared with the community, *Clotilda* descendants, and the public. That sharing came with a recommendation to preserve it in place at the final scene of the crime that its owners and captain had committed.

The focus and the importance of this story therefore rest with the people carried on board the ship, their resilience and survival, and the ongoing saga of the communities they have left as part of the fabric of Alabama, the United States, and the world in the 21st century. In that context, the story of *Clotilda* and the people involved in its saga represent a local convergence of events that were both global and national in scope—the slave trade, both in Africa and transatlantic, the role of slavery in America, and the formation of the United States, Alabama, and Mobile, and especially of Africatown. *Clotilda* is the nexus of this story, as the vessel in which the primary act, accomplished through force, brought the people carried in it against their will to the United States.[8]

As governments, historians, and archaeologists consider what makes a shipwreck significant, there are different aspects that come into the discussion. One is the trade or type of work it was used for, whether that was a trade we deplore in modern times—like the slave trade, or whaling—or vital parts of an economy now vanished, like the trade in fertilizers, especially guano, or bird excrement, which was a lucrative business even if unpleasant. Ships can be historic if they were the work of a famous shipbuilder or shipyard. The events in which a ship participated—a famous battle, an epic voyage, or a discovery made on board, like the British ships engaged in the quest to navigate the Northwest Passage in the Arctic—make them historic. Ships can also be significant if they are the first of a type, like the first iron ship, or the first steel vessel, the earliest steamships, the first to use propellers instead of sidewheels—or the first type of a new warship.

Wrecks significant for these reasons also include numerous warships from battle, including well-known examples with losses in the hundreds and at times over a thousand; these are ships from the fleets of Britain, Germany, Italy, the United States, Japan, and other nations. They also include the thousands of merchant ships lost in the two world wars, and enduring symbols of tragic loss, such as *Titanic*, or *Lusitania*, and other such incidents with a large loss of life. They can also be wrecks that captured public attention, such as *Andrea Doria* sinking after an oceanic collision in fog. In modern times, shipwrecks that created ecological disasters on a vast scale, killing marine life and seabirds, leading to massive clean-ups and changes in regulations, as well as the design of oil tankers, are also historically significant. These include the crude oil carrier *Amoco Cadiz*, which spilled much of its cargo of 69 million gallons of oil on the coast of Brittany in 1978, and the notorious *Exxon Valdez* that spilled over 10 million gallons of crude oil in Prince William Sound in 1989 after running onto a submerged rocky reef. The oil spread over 1,300 miles of marine habitat on the Alaska Coast. It was the largest marine oil spill in U.S. history until the explosion and sinking of Deepwater Horizon in the Gulf of Mexico. *Exxon Valdez*'s disaster led to the establishment of new regulations to prevent marine pollution, MARPOL, which were established by the International Maritime Organization. *Exxon Valdez* also entered pop culture as the floating headquarters of the villain in Kevin Costner's 1995 film, *Waterworld*. Shipwrecks do not need to embody "feel good" messages to be significant.

Shipwrecks as Graves and Memorials

The ocean is one of humanity's largest graveyards, both for individuals who drowned or were otherwise lost on the water, as well as those whose bodies were committed to the deep after dying on board a shipwreck, to await the time when, as the Bible's Book of Revelation promised, "the sea gave up its dead."[9] That verse inspired a powerful artistic response in British artist Frederic, Lord Leighton's *And the Sea Gave Up the Dead Which Were in It* (1892), which depicts as its central figure a resurrected man, holding his drowned wife and child, rising from the ocean and ascending to heaven as a shrouded sailor and other specters rise behind them. Going to sea was the deadliest profession. It is "hard, dirty, dangerous work."[10] From 1871 to 1886, the British government recorded the deaths of 25,395 seamen on British-registered ships; this short window of fatalities in peacetime included only losses of life due to accidents at sea, drowning at sea, foundering and shipwreck, and did not account for death on a ship in port, or death from disease at sea.[11] With death so commonplace, a fatalistic acceptance that it could come at any time to anyone on a ship led to an acceptance by most sailors that the sea was "the natural sepulcher of a sailor."[12]

However, sailors were superstitious, and to ensure that the dead remained at peace and did not haunt the living, a dedicated set of rituals were stablished for a proper burial at sea "to separate and place the dead."[13] These rituals included fellow sailors washing a shipmate's body, dressing them, and rendering honors, all part of showing respect to prevent the spirit of that dead shipmate from returning from the dead to haunt the ship. Sailors were, and still are, superstitious. Sudden death at sea, whether from injury, falling from the rigging onto the deck or into the water, in battle, or from illness, was cause enough, for a superstitious seaman, to believe that his dead shipmate would remain as a spirit to haunt the ship. There are many ghost stories associated with ships, some of them related personally to me by caretakers and curators who have worked on historic naval ships preserved as floating museums.

In addition to honors rendered and religious ceremonies to keep the dead from returning as a ghost, the more pragmatic ritual was a quick burial, usually within a day, and wrapping a dead shipmate's body in a shroud. This was usually a piece of sail, spare canvas, or the dead man's hammock, and placing a weight near the feet. Once the body was lying inside the canvas, the sailmaker would stitch it shut with thick twine and a large sailmaker's needle capable of piercing the thick cloth, and then at the face, the final stitch meant running that needle through the corpse's nose just to make sure they were dead before being buried. Laid on a plank, with a flag covering the shrouded body, the funeral service ended with the tipping of the plank, and the body falling, feet first, into the water in a symbolic one-way journey down, facing away from the ship to help prevent a ghost from returning.

However, as archaeologist Elena Perez-Alvaro has noted, death at sea and how that was handled have different meanings to different groups, and meanings that can change over time, and not everyone agrees about what is important or acceptable.[14] The emotions associated with death and what to do with the dead can bring closure for some families but may offend others. Some cultures need to "see" a body; others do not. For some, acknowledging the presence of the dead compels society to recover and "properly" inter them. When that is impossible, memorials, such as names of those lost at sea inscribed on a family monument in a cemetery, provide the means to remember and honor the dead. One form of remembrance was the physical memorial to those who had died at sea, for whom the ocean was their grave, be they victims of accident, such as falling from aloft or going overboard in a heavy sea, or disease, or through shipwreck. Widows of seafarers, families of drowned sailors, as well as the kin of passengers who died at sea, placed memorials in churches and placed the names of their unreturned dead upon grave markers in cemeteries. These included individual tombstones as well as those including the names of fathers, brothers, husbands, sons, and other kin lost at sea. I've seen countless examples around the world, all poignant and sad. Grief and our response to loss span cultures, politics, and millennia.

A family stone at St. James's cemetery in Liverpool marks the graves of the family of Wilfred Mossap, a mariner who died in 1848. Also noted on the stone are his daughter Hannah, who died in 1854, his nephew, Wilfred Gilberry, and Gilberry's wife Isabella, who both died in 1883. The inscription notes that Wilfred Gilberry, age 40, "left Callao 30th May 1865, in command of the ship 'Andacollo' bound for Valparaiso, and has never since been heard of."[15] The disappearance of Franklin's expedition, with subsequent searching expeditions finding only relics and a relatively small number of bodies scattered across the Arctic landscape, left their relatives to also mark their family plots with cenotaphs. Franklin's memorial at Westminster Abbey is the most famous, with a white marble bust and a dramatic image of a ship trapped in ice. The epitaph, written by Alfred, Lord Tennyson is short and powerful:

> Not Here: The White North Has Thy Bones; And Thou, Heroic Sailor-Soul, Art Passing On Thine Happier Voyage Now Toward No Earthly Pole.

A cenotaph in the New Bedford, Massachusetts, Rural Cemetery, erected by Paul and Louisa G. Ewing, commemorates their only son, Walter C. Ewing, "who was lost at sea from Brig *Zoroaster* on her passage to California," on March 18, 1850. The monument then lists the latitude and longitude of the ship's position when he died, and hence where he likely was laid to rest.[16]

In cases where there was a large loss of life in a maritime disaster, and the wreck remained either undiscovered or unreachable, cenotaphs and memorials were commonly erected. Whether this was a satisfactory solution for all concerned, especially those from non-Western cultures, was another matter. Japanese tradition insists that human remains, even from shipwrecks, need to be recovered and buried "properly" or cremated ashore. Maritime archaeologist David Stewart divides maritime memorials into three classes: state (government-sponsored), community, and individual. The memorial to the dead of USS *Arizona* is one powerful and iconic example.

Another is the *Russalka* Memorial in Tallinn, Estonia, which commemorates the loss of the Russian ironclad *Russalka* and its 177-man crew. *Russalka* sank in a storm in the Baltic after leaving Tallinn for Helsinki on September 7, 1893. Only one body was recovered, that of a sailor found in a dinghy that washed ashore. The monument, a stone cenotaph topped with a bronze statue of an angel holding a Russian Orthodox cross and looking out to sea, has stood since 1902. It remains a site of remembrance, even after the wreck's discovery in 2003, just off Helsinki, intact, and with the bodies of its crew entombed inside. A technically difficult dive, *Russalka* is now a rarely visited historic site and

Image 3.3. Tourists disembark to visit the USS *Arizona* Memorial at Pearl Harbor. Photograph by MC3 Diana Quinlan, U.S. Navy.

grave. The memorial in Tallinn is the only means by which those onshore can connect to the ship and its lost crew. I remain powerfully moved by the fact that when I dived it, as one of the few who were allowed, one of the ship's small boats lies next to the wreck on the sea bed, with what appear to be the bones of some of the crew. We did not get close enough to examine that scene.

The two world wars, with previously un-thought-of casualties, included horrific losses both on land and at sea, and in both arenas of war, with bodies never found. Other powerful moments I have shared with families and colleagues have been at memorials to those dead. On the anniversary of the start of World War I, I was one of the American representatives at UNESCO meetings in Belgium; our itinerary took us to Ypres, and its massive cemetery and memorial, where we laid poppies and prayed. There, at the Menin Gate that leads into the cemetery, the Hall of Memory contains the names of 54,395 dead whose bodies were not found. By way of comparison, the U.S. Navy's records indicate that 36,950 officers and enlisted personnel died in combat in World War II, and many of them who went down with their ships were never found. That number does not include U.S. Coast Guard or U.S. Merchant Marine sailors lost on convoys. In the United States, national cemeteries include walls of inscribed names of those tens of thousands lost at sea in service to country. At Arlington National Cemetery in Washington, the graves of 230 men lost in the explosion and sinking of USS *Maine* in 1898 lie before a circular monument topped by the ship's mast. I visit it every time I've been to Arlington, along with other monuments and graves that honor service and sacrifice.

There are numerous memorials to the unrecovered dead of *Titanic*; I've visited a number of them. That was a quest I felt necessary after my submersible dive to the wreck. One is the *Titanic* Memorial in Washington, D.C., dedicated to the men who stood back so that women and children might live as the lifeboats were loaded. Another is the small park in New York with the memorial to Isidor and Ida Straus. It powerfully honors her choice to die with her husband, with a biblical passage, "Lovely and pleasant were they in their lives and in their death they were not parted" (Second Samuel 1:23). The *Titanic* Memorial Lighthouse at South Street Seaport in New York is a less personal, but imposing tribute. Next to City Hall in Belfast, in Donegall Square, is the memorial erected by the city that powerfully felt the loss, as it had been built there and among the dead were some of those who had built the ship. The original memorial, a statue of a woman standing over the drowned body of a sailor lifted out of the water by mermaids, was erected in 1920. Originally commemorating the "gallant Belfastmen" whose "devotion to duty and heroic conduct" had helped save lives at the cost of their own, it listed the names of most but not all, starting with Thomas Andrews, the ship's designer, who stayed and died, and other Harland & Wolff employees who had joined him on the maiden voyage, as well as locals who had served as crew. A memorial garden, which opened in 2012, now surrounds the monument, and includes the names of all 1,512 victims of the sinking on bronze plaques. It is said to be the only memorial in the world that honors all of *Titanic*'s dead. It, too, is a powerful place to visit. The rows of names, as you walk along them, remind us of individual lives lost, not a number that has become a statistic.

The same is true for another memorial, this one to a modern Baltic shipwreck. The car ferry *Estonia* sank on September 28, 1994, after leaving Tallinn for Stockholm. In the midst of a heavy storm, the seas forced open the bow door and tore it off. The ferry rapidly flooded and sank with very little time for rescue. While 137 were saved, 852 lost their lives, making it one of the greatest peacetime maritime disasters in European waters. There is a memorial to *Estonia* in Stockholm, engraved with the names of the dead; another memorial was erected in a public square in Tallinn to commemorate the locals who were lost in the disaster. A tall leaning tower with a bell that rings as it is buffeted by the wind overlooks the Baltic at Korgessare, Estonia. The loss of *Estonia* also inspired an international movement to make the wreck a memorial with the dead entombed within it.[17] While some families wanted bodies recovered, an international agreement was signed in 1995 by Denmark, Estonia, Finland, Great Britain, Latvia, Poland, Sweden, and Russia. The agreement was done "to protect the M/S *Estonia*, as a final place of rest for victims of the disaster, from any disturbing activities," and urged "the public and all other States to afford appropriate respect to the site of the M/S *Estonia* for all time" through legislation passed by each signatory country. It sets out the "criminalization of any activities disturbing the peace of the final place of rest, in particular any diving or other activities with the purpose of recovering victims or property from the wreck or the sea-bed" and that the wreck would never be raised.

Any memorial to lost seamen and ships was a powerful aspect of how societies deal with mass death, especially at sea, as these memorials provided a place for families to mourn. While some grieve privately, at a family plot, others find comfort in a more public place. I would argue that the need for public memorials emerged as the modern era approached, and ships increased in size. When they wrecked, it wasn't dozens of deaths. Hundreds, and later, as ships grew larger, thousands of people could and did die in major shipwrecks. Shipwrecks did not just bring grief to a few families. They devastated entire communities. When a major disaster like *Titanic*'s sinking happened, the shipwreck was an event that shook the world. These massive losses of life as collective catastrophes grew in scale, both in terms of lives lost and cumulative effect, in the 19th and 20th centuries. The sea truly is our greatest graveyard, and many shipwrecks are undersea tombs. That aspect—the shipwreck as tomb—is one that I've always respected; dives on wrecks where the dead remain inside have always been somber and humbling experiences.

Not everyone was content with leaving their dead in the sea, however. Contemporary accounts of maritime disasters centuries ago clearly state that surviving family and friends knew that the bodies of those lost, if they had not floated ashore, could lie scattered on the seabed, "violated by the effects of water and marine life."[18] In the 19th century, as "sub marine armor" (diving equipment), allowed salvagers to journey below and into shipwrecks, they published accounts of encountering the dead in shipwrecks, lying in "their watery beds," as well as those who had drowned, trapped in cabins. As decomposition set in, gases in the body caused them to swell and rise "until it assumes an almost vertical position," a "sight such as timid souls would quake to look upon."[19] The horrors of such scenes notwithstanding, many families wanted the bodies of their loved ones recovered and buried ashore.

A powerful example of the extent to which families would go is illustrated in the case of the Canadian Pacific Railroad (CPR) steamship *Princess Sophia*, which wrecked on Vanderbilt Reef in Alaska's Inside Passage on October 25, 1918, and all 364 persons on board were lost. Approximately half of the bodies washed ashore. The CPR demurred on launching an effort to dive into the wreck, which lay in only 75 feet of frigid water. Al Winchell, whose ailing wife Ilene, heading home to recuperate, had died in the wreck, used his own money to hire a hard hat diver, Selmer Jacobsen, to find and recover her body. Accounts of the two men's ordeals are harrowing. As historians Betty O'Keefe and Ian Macdonald described in their comprehensive book on the disaster, Selmer brought up a woman's body, but it was not Mrs. Winchell.

Selmer returned to the wreck and made his way to her cabin, which had a large window that looked out onto the deck. Through the unbroken glass, Selmer saw two women's bodies floating inside. He broke the cabin window to get to them, but currents pushed the bodies out of the cabin and deeper into the ship. When recovered, neither of them was Ilene Winchell. Repeated dives found more bodies, but as time passed, the corpses were increasingly "creepy," according to diver Jacobsen. At this stage, Al Winchell had exhausted most of his funds. The publicized search and his sorrow, however, shamed the CPR into hiring divers who systematically searched the ship, recovering many bodies that had been trapped below, some in public rooms and others still in their cabins. They brought up 86 bodies, and on that dive barge, Al Winchell examined every one of them to see if they were Ilene. Finally, in July 1919, they brought up Ilene Winchell. Al had promised that if something happened, he would bury her next to her mother. He spent the last of his money to do that.[20]

The effort to recover the dead from the wreck of USS *Maine* is yet another example. Following the explosion that sank the armored cruiser in Havana Harbor in February 1898, killing 253 of its 355-man crew, the broken hulk remained partially visible above the water. While it lay awash in Havana Harbor, the U.S. Navy buried, and then later disinterred and shipped to Arlington National Cemetery the bodies of most of the dead who had washed ashore or were pulled from the water. The wreck, however, was left untouched, despite the fact that there were still men whose bodies had not been found. Years of intense lobbying by those families whose loved ones had been left inside the USS *Maine* led Congress to appropriate nearly a million dollars to salvage the wreck and recover bodies. After building a cofferdam around the wreck in 1911, contractors pumped out the water and cleaned out the shattered hulk, cutting off badly damaged portions. They also found the bones of 36 men, who were shipped home to join their shipmates at Arlington. The stern of the ship, patched and raised, was then towed out to sea and was scuttled on March 16, 1912, with a large American flag flying from it. Rediscovered in deep water a century later, the remains of *Maine* are an empty deep-sea relic, no longer a grave, and not a memorial. Those are ashore.

The major memorial to USS *Maine* is at Arlington National Cemetery, as previously discussed. Other USS *Maine* memorials, both in Cuba and throughout the United States, include pieces and parts of the lost ship. These preserved relics of the ship recall the much older practice of saving and holding sacred the bones and effects of Christian martyrs in reliquaries. They include two of the primary armament, the cruiser's 10-inch guns, which are displayed at a memorial to the ship on Havana's waterfront, the USS *Maine* Monument in New York City, where it was built, and at a memorial to the ship at Davenport Park in Bangor, Maine, which features the ornate cast scrollwork and American shield from the bow, and various fittings including the ship's guns and anchors in various parks and other settings. Like *Titanic*'s memorials, I've visited many of them, and also have sailed over the site of the explosion in Havana Harbor, where fragments of *Maine*'s hull and one gun turret lie buried in the mud. Brass recovered from the wreck, melted down, was cast into some thousand plaques to a design by sculptor Charles Keck; the plaques were distributed throughout the United States.

While some monuments to lost ships are reliquaries, a Chilean warship lost in battle with most of its crew is an underwater grave that has over time yielded its dead for interment in a reliquary/monument ashore at Valparaiso. The wooden-hulled Chilean steam corvette *Esmeralda* was sunk during Chile's war with Peru and Bolivia, the *Guerra del Pacifico*. *Esmeralda* met the Peruvian ironclad monitor *Huáscar* and the armored steam frigate *Independencia* in battle on May 21, 1879, off Iquique. Outgunned and unable to effectively damage his opponents, Captain Arturo Prat of *Esmeralda* stayed in the fight for hours. It ended when Admiral Miguel Grau Seminario, the commander of *Huáscar*, ordered his crew to ram the disabled *Esmeralda*, striking it and opening a large hole in the starboard side. Captain Prat shouted, "Let's board, boys!" and leapt onto the deck of *Huáscar* with two of his crew. The Peruvians shot them as they boarded, and as more men from the Chilean corvette followed, they were also shot down as *Huáscar* rammed *Esmeralda* again, and the Chilean ship sank.

The victorious Peruvians buried Prat and his crew ashore, where the bodies remained until 1888, when they were returned to Chile to rest in a crypt below a large monument on Valparaiso's waterfront that honors the "Heroes of Iquique." The bodies of Prat's men who sank with *Esmerelda* were not recovered, although Chilean naval divers retrieved a number of artifacts from the wreck to place in the naval museum. Dive groups have also visited the wreck, and in 2010, a report that a diver had seen a human skull led to a thorough examination inside the substantially intact shipwreck, led by Chilean archaeologist Diego Carabias. Carabias located the skull, which was recovered after much debate. While the decision was made to recover it and inter it with Prat and the others who died with him on the deck of *Huáscar*, there was no further work to seek other remains. The Chilean Navy's decision was to retain the status of the wreck as a grave. No more bodies were to be sought.

With many other wrecks the recovery of bodies is not possible, due to the location of the ship being unknown, or when it lies beyond the practical limits of recovery. Perhaps the most famous example is *Titanic*. Steamships sailing through the area after the tragedy reported spotting floating bodies, including one of a mother still holding her child; the published accounts and outrage led the White Star Line to hire the Cable

Ship *MacKay-Bennett*. It steamed from Halifax five days after *Titanic* sank, and stayed at sea for nearly two weeks, collecting 306 of the dead. The condition of some of the bodies was such that 116 of them were buried at sea, and the ship returned to Halifax with 190 bodies, which were laid out in a local ice rink and photographed. Both on the ships and in the makeshift morgue, morticians collected personal items in an effort to help identify the dead. Among those identified were nine-year-old third-class passenger Walter Van Billiard, who had boarded in Southampton; one of the ship's firemen, J. Smillie; a number of engineers and others from the engineer department; Isador Strauss; John Jacob Astor; and *Titanic* Purser Hugh McElroy.

The number of dead found afloat overwhelmed the capacity of *MacKay-Bennett*, so the White Star Line hired the steamer *Minia*, which recovered 17 bodies, including that of Charles Melville Hays, the president of the Grand Trunk Railway, who was still wearing his gloves, and returned to Halifax with 15 of them, as well as the steamer *Montmagny*, which recovered four bodies, one of whom, a ship's steward, was buried at sea. The fourth ship hired by White Star was the steamer *Algerine*, which searched for three weeks in May and found only one body, that of Saloon Steward James McGrady. In all, 23 percent of *Titanic*'s dead were recovered; 125 were buried at sea, and the others were buried ashore. Other ships at sea found three men in Collapsible Lifeboat A, and two others were found still afloat in June. The recovery of the bodies, the question of identity, and the retention of the personal items from the unidentified dead, as well as the photographs of the bodies, led to an ongoing quest to identify these people, which continues to this day, and has involved DNA testing that identified two-year-old victim Sidney Leslie Goodwin.[21]

The families of wealthy victims hired the Merritt-Chapman Derrick and Wrecking Company to try to find the wreck, but given the great depth, it was impractical, and the plan was abandoned. *Titanic* was one of many cases where the pragmatic decision was to finally consider the wreck in and by itself a grave. When Dr. Robert Ballard and team discovered the wreck of *Titanic* in 1985, the fact that the ship, a broken but recognizable hulk two and half miles down, was suddenly accessible both shocked and fascinated the world. The act of discovery and filming of the wreck discomfited some who thought it best to leave it forever in the darkness. Inevitably, this takes us to the question about bodies. There are no bodies, only items from the dead—shoes, some in pairs, clothing, some of it nothing more than what Charles Pellegrino, who participated in early dives and recoveries of artifacts, described as "shreds of fabric." Pellegrino calls the site an anoxic "fossil bed" that contained a range of small artifacts, including broken ceramics and buttons. These finds, according to Pellegrino, led to the sensitive decision to stop work in that area of the wreck.[22] Are there more artifacts that remain after a body decayed inside the wreck? Some of the intact cabins and other compartments inside *Titanic* may have more tangible reminders of lives lost. The topic is debated in *Titanic* forums. Regardless of opinion, *Titanic* remains, and powerfully so, a gravesite in the minds of most of the public.

While human remains have been found in shallower sites, the presence of remains in deep water sites and what rests around and within them remain for the most part either "undiscovered," or we simply look away in tacit agreement to neither speculate, seek visual proof, nor provide a spectacle for the viewing public. However, in 2012, during the centennial of the sinking, I made the decision as the director of NOAA's Maritime Heritage Program to re-release (note that I said *re*-release) a provocative photograph from the 2004 NOAA expedition of a long coat and boots lying on the *Titanic* wreck site, near the stern, in response to widely announced plans for commemorative cruises and parties floating above the wreck site. That was done to remind everyone that while people attend "last night on the *Titanic*" dinners and other commemorations, those types of events do not take place at sensitive sites on land; I've never heard of a Civil War–themed ball and banquet set in the graveyards of Gettysburg. The point was made, but interestingly, there were some who wanted to argue that there were no visible human remains, the inference being that we were overly sensitive. I don't think so; I have met and know a number of families whose dead remain in the ocean and who appreciate sensitivity.

The *New York Times* described the mixed reaction to the photo as differing opinions, while others confused the issue with a debate on whether there were skeletons on the wreck (which no one has seen). What was notable were the comments calling for declaring the site a "nautical grave" and leaving it to rust in peace, while others called for ending what they termed "disaster tourism." The issue for them was the same—whether you *see* the bodies or not, it was (is) a graveyard. That was my point in releasing the image. That same point was one aspect of the first calls for a protected status for *Titanic*, in 1985, much like that for lost warships that are military gravesites. As early as 1985, and then again in 1995, national governments took steps to see the wreck itself protected as a memorial, arguably the paramount value of the site in some eyes. The RMS *Titanic* Memorial Act of 1985, signed into law by President Ronald Reagan, led to discussions and the drafting of an international agreement initially modeled on the *Estonia* Agreement. The *Titanic* Agreement entered into force in late 2019. Salvage from the wreck site, as overseen by the U.S. District Court, has followed principles put in place by the Court that prohibit cutting into the hull to recover objects from the wreck that rest on or inside it. While there are critics of the salvage, the general consensus is that it and other activities, including tourist dives to the wreck, have generally acted with respect. A number of memorial plaques have been placed on the wreck to commemorate the loss of life. I'll return to the subject of *Titanic* tourism and the *Titan* submersible in a later chapter.

This modern practice of placing plaques as memorials on sunken ships is also happening on other wrecks to acknowledge loss and to honor the dead. In recent years, plaques have been placed on a number of warship wrecks rediscovered decades after their loss, including the Australian cruiser HMAS *Sydney* and the battleship HMS *Hood*, both lying at extreme depths in the ocean. Once "lost" and "beyond reach," these wrecks are a reminder that modern technology makes them accessible. While not available to families for regular visits, as they would be as a grave on land, a strong argument has been made that even as they may not be accessible by tourists, salvagers, and scrappers, that they be protected and preserved in situ as memorials.

The most unique memorial to naval loss that incorporates a wreck is the USS *Arizona* Memorial at Pearl Harbor. During the Japanese Navy's attack on Pearl Harbor on December 7, 1941, *Arizona* exploded and its broken hulk burned for days. It was not alone, as the attack sank four battleships and the former battleship *Utah*, then being used for training, as well as a harbor tug; in all, 18 ships were put out of action and 2,493 Americans were killed, the majority of them trapped inside their sunken ships, and the majority in *Arizona*. Of those sunken ships, USS *Oklahoma*, with 439 dead, USS *West Virginia*, with 106 dead, and USS *California*, with 100 dead, were all raised, and their dead recovered. Navy divers recovered some of the dead from USS *Arizona*, which had lost 1,177 of the crew. They also removed three of the battleship's turrets and guns, secondary armament, and ammunition before abandoning efforts to raise the ship.[23]

USS *Utah*, with 64 dead still on board, also could not be raised, and salvage was abandoned. The hulk of USS *Arizona* still sits awash where it sank. The Navy made a pragmatic decision not to attempt to recover more of the dead following wartime dives' discovery of 105 men in 1942. The wreck's ongoing presence sparked debate, with some viewing it as a rusted "mass of junk," while others saw it as a lasting symbol of service and sacrifice, and the tomb of its dead. Because, unlike *Maine*, it rested not only on U.S. soil but also within a naval base, it was left and ultimately spanned by the arched memorial that straddles but does not touch the wreck. Painted white, with the U.S. flag flying over it, the *Arizona* Memorial is the focal point for visitors to Pearl Harbor. Disembarking from a tour boat that ferries them to the memorial, visitors read the names of *Arizona*'s dead crew. They gaze down into the oil-stained waters and see rusted portions of the ship that rise above the surface and coral-encrusted sections of the battleship through the water. Family members of the lost have come to pray and drop family photos and notes into the water. They do so to connect with dead husbands, sons, fathers, brothers, uncles, and now grandfathers and great-grandfathers lost with the ship.

The open barbette of the number four turret, its exposed edges just below the surface of the water, is the location where those *Arizona* survivors who died long after the war now spend eternity with the shipmates they lost on that December morning in 1941. I have personally participated in one of those dives. Others have had their ashes scattered over the wreck. Archaeological dives, corrosion assessment work, and studying the possibility of a major oil leak from the battleship's fuel bunkers have proceeded since the 1980s. *Arizona* is a National Historic Landmark, managed for the U.S. Navy by the National Park Service, but its symbolism and role as a memorial and grave have always been the paramount value that guides how the U.S. government manages the site. The wreck is rarely disturbed, diving is restricted, and the National Park Service "takes its stewardship of the site very seriously" because "*Arizona* is a sacred place for Americans."[24] In the decades after the war, the memorial also became a site for Japanese pilgrims, some of them descendants of those who took part in the attacking raid, others who see in the wreck the opening act of a long war that ended in the devastation of their country.

Not all wrecks with loss of life have been left to the sea. One of the greatest social crises of the early 21st century was the Syrian civil war and the flight of immigrants by land and sea to Europe. This has brought many tragedies, among them a shocking shipwreck that took place off the Mediterranean island of Lampedusa. A 90-foot-long fishing vessel from Libya, packed with as many as a thousand immigrants from Eritrea, Somalia, and Ghana, sank after colliding with a rescue vessel responding to its distress call. When the vessel capsized, with hundreds of people, crowded on it, nearly everyone on board died as the ship sank, leaving only 28 survivors. Italian authorities raised the ship, which lay 1,214 feet deep, and took it to a naval base where forensic teams recovered the remains of several hundred people.[25]

The wreck was then to be demolished, but artist Christophe Büchel, working with the Sicilian community of Augusta, asked for the ship to be made into an exhibition. First displayed at Venice during its annual Biennale in May 2019, and then ultimately moved to Augusta as the center of a "Garden of Memory," it is known as the *Barca Nostra* (Our Ship) Project. It has been the subject of fierce debate. The comments of one art critic underscore the power of shipwrecks as physical reminders of settings for often violent death. Waldemar Januszczak wrote that he found it "dark, upsetting, accusatory and powerful...to suggest that the piece somehow glorified or ignored death is, at best, plain wrong."[26]

Others argue that emptied of its dead, the raised hulk is more than a memorial. It is a potent, powerful symbol. Exhibition curator Maria Chiara Di Trapani in an interview stated her hope that displaying the wreck would focus on the ongoing humanitarian crisis that led to an overcrowded ship, in unsafe conditions, sinking and killing innocent victims. Confronting the reality of the tragedy by displaying the "ship of the dead," she said, would hopefully move visitors to be silent to "listen and reflect" on what had happened.[27]

Another example of this type of monument is the display of the Albanian ship *Kateri i Radës* at Otranto, Italy. The end of Communist rule in Albania introduced a wave of Albanian immigration into nearby countries in 1990–1991, including fleeing by water into Italy across the narrow Straits of Otranto. Anti-immigrant sentiment was high, and when an economic crisis gripped Albania in 1997, a second wave of Albanians fleeing their country again began arriving in large numbers, this time meeting a de facto blockade by Italian warships, in an agreement with the Albanian government, to board vessels, and turn back or return the immigrants to Albanian soil. One of those vessels was *Kateri i Radës*. The Italian naval corvette *Sibilia*, while maneuvering to board in the late afternoon of March 28, 1997, inside Albanian territorial waters, struck *Kateri i Radës* and sank it in 800 meters of water.

The ship was crowded with some 120 persons (some accounts say 142), and as many as 58 died in the sinking; there were only 34 survivors rescued. After several months, the wreck was raised from the seabed, and forensic pathologists recovered 52 bodies from inside the ship. The recovery was driven by the ongoing legal inquiry, and so another important task was to look at the damage to *Kateri i Radës* to try to determine if the use of force that led to the sinking was disproportionate to the threat of letting illegal immigrants into Italy. Accounts of the disaster claimed that the Italian warship had come too close in an effort to force *Kateri i Radës* to turn back to Albania; given the disproportionate size of *Sibilia*, Albanian survivors claimed that the "harassment" of their ship turned tragic when *Sibilia* hit them three times, tearing off a small boat, then scraping along the side, and then riding over *Kateri i Radës* and capsizing it. The Albanian ship, upside down with many of its passengers trapped below, sank eight minutes later. *Sibilia* did not stay close by, and according to the survivors, returned a half hour after the collision. Assessing the damage to the sunken *Kateri i Radës* verified the stories that *Sibilia* had hit it twice. That was damning. But the recovery of the dead from inside *Kateri i Radës* was a public relations disaster for the Italians.

The evidence presented by the bodies was sufficient to identify 49 of the 52 dead because they had been inside sealed compartments in a constant temperature of 4°C and were still wearing thick layers of clothing to protect them from the extremely cold weather. That clothing kept marine organisms from scavenging the bodies, other than their faces, necks, and hands—a horrible detail that any of us familiar with the sea know about or have seen, but which is often not a publicly discussed fact.[28] One of the things that we can all identify with is that the hands and faces are what we most commonly see and react to as personal identifiers. Raising *Kateri i Radës* was not in the best interests of the Italian government, as a tragedy offshore had literally come ashore in gruesome, graphic detail.

Ultimately, modern forensic science was able to identify the victims; this was, like the earlier recovery of *Titanic* dead, an important thing to do. However, the response to *Kateri i Radës* and the hearings and criminal proceedings that followed would not bring closure to the families of the lost. As well, the toll of Mediterranean immigrant deaths in shipwrecks in the Mediterranean continued to climb, be they Albanians, or later Syrians, Libyans, or Africans. *Kateri i Radës* and other "illegal" migrant ships that wreck speak to a humanitarian crisis. With *Kateri i Radës*, the shipwreck became a symbol of the failure of humanitarian values.

Legal proceedings over the "Tragedy of Otranto" lasted for several years, with the international tribunals finding Italy liable, and the two captains were both prosecuted and convicted of manslaughter as an

Italian court ruled that they were responsible for the accident and the deaths. Emotions ran high, especially as many of the victims were women and children, some of them infants. The dead from this one shipwreck represented a portion of over 500 Albanian lives lost in the crossing in the span of a few years—a harbinger of the tragedy that later arrived with the Syrian refugees. It also inspired an ongoing quest to expand forensics to take a more active role in such disasters—a shift from the "shipwreck as a grave" approach to a more active assessment, especially if the wreck is seen as a potential crime scene. By 2017, the number of maritime fatalities had doubled from previous years as a result of the ongoing refugee crisis.

The wreck of *Kateri i Radës* after it was raised was taken to Brindisi, where it sat in a non-public area of the port, in pieces and rusting for over a decade. A public project, *L'Approdo. Opera all'Umanità Migrante* (*The Landing. Work Dedicated to Migrating Humanity*), led by sculptor Costas Varotsos and completed in 2012, moved to the waterfront of Otranto, despite requests from Albanian families of the victims to the Italian government to return the wreckage to Vlore, the port it had sailed from. Varotsos reassembled rusted, battered pieces of the wreck, shrouding the hull and superstructure with sheets of glass to create a sense of water flowing over it—as if it were still under the sea.[29] As Varotsos stated, "to extract something positive from the tragedy, optimist, I wanted us to remember the event with horror but at the same time make this ship travel again." Utilizing the glass gave the sculpture a sense of "energy," according to Varotsos, as well as a "fascination with the sea and the dangers it holds."[30] At the same time, the wreck of *Kateri i Radës* is a visible one-time sepulcher and a focal point for ongoing Albanian anger; the process of turning it into a monument could be seen as hiding the evidence of a crime in plain sight. It is perhaps a reminder, as the Lampudesa wreck shows, along with the Steccato di Cutro wreck, both lost on the Italian coast during the African immigration crisis of 2023, of the deadly nature of immigration when it is deemed inconvenient or illegal. It is also reflected by *Titanic*'s harsh and damning statistics of first-class survival and third-class (migrant) deaths in that tragedy. History inevitably repeats itself.

Such is the power and the value of shipwrecks as symbols, landmarks, memorials, and graves. They serve as reminders of the costs of interacting with the sea, in the face of the forces of nature, the power of the sea, in times of war, or when incompetence, greed, inaction, or other human failings lead to their loss. As sites, shipwrecks are mirrors that reflect the various aspects of humanity's millennial relationship with the water that covers and connects much of the planet, as well as a stage on which every aspect of human nature plays out. At times that tragedy inspires quests to seek out and visit the places of their demise. As Shakespeare noted in *The Tempest*, and as Sara Rich, with an approach to wrecks as physical entities that inspire reactions, has powerfully documented, wrecks are places where the sea transforms them into something altogether different.

However, these aspects of why people care about shipwrecks draw from the physical survival of the wreck—be it intact, or in pieces, but as a tangible link to real and imagined pasts, near-mythic events, past victories and glories, or as reminders and shrines that reflect great tragedies. And yet, there is another aspect to our fascination with wrecks. That aspect of the allure of shipwrecks is captured in Ariel's song in *The Tempest*. People have been fascinated with the changes wrought on that which we built, whether the result of catastrophe or of decay, as discussed earlier. The romance of ruin, the nuances of decomposition, and metamorphosis, all aspects of what happens when a ship becomes a shipwreck, and in that "doth suffer a sea-change into something rich and strange," is where we now turn our attention. Shipwrecks compel our visitation, investigation, and study.

4

In the Solitude of the Sea

> One would have thought it a ruin buried under a coating of white shells, much resembling a covering of snow. Upon examining the mass attentively, I could recognize the ever-thickening form of a vessel bare of its masts, which must have sunk. It certainly belonged to past times. This wreck, to be this incrusted with the lime of the water, must already be able to count many years passed at the bottom of the ocean. What was this vessel?
>
> —Jules Verne, *Twenty Thousand Leagues Under the Sea*, 1872

As a ship is wrecked, it undergoes a physical transformation. It ceases to be the ship that it was, once it is torn apart, crushed, burned, or blasted by gunfire or explosions. Some parts—sails, wood fragments, bodies—float away. It then sinks, either as a more or less intact hulk, or as scattered pieces of wreckage dropping down to the seabed. Ships wrecked on the shore bed down, partly swallowed by wet sand, and in time break apart and are scattered over miles of beaches or are gnashed in the teeth of rocks that gradually turn stout timbers into splinters, and iron or steel into shattered, worn pieces of debris. The inexorable physical power of the sea continues the destructive process by which even the largest and most powerful ships are reduced to fragments, unless they fall into the deep.

In the ocean, the natural environment continues to transform a ship into a different entity; a dark hulk, slowly consumed by chemical processes that rust metal and digest wood, or scatter pieces undergoing the same transformation. Whether it rests in a river, lake, or the ocean, it is colonized by marine life, large and small. This includes bacteria and a variety of plant and animal life that can partially or in time completely consume a wreck, as well as colonize it. The oceans are where life began on this planet, and it is there that the greatest diversity of life is found. What we have begun to understand is the role that shipwrecks play in that biodiversity. A Belgian study looked at 10 shipwrecks in the North Sea and found 224 species larger than a millimeter, 46 species new to Belgian waters, and "several species said to be rare to the Belgian marine fauna" on those wrecks.[1]

Shipwreck Biodiversity

The study of what colonizes shipwrecks is more than a catalog of species, or the realization that a shipwreck is an "artificial reef" and home to corals as well as fish that inhabit the area around it. For many years it has been commonly known that fish like to congregate around wrecks; fishermen plot the locations of wrecks so they can fish close to them and make a good catch. Science is increasingly demonstrating that there are other creatures—"aliens of the deep," as some term them—that have not been seen before, or which exist deeper than ever thought possible. Italian marine scientists studying a deep-water wreck in 490 meters of water in the western Mediterranean found large tube worms whose DNA was similar to worms in the eastern Mediterranean, as well as a new species. Scientists are working to determine which type of energy source the worms are feeding on.[2] That's because they ordinarily consume sulfur, but that wasn't present on this shipwreck. However, because the wreck had some wood and was carrying a cargo of cotton balls and oil seeds, this was their food source, and wrecks might be a "possible stepping stone habitat for large scale dispersion" of the worms. In other words, the study is about the proliferation and dispersal of life itself.

Dutch scientists investigating wrecks in the North Sea came to another important conclusion; in studying wrecks on the Dutch continental shelf from 2010 to 2012, they discovered that the number of species found on the wrecks alone was similar to the numbers found on their entire section of the continental shelf. In short, as many species were found on a finite number of wrecks, representing a much smaller area, as on the entire seabed off Holland. The "presence of these important species and their absence from many other habitats, illustrate that shipwrecks function as key habitats, nurseries, and *refugia* that are rare or absent anywhere else in the Netherlands."[3] *Refugia*, the plural form of the Latin *refugium*, is, as the name implies, a refuge—a safe place where an endangered population can find a haven.

Shipwrecks are increasingly seen as havens for threatened marine life. A recent study by Greg Asner of the Center for Global Discovery and Conservation Science at Arizona State University studied coral growth on the wrecks of various warships sunk in the atomic tests at Bikini Atoll in July 1946, as well as the ships at Chuuk Lagoon sunk by aerial attacks during World War II. There are some 800 known species of hard coral in the world's shallow tropical oceans—a key fact, as climate change is killing off this coral. Coral are key to ocean life, for as Asner has explained, hard corals form the basic architecture of a reef, serving as the home for other species. Asner further explains that hard corals "are to reefs what trees are to forests; habitat makers."

These collections of wrecks turned out to be an incredibly robust habitat for coral. Asner's research suggests that this is because, despite the exceptionally violent forces that sank these ships, they are now isolated from regular human contact; there is less pollution, fishing, or the effects of climate change—ocean warming. The wrecks in question lie deep enough that, for now, they are not affected by marine heat waves, the number-one cause of coral death. The larger size of these sunken warships also makes them ideally sized to serve as artificial reefs. The wrecks at Chuuk host some 35 percent and the wrecks at Bikini harbor 27 percent of the world's known population of hard coral genera. The aircraft carrier USS *Saratoga* at Bikini, the largest wreck there, hosts 28 types of coral.[4] These surveys are significant because ocean heat waves, which trigger coral die off or "reef bleaching," reach only 10–15 meters deep.

The wrecks at Bikini lie at 58 meters, and so they are below what the lead scientist terms the "danger zone" of shallow water. He calls them "arks" of coral diversity. While the wrecks at Bikini and Chuuk have cultural significance and value as historic craft, and as war graves (some of them hold the bones of lost crew), and are also active tourist dive destinations, Asner's findings suggest a greater value. They are a previously unquantified key factor in preserving ocean life in the face of climate change. If the marine ecosystem crashes, as a foundation for life on earth, it will trigger a catastrophic chain of events as the oceans die. If the oceans die, so do we.

Touring Shipwrecks

When a wreck is transformed by marine colonization into an oasis of marine life, abundant in coral, fish, and other creatures, that attracts recreational scuba divers and snorkelers. The attraction is different than visiting a historic site or a compelling ruin. Wrecks on the reefs of Bermuda, along the Florida Keys, and throughout the Caribbean, as well as in the Mediterranean, have attracted many snorkelers and recreational divers who can float and observe, or make shallow-water scuba dives. Many of these wrecks are valued more for the experience of exploring and encountering marine life than for offering a brush with a relic from the past.

Bermuda, ringed by reefs, is a graveyard of hundreds of ships. A few dozen are popular dive sites, and among them is the wreck of the four-masted wooden motor schooner *Constellation*. Built in 1918 in the midst of a hurried rush to replace cargo ships lost to German U-boat attacks, *Constellation* was one of nearly 400 schooners of its type built in the United States between 1880 and 1919, and one of 125 specifically built as part of the emergency shipbuilding program of World War I. Launched in the fall of 1918 as *Sally Persis Noyes*, the schooner did not enter the war effort. It carried cargoes of coal and lumber along the Atlantic Seaboard until the Great Depression. It was hardly unique.

When World War II came, the schooner, renamed *Constellation* in 1932, was pressed into duty carrying war cargoes. Leaving New York for

Venezuela and carrying a mixed cargo of building supplies, bags of cement, medicinal supplies, including glass ampules of morphine, and 700 cases of Johnny Walker whiskey, *Constellation* ran into rough weather and began to take on water. The captain diverted to Bermuda, where on July 31, 1943, the schooner hit Western Blue Cut Reef. Stranded in the shallows, *Constellation* gradually broke up; locals and U.S. Navy personnel stationed in Bermuda salvaged much of the medicine and whiskey and stripped the wreck of its rigging and sails.

Constellation, as noted in Chapter 2, lies near the Civil War blockade runner *Montana*, which hit the reef and sank just off it in December 1863. The two wrecks inspired Peter Benchley's *The Deep*. What attracts visitors, however, is the incredible beauty of *Constellation* as a snorkel and dive site. The wood of the hull is largely gone, exposing the hold, which is defined by hundreds of now solid bags of cement, glass bottles, rusted metal, and sheets of glass cut into window panes. Snorkelers pass over the wreck in just a meter and a half of water, with sunlight slanting through the water to light the wreck and glint off the iridescent glass. Covered in marine algae, coral, and sponges, the nooks and crannies of the wreck are home to eels, lobsters, and fish; clouds of hundreds of tightly clustered damselfish known as "Sergeant Majors" glide past delighted divers, who may visit *Constellation* because of its accessibility and its fame associated with Benchley's book and the movie adaptation, or simply because of the beautiful artificial reef it has become.

The "ghost town" quality of other wrecks attracts divers. The cold, darkness, and lack of oxygen in deeper waters act as a preservative for wooden wrecks, especially in fresh or brackish environments. In contrast to the wooden hull of *Constellation*, torn apart by waves and consumed by voracious marine organisms that eat wood, wooden wrecks in the Baltic Sea, or the Great Lakes of Canada and the United States, are virtually intact ghost ships. In the lakes, in particular, wooden wrecks lie barely beneath the surface.

Thunder Bay National Marine Sanctuary on Lake Huron has over a hundred known shipwrecks. Among them are the well-preserved lower hull, stern, and massive propeller of the wooden steamship *Monohansett*,

Image 4.1. A diver snorkels over the wreck of the steam barge *B.W. Blanchard* at Thunder Bay National Marine Sanctuary.

Photograph by David J. Ruck, National Oceanic and Atmospheric Administration.

lost in just five meters of water in November 1907. The waters of Lake Huron, even in summer, are too cold for vacationing snorkelers. A glass-bottom boat tour, however, glides over the well-preserved bones and the wreck's large firebox boiler.

Other wrecks require technical diving gear and special training. These include deep-water wooden wrecks in the lakes, as well as metal-hulled ships that lie below the hundred-foot (30-meter) mark, which is considered the dividing line between non-specialized, advanced scuba and technical diving. Thick diving suits, sealed to keep the water out, more than one diving tank, filled with mixed gases as air becomes toxic under pressure, are used by some divers. Others use rebreathers, computerized gear that processes breathing gas by absorbing exhaled carbon dioxide and recycling and adding oxygen because the human lung does not absorb all the oxygen that is breathed in. That type of system is basically the same that is used in space suits, space craft, and submersibles and submarines. Highly technical and requiring detailed training, rebreathers opened deep wrecks to divers who enjoy the challenge (they refer some wrecks as "Everests") as well as the ability to explore a shipwreck that seems frozen in time.

The human body can only go so deep. Cold and the amount of time required to decompress and allow the body to release highly pressurized gases that the body has absorbed into the bloodstream limit both the depth as well as time spent, unless divers stay in a pressurized habitat for an extended mission. That type of diving, known as saturation, simply means that once you're down there, your body cannot absorb any more gas because the gas inside of you reaches equilibrium. You can stay down for hours, or days, and in some cases, for weeks. You only decompress once when the mission is done. Years of experiments in undersea habitats proved that it works. It is primarily used commercially, either for work on offshore oil and gas rigs, or deep-sea salvage.

For those who wish to explore wrecks beyond the limits of diving, submersibles offer explorers, scientists, and tourists an opportunity to reach shipwrecks in the abyssal deep. In the late 1990s, and into the new millennium, Russia's *Mir* submersibles took passengers to *Titanic* and to *Bismarck* through a partnership with Seattle-based Deep Sea Expeditions, a subsidiary of a culture- and nature-themed tourism company, Zegrahm

Image 4.2. A diver inspects the wreck of the German submarine U-701, off the North Carolina coast.

Steve Sellers, National Oceanic and Atmospheric Administration.

Expeditions. The 1998 price for a dive to *Titanic* was US$32,500, and several expeditions were filled. I was invited to participate and audit the dives by Zegrahm's Werner Zehnder and Scott Fitzsimmons in 2000. Archaeologists and museum professionals asked how the tours were conducted, both in terms of respect for the site's values and in regard to safety, and what had over a hundred salvage dives done to change the archaeological integrity of the wreck site. The first answer was simple. The Russians knew the wreck better than anyone else, including the company RMS *Titanic*, at that stage. The *Mir* submersibles were heavy-built, dependable, Cold War technology that, while not luxurious or comfortable, were reliable and were professionally well handled. They had been chosen by submersible expert and one of the initiators of submersible tourism, Rob McCallum, Zegrahm's partner in Deep Sea Expeditions because of their reputation, and that of the Shirsov Institute of Oceanology and its leader, Anatoly Sagalevitch, as well as his pilots. McCallum is to my mind a global leader and explorer who combined responsible tourism—as did the Russians—to fund missions.

Image 4.3. The author (right) with Zegrahm Expeditions President Scott Fitzsimmons (left) and *Mir 2* pilot Genya Chernaiev (center) on the *Akademik Mstislav Keldysh* in 2001 after diving to *Titanic*.
Author's photograph.

While the *Mirs* landed on *Titanic*, including on my dive, as all submersibles did (including Woods Hole's and IFREMER's) until it became a point of protocol to not land on the wreck, there was a careful approach, soft landings, and a reverence that the Russians brought to the dive I made. Their dives followed careful protocols, with a margin of risk if the pilot deemed the conditions right; we were stuck under the stern of *Titanic*, between the mud and the bottom of the hull, for about 20 minutes until our pilot, Evgeny "Jenya" Chernaiev, carefully worked us free. We were not alone—that was a tricky spot to navigate with erratic, strong currents. As we examined items scattered outside the hull on our dive, we and others in their subs saw a range of ceramics, corroded iron, brass, glass bottles, a small lantern, and shoes. They were close together, splayed out, side by side, and still laced. We did not tarry, as Jenya moved away, as we all had a clear sense that this was the resting place where someone had fallen with the ship to the bottom of the sea, only to vanish, leaving only those boots. The Russians clearly respected the site and saw it for the graveyard it was, as well as a historic site. On this and subsequent expeditions, the divers stayed aboard the research ship *Akademik Keldysh*, dived in the *Mir* submersibles, were treated to briefings by experts and scientists, and participated in ongoing deep-ocean research. I gave a positive report to my colleagues—those tourist dives were not harming the wreck, and the conduct of all on the ship and sub on my visit were respectful. There was no morbid humor, nor any sign of disrespect. The sense I had, then and now, was that this site carried such an emotional impact that your only response was sober reflection, tears for some, and wonder at what was visible both with the wreck but also the "aliens of the deep," as the marine life that inhabits the abyssal dark and its seabed have been called.

The Russians utilized the ongoing tourism dives to continue oceanographic, geological, and marine biological studies, data that they shared with their American colleagues from the National Oceanic and Atmospheric Administration (NOAA) in 2003 on a joint dive to better understand the wreck. They also hosted James Cameron and his team, starting in 2001, as Cameron made his extensive investigations and filmed the wreck. They also partnered with RMS *Titanic*, Inc., the salvors in possession of *Titanic*, for their recovery dives, following the earlier work done by their colleagues from France, IFREMER, who had worked with RMS *Titanic* since the first salvage dives and up to 2000. The Shirsov Institute retired the *Mir* submersibles, both of which are now museum displays, effectively ending active Russian participation in *Titanic* dives.

Tourism dives resumed in 2021 when Seattle-based OceanGate began to market dives using the *Titan* submersible, which had been developed by them using a titanium/carbon fiber composite hull. With up to five people, *Titan* made a series of dives to various sites, but then focused solely on *Titanic*. I knew OceanGate CEO Stockton Rush fairly well, but never was on of any of their sea expeditions. Our discussions were focused on the question of meaningful science and observation being performed during deep-sea missions, as Zegrahm had done with the Shirsov Institute, and I briefly served as an unpaid advisor to Ocean Gate's nonprofit foundation, which had assisted in the documentation of shallow-water shipwreck sites. That ceased when I returned to government service in 2010.

Titan, as the world knows, suffered a catastrophic failure, and imploded on the *Titanic* site on June 18, 2023, instantly killing Stockton Rush, Paul-Henri Nargeolet, Hamish Harding, Shahzada Dawood, and Suleman Dawood. There has been a considerable amount of speculation and a range of reports in the media about the demise of *Titan*. Stories about the craft's flaws and about the arrogance and disregard for warnings are replete in the media. An active investigation was launched that, as of November 2024, has not publicly announced any conclusions. I personally would not have made that dive, and I know others who also chose not to go. Diving *Titanic* the one time I personally saw the wreck through the viewport of a *Mir* submersible was enough for me to see it; what would have compelled me to go back, and ultimately did, was to document and learn more. We were able to do that with remote and autonomous vehicles in 2010, as have others since.

Comparisons between the fates of *Titanic* and *Titan* have been made. As a result, submersible tourism dives might not be made to *Titanic* or any other deep-sea wreck for a very long time, if ever. As I say that, the tech billionaire Jared Isaacman just made the first private trip to space on September 12, 2024. He is the first nongovernment or military astronaut to do so. To be clear, I have no problem with ocean, space, or shipwreck tourism, and many missions, discoveries, and explorations have come from private funders whose fortunes came from other endeavors. I respect them and their bold quests—and especially the non-wreck quests to not only go deep, but to do so to again highlight the importance of inner space exploration in an age of renewed interest in outer space. I applaud James Cameron and Victor Vescovo, both of whom followed Don Walsh and Jacques Piccard's epic seven-mile deep dive into the Challenger Deep. I'm not opposed to exploration, or adventure tourism, as long as it is responsibly done with diligence and care for the tourists and the places and people "explored."

For non-divers, shallower shipwrecks have been part of the tourism draw through shallow submersible diving. Individual *Atlantis*-class tourist subs, manufactured in British Columbia, have provided undersea tours in Aruba, Barbados, Grand Cayman, St. Thomas, Cozumel, and Guam. Three different *Atlantis* subs operate in Hawai'i at Waikiki, Kona, and Maui. Some 12 million people have visited the depths in *Atlantis* submarines, which can dive to 150 feet and carry up to 64 passengers. While reefs are popular, the Waikiki dives take passengers past two wrecked ships and two aircraft on the bottom. The Barbados sub also dives to a coral-encrusted wreck hanging on a submerged reef. At Maui, a former "replica" museum ship, *Carthaginian*, was purposely scuttled at the end of its floating life to become a dive attraction for *Atlantis* tours.

Shipwrecks in Parks and Marine Sanctuaries: Undersea Museums

Dive tourism to shipwrecks has been and remains a key part of visits to various marine areas around the world, with some standing out as exceptional experiences that are featured in industry magazines such as *Wreck Diver, Skin Diver, Diver, Advanced Diver, Alert Diver, Scuba Diver, Scuba,* and *Undercurrent.* For example, 20–30 percent of nearly 3 million visitors to the Florida Keys, according to a NOAA survey in 1999, a time when diving was at a peak in the country, went scuba diving or snorkeled, and spent about $31 million a year to do so. The excitement of diving to a shipwreck is magnified for divers when they see a wreck that is substantially intact, and so popular dive sites include ships sunk deliberately as artificial reefs, in the United Kingdom, off British Columbia in Canada, in Florida, and in other U.S. waters. When wrecks are not as intact and resemble more of a jigsaw puzzle than a storybook shipwreck, heritage trails, such as those championed and expertly done by the Florida Preservation Network (FPAN) with Florida Panhandle Shipwreck Trail, offer a guided experience that explains just what the diver is seeing, and how it relates to the ship that once was.[5] As well, some sites offer programs that involving sport divers in hands-on archaeology.[6]

International dive destinations that attract attention and generate significant tourism revenues include the Red Sea, Chuuk (Truk) Lagoon, with its fleet of sunken Japanese war and merchant ships from World War II, Scapa Flow in the United Kingdom, the Great Lakes of Canada and the United States, especially in marine reserves like Fathom Five Provincial Park, Thunder Bay National Marine Sanctuary (and Michigan's many other state marine preserves), Isle Royale National Park, and Sleeping Bear Dunes National Lakeshore. The Great Lakes as a major focal point for shipwrecks and wreck diving may sound incongruous. However, these five massive bodies of freshwater are the largest (by volume) freshwater lakes on earth; locals know of them as the "Inland Seas." They hold just over 20 percent of the planet's fresh water, and in size, they cover the same areas as the entire United Kingdom. They are also a vast underwater museum, with more than 6,000 known wrecks in the Great Lakes; a number of communities in every state and province, and on every lake, offer access to divers who explore the amazingly well-preserved shipwrecks in the cold freshwaters of the lakes. Even with the deleterious effects of freshwater mussels that now cover the surfaces of the shallower wrecks, the cold freshwater of lakes acts as a remarkable preservative; wooden wrecks that would be consumed by marine organisms in the ocean remain intact, some from the early to mid-19th century. One of the most amazing dives I have made, decades ago, was into a small wooden schooner that still had traces of paint; inside the captain's cabin, overturned furniture still lay on the deck, as did his hat. That type of preservation was and remains why the Great Lakes are a wreck diving mecca, as is the Baltic, with its similar levels of preservation.

But while divers love the lakes, managing them for their protection and for ongoing study was not initially popular in the neighboring towns and cities. It was primarily due to the success of tourism attracted by Thunder Bay National Marine Sanctuary in revitalizing the economy of Alpena, Michigan, that brought a shift in local attitudes from folks initially opposed to a federal presence managing "their wrecks." A number of communities surrounding Alpena worked with NOAA's Office of National Marine Sanctuaries to expand the sanctuary from 448 to 4,300 square miles of Lake Huron, an area known locally, and now for many visitors, as "Shipwreck Alley." That inspired other communities on other lakes to nominate their local and regional waters for consideration as new sanctuaries. Rather than a government-led process, this has been a community process. There are many criteria considered in designating these sanctuaries, but the dominant considerations are maritime heritage, represented primarily by shipwrecks, and their economic value through tourism. The nomination for the proposed Shipwreck Coast National Marine Sanctuary in Lake Superior summed up what they felt a sanctuary could do for their economy:

> Creation of a National Marine Sanctuary in our area will provide a critically needed boost to our economy. The shipwrecks are a truly unique asset that will draw divers from a broad area. Tourism will be greatly enhanced, and jobs will be created in the hospitality segment of our economy. Creation of a National Marine Sanctuary will stimulate creation of new businesses such as a dive shop, support charter dive operations from our harbor, improve our harbor facilities, expand motel room availability, promote the use of our campgrounds, improved sales of fuel, restaurant meals, as well as food sales in our stores. Ripple effect impacts will include

more charter fishing operations, expanded use of all of our other tourism related facilities and enhance sales for local stores, and repair shops.[7]

Outside of the Great Lakes, in late 2019, working with the State of Maryland, NOAA designated a new National Marine Sanctuary at Mallows Bay, on the Potomac River outside of Washington, D.C. Accessible to kayakers, an assemblage of wrecks, many of them World War I–era wooden ships laid up for scrapping at the end of the war, were selected to be the next tourism draw in the greater Washington, D.C., area. The wrecks thickly pack Mallows Bay, with the lower portions of the wooden hulls dotting it like a series of small islands. The hulls, filled with soil, rotten wood, and with grasses and trees sprouting from them, are habitat for wildlife. Fish dart between the hulls in the shallows, making Mallows Bay National Marine Sanctuary a destination for recreational kayakers, bird watchers, and anglers. While the wrecks have an interesting history as part of a wartime revival of wooden sail and steamship building to offset losses to German U-boats, most never entered service. Laid up waiting for a call to service that never came, they were ultimately sold for scrap, but even that effort came short, leaving a ghost fleet that finally succumbed to neglect, dry rot, and storms. There are some 100 known wrecks in and around Mallows Bay, and they are listed as a group on the National Register of Historic Places. But that is not their paramount value.[8] These mundane shipwrecks are a captivating tour, a wildlife habitat worthy of being a sanctuary, and make a substantial contribution to the local and regional economy through tourism. In parks and sanctuaries, the value of shipwrecks as historic sites, as tourism draws, as habitat for marine life, or even as favorite sport fishing sites are balanced and managed. Instead of viewing wrecks as "cultural" or "natural" resources, managers realized that they could be both. Balance means choosing a path that tries to not sacrifice the multiple values of a shipwreck unless one value is of such exceptional importance that it is paramount. This can be a wreck that is habitat for endangered species of coral, a wreck with tremendous potential through archaeology to teach more about the past, or one that is most valued as a favorite place to snorkel or sport fish.

Perhaps one of the most creative ways of using a shipwreck as a "museum in the sea" was in Florida Keys National Marine Sanctuary in 2013. That year, artist Andreas Franke mounted the world's first underwater art gallery with 12 scenes set on the 27-meter-deep wreck of the USNS *General Hoyt S. Vandenberg* in the Florida Keys. Sunk as an artificial reef and diving attraction in 2009, *Vandenberg* captured international attention with Franke's stunning and eerie selection of 12 images. Using his earlier underwater images of the wreck, Franke merged them in the studio with models dressed in period clothing in a variety of poses. He then printed and mounted his images using the actual wreck as his gallery. It was haunting. It was as if ghosts inhabited the submerged decks, caught up in everyday activity but oblivious to the viewer's reaction. The project spurred an extensive popular reaction. In the four-month showing of his art on the wreck, Franke's photos attracted visits by thousands of divers.[9]

In its way, the exhibit on the wreck of *Vandenberg* captured a sense of intact and near-intact shipwrecks as underwater "ghost towns." It is not unlike the approach taken by James Cameron in "Ghosts of the Abyss," but it is obviously fictional and not a depiction of actual people who were on the ship when it sank. The wreck of *Titanic*, miles deep, lies in eternal darkness until visiting craft, either submersibles or remotely operated vehicles, light up for a brief moment. With some stories of the wreck being so well known, the experience of visiting *Titanic* can be a powerful journey of imagination in which scenes play out in the mind of what happened on that night. Cameron's documentary merges footage from his blockbuster feature film with that of the wreck from a 2001 expedition led by Cameron to "ghost in" people and events; the wrecked, largely vanished bridge is the setting for the cinematic ghosts of the quartermaster and the first officer at the moment of the impact with the iceberg, a father kneeling and speaking to his child in a lifeboat from the edge of the now empty, corroded deck, or diners at their tables inside the sunken hulk. Eerie and compelling, "Ghosts of the Abyss" took the wreck of *Titanic* from depths and made it "live" again, which reinforced the view that this wreck, an undersea museum, compels visitation and ongoing social interaction because of the powerful human stories associated with it.

Shipwrecks as Aesthetic and Romantic Sites

The physical remains of a lost ship, even an abandoned one, have cultural value. Certain wrecks, as they exist on a beach, underwater, or even in a museum, have value as both muse and as a means to profit. A wreck as a visible entity that inspires artistic creation or tourism is a wreck that makes money, and in a renewable way if managed properly. One of the more fascinating wrecks in U.S. history is a small wooden craft, which might be America's first "celebrity shipwreck." The bones of the wreck appeared on a Cape Cod beach after a fierce storm stripped away the sand in early May 1863.[10] It was the first "old" wreck to capture public attention in the United States, as opposed to a contemporary loss that attracted the curious and thrill seekers drawn to the scene of an accident.

Locals identified the wreck, partially preserved by swamp mud and the sand that buried it, as the "antient wrecke" *Sparrow-Hawk*, a colonial vessel blown ashore in 1626 and last exposed by storms in 1782. Hundreds visited, and many took a small "souvenir," including chips or pieces of wood. Two local citizens, inspired by a sense of history, and perhaps profit, as it was a "Pilgrim" ship, raised the wreck from the sand and put it on display, for a fee, on Boston Common, and then for a while in P. T. Barnum's museum, before being transferred in 1889 to the Pilgrim Society for display at the Pilgrim Hall Museum. After a century at Pilgrim Hall, the bones of *Sparrow-Hawk* went to the Cape Cod Maritime Museum for display.

Sparrow-Hawk is the first known old wreck taken off a beach in America and put into a museum, while other shipwrecks were left where they lay, or were allowed to be taken back by the sea. Others still rest on stretches of beach. They are attractions in their own right, just like the ruins of a castle, a fallen Greek temple, or an ancient city. This is a concept captured by Rose Macaulay in *Pleasure of Ruins* (1954), in which she examines humanity's reaction to decay and ruin as a compulsion to see and confront them because of "their shattered intimidations that strike so responsive a nerve in our destruction-seeking souls."[11] The rusting,

Image 4.4. The wreck of the colonial vessel *Sparrow-Hawk* displayed on Boston Commons, ca. 1865.
New York Public Library/Wikimedia Commons.

stranded wreck of the small steel freighter *Panagiotis* lies on a sand beach in a small cove on the island of Zakynthos, a beach now known as *Navagio*, or Shipwreck Beach. It is one of the most photographed shipwrecks in the world, caught between two small promontories in a small, sandy cove. A humble, working craft with no real historical significance, this 1937-built freighter ran aground on the beach in 1980, reportedly as it was being chased by the Greek Navy while smuggling cigarettes. The stranded hulk, high and dry on the sand, has drawn thousands of visitors for four decades. While not historically important, the compelling need to see and walk around the ship led to calls in 2016 for restoration to keep it as a viable tourist attraction.

Another beached wreck with a tremendous tourist draw is the rusting skeleton of the steel-hulled *Peter Iredale*. The four-masted bark, built in 1890, was one of a number of multi-masted vessels built, mostly in British shipyards, at the end of the era of metal-hulled sailing ships. Ocean steamers were ruling the seas and trades, but vessels like *Peter Iredale*, running with the wind, could still eke out a profit in bulk trades. *Peter Iredale* wrecked at the mouth of the Columbia River while heading to Portland, Oregon, to load wheat on October 25, 1906. The mouth of the

Columbia, known to sailors as the "Graveyard of the Pacific," is studded with a few hundred wrecks. Caught in a heavy wind on a rough bar with the seas breaking over it, *Peter Iredale*'s crew could not anchor and hold the ship off the beach. The wind and seas drove it ashore with so much force that the impact snapped three of the masts. Lying on Clatsop Spit, heeled offshore, with the waves digging the wreck deep into the sand, *Peter Iredale* was a total loss. The sight of the huge ship, festooned with fallen rigging and torn sails and lying stranded on the beach, brought thousands of tourists to see it. Over the course of the next century, the stranded hulk, battered by waves and rusting, has slowly collapsed, but its bowsprit stood well past mid-century. Known as Oregon's "iconic shipwreck," *Peter Iredale* is a much-visited, oft-photographed landmark that reveals more of its buried secrets when winter storms strip sand from the beach and low tide reveals the lower hull, with deck beams and the stubs of the masts in a row defining the length of the hull as beachcombers and picnickers walk and play amid the ruins of the ship.

Raising the Wreck: Shipwrecks in Museums

Shipwrecks also make fascinating exhibits in museums. This includes finds raised from wrecks, or entire shipwrecks that have been raised from the water. Early recoveries from ships—and of ships—include the 19th- and early 20th-century excavations of the previously mentioned Viking ships that had been hauled ashore and used to bury chieftains and high-status warriors between 1,100 and 1,000 years ago. The well-preserved hulls of the Gokstad and Oseberg ship, and the remains of a third, the Tune ship, and the grave goods found in them are displayed in a specially built museum in Oslo, Norway. The *vikingskipshuset* (literally "Viking ship house") has three white-washed "halls" for each ship; the museum has been compared to a series of chapels, with each Viking ship displayed as an exquisite relic.

Scandinavia is home to other museums that prominently feature wrecks raised from mud and water; the other well-known Viking ship museum is outside Copenhagen in Roskilde. There, excavations in the 1960s in the shallows of the bay raised the broken remains of five ships used to block the harbor in the late Viking age, around the year 1070 AD. Additional excavations in the 1990s revealed the remains of nine other ships. After excavation, archaeologists treated the fragile wooden hulls from Roskilde to preserve them and then mounted them on display inside the main museum building, the architecturally simple Viking Ship Hall, where visitors walk along the sides and above the ships as they rest on steel skeletons that fill out the missing parts and support the fragile planks.

Roskilde also features an open-air display of Viking technology and a shipyard where accurate replicas are built and sailed, and visitors can join in the experience. The Viking Ship Museum at Roskilde, like the one in Oslo, is highly popular and heavily visited. The Roskilde ships, unlike the ones in Oslo, are regular craft used for work, trade, and war, while the Oslo ships are royal "dragon ships." Scandinavian museums display other archaeologically recovered and well-preserved wrecks of wooden ships from the post-Roman period in Northern Europe, but the Viking ships, displayed as they are in their specially built halls, are cultural icons and the source of national and pan-Scandinavian pride.

Another Scandinavian wreck, from Stockholm, is the world's most famous shipwreck in a museum. The Swedish warship *Vasa*, with its massive, magnificently decorated, heavy hull built to demonstrate the power and majesty of the Swedish throne in a time of wars to control the Baltic region, sank on its maiden voyage in Stockholm harbor in 1626. Some of the cannon were salvaged, but *Vasa* was gradually forgotten until researcher Anders Franzen decided to look for it. In 1956, Franzen found the wreck in relatively shallow water in the middle of the active harbor. What followed was a three-year project to clear the wreck from the mud, cut tunnels beneath it to pass cables, and then lift the still-intact hulk of *Vasa* to the surface in April 1961.[12] A symbol of royal power from a time when Sweden controlled the Baltic, *Vasa* was once again a symbol of national pride. Once raised from the sea, years of work to preserve *Vasa* and gradually dry it out followed, as archaeologists explored inside to recover tens of thousands of artifacts, including the remains of some of the crew lost with the ship when it sank. *Vasa* was a time capsule. It took until 1977 for the preservation treatment to end its first phase. Then the work to restore and replace hundreds of carved decorations and put the lower masts back in place followed, as a custom-built museum, the *Vasahusset*, or *Vasa*'s house, was erected around it.

The *Vasa* museum is Sweden's most popular museum, with the complete hull of the warship displayed inside as an almost sacred icon, while the artifacts, including the skeletons of the dead with their belongings and CSI-style reproductions of what they looked like, are displayed. It is this exhibit, the dead of the *Vasa*, that I find as fascinating as the ship itself. The skeletal remains of at least 17, and possibly 19 people emerged from the mud as the interior of the wreck was excavated after it had been raised. In at least one of them, the brain had been preserved in the cold, oxygen-free conditions of burial (I've seen it in the lab), as well as hair and fingernails. Forensic analysis has revealed much about the men, two women, and a child whose skeletons are displayed in a sensitive matter. Visitors can choose to view this particular exhibition. Their life stories are told, in a way, through the isotopes in their bones that tell where they were from and their diet; injuries, illnesses, including in some of them scurvy, anemia, or chronic diarrhea; and in one case, that one of the dead, a man, was a lifelong vegetarian. The child shares DNA with one of the men.

But because archaeologists, as curators of the past, have a focus on what makes us human, the team at *Vasa* also displays and interprets these bodies as people. Facial reconstruction of as many as could be done, including the two women, reveals what they looked like, with DNA also providing details such as hair and eye color. Another powerful and emotional part of the display includes life-sized screens where actors wearing reproductions of the clothing associated with some of the dead step forward, as if from the mists of time—or the beyond—to silently greet the visitor. It's eerie, and yet compelling, at least for me and the many others who were visiting the day I was in that gallery, which is named "face to face." There is careful sensitivity in what the *Vasa* displays do, and the example from their museum has guided facial reconstructions from the skulls from other wrecks, including the faces of Civil War dead in the United States.

Vasa inspired other nations and museums to display all, or significant parts, of historic wrecks raised from lakes and oceans, or in some cases, from land where landfill or the shifting course of a river left a former bend in a corn or soybean field in middle America. The ancient Kyrenia ship, lost in the 4th century BC, was excavated in the late 1960s under the leadership of the late Michael Katzev; it was raised, conserved, and placed on display in the Crusader Castle at Kyrenia, Cyprus, where it remains to this day. Roman riverine warships discovered in early 1982 in the Rhine were raised, conserved, and placed in a custom-built facility, the *Museum für antike Schifffahrt* in Mainz, Germany. The preserved remains, in some cases fragmentary, are displayed next to full-scale modern replicas. The remains of the hull and artifacts from the Dutch ship *Batavia*, wrecked off the coast of Western Australia in 1629, were rediscovered and excavated in the 1970s and, after conservation, placed in the Western Australia Museum in Perth and in other satellite locations for the museum. The substantial remains of Henry VIII's warship *Mary Rose* and its thousands of artifacts are displayed in their own custom-built museum at Portsmouth, England. But like *Vasa*, at the *Mary Rose* Museum in Portsmouth, the focus is on more than the ship.

The *Mary Rose* Museum is stunning, starting with the upright half of the hull of King Henry's once mighty warship, displayed in its own hall. The truly amazing portion of the museum, for me, is the area in which the artifacts depict life, war, and loss from half a millennium ago. The ongoing study of the collection, like that of *Vasa*, continues decades after the initial excavation. New finds and revelations emerge from that study—in essence, as is the case with other museum collections where all that was excavated is kept together for ongoing preservation and analysis, the emergence of new DNA technology has revealed more about the people whose remains were found; *Mary Rose*'s complement of warriors and sailors included men who were not English, including some who were French, ironically lost in a battle with other French as they served Henry VIII, or more likely, worked for him for higher wages.

The examples in the United States include the turret and machinery of the Civil War ironclad USS *Monitor*, still undergoing conservation, which are in a purpose-built, $30 million center at the Mariners' Museum in Newport News, Virginia; and the former Confederate Naval Museum, now the National Civil War Naval Museum in Columbus, Georgia, which displays the lower hull of the CSS *Jackson*, an ironclad scuttled at the end of the war, as well as the stern and machinery of the CSS *Chattahoochee*, an armored gunboat. The previously mentioned USS *Cairo*, discovered intact but broken in the attempt to raise it, was reconstructed and is displayed outside its museum at Vicksburg Military National Historical Park in Mississippi. As is the case with other museums that display shipwrecks, there is more in all of these museums and historic sites than the bare bones of hulls and machinery. The personal effects of the crew, raised from the time-capsule-like *Cairo*, are displayed in its museum.

Artifacts from *Monitor* include items from the crew, but by far the most powerful part of the exhibit is the display of not only personal effects but casts of the skulls, and forensic-reconstructions of the faces of two men whose skeletal remains were found inside the turret of *Monitor* as Navy divers prepared to raise it from the wreck in 2002, all part of a focused plan to raise some but not all of the ironclad in response to ongoing deterioration and collapse of the hull. Sixteen of the crew had died, and the possibility of finding bodies was ever present. I've described the background and events from the archaeological work on *Monitor* in a previous book, *War at Sea: A Shipwrecked History from Antiquity to the Twentieth Century*, so I will only go into details on the discovery of the two skeletons in the turret and the facial reconstructions.

The display of the two facial reconstructions at the *Monitor* Center is a powerful exhibit that reminds the visitor that real people lived and died on the ironclad, but there's more to the story. David Alberg, superintendent of *Monitor* National Marine Sanctuary; Daniel Basta, the director of NOAA's Office of National Marine Sanctuaries; and I, as then director of NOAA's Maritime Heritage Program, which was part of the Office of National Marine Sanctuaries, were all frustrated by the fact that, after a decade of fascinating but inconclusive forensic analysis by the nation's best military lab, in Honolulu, there was no match to samples they were able to obtain from descendants of the lost 16 men on *Monitor*. And so they stayed in the lab. There are strong protocols for the burial of U.S. military dead; there are not to be any more interments of "unknown" military casualties. But we felt the need to bury those two men, and to do so in a way that did not fly in the face of a good and sound policy.

An interment of those two men, which we felt should be at Arlington, would also again focus attention not on rusted iron and Civil War history, but on people. The facial reconstructions were a key first step. From the clay models that covered the casts of the skulls, software produced life-like images—essentially, driver's license–style photos of each man, albeit clean-shaven, as we had no idea about facial hair. Releasing those images to the press humanized the two men in a way that images of their skulls could not. We unveiled the photos and the forensic reconstructions at the National U.S. Navy Memorial in Washington, D.C., telling the *Washington Post* that even if no one knew exactly who they were, their mothers would have recognized them. That was, I felt, the right way to humanize them, although the younger sailor's facial reconstruction photo ended up being featured on the website "Bangable dudes in history." Ahem.... We'd made our point about these two dead men being relatable to a modern audience. I just hadn't realized how relatable.

Meanwhile, research by friends at the Mariners' Museum determined that there was no monument to all of the 16 who had died, so, in response to a pointed question asked at a meeting with the Navy and Arlington staff at the Pentagon, when asked how the government could place a stone and ensure that the two men were properly identified on it, I answered that a stone with all 16 names on it would make sure the right names were there. And with that, in March 2013, a year after our public unveiling, a caisson with the two bodies in caskets, their bones draped with modern U.S. Navy uniforms, slowly moved through Arlington

National Cemetery. Hundreds gathered to watch, including descendants of *Monitor*'s 16 lost sailors, as well as those who had lived out the war. They were joined by historians, archaeologists, the Navy divers who had raised the turret and those two men, and our colleagues from NOAA and the Mariners' Museum. Secretary of the Navy Roy Mabus spoke at the service for the two *Monitor* sailors. He said that "while Naval tradition holds the site of a shipwreck as hallowed ground and a proper final resting place for sailors who perish at sea," the ceremony and burial at Arlington paid tribute not only to two men but to all who were lost when *Monitor* sank; "little is certain in military service, but we can guarantee the Navy will always remain committed to honoring those who pay the ultimate price defending our nation." Every time I visit the *Monitor* Center, it is those reconstructed faces that hold the most meaning for me. It is for me always about the people. But that is not to say that the only way to connect to people in shipwrecks is through their remains. We rarely find human remains in older wrecks. But we almost always find artifacts made by, for, and used by people.

The wreck of the river steamboat SS *Bertrand*, wrecked in 1865, rediscovered and excavated from a Nebraska field in 1968, is not displayed in its own museum. It lies underwater. However, hundreds of thousands of artifacts from the wreck are on display. That museum is one of my favorites; it does not focus on the remains of the lost steamer; it instead tells the story of a growing America at the close of the Civil War, and of life in boomtowns as people flocked to settle in a rapidly changing part of America. A gold rush in the Montana Territory that began in 1863 led to boom times and towns, and on its final voyage, *Bertrand* was carrying passengers and some five tons of cargo and baggage. North of Omaha, *Bertrand* hit a submerged log on the Missouri River and quickly sank. No one died, but the cargo was lost, as were the bags of the steamboat's passengers. While some of its goods were salvaged, it settled into the mud, where over the next century, the changing course of the river left it entombed beneath a field. Deep below that field, the wet mud of the former river bed, however, sealed the hull and over half a million artifacts in cold, damp conditions that nearly perfectly preserved them.

Two salvagers seeking both gold and flasks of mercury bound to the gold diggings in Montana to help extract the metal from crushed ore, as well as what they suspected might be perfectly preserved whiskey in its wooden casks, found the magnetic signature of the wreck 28 feet below the surface of the field. Using a borer, they drilled test holes that brought broken glass, lead shot, pieces of leather boots, wood, and brandied cherries. Because the wreck sat on government land, and because the wreck was presumed to likely be intact and well-preserved, the government set conditions for the excavation and recovery in the permit that allowed the salvagers, Jesse Purcell and Sam Corbino, to start work in 1968. As excavation took place, the removal of the soil and mud that covered the wreck meant that the site flooded because of the high water table. That led to pumping to lower the water and reveal the intact hull of *Bertrand*, still packed with goods and passenger baggage. One of the first finds was a wooden crate that was marked "*Bertrand* Stores." Another find that confirmed the identity came from passenger luggage. The name "Fannie" was cut into the wooden frame of a small chalkboard. These were used by schoolchildren in their lessons at that time. This artifact, with the other items, were the possessions of the family of Major J. B. Campbell, and the chalkboard belonged to his daughter Fannie, who was on *Bertrand* with her sister Annie. They, as did all the other passengers, survived the wreck.

The excavation of *Bertrand* continued through 1969, as the hull was completely exposed, and the intact deck was removed to get into the holds. Early salvagers, likely at the time of the sinking, had pulled off the superstructure on the deck, removed much of the machinery, and recovered the mercury and any gold. The wreck was a near-intact time capsule from 1865, but there was no "treasure." The intact lower hull, after excavation and documentation, was left to rest in the pond that now covers the excavation site. The amazing time-capsule nature of the wreck is on full display, however, with a wide range of frontier-bound artifacts preserved by their anaerobic burial in water-saturated silt. *Bertrand*'s museum is operated by the U.S. Fish and Wildlife Service at the De Soto Wildlife Refuge.

The artifacts—all half million—were not sold, but were kept together, and are displayed in a publicly accessible visitor center at the Refuge that is both a massive storage facility and a museum. When you walk through it, it is like you are in a Costco from 1865. Tools, clothing, food, some of it packed in bottles, canned food with paper labels intact, and the perfectly preserved and labeled crates they were shipped in, as well as alcoholic beverages, boots, household items such as brooms, candles, cooking utensils, butter churns, cutlery, and chinaware, lamps, matches, sewing supplies, shoe polish, washboard, glassware, plows, hayforks, axes, tools, and nails, and tar paper, and the baggage of three families. That's quite a list, and I have not included everything displayed or cataloged. This small museum is worth the visit, and an example of why we archaeologists love shipwrecks as sites, because they can provide a detailed glimpse into the past through that which was once common, in near time-capsule circumstances that we get to excavate, study, and share with the public.

Another "time-capsule" wreck is being excavated in a unique way; rather than excavate the artifacts underwater, preserve, study, and display them, Chinese archaeologists raised the entire, unexcavated hull of a medieval Chinese trading ship, known as the Nanhai #1 wreck, and placed it inside a large pool in a custom-built museum in Guangdong. There it is slowly being excavated by archaeologists in front of the visiting public. These are just a few examples of entire shipwrecks taken from the sea and made part of popular and highly visited tourist destinations. A number of museums display collections of significant artifacts from shipwrecks, not only those recovered at the time of a wreck event, but also those from later dives and archaeological excavations. A modern example that draws on the power of tragic shipwrecks is in Halifax, Nova Scotia. Pier 21 in Halifax is Canada's national historic site dedicated to immigration by sea. It displays a large collection of artifacts recovered from Canada's most tragic shipwreck, the liner SS *Empress of Ireland*. Rammed and sunk in a collision on the Saint Lawrence River on May 29, 1914, *Empress of Ireland* sank in 14 minutes, taking more than a thousand people with it. The items from this immigrant steamship give visitors a powerful, physical connection to the ship and the people on board.

Perhaps the most famous and most visited is the Museum of Underwater Archaeology in Bodrum, Turkey. It is Turkey's most popular archaeological museum. It features the results of decades of exploration, excavation, and research by Turkish and American archaeologists from the Institute of Nautical Archaeology. The museum shares not only the finds, but the results of decades of dedicated scholarship, as well as CSI-style forensics that reconstructed largely vanished ships from fragments on the seabed, analyzed where items once were located inside a ship through the precision mapping of every item as it was excavated, and gave the world its first view of decorated medieval Islamic glass, hitherto unknown but from a few fragments found in the desert outside of Cairo, by working for years in painstaking fashion with a million fragments to rebuild, at last count, nearly 250 complete glass vessels.

The most famous shipwreck in the world, *Titanic*, has inspired more than one *Titanic* museum and many exhibitions. From the ongoing recovery of artifacts from the seabed, salvager RMS *Titanic*, Inc., created a permanent exhibition in Las Vegas, as well as touring exhibitions that travel the world. Displayed with full-scale recreations of cabins and the grand staircase of the ill-fated liner, a freezing section of ice so visitors can "touch the iceberg," and a lifeboat that one can step into, merged with the powerful personal stories of the people on board who lived and died, the *Titanic* exhibitions have been seen by millions globally. The *Titanic* Museum in Pigeon Forge, Tennessee, and its sister attraction in Branson, Missouri, advertised as the world's largest museum attractions, take visitors through a half-scale replica of the ship, where they experience "*Titanic*" and see artifacts associated with the ship. They are both very popular attractions, as is *Titanic* Belfast, a purpose-built museum at the former Harland and Wolff (H&W) shipyard, where *Titanic* and its sister ships were built. Sited next to the offices of H&W, where *Titanic* was designed (now a boutique hotel), and the slip where the ship was built and launched, the museum tells the story of *Titanic* from the perspective of the community where it was born. It is also a highly popular attraction.

In summary, shipwrecks are magnets for both marine life and for people drawn to their mystique, history, or the opportunity to explore the undersea world and seek out reminders of our own human past. They are also places where, like other archaeological sites, relics and physical evidence of past events and human enterprise come to light when raised and placed in a museum. Can all of these values or reasons to care about shipwrecks coexist? I think so.

The powerful human stories associated with shipwrecks, the cultural impact that shipwrecks have made on society over time, and the otherworldliness of a wreck rusting, decaying, or overgrown, or seemingly half-frozen in time in the deep and cold, have captured people's imaginations. That has sparked not only commemoration but also a desire by some to see and connect to them. On the beach or in the museum or under the water, wrecks put the modern viewer onto that deck, and physically connect them to those stories of the past and to lives lost and saved.

The invention of SCUBA after World War II led to an explosion of interest and a surge in the number of people being certified to dive in the 1950s and 1960s. Recreational divers were drawn by many things, among them wrecks, and when I started diving in the 1970s, I joined a group of men and women whose numbers grew, according to SCUBAPRO, one of the leading manufacturers of dive equipment, to some 6 million certified divers worldwide. Over the five decades I have been diving, technology continues to advance to allow divers to go deeper, and stay longer, and to bring equipment to document their adventures in far better detail than we did half a century ago. But I want to make it clear that you do not need to dive to explore a wreck, thanks to the new, interactive, three-dimensional experiences provided by detailed scans. You can see all that we see as divers by clicking a mouse or navigating a touchscreen with your finger. But for those who dive, there is the thrill of "being there."

But there is also the desire to retrieve artifacts and at times even complete ships from the deep and not leave them in that great museum of the sea. For decades, projects have raised ships and their contents, and have displayed them ashore. The fascination that these finds convey is also shared by those who beachcomb and encounter a wreck. But this interest and these pursuits are at times in conflict with the other values of shipwrecks. Not every wreck is historic or archaeological, nor may it be the subject of romantic reflection or discourse. There are other reasons we as society interact with shipwrecks, and a key focus is economic value, as salvage of ships and cargoes is a major, often unseen aspect of the world of shipwrecks.

The concept of shipwrecks as biological colonies, as *refugia* or "oases" for certain marine life, from bacteria and coral to the fish that swarm around wrecks, has meaning. One constant I have observed in many years of marine exploration is the wreck as a "reef," no matter how deep it is. It's easy to imagine in shallow water, but I also want to share how whenever we lower a remotely operated vehicle (ROV) into the ocean to explore a wreck, there are times when the sonar is just picking up the shadow of a hull still hidden in the darkness, but we are also seeing the ROV pass through schools of fish. They *love* wrecks. Let's remember that.

5

The Bounty of the Sea

> Sahei told him that *O-fune-sama* referred to the ships that were wrecked on the reef that stretched out in front of the village. These ships normally carried such things as food, utensils, luxury goods, and cloth, which would substantially improve the lives of the villagers.... The late autumn village ritual was carried out in the hope that passing ships would founder on the reef.
>
> —Akira Yoshimura, *Shipwrecks*, 1982

In his book *Shipwrecks*, Japanese novelist Akira Yoshimura tells the fictional tale of an impoverished medieval Japanese village whose inhabitants made a living by luring unsuspecting ships onto the rocks. The late autumn ritual, a time to honor ancestors and celebrate, has powerful symbolic meaning in Japan; crops are harvested, and autumn is seen as a time of hope and celebration. Yoshimura is arguing that, for people whose prosperity depended on the plunder of deliberately wrecked ships, their fortune was the result of their victims' misfortune. That novel is based on historical events that span the globe and many cultures; coastal communities reaping the bounties of the sea was a widespread practice. Historian David Cressy convincingly argues in his book *Shipwrecks and the Bounty of the Sea* that they were not just disasters or "catastrophes" for owners and crews. They were also considered benefits of coastal life for local communities living at the "margins," a transitional zone between land and sea, where a shipwreck was a social event.[1]

It is important to remember that a shipwreck is usually not a happy social event for any. Coastal wrecks were no guarantee of rescue or survival. Ships didn't just strand on a sandy beach; some hung up on offshore rocks, where heavy surf made it dangerous and at times impossible to launch lifeboats. The coastal steamship *Independence*, with several hundred passengers, struck rocks off Baja California on a February 1853 voyage, and taking on water, headed for the shoreline. Stranding at high tide, far from the beach, as boats were launched, most of them capsized in the surf, drowning some passengers and destroying the boats. The *New York Times*' account of the disaster, published on April 26, described what happened next as "one of the most harrowing scenes ever recorded in the history of shipwreck."

When hot coals tumbled out of the boilers as the wooden hull pounded in the surf, *Independence* started to burn. The wind blew the flames toward the bow, where passengers and crew desperately ran to escape. Families leaped into the surf and drowned, while others burned. One hundred and twenty-nine people died; one of the stories of the loss of SS *Independence* is that of a man who searched for his family and was told they had washed ashore dead and had been buried in the sand. He brushed the sand away and found his family. He kissed their faces and reburied them. When wreck-diving friends rediscovered the wreck on Baja's Isla Margarita more than a century later, they told me that the sand dunes, as they shifted in the wind, still exposed human bones, and the twisted iron machinery of *Independence*'s engine was revealed at low tide during storms.

There are worse stories of shipwrecks on the shore; globally, there are thousands of these tales. Another I know is also on the Pacific Coast, on the rocky shores of Vancouver Island. In January 1906, the iron-hulled steamer *Valencia*, bound for Seattle from San Francisco, ran aground in stormy weather after missing the entrance of the Straits of Juan de Fuca, struck rocks offshore, and started the flood. I know that shore; the open power of the unimpeded Pacific beats against those rocks. "My God, where are we?" the captain reportedly asked his second mate. To keep from sinking in deeper water, the captain ran his ship aground. *Valencia* was stranded in the rocks a few hundred feet offshore. As one surviving member of the crew later testified, "it was thick dark, sleeting and blowing a stiff breeze." In a panic, the crew launched all but one of the lifeboats. Boats smashed against the side of the ship, and others capsized. On deck, as the hull settled into the rocks, heavy waves washed passengers into the freezing cold sea.[2]

In desperation, women and children were carried up into the rigging of the masts and tied in place; another survivor later testified it was a "pitiful sight," as many of the women were "wearing only night dresses, with bare feet on the freezing ratlines, trying to shield children in their arms from the icy wind and rain." Only a few survivors made it ashore. An accurate count of the dead was never determined, but most numbers range from 124 to 136. Not one of the women or children aboard survived. The local people continue to insist, as they have since the wreck, that this spot of the coast is haunted by the spirits of *Valencia*'s dead. Years later, one of the lifeboats was reportedly found wedged into a sea cave with the skeletons of the dead still inside.

It is inevitable that assigning blame always follows an accident. For survivors of a wreck, watching locals salvaging goods, luggage, and personal possessions from the dead who washed ashore was devastating and horrifying. It is also easy to understand that survivors or the families of the dead would question whether those on shore who benefited from the flotsam had profited from sinister motives. The reality, David Cressy argues, was that what was plunder to some observers was salvage to others. Wrecks were both emergencies and opportunities, and when a ship came ashore in a coastal community, it tested that community's bonds of authority, morality, and discipline.[3] In his assessment of centuries of coastal English shipwrecks and the "barbarous country people" on those shores, Cressy examined the "myths of murderous wreckers" and found a more complex reality where shipwrecks connected people who ordinarily did not interact; nor did they necessarily understand each other.

The idea of "wrecking," or salvaging or luring ships to their doom for economic benefit, is an old one, as are the less sinister but equally chilling tales of isolated, hardscrabble maritime communities who saw a wreck as a boon. There is also a powerful narrative associated with this in which a shipwreck helps address the disparities in society and between cultures. It is a global story that spans millennia. The wrecking of a craft on one's shore, whether an accident or one deliberately caused by luring a ship, is a powerful subject in maritime history and literature. Robert Louis Stevenson wrote of a village in the Pentland Firth off the northeast coast of Scotland "who stood by on the shore as a ship struggled to get free of the pull of the sea that threatened to pull it ashore." There was "no emotion, no animation, it scarce seemed any interest, not a hand was raised; but all callously awaited the harvest of the sea."[4] "Please, God, send us a wreck" was a common prayer on more than one coast. Whether through deliberate, malicious intent, or opportunistic salvage, the key value of a shipwreck for the disadvantaged in Western society has always been a chance to make even a small improvement in the standard of living, and in some cases to remedy desperate circumstances.

Indigenous Peoples and Shipwrecks

Shipwrecks represented not only cross-cultural contact but also trade with indigenous peoples. "Wrecking" takes on a very different meaning when a trading ship was stranded or wrecked and "plundered" by the indigenous peoples who lived there, or when vessels were seized and "plundered" as a result of unequal trade relationships, or as an assertion of indigenous rights and power. While the stories of "wreckers" are often ascribed to impoverished or subsistence communities—the town of Nags Head, on North Carolina's Outer Banks, reportedly gained its name from the hardscrabble townsfolk tying a lantern to the neck of an old horse that would wander up and down the beach to lure unsuspecting ships ashore—or Yoshimura's fictional Japanese village, there were many "wreck" events that appear to have been opportunities that were seized by the locals. In some cases, it was reaping what the sea had delivered; on others, ships were taken and, in a number of those cases, destroyed.

In my decades on the Pacific Northwest coast of the United States and Canada, I learned and appreciated the First Nations' indigenous perspective: that which washed ashore was a gift of the sea. A stranded ship was no different than a whale's carcass. That meant, in the 17th, 18th, and 19th centuries, that the ships themselves, their cargoes, such as they were, and the crew and passengers became the property of the indigenous peoples. One of the most fabled shipwrecks on the coast is in Oregon, and in the shadow of Neahkanie Mountain on Nehalem Bay. When explorers Lewis and Clark reached the mouth of the Columbia River in October 1805, they were told by local people of a wreck which had left large blocks of beeswax strewn along their shores. There was more to the story, and as Americans arrived in larger numbers and settled the coast in the mid- to late 19th century, more than beeswax emerged—fragments of porcelain and the hardwood timbers of an "ancient" wreck, as well as more stories from the local tribes. The wreck had drifted in with survivors. The survivors had lived with the tribes until a dispute over women arose, and they were killed.

What also became clear through time was that there had been more than one wreck, and that some survivors had stayed and married into the tribes; Lewis and Clark met one man, whose name was Soto, whose father or grandfather had been on one of those ships. His name infers that the wreck was Spanish and dated to the 18th century. Spanish settlement of Mexico and Central and South America had ultimately extended north in the 18th century into what is now the United States. San Francisco was the northernmost site of permanent settlement. Spanish voyages of supply and exploration had traversed the length of the Pacific coast as far north as Alaska and included a temporary settlement in what is now British Columbia. Another Spanish trade, from the Philippines, brought valuable commodities from Asia—porcelains, spices, and beeswax among them—in exchange for silver mined in the Americas.

The Manila galleons, so called because of their origin in the Philippines, sailed across the Pacific until they reached the West Coast, often sighting land as they approached either the southern Oregon or northern California coast, before tacking south to head for Acapulco. Two of them, *Santo Cristo de Burgos*, wrecked in 1693 or 1694, and *San Francisco Xavier*, wrecked in 1705, came ashore and resulted in a powerful cultural connection with the local Nehalem-Tillamook peoples. That cultural connection is represented by the stories passed through generations of tribal members and their artifacts. While much of the modern lore focuses on the blue and white porcelains and beeswax, for the people of the time of the wreck, the survivors brought metal and the knowledge of metalworking, and the shipwreck brought benefit. The porcelain was repurposed; broken up, its hard ceramic nature was adapted through hand-flaking to become projectile points. The same is true for the porcelain washed ashore from another Manila galleon, *San Agustin*, which wrecked north of San Francisco in Drakes Bay, in November 1595.

I've visited both of these wrecks' sites many times. At Nehalem and on Drakes Bay, archaeological excavations have yielded Spanish artifacts and modified porcelains in burials and village sites, and winter storms expose porcelains on the sands of both beaches. Most recently, winter storms exposed the surf-worn hardwood timbers of a portion of the beeswax wreck's upper hull in sea caves north of Nehalem Bay. I was one of those on the team that rescued them before subsequent storms swept them out to sea again. I'd like to think that the story of that rescue, which was a nationally reported news event, was publicized because of its amazing history. That history, especially the cultural impact of this massive Spanish ship coming ashore three centuries ago, is newsworthy. But I suspect that the tale of the "Beeswax Wreck" had more currency for modern audiences because it is credited as an inspiration for Steven Spielberg's 1980s movie *The Goonies*.

The Beeswax Wreck is now known to be *Santo Cristo de Burgos*, thanks to archival research, and geomorphological studies show that the exposed wreck, on the beach of Nehalem Bay, was overwhelmed and further broken up by an earthquake-generated tsunami in 1700. With *San Agustin*, it is one of three of the oldest known shipwrecks on the Pacific Coast of North America, with another Manila galleon wrecked on the Mexican coastline of Baja California that dates to the 17th century. At least two, as noted, took place with indigenous observers who were "gifted" by the sea with items that represented a cultural contact, some of which could be repurposed. This pattern would continue in the next three centuries as ships belonging to Spanish, Russian, and American explorers and traders wrecked, stranded, or were seized by tribes along the coasts of present-day California, Oregon, Washington, British Columbia, and Alaska.

A favorite topic for many on this coast is the story of Japanese "drift junks." Beginning with the edict closing Japan to foreign trade and banning overseas travel in 1636, Japanese vessels were redesigned for coastal travel, not extended voyages. Storms and ships being caught in the Japan Current (known as the *Kuroshio*, or Black Current to the Japanese) swept an estimated 1,000 vessels out to sea, and there is a considerable 19th- and 20th-century body of literature on the subject. There is also a range of iron artifacts of Asian origin in coastal First Nations archaeological sites, and an oral tradition of pre–European contact Japanese vessels washing ashore, usually with dead crews, with increased reporting in the 19th century in Russian accounts, as well as by American maritime fur traders and whalers.

Are there wrecks waiting to be found? Yes. Fishing vessels have trawled up pottery of Asian origin, one of which, a dark-glazed Japanese *tsuba*, is in the collections of the Vancouver Maritime Museum. That came in when I was director of the museum, and I met with the fisherman who snagged the wreck in some 300 meters of water off Vancouver Island; he reported repeated hits on a "mound" of this pottery by his nets over the years. As I held it in my hands, I wondered what stories it could tell; the hands that had shaped it from raw clay, and fired it; what it had carried, the voyage that ended in despair and death, and the centuries it had lain in the dark on the seabed until caught by the fisherman's net. It's that active imagination that I still have, decades after the same questions fired my teenage enthusiasm for the past, that inspires me as an archaeologist to this day.

One of the best-known stories on the Northwest Coast is that of the survivors of the Japanese merchant ship *Hojun-Maru*. Damaged by a storm and unable to navigate, it was caught in the *Kuroshio* and drifted for months across the North Pacific. Only three of the crew survived.

Hojun-Maru washed up on the rocks of Cape Flattery, in what is now Washington State, in early 1834. The ship was salvaged, and the Japanese survivors were taken as slaves by the Makah people. The story of this shipwreck and the tale of the three Japanese mariners is not unique. The British Columbia coast was the setting for a number of gold rushes that followed the 1848 discovery of gold in California. The Haida, a powerful maritime people, literally took prisoners. There were a number of times they attempted and succeeded in capturing vessels, taking their cargo and ransoming the crews.

The ship *Susan Sturgis*, while sailing near the coastal village of Massett, stranded on a sand bar. The Masset people seized the vessel, stripped and burned it, and ransomed the crew. When I was in Haida Gwaii (formerly known as the Queen Charlotte Islands, on the northern coast of British Columbia and bordering Alaska) in the early 1990s searching for the wreck of the coastal schooner *Vancouver*, stranded and seized in 1834, I visited Massett and was told the story of *Susan Sturgis* by a Haida elder who related the story to me as he had heard it from his ancestors—who, he said, stood with him, unseen but telling him what happened in their own words. The location of the remains of *Susan Sturgis* is "known" but not officially located—in short, they were not going to share where it was to any one of us. As for the schooner *Vancouver*, I went to the wreck site and found nothing. The Haida had gathered up and used everything from that craft. The accounts from the Hudson's Bay Company's archives tell a tale of tense negotiations, the surrender of the schooner, but not the crew, who were taken away by another Hudson's Bay Company ship—which was armed.

Another site on the Northwest Coast has revealed no remains of the ships themselves, but the rocks at the coastal village of Clo-ose on Vancouver Island tell a story of many passing ships and wrecks through petroglyphs depicting those events. The site is curated and controlled by the Ditidaht Band, who allowed the Royal British Columbia Museum to document them. Some of the petroglyphs appear to depict the loss in 1869 of the ship *John Bright*. The tribe was falsely accused of murdering wreck survivors, with terrible retribution. A Royal Navy ship burned the village, shelling and destroying canoes, and colonial officials hanged members of the tribe after a trial. The vessels depicted on the rocks include what are believed to be European ships, maritime fur traders; one image depicts *Beaver*, the first steamship on the coast, likely dating to the only time it would have passed the village in 1836. Other petroglyphs are thought to represent not only the ill-fated *John Bright* but also HMS *Sparrowhawk*, the warship that devastated the village in retaliation for the supposed massacre.

The area around Clo-ose was one of the key encounter sites of the 18th century on the Northwest Coast as Spanish and British explorers landed and traded, followed by maritime fur traders in the 19th century. Neighboring Nootka Cove, within the territory of the Nuu-chah-Nulth tribe (of whom the Didtidaht are one of three bands) was the setting for violent encounters that included seizing ships and killing their crews in the late 18th and early 19th centuries. The most famous encounter was Mowachaht tribal chief Maquinna's violent seizure of the ship *Boston*, and its destruction after it was stripped. An American fur-trading ship, *Boston* was attacked while at anchor in Nootka Sound in March 1803; only two of the crew were spared, and 24 others were killed. The ship's blacksmith and the sail-maker were enslaved as they had valuable skills. The blacksmith was also the "armorer," the only man on board with the skill to repair guns. The exchange of fur for weapons by some traders led some canny chiefs previously exploited in earlier negotiations to demand a higher price, namely muskets. Taking a ship also provided access to a non-trade item, cannon. The account of survivor John Jewitt, who escaped his captivity and enslavement after two years, was an early 19th-century "bestseller."

In another famous incident, the American fur trader *Tonquin*, owned by John Jacob Astor, was boarded while at anchor in Clayaquot Sound off Vancouver Island in June 1811 by members of the Tla-o-qui-aht tribe, who killed all but four of the crew. One of the survivors detonated the ship's powder magazine, destroying it and killing most of the tribal members who were on board. Some accounts suggest over a hundred dead. Only one survivor of the crew made it back to Astor's Fort Astoria, at the mouth of the Columbia River, to tell the tale. Stories like these, remembered for decades on the Northwest Coast, likely played into the brutal response to the *John Bright* wreck by British Columbia officials. Neither the wreck of *Boston* nor that of *Tonquin* has been located by wreck divers or archaeologists; if anyone has, neither they nor the tribes have talked about it. Some of these wrecks represent painful stories for tribes—of unequal encounters, violence by traders, and brutal reprisals by colonial authorities. They also speak to brutality by tribes against traders. Not all encounters were violent, however. The following are three examples of shipwrecks that were salvaged by local indigenous tribes on the Pacific Coast; I was able to participate in their study as a maritime archaeologist. In each of these cases, the discoveries were made on land during excavations of tribal sites, and the discovery of salvaged maritime objects brought me into the team to help identify them.

The first came as a result of a land dig on the Mendocino coast of California, 120 miles north of San Francisco. While excavating a site in the hills near the coastal community of Caspar, archaeologist Tom Layton and his students from San Jose State University found 50 sherds of broken Chinese blue-and-white stoneware and 148 fragments of green bottle glass, mixed in the material evidence of life in a mid-19th-century Mitom Pomo village. The Pomo had broken the pottery and tried to make shells, much as they did from raw clam shells; the glass had been broken to make projectile points. This find led Layton to learn about the wreck of a "Chinese" ship on the coast discovered by sport divers decades earlier. What emerged from research and from the collections of many of the divers was that the wreck was a former opium trade clipper, the brig *Frolic*, which wrecked in July 1850.

Frolic ran into the coast, thanks to faulty charts while sailing from Hong Kong with a speculative cargo of manufactured goods, mainly from China, bound for the booming Gold Rush market of San Francisco. The captain and crew survived, and some made an open-boat journey down the coast to San Francisco, while others walked through the coastal forest. News of the wreck and a "valuable cargo of Chinese goods" led to an overland expedition to salvage what could be saved. The local Mitom

Pomo were the first to salvage, however, and American salvagers arrived to find Mitom women wearing silk shawls, while others found lacquered wares, camphor wood trunks, and "huge China jars." Local settlers traded with the tribe for some of the silks, but as Layton's excavations showed, tribal members made use of those items that could be converted to indigenous use.

Layton's find of cargo led Tom to conduct research into *Frolic* after the excavation of the village site was finished. I was one of the two maritime archaeologists brought in by him to dive the wreck; the other was California State maritime archaeologist John Foster. Layton reached out to the wreck divers who had dived and collected from the wreck since the 1960s, and the donation of their collections led to a detailed study as part of an award-winning project of many decades. With friend and colleague Richard Everett of San Francisco Maritime National Historic Site, I was able to work with Layton on the collections and to identify maritime equipment, fasteners, and ship parts. Layton's project included working with current-day tribal members; this expanded into a series of books and saw the wreck nominated to and listed in the National Register of Historic Places. It also inspired a modern re-creation of the alcoholic beverage that was in the green glass bottles, "*Frolic* Ale," and a performance of the tale of *Frolic*, created by Sandy Metzler, in which one of the shards of porcelain was passed to various actors representing people who had handled that porcelain through time. The indigenous salvage of *Frolic* in 1850 ultimately sparked one of the most amazing tales I know of where a seemingly innocuous shipwreck became a powerful muse a century and a half later. And the *Frolic* Ale had to have tasted great on a hot day after diving on the wreck in subsequent surveys of that site.

The second wreck with an indigenous context was the 1852 loss of the U.S. Army–chartered schooner *Captain Lincoln*, bound from San Francisco to Port Orford, Oregon. With the schooner leaking and in danger of foundering after a storm, the captain of *Captain Lincoln* ran it ashore in Coos Bay, Oregon. Using the schooner's spars and sails to build shelters, and trading supplies and copper from the ship's hull to the local tribes for food, the soldiers and ship's crew survived at "Camp Castaway" for four months until rescued. After seeing the wreck site depicted on a U.S. Coast Survey manuscript chart, archaeologist Scott Byram located the site through historical manuscript chart analysis. Archaeologists Steve Samuels and Mark Tveskov assembled a team from Southern Oregon University Laboratory of Anthropology, the Confederated Tribes of Coos, Lower Umpqua and Siuslaw Indians, and the Coquille Indian Tribe to excavate it. I analyzed maritime artifacts for the team, along with my colleague Robert Schwemmer. It may not have been a "big name" wreck, but *Captain Lincoln*'s loss was yet another example of how the bounty of the sea came into indigenous hands, in a positive exchange and cultural connection.

The third wreck was that of the former packet ship *Oxford*, inbound with a cargo of whiskey, ice, and merchandise for Gold Rush San Francisco, stranded in the mudflats of Tomales Bay, about 50 miles north of the Golden Gate, when the captain mistook his bearings at nearly the same time as *Captain Lincoln* went ashore farther north in January 1852. The cargo was salvaged, but *Oxford* was left to the tide. The vessel remained visible, stranded in the mud, for decades and was noted in U.S. Coast Survey charts through the 1870s. With archaeologist Jim Allan, I relocated the wreck while with the National Oceanic and Atmospheric Administration (NOAA), probing the site to find the mollusk-eaten, crunchy bits of *Oxford* under a mud-covered sand bar that marks the wreck. It is within Greater Farallones National Marine Sanctuary. What inspired our hunt for the wreck was work by archaeologist Tsim Schneider. Schneider and colleagues excavated the site of a trading post inhabited by American seaman George Thomas "Tom" Wood, who deserted his ship and married a Coast Miwok woman and settled at the point now known as "Tom's Point" at the mouth of Tomales Bay. Wood, his wife, and other local Coast Miwok lived there, and the Miwok worked on the local ranches at Point Reyes. Schneider's excavation yielded a rich archaeological record of mixed indigenous and manufactured North American and European goods, as well as fasteners from the ship, which Wood and the Coast Miwok had salvaged from *Oxford* to build homes and other structures. I analyzed the fittings and fasteners for them. A key take-away from their research is that the archaeology at Tom's Point counters previous assertions that Spanish-Mexican and Russian settlement, the subsequent American conquest, and increased settlement with the Gold Rush resulted in cultural extinction. Cultural extinction did not happen, and indigenous groups survived colonization; the wreck, the Tom's Point site, and the fragments of *Oxford* all help make that point.[5]

Another region where indigenous peoples interacted and clashed with mariners, with shipwrecks playing a central role in the drama, is the larger Pacific, especially what sailors knew as the "South Seas." The commodities of the Pacific island were of particular interest as trade with China opened to English and American ships in the 18th and 19th centuries; that same trade and the value of sea otter pelts in the Chinese market is also what sent ships to the Northwest Coast of America. While the best trade relationships are mutually beneficial, cultural misconceptions on both sides, disagreements over reciprocity, and sex all played a role in the occasionally violent encounters. For perspective, the introduction to an early 20th-century edition of a South Seas trading adventure noted that a musket would bring a dozen large hogs to feed a crew, and a pair of scissors or a jackknife would bring a bunch of plantains or 40 coconuts.

When ships in the Pacific trade wrecked, that was often an occasion for seizure of wreckage, cargo, and supplies, as well as survivors, as was the practice on the Northwest Coast. There were also bad actors on either side—captains who cheated and demeaned indigenous leaders, and indigenous leaders who opted to seize a ship and its goods. One example is the ship *Glide* of Salem, which wrecked at Fiji in 1831. William Endicott, the Third Officer, survived and wrote an account, *Wrecked Among Cannibals in the Fijis*, on his return. When their vessel wrecked, and went over onto its side, they surrendered the wreck to a local chief and went ashore to avoid being on board when others arrived to join in the plunder who "would not scruple to take our lives."[6] When they landed, however, they were seized, stripped, and left to wait for two days while the chief and his people stripped their ship. They were later allowed to remove some of their provisions from the wreck and were treated well until another American vessel arrived and took them aboard.

A less fortunate group were the crew of the ship *Charles Eaton*, a passenger which wrecked off Cape York in Torres Strait in August 1834. After striking a reef, the ship was abandoned, and the crew and passengers took to the boats and two rafts in separate groups. One group on a raft encountered Torres Strait Islanders, who took them ashore and killed all but two of the crew after learning they had no weapons or anything to trade. Loaded into a canoe, the two crew members were taken to another island. There, they saw personal items and clothing, and then heads of the passengers and crew who had left on the other raft and in the boats, but also two young children who had been spared while their parents had been murdered. The bodies of the massacred crew and passengers had been eaten. Rather than being killed, however, the two crew members who survived were enslaved before being sold to another indigenous community. They remained in the islands for two years, learning the language and adapting to their captivity. Their new "captors" adopted the narrator of the account, sailor John Ireland, as well as the young boy, William D'Oyley, and treated both of them well. On the other island, however, the other crew member, John Sexton, was speared to death, and the other boy, George D'Oyley, died of illness. In June 1836, the then 17-year-old Ireland and 4-year-old William D'Oyley were rescued by the Australian government schooner *Isabella*, which had been dispatched to see if any survivors of the wreck of *Charles Eaton* were still alive.

The story of the two boys captured the attention of the Australian public, and then the world. Ireland's account was published as a children's book in 1845, and their rescue was depicted in two oil paintings, dated 1839 and 1841, one of which is in the collections of the National Gallery of Australia. Recent scholarship has made a powerful point that the paintings look at the event from a European worldview, with a triumph of colonial power in the "rescue" of the two boys, rather than the complex tale of indigenous response to disparities, cultural misunderstanding, and ultimately, a compassionate adoption of both Ireland and

D'Oyley by a Torres Islander who acted as a father, not a captor, and wept when the boys were "rescued."[7] Those 19th-century narratives also looked only at the events as "savagery," but modern scholars question whether *Charles Eaton* might have grounded in a sacred area, thus breaking a taboo, and for this, those on board were punished.

The reality of indigenous encounters with ships and shipwrecks was complex—at times cooperative, at other times contentious. Whether attacks on ships and crews occurred as revenge against an assault or insult from a previous captain, crew, or ship, or were opportunities to raid an unarmed or poorly armed vessel, or were considered compensation for bad-faith trading or breaking a taboo, they happened with relative frequency. Preexisting, pre-European trade networks and practices were often at odds with the Europeans and the cultural interactions that followed the European "discovery" of the various island groups.[8] The indigenous response varied from peaceful to violent encounters, and the literature associated with these encounters in the early 19th century became a significant subset of maritime literature, either as a specific type of shipwreck narrative or yet another book on the plight of "castaways." Not all of those who were castaways were enslaved or murdered, nor were they deserters who joined indigenous communities. And yet the colonial response was occasional naval expeditions sent to "punish" indigenous communities, and not always fairly as entire villages were shelled or burned and canoes were destroyed. These encounters—attacks, raids, shipwrecks, and retaliation—persisted into the late 19th century. Much like the myth of sinister coastal communities populated by "barbarous" denizens who lured ships ashore, murdered survivors, and robbed the dead, while incidents did occur, the narrative of shipwreck is often mythologized. The realities are often more profound and inconvenient reflections on how communities and individuals respond to disparity, and the bounty of the sea offers a boon.

What then, of the stories and the remains of wrecks that speak to the experience of ships that are lost in these circumstances? I'd like to close on the subject of a famous ship and its wreck, *Bounty*. The name is appropriate to the chapter, but its legacy was no bounty for any who encountered the ship. The wreck lies in shallow water, where it was burned at the end of its infamous voyage. The April 1789 mutiny against the authority of Lieutenant William Bligh on the armed transport *Bounty* was a cause célèbre of its time in Britain, as Bligh made a near-miraculous voyage in an open boat in one of the most epic tales of survival at sea. That was followed by publicity that came with the capture, trial, and execution of some of the mutineers, but also because some of the mutineers, including its instigator, Acting-Lieutenant Fletcher Christian, had vanished into the open Pacific. Early 19th-century mariners ultimately reached the island to which they had fled and scuttled *Bounty*, and found one surviving mutineer on an island of Polynesian women and children. That led to another flurry of interest.

However, 20th-century fame came with bestselling novels and feature films, including one that debuted Errol Flynn (as Christian), another with Clark Gable and Charles Laughton, the Marlon Brando and Trevor Howard film, and the most recent cinematic offering with Anthony Hopkins and Mel Gibson. The media and cinema made *Bounty* famous in our time, or as National Geographic once termed it, a "ship of legend." When the wreck was identified in 1957, *National Geographic Magazine* published photographer and writer Luis Marden's account, "I Found the Bones of the Bounty," with a map and 53 photos. Does *Bounty* deserve status as a celebrity wreck? I argue that celebrity often masks true stories, or aspects of tales that are ignored. The story of *Bounty* is more than a mutiny. It is a wreck that also reflects the disparities and the realities of encounters between colonial ships and indigenous communities.

The reality of the wreck, Hollywood's portrayal of the ill-tempered Bligh as a monster notwithstanding, is that it is an artifact that speaks less to the mutiny and more to the aftermath. The mutiny was the result of sexual tensions occasioned by British sailors' lack of understanding of Polynesian customs; this was not a tale of fabled romance. *Bounty* lies as a wreck off Pitcairn Island because Fletcher Christian encountered sexual freedom in Tahiti after a protracted voyage of sexual repression. The mutiny, the voyage to Pitcairn, and the destruction of the ship to avoid

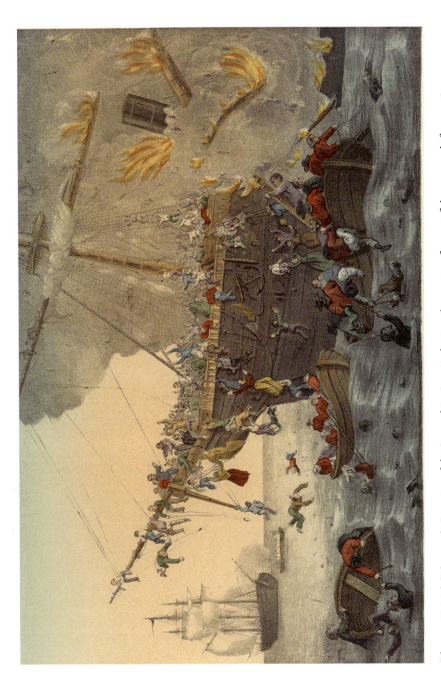

Plate 1. British lithograph *Burning of the Steamship Austria* depicts the rescue of some of the steamer's few survivors. Royal Museums, Greenwich, PAH0297/Wikimedia Commons.

Plate 2. Title sheet for the "Marine Redowa, Dedicated to the brave, energetic and whole souled Capt. Hiram Burt, of the Brig. *Marine,* who rescued from a watery grave a large number of the passengers of the ill-fated *Central America*."

Published by Oliver Ditson & Company, ca. 1857. Library of Congress, LC-USZ62-64401.

Plate 3. *The Raft of the Medusa*, by Jean Louis Théodore Géricault. Collection of the Louvre, Paris. Wikimedia Commons.

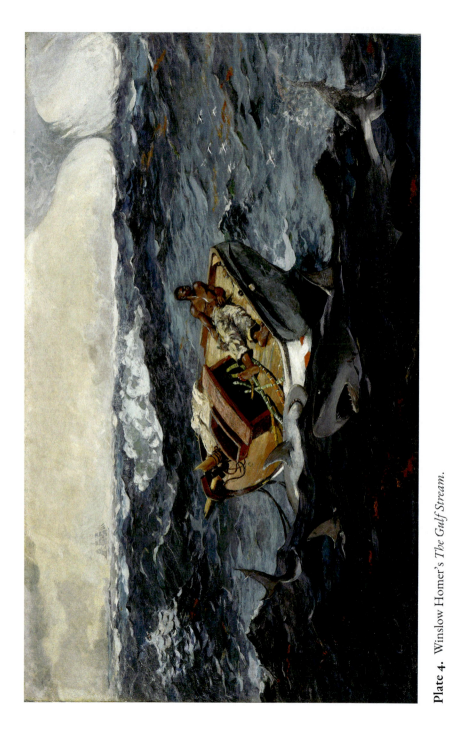

Plate 4. Winslow Homer's *The Gulf Stream*. Collection of the Metropolitan Museum of Art, New York. Wikimedia Commons.

Plate 5. The BlueView© scan of the wrecked steamer USS *Hatteras*, in the Gulf of Mexico, 2012, juxtaposed with a drawing of the sinking warship by Francis H. Schell, 1863.

The Becker Collection, Boston College; Sonar Image by James Glaser, Northwest Hydro, courtesy of the National Oceanic and Atmospheric Administration.

Plate 6. Ceremonies and a wreath laying at the USS *Maine* Memorial at Arlington National Cemetery on February 15, 2023, commemorated the 125th anniversary of the warship's loss with 260 of its crew, 65 of whom are interred at Arlington. U.S. Army photograph by Elizabeth Fraser/Arlington National Cemetery.

Plate 7. This coat and sea boots are thought to be the surviving traces of a victim of the sinking of *Titanic* on the seabed at 12,426 feet.

National Oceanic and Atmospheric Administration/University of Rhode Island.

Plate 8. An octopus inhabits the anchor hawse pipe of the wreck of the U.S. Navy tug *Conestoga* in Gulf of the Farallones National Marine Sanctuary.

National Oceanic and Atmospheric Administration.

Plate 9. The Swedish warship *Vasa* on display in Stockholm. Jorge Láscar, Wikimedia Commons.

Plate 10. U.S. Navy divers from Company 2-6 of Mobile Diving and Salvage Unit (MDSU) 2 being lowered into the water using a staging platform.

U.S. Navy photograph by Chief Mass Communications Specialist David Collins.

Plate 11. The bow of Wreck 15537, a possible immigrant packet ship of the 1830s–1850s, lying in 1,000 meters of water in the Gulf of Mexico.

National Oceanic and Atmospheric Administration, Office of Ocean Exploration and Research.

Plate 12. *Sub Marine Explorer* exposed on the beach of Isla San Telmo at low tide. Photograph by James P. Delgado.

Plate 13. Archaeologists excavating the Alonissos Shipwreck, a fifth-century BC amphora-carrying merchant ship, in the fall of 2000.

Elpida Hadjidaki, Wikimedia Commons, https://creativecommons.org/licenses/by-sa/4.0/deed.en.

Plate 14. A gold octagonal footed cup from China salvaged from the Belitung shipwreck. Photograph by Jack Lee, Wikimedia Commons.

Plate 15. Octant on the Blake Ridge Wreck.
National Oceanic and Atmospheric Administration, Office of Ocean Exploration and Research.

Plate 16. A young visitor to the African American Museum of History and Culture engaged with a touchscreen guide to the wreck of the slave ship *São José*.
Photograph by James P. Delgado.

detection was the result of the liaisons made in Tahiti. The voyage to Pitcairn with Tahitian women and men was undertaken without telling them they were leaving their homes and families. Instead, they sailed with a group of alcoholic, violent mutineers into hiding to Pitcairn, and were trapped there when the ship was burned to avoid being spotted by Royal Navy ships hunting for them.

The island community was ultimately doomed by racial tensions and the behavior of the British sailors, leading to a massacre that left only two of the Britons alive, along with the women and children. The site of the wreck was known by the islanders, but not disturbed until 1957, when it was "discovered" by Marden.[9] Artifacts including an anchor were subsequently raised; when you land at Pitcairn, the wreck is not far away, and inaccessible by land and usually by boat. On my one visit, as I stood looking at the anchor, I realized that the wreck, despite its celebrity, is not as important as a historical or archaeological site as it is a reminder of maritime encounters between the indigenous and foreign visitors with at best unpleasant consequences, and in the case of *Bounty*, with tragedy.

6

Shipwreck Salvage

> It is difficult enough for the average man to find his way about a strange liner when she is afloat, so it can be imagined how difficult it must be for a diver to wander about such a vessel when she is 90 feet under water. All the time he is adventuring through the saloons and other compartments, he is running continual danger of his air-pipe catching on something and tying him up. He may lose himself. Doors may slam to with the current and imprison him while cutting off his air supply. The man manning the air-pumps will quickly find out that something is wrong, but by the time assistance is sent the imprisoned diver may easily be in a sorry state.
> —David Masters, *The Wonders of Salvage*, 1924

Ships are part of economic systems when they are afloat. Even in antiquity, many were owned by merchants in the business of maritime trade, or the owner was the captain. Starting in antiquity, the risk of going to sea was shared by those who loaned or participated in the venture of a voyage. A ship, its cargo, and its voyage were commercial ventures. Marine insurance facilitated the spread of trade by sea, compensating an owner and investors for losses. Both the ship and its cargo were commodities with monetary value. That monetary value was not lost to investors and owners even if a ship was wrecked and the cargo went down with it, because it was insured. Geographer and historian Peter Hugill argues that shipping "has been central to the emergence of the capitalist world system."[1] In time, as larger economies emerged, particularly the emerging global economy of the past 500 years, ships were owned by businesses, companies, and corporations. To mitigate losses, the business of marine insurance began, famously in London around 1686, expanded with rising global trade, and then was dominated by Britain in the 18th and 19th centuries. Both ships and their cargoes were insured, with different underwriters, or a group of underwriters assuming the risk, depending on the potential impact of a loss of either or both ship and cargo. This economic value of shipwrecks goes back centuries. To recover at least some of that value, salvage by another vessel or a professional salvage crew aimed to rescue cargo or a ship that lay awash, in danger of sinking. Salvage also included work to grapple and raise cargoes, and all or portions of a sunken ship. Cargoes, especially highly valuable or perishable, were high priority, followed by salvaging ships that had stranded and lay partially exposed in shallows, on the rocks, or on a beach where quick rescue would return them to service. Salvage also included raising cargoes and wrecks from deeper water, a practice that began as early as the 17th century and which continues to this day. Starting with the 19th century and continuing into the 21st century, marine salvage has evolved into a substantial business. A body of salvage law has also evolved with the basic premise of assuming financial and physical risk to recover a ship or property from peril.[2]

In the 21st century, marine salvage includes large international corporations that work globally, as well as regionally based companies and small firms that work locally. A recent (2018) speech by Charo Coll, president of the International Salvage Union (ISU), the global trade association, which handles about 90 percent of global marine salvage work, listed 57 full members from 32 countries. Some are part of larger marine or industrial corporations and privately owned companies. According to Coll, ISU gross revenues ranged from a high of US$717 million in 2015 to US$456 million in 2017.[3] Not all are big companies. The waterfronts of the world have always been the home of small companies and sole-proprietor salvors. Rugged and independent, they epitomize the "jack of all trades" when it comes to marine rescue, recovery, and salvage. Intelligent, learning their craft by working up the ranks, either in military

Image 6.1. A diver descends from a salvage ship during wartime training in the United States.
United States War Department Photo, National Archives NAID 45499814.

or commercial service, and entrepreneurial, they use a practical approach to get the job done. The same holds true for the larger companies.

Is there enough work? William Langewiesche, in a 2014 *Vanity Fair* profile of master mariner Nick Sloane, noted that with a global population of around 100,000 ships on the water in any given year, within a decade, a quarter of them will become an insurance casualty and 1,600 will be lost at a rate of one every two and a half days. That's where highly skilled people like Nick Sloane come in, a "marine salvage master with a taste for chaos and a genius for improvisation."[4] Sloane headed the salvage of the cruise ship *Costa Concordia*, perhaps the greatest marine salvage operation of the past quarter century.

The 951-foot (290-meter) long cruise ship *Costa Concordia*, with 4,252 passengers and crew on board, famously capsized when its captain came too close to shore at the Tuscan island port of Giglio, Italy, on January 13, 2012. The cruise ship struck an undersea rock that tore a 174-foot long (53-meter) gash in the port side of the ship. As the water poured in, flooding the engine room and killing the ship's power, *Costa Concordia* began to roll, and panicked passengers scrambled to get to lifeboats. The wreck killed 32 passengers and injured many. The aftermath of the disaster saw the captain and several of the officers and crew prosecuted, convicted, and sentenced to prison for negligence, manslaughter, and in the case of the captain, for abandoning his ship while as many as 300 of the passengers and crew remained on board the stricken vessel. A haphazard evacuation, punctuated by power failure, poor communication, and a continually tilting deck that made launching lifeboats difficult, and then

Image 6.2. The wreck of *Costa Concordia* during salvage efforts to right the ship with the heavy lift vessel SAL *Lone*.
Isjc99/Wikimedia Commons.

impossible, contributed to confusion, injury, and death. The ship was finally evacuated in the early morning hours of January 14.

The accident made global headlines. *Costa Concordia* could not be refloated, and so a massive nearly two-year-long salvage operation followed. The first task was removing some 2,000 tons of fuel still in the ship's bunkers a month after the sinking. What then followed, after a competitive bidding process and the award of a contract to re-right, refloat, and tow the liner away to be scrapped, was a massive salvage effort led by Sloane for Titan and Micoperi, an Italian subsea engineering company that partnered with the U.S.-based Titan to win the job. The task of raising *Costa Concordia* began in mid-2012 and lasted for nearly two years. Sloan managed over 500 people on a team whose job was to raise the ship, first by rolling it upright. Once righted onto an artificial seabed made of sandbags and cement in September 2013, the wreck was refloated and towed to Genoa in July 2014, where over the course of the next three years, scrappers broke down and recycled nearly all of *Costa Concordia* by July 2017. It was one of the great, epic salvages of a shipwreck in modern times. The billion-dollar job was also the most expensive ship salvage in history.

Another modern ship salvage job was undertaken by Resolve Marine, a Florida-based global company, to remove hundreds of thousands of gallons of oil from the sunken tanker *Coimbra* off Long Island. The five-year-old *Coimbra* was a victim of Nazi Germany's U-boat campaign against the United States during the Battle of the Atlantic, an epic struggle at sea that spanned the entirety of World War II and saw the loss of thousands of merchant ships, hundreds of warships, and hundreds of U-boats. Following the Japanese attack on Pearl Harbor and U.S. declaration of war against Japan, Germany declared war on the United States in support of Japan. German U-boats quickly unleashed a campaign against shipping directly off American shores, known as *Paukenschlag* (Operation Drumbeat), in January 1942. The first U-boats arrived on January 13. The following day, January 14, *Coimbra*, loaded with lubricating oil, steamed from New York. The following evening, while off Long Island, the submarine U-123 spotted the lights of *Coimbra* and fired a single torpedo that struck the starboard side, just aft of the superstructure. As the tanker began to sink by the stern, and the fuel oil leaking from it caught fire, a second torpedo sent

Coimbra to the bottom, broken into three pieces, in 180 feet of water. The attack killed the master, 29 of the crew, and 6 naval personnel put aboard the tanker to man anti-submarine guns. Only 6 men survived.

Coimbra is a National Register–listed historic wreck, an occasional dive and fishing site, but also a wreck that for decades continued to leak oil. Identified in a 2013 study as a high risk for a substantial, catastrophic release if the hull collapsed, *Coimbra* was assessed by Resolve Marine at the request of the Coast Guard in May 2019 after more oil began to leak from the hull. That assessment found that there was an imminent risk, and so the Coast Guard tasked Resolve with removing all of the oil while protecting the remaining structural integrity of the wreck, as well as its value to fishermen and wreck divers as a historic shipwreck. The task was completed in July 2019. When torpedoed, *Coimbra* had been carrying an estimated 2.7 million gallons of oil, but the amount left in the wreck was unknown. It turned out to be close to 450,000 gallons. If the oil had leaked, it would have potentially impacted beaches and marine life from Cape Cod to Cape Hatteras.

Interestingly, a Hamptons newspaper article suggested that the vintage oil inside the wreck, an amount estimated in the story at 9,000 tons, could be sold to those "who only use antique oil in their antique machines," and sold at $1,500 for a two-ounce vial of the oil.[5] It turned out there was no monetary value in *Coimbra*'s oil, as it had undergone chemical changes and was no longer viable after nearly eight decades beneath the sea. Monetary value in shipwrecks rarely comes after a prolonged period underwater; the business of recovering monetary value usually happens only if it is done expeditiously. However, salvage of World War II losses did recover monetary value when it was done within a few decades of the war. One of the more profound stories of the business of marine salvage comes from the saga of the firm known by the name of its founder, Risdon Beazley.

Risdon Beazley

Risdon Archibald Beazley (1904–1979) formed Risdon Beazley Marine Ltd. in 1926 in Southampton, England. Beazley's salvage work grew dramatically during World War II. That included the award of a contract by the British Admiralty to provide and load most of the merchant ships sent to support D-Day landings. It also included a wartime contract to salvage sunken ships and clear ports of marine debris and wrecks. Postwar, the firm continued to actively recover cargoes lost during wartime but unreachable until hostilities ended. There were thousands of wrecks potentially worthy of salvage. What Beazley focused on were those that lay beyond standard diving depths. They lay on the continental shelf, where only an industrial-scale effort could reach them.[6] There were enough wrecks on the continental margin that lay off the coasts of Europe, Canada, and the United States to make the company profitable. Cutting a deal with the War Risk Insurance Office, which covered losses on behalf of the British government during the war when private insurers could or would not, Risdon Beazley was able to get government contracts for salvage of all of Britain's wartime shipping losses. The company located and then recovered what they could. They reportedly salvaged lost wartime cargoes from as many as 85 wrecks. These were selected because they were known to be laden with important cargoes of lead, copper, tin, and other metals that had been lost when the ship carrying them had sunk after U-boat attack. The firm's business model was based on non-ferrous metals; gold bullion cargoes were rare, but 3,000–4,000 tons of copper would be more valuable. Tin was also valuable, and as an inert metal, it did not corrode or change even after decades of submersion in the sea. It retained its value. All that was needed was rinsing it off after recovery and inventorying it. In all, between 1947 and 1980, the firm reportedly recovered over 51,000 tons of "non-ferrous cargoes" from wartime wrecks.[7]

Risdon Beazley's fleet shifted from prewar and wartime salvage ships and armored one-man diving suits to custom-built ships in the 1950s. The salvage ships *Twyford* and *Droxford*, the world's only purpose-built salvage and recovery ships at the time, and diving bell/observation chambers lowered from the ships, were the new state-of-the-art approach to deep-water recoveries. A salvage master in the bell, connected to the surface by a telephone line, guided the work as underwater explosive charges opened up a ship, peeling back the sides and collapsing decks. Drop claws would shift dislodged hull sections, and then grab stacks of tin, copper, or aluminum ingots in water up to a thousand feet deep. Most of the work was done quietly. Beazley was a secretive man. Those who knew him, especially in government salvage circles, highly respected the man, his company, and his team.

I was part of the dive study of the wreck of the German submarine U-215, which was attacked and sunk by the antisubmarine patrol boat HMS *Le Tigre* off Georges Bank in the North Atlantic on July 3, 1942. We also explored the wreck of the nearby Liberty Ship *Alexander Macomb*, which had been sunk by the U-215. Ten of the crew died in the sinking, with 56 survivors. The dives on the wreck provided clear evidence of the professionalism and thoroughness of the Risdon Beazley team. They relocated the wreck in October 1964 and quickly recovered its non-ferrous metal cargo. The wreck of *Alexander Macomb*, as we documented it in 2004, had been methodically cleared on a site that was a very difficult place to work and dive, with powerful currents. There was practically nothing left but scattered tanks and ammunition too small and too dangerous to recover.

Another wreck in Canadian waters we also studied offers mute testimony to the work done by Risdon Beazley's crews. The Dutch ship *Kaaparen*, while departing Halifax to join a convoy, collided with another ship and sank just outside Halifax harbor on June 14, 1942. Like other Risdon Beazley targets, it lay beyond the reach of then conventional salvage. What survived on the seabed in 2004 was a wreck that had systematically been cut down by shaped explosive charges that peeled back hull plating and opened up the ship to expose the cargo holds. It was done with surgical precision. All of this work, supervised by the salvage master in the observation chamber, was then followed by a steady, methodical recovery of the ingots. Simple, effective, and thorough, this type of marine salvage set the standard for decades and returned a great deal of metal to the stream of commerce.

Recovering Lost Bullion and Specie

Shipwrecks with monetary value also include those that were transporting specie or bullion. The companies who are hired by governments and insurers to recover these are not "treasure hunters." They are marine professionals who work under the rules of law to return the bullion and specie to the owners or insurers. Over the decades, misuse of the term "salvager" and confusing professional marine firms with treasure hunters have muddied the waters of public perception. Archaeologists have issues with the commodification of artifacts from wrecks (which will be discussed in subsequent chapters), but in legal and government circles, the recovery of gold or silver that still belongs to someone is a valued and accepted aspect of maritime practice and tradition.

Two examples speak to the lasting monetary value found in World War II shipwrecks that carried bullion and specie. The first is the gold of the heavy cruiser HMS *Edinburgh*, torpedoed on May 2, 1942, out of Murmansk, Russia, in the Barents Sea. The cruiser carried a secret cargo of five and a half tons of gold bullion, in the form of 465 bars packed in 93 wooden crates. The Soviets were shipping it on the British warship to pay for war materiel delivered by convoys to help the beleaguered Soviet Union fight back German invaders. The gold had been insured, and the War Risk Insurance Office paid off Lloyds for the one-third they had covered; the other two-thirds belonged to a subsidiary of the Soviet government's state insurance company. When the time came to mount a salvage expedition, the salvors negotiated a deal with the governments of the United Kingdom and the Soviet Union, each of whom held a stake in the gold, and with the United Kingdom because *Edinburgh* was still a government-owned ship, as well as a grave, and nothing could be done without the permission of the British government even if they had no stake in the secret cargo of gold.

The salvage that followed in 1981 was a challenging venture. *Edinburgh* lies in 800 feet (244 meters) in the cold depths of the Barents Sea. At the time of the salvage, it was deeper than commercial divers had ever ventured. The salvors were a consortium made up of Jessop Marine Recoveries, Ltd., led by veteran UK salvor Keith Jessop; Wharton & Williams, also known as 2W, a commercial dive firm, led by Ric Wharton; German-owned Offshore Services Association (OSA), which provided the ship, *Stephaniturm*; and marine surveyors Racal-Decca, who answered to the British Ministry of Defence (MOD) and operated under a standard "no cure, no pay" salvage contract. If successful, they received 45 percent of the gold. If they failed, they got nothing.

The divers worked in the dark, freezing cold, cutting into and going inside a corroding, broken ship that could collapse and seal them in a steel tomb. Wearing dive suits that pumped in hot water to fend off hypothermia, they deployed from diving bells that remained under pressure even when raised back to the deck. Known as saturation diving, this approach eliminated the need for regular decompression. Essentially, once a diver exceeds the no-decompression limit and remains at that pressure, they only need to decompress once, at the end of the dive, be that hours, a day, or even weeks.

The systems aboard *Stephaniturm* were complex. The diving bell was suspended from an open "moon pool" in the hull, with computer-assisted dynamic positioning to keep the ship hovering directly over the wreck, and divers deploying from the bell with umbilical lines linking them to the bell and carrying the hot water, the mixture of gases they breathed (regular air would be fatal), and hard-wired communications. It was, as Ric Wharton would later write, "the diving equivalent of the first moonwalk."[8] Twelve divers worked from the bells, from early September through early October 1981. Cutting through four-inch-thick armor, they worked their way through debris, silt that blocked visibility, and removed live ammunition blocking access to the storage compartment where the 93 crates of gold were buried under a tumble of silt and wreckage.

The dives ended on October 7, 1981, with 431 of 465 bars recovered; dive operations ceased and *Stephaniturm*'s crew began preparations to return to port as weather worsened. The Soviets received 158 bars in Murmansk, and the British government took 111 and the salvors received 161, for which they had to pay income tax.[9] In 1986, Jessop and 2W returned to the wreck to recover the remaining 34 bars inside the wreck and found 29. It was an epic feat in the history of marine salvage. The wreck's status as a war grave had been a consideration, as 57 of *Edinburgh*'s crew were lost with the ship. What the UK government faced, specifically the Ministry of Defence, was "whether to leave the war grave unprotected to the depredations of would-be salvors, or to forestall them by permitting recovery of the gold under controlled conditions."[10] The answer was controlled salvage that went beyond the earlier "blast and grab" limitations of deep-water salvage.

Despite lurid accounts of divers encountering and disturbing the remains of some of the crew, Wharton notes that at no time did the salvage divers find human remains, and a Ministry of Defence investigation found there was "absolutely no evidence to suggest any inappropriate incidents occurred." They recovered artifacts from the wreck that included the ship's bell, which was turned over to the Royal Navy 45 years after it had been lost in the sinking in 1986.[11] With the gold recovered, the wreck's significance as a war grave and a historic site are now the paramount values associated with HMS *Edinburgh*. A recent analysis of the project by historian Michele Blagg notes "perhaps the greatest lesson that came from the salvage" was that "advances in diving technology had put a great many wrecks within the reach of the modern diver." The two salvage dives, notably the final one, she notes, ensured that "this war grave may forevermore rest in peace."[12]

The other notable salvage of the 20th century was that of the cargo-carrying steamship *John Barry*. A Type EC2-S-C1 Liberty Ship, *John Barry* was built to standardized plans. Launched from the Kaiser Shipyard in Portland, Oregon, in November 1941, *John Barry* was completed three months later, in February 1942. *John Barry* was one of more than 2,000 standardized Liberty ships that rolled down the ways at a pace of nearly one every three days from American shipyards in World War II. It was remembered only by survivors and the families of the two men lost in its sinking. What made it famous was the recovery of a secret cargo of silver that went down with it, and the extraordinary deep water salvage of much of that treasure.

The U.S. government minted 3 million silver Saudi riyals in Philadelphia to pay the Saudi oil company ARAMCO as part of a wartime deal and shipped the coins in wooden crates loaded on *John Barry*, which left its convoy after entering the Arabian Sea, and headed for Dhahran, Saudi Arabia, to deliver the money. On February 28, 1944, the

German submarine U-859 torpedoed *Barry*, which broke into two and sank 100 nautical miles off the coast of Oman in 8,400 feet (2,600 m) of water. The "secret" was soon out, with a claim that as much as $26 million in silver lay inside the wreck, too far down to reach at the time.

The late Captain Brian Shoemaker, a retired U.S. Navy officer (1937–2017) and a veteran of Arctic and Antarctic missions and research, had learned of *John Barry* and its wartime secret cargo. He and a group of three partners, attorneys H. McGuire Riley and Hugh O'Neill, and restaurateur Jay Fiondella, formed the "*John Barry* Group" and sought the rights to locate the wreck and recover the silver. Shoemaker was convinced that in addition to the coins, another secret cargo of silver bullion also lay inside *John Barry*'s holds. U.S. government records in the National Archives, however, noted only the loss of Lend-Lease requisition SZ-505 A2 (AB), or 1,031,250 fine ounces of silver, valued then at $753,607.99.[13] Brian was convinced that as much as 1,500 tons lay inside the wreck, based on *Barry*'s captain's statement to U.S. naval intelligence officials that a $26 million dollar cargo of silver had been lost after the sinking.

The U.S. Maritime Administration called for bids to salvage the cargo in 1989, not long after the discovery of *Titanic* showed that the technology to not only find but also reach wrecks in the deep ocean was at hand. The *John Barry* Group won the rights with a $51,000 bid in August 1989. The salvage that followed was complex, first diplomatically and then technically. The Sultanate of Oman, with the wreck lying within its exclusive economic zone, had been planning a salvage with Keith Jessop of HMS *Edinburgh* fame, through an Omani-British partnership known as the Ocean Group. After stalled discussions, Shoemaker, a masterful negotiator, arranged a deal with the lead Omani, Sheikh Ahmed Farid al Aulaqi, and the *John Barry* Group sold their rights to the wreck for $750,000. The whole tale is told by John Beasant in *Stalin's Silver* (1995).

After a survey that located the wreck, a 1992 ROV dive by David Mearns, then with Eastport International, identified the wreck, still loaded with tanks and trucks and other military equipment. While broken in two, it was in "excellent condition." That was followed by a two-phase recovery project. The Omanis turned to France's ocean research agency, the quasi-governmental IFREMER, which had submersibles and experience. The first efforts to blast open the wreck failed, but IFREMER turned to a new take on Risdon Beazley's old "smash and grab" technology. They contracted with Robert Hudson and David Mearns, who formed a new company, Blue Water Recoveries, to do the project.

Bluewater Recoveries designed and built an "intelligent grab." This was a giant claw capable of being carefully guided to areas of the wreck to exert up to 200 tons of pressure to peel back steel and open the ship. It would then delicately reach into the holds to grab and raise the coins to the surface. Suspended from an oil rig drill pipe and lowered through the moon pool of the drill ship *Flex LD*, the "Grab 3000 System" removed the deck cargo, then the decks, and raised 18 tons of silver coins in October–November 1994.[14] In total, some 1,300,000 riyals were recovered, leaving about half of it on the bottom, as a number of loose coins spilled back into the sea, and others could not be reached. No trace of silver bullion was found. While some believe it remains somewhere on the wreck or buried beneath seabed sediments, others doubt it was ever there.

The disappointment for the investors was that the entire cargo of recovered silver, less the 10 percent returned to the U.S. government, failed to reach the minimum bid of $8 million at Sotheby's in November 1994. Sotheby's removed the lot from sale after no bids were made. *John Barry* coins reportedly now sell online from $5 to $12 each, although a September 2019 online search found a few offered on eBay for up to $49. The monetary value of *John Barry*, despite the amount of silver in the ship, proved insufficient to recoup the millions reportedly invested in the salvage. This has happened on other salvage jobs, including those focused as treasure hunts. While some commercial salvors have recovered lost specie, bullion, and other treasure, they are not "treasure hunters."

A shipwreck with monetary value that continues to excite interest is a Klondike Gold Rush passenger and freight steamer, SS *Islander*, which struck ice in the Inside Passage just 12 miles from Juneau, and sank, killing 65, on the early morning of August 15, 1901. Along with the steamer sank a shipment of gold bound for Victoria, British Columbia. Various efforts to find and then salvage the steamer failed, until Frank Curtis of Curtis-Wiley Marine Salvors took on the task. Between 1933 and 1934, using cables passed under the sunken hulk by hard hat divers and the power of the tides, they slowly pulled *Islander* from the depths 33 years after it had sunk. The effort did not pay off, as the gold shipment was not found, and only a small amount of personally shipped gold was recovered. The purser's office did not hold the boxes of gold known to have been loaded aboard. An amazing feat of engineering and human ingenuity has left the cut-down, partially scrapped remains of *Islander* on the rocky shores of the Lynn Canal, alongside the remains of one of the vessels used to lift the hulk, the schooner barge *Griffson*.[15]

The gold, as it was later learned, had been loaded in the bow. It was not until 1996 that a new team formed a Seattle company to survey and raise the gold from the bow, which still lay in the shipping channel. They bought the rights to salvage from the insurance company that retained rights to the gold. What followed was a flurry of legal proceedings as another company claimed the rights to the wreck and the gold. At the same time, with the thought that the sunken bow might be historic, the State of Alaska went through a formal process to determine if what was left was eligible for the National Register of Historic Places. It was not determined to be eligible, and the state entered into an agreement with the salvage company. They proceeded to the bow in 2012 and recovered some of the bullion boxes which had fallen free of the wreck. Reportedly $1.4 million in gold was recovered in six leather bags, known as pokes, that collectively held 1,200 ounces of unrefined gold dust, but at a cost said to be $4 million. The costs of the recovery were not met. The Salvage Association of London still retains the rights, and as of this writing, reportedly was looking to mount its own expedition to recover the gold for which it had paid out claims over a century ago. They have reportedly engaged a major international marine salvage company to do the work. Time will tell whether the latest effort will recover not just gold, but the expenses of recovery.

Recent discoveries have again triggered the imagination. The galleon *San José*, often referred to as the richest shipwreck in the world, was lost in battle with a fleet of British ships that ambushed it and others in Spain's Tierra Firme fleet off Cartagena, Colombia, on the evening of June 8, 1708. The massive, 64-gun galleon exploded and sank during the fight, killing nearly all of the 600-man crew, and taking a large amount of treasure, reportedly at least 12 million reales worth of gold and silver coins, emeralds, and porcelain, to the bottom.[16] The sheer size of the treasure led to a series of searches, including one that was going to use a large submersible. That company, Sea Survey Armada (SSA), ultimately claimed the wreck's discovery in 1982. In a conversation with one of those involved with that search, at that time I was told that it was covered with coral and not readily apparent as a wreck. What they found, however, turned out to be not the wreck of *San José*.

The survey that ultimately found the wreck in 600 meters of water in late November 2015, according to Colombian accounts, was conducted with and from a Colombian navy ship by the Deep Submergence Laboratory at Woods Hole Oceanographic Institution using one of the REMUS 6000 autonomous vehicles—the same type that had previously been used on the first full scientific mapping of *Titanic*, as well as other projects, including the successful deep sea search for Air France flight 447 in the mid-Atlantic. The project was undertaken by the Colombian Navy with Colombia's Instituto Colombiano de Antropología e Historia (ICANH), Dirección General Marítima (DIMAR), and Maritime Archaeology Consultants (MAC). The news of the discovery was released three years later, in May 2018. The announcement of the find of what was touted as the "Holy Grail" of shipwrecks led to global media coverage and speculation, as news reports estimated the modern value of the "treasure of the *San José*" to be anywhere from $16 billion to $20 billion. It also spawned a protracted—and still raging—series of disputes in court and in diplomatic discussions over the ownership of the wreck and rights to its treasures. As an article that summarizes four decades of disputes stated, "the galleon is once again in the middle of a battle, but this time not with guns and powder, but with diplomatic, archaeological and legal arguments before various national and international courts, and between various actors."[17]

In addition to legal battles with private companies with a claim, there have been ongoing diplomatic discussions and in some cases disputes between Colombia, Spain, the United States, and Bolivia. UNESCO and ICOMOS have also weighed in to the arguments. Major points include the questions of who owns the wreck, which is a key focal point of the discussions between Colombia and Spain. Colombian officials voiced strong concerns over ceding their nation's sovereignty over what occurs in its waters, but also argued that the preservation in situ—looking but not touching, as outlined in the UNESCO, ICOMOS, and the UNESCO Convention on the Underwater Cultural Heritage—did not make sense for what was being touted as the richest shipwreck in the world.[18] It does not seem that either of the extreme options—of complete salvage and sale of treasure, or leaving the site as an undersea museum—is likely.

What will ultimately happen with this "holy grail" of shipwrecks? It could be recovery of the treasure and placing it in a museum, as Spain did with the treasure from *Nuestra Señora de las Mercedes* after winning the legal dispute with Odyssey Marine Explorations, or some other alternative, such as the sale of some or all of the coins. Private litigation is ongoing with Sea Search Armada (SSA), who, as noted, had claimed that they discovered the wreck in 1982 and are suing for a 50 percent award of the treasure. In addition, there are questions of Colombian domestic law and policies regarding cultural heritage, the laws pertaining to marine salvage, particularly if "salvage" as a law designed to rescue property from marine peril is appropriate for centuries-old vessels and their contents, and the legal status of "treasure." Colombian courts ruled that none of these were applicable to *San José* prior to its 2015 discovery.[19] Instead, the courts ruled that, if found, the wreck "should be treated as potential underwater cultural heritage." When discovered, the president of Colombia, Juan Manuel Santos, announced that Colombia would enter into an agreement with private investors who fund the recovery of the treasure and other artifacts and then fund and create a museum in

Cartagena to display "the remains" of the galleon; none of this would cost the people of Colombia, and no other party, including Spain, had any right to make decisions about the wreck. That assertion met with criticism and ultimately a change in that policy with a new administration in 2018 that "moved past commercial extraction."[20]

However, prominent Colombian archaeologists have argued that the nation's Submerged Cultural Heritage Law, enacted in 2013, "opposes basic archaeological principles as well as the 2001 UNESCO Convention."[21] In early 2024, Colombia announced a return expedition to the site, at an estimated cost of $4.5 million, that will not involve private companies, but would involve Colombian archaeologists working off a naval vessel and utilizing a remotely operated vehicle to assess artifacts that speak to life on board, with the minister of culture, Juan David Correa, telling the media "it is time to claim the heritage elements for which the remains of the galleon should be valued. History is the treasure."[22] Where and when will the ultimate disposition of *San José* and its artifacts—including the treasure—be decided? Facing off against my archaeological colleagues are those who focus on the media-touted estimates of up to $20 billion. Whether those estimates are accurate, I have argued in the past that the flash of gold and silver obscures or overwhelms the type of careful work that yields treasures of a different sort. But there is more to the conundrum that a "treasure wreck" incurs.

Shipwreck recovery and treasure salvage, in my experience and opinion, inevitably lead to litigation. Litigation, notably legal fees, is often the highest cost. Millions of dollars in investor and corporate money have been spent on shipwreck litigation, including cases where rival firms or investors litigate, or when a recovery is contested by an original owner, be they an insurance company or a government, or when allegations of improper actions and activities are made. This point can be illustrated through many examples. To pick just one, the case of the Columbus America Discovery Group is illustrative. The Columbus America Discovery Group is known for its discovery and the recovery of gold from the 1857-wrecked steamship *Central America* in deep water off the coast of South Carolina.

Their discovery of the vessel became tied up in years of expensive litigation after it declined to purchase the salvage rights for the vessel from the original insurers for a suggested $50,000. When they filed an Admiralty claim, a counterclaim of ownership by a consortium of the original and successor insurance companies was filed in opposition. This litigation extended for years through appeals before a major portion of the treasure was finally awarded to the Columbus America Discovery Group. The treasure, initially claimed and marketed as potentially worth $500 million, was, after being awarded, then sold by the Columbus America Discovery Group's CEO for a mere 10.4 percent, or $52 million, of the $500 million "value" in 2000. The litigation continued as shareholders and employees sued for a return on investments and proceeds promised to employees for their work. The CEO, Tommy G. Thompson, disappeared. In November 2018, Thompson, after being a federal fugitive for three years, was arrested and imprisoned until he revealed where he had placed the unsold assets of the company, and was sued by his former investors. In 2018, a jury awarded the investors $19.4 million in damages. This is just one example of how treasure hunting does not pay all those involved.

In 1924, master salvage diver David Masters wrote that "so fascinating is the idea of treasure that men gladly risk their lives to go in search of it," and that even the "keenest of business men, who boast of their hardheadedness, seem to lose their heads where treasure is concerned," eagerly providing funds "in return for the promise of the most shadowy spoils."[23] I'll discuss this later, but treasure hunting has been criticized as the world's worst investment. The richest shipwreck, *San José*, may only yield wealth to some, but not all. It is also important to remember that what gets lost in discussions of riches is that there are other values; and shipwrecks, as mentioned previously, may also have profound value as archaeological sites, including those which encompass treasure. The treasure for archaeologists is learning the secrets of the past that a wreck can reveal. It is not the value of its material contents.

Coming back to the point of shipwrecks as the "bounty of the sea," but as bounty that comes at the expense of other values—like heritage, belief, culture—in some countries, where an old shipwreck is found, for a community it means selling their own heritage. But what is the value of heritage and archaeology to a subsistence farmer, fisherman, or a laborer when you need to feed your family? For archaeologists who want to try to "solve" the problem of tomb robbing, pot-hunting, or shipwreck salvage around the world, the issue is as difficult as trying to stop people elsewhere who grow opium poppies or coca leaves. Larger, global efforts to resolve poverty and hand-to-mouth subsistence are necessary to deal with systemic problems like these.

To deal with shipwreck exploitation and looting, the approach has been focused, as it has been with other archaeological sites, on tackling the global antiquities trade. This starts with demanding ethical behavior from major auction houses. Another means by which archaeological sites including wrecks can be better protected from looting is the type of action being taken by Interpol and various national police and intelligence agencies. They have found that the antiquities trade is being used by international terrorist and criminal organizations as a convenient means to generate funds and to launder money. This was highlighted by investigative journalists who disclosed that the Islamic State was marketing antiquities it had looted to raise funds for their jihad. The global antiquities trade is now estimated to be approximately $45 billion annually in both legal and illegal revenue. It is unregulated, and it has been unpoliced at an international level. However, in September 2019, an international meeting in Brussels called for new laws to apply a "systematic approach" that would "clamp down on art galleries and auction houses to ensure the legitimacy of the artworks they handle."[24]

Another approach has been a concerted push within the archaeological community to share their perspectives on what archaeology contributes to knowledge and try to change the point of view of collectors. Some people collect because they have a strong interest in the past, or a specific aspect of the past. Having something from a site helps connect them to that past; this has been the motive for many antiquarians and other collectors for centuries. The very human desire to have and hold something will never go away for some. But sharing the "magic" of what finds can mean, especially when excavated and studied scientifically, is one means of positively pointing out an alternative to looting and the illicit trade in artifacts. What is key to remember is that an archaeological site such as an ancient shipwreck is like the only copy of an old, rare book full of knowledge. If that book is pulled apart, page by page, to cut out and sell the hand-drawn illustrations, and the text itself is thrown away, it is no longer a book. Archaeological sites are fragile and irreplaceable. Maritime archaeologist Daniel Lenihan notes that shipwrecks in the sea represent a bank account in which the value lies in what you can learn, but one from which you can only make withdrawals. Once removed, what was in that account, unless it was meticulously documented, and the evidence held together for study by future generations with new perspectives, different questions, and new techniques, is lost forever.

Lenihan's observation is based on firsthand experience. He and other archaeologists have seen this loss played out through decades as treasure hunters systematically strip-mined shipwrecks in various locations in the United States, most notably in Florida. There, the tip of Florida includes the narrow passage between Cuba and the American mainland. Spanish ships entering and leaving the Gulf of Mexico had to navigate that passage, and then turn north and make their way through another passage outlined by the reefs of the Bahamas and Florida's shores. Shoals, storms, and piracy, among other factors, wrecked many Spanish ships along that route. A number of them lie off the coast of Florida, especially on the coral reefs of the Florida Keys and the beaches of the "Treasure Coast" stretching from Palm Beach to St. Augustine.

Beachcombing discoveries of gold and silver coins in the surf in the 1950s led to a boom of open sea treasure hunting. This came at a time when scientific archaeology underwater was also in its infancy. Diving to "a flash of gold" at the same time led to a great deal of public confusion over what archaeology was. Only archaeologists understood, it seemed, that simply recovering something was not in and of itself archaeology. It was also difficult to argue to the public that a centuries-old ceramic jar full of olive pits, for example, had "value" compared to a pile of gold and silver coins and bars. It also did not help that maritime archaeology emerged at the same time as treasure hunting, leading to popular misconceptions also fed by deliberate hijacking of the term "archaeology" by treasure hunters.[25]

The result is that, 60 years later, we know more about ancient Greek and Roman ships than we do about the Spanish ships involved in the conquest, colonization, and exploitation of the New World. A large number of other ships were also collateral damage as treasure hunting operations moved offshore, diverting the powerful blast of their propellers to scour the seabed and "blow" open wrecks to see what they held. Known as "prop wash deflection," it has proved to be a highly destructive tool. Journalist Steven Kiesling, in writing about Massachusetts treasure hunters who worked on the wreck of the *Whydah*, a former slaver turned pirate ship that wrecked off Cape Cod in a storm in 1717, disclosed just what such a technique can do to a wreck. Found and excavated by a group led by Barry Clifford, the *Whydah* project was required to work with archaeologists as part of a permit granted by the State, which controlled the seabed. Careful excavation was required, and under archaeological supervision. The project, nonetheless, was controversial in archaeological circles. It was strongly felt that no matter what was required under the permit, and no matter how good the intentions of the archaeologists were, a profit motive would get in the way of archaeology.[26]

With that, Kiesling's book includes an interview with one of the project team, treasure hunter Rob McClung. McClung stated that before the archaeologists arrived, he led a team for Clifford, who used a prop wash deflector to quickly open up the entire site. McClung said that "the wreck was in different planes. The more we blew the more everything settled to the same place...the original wreck was under eight to ten feet of sand. We blew it to twenty feet. Archaeology? You could forget about it."[27] McClung's account of the project is disputed by Clifford and others in the treasure-hunting community. An article by Alex Heard in *Outside Magazine* in 1995 includes some highly disparaging remarks about Kiesling by Clifford. The crux of the dispute, according to Heard's article, is the allegation by McClung and Kiesling of a complete exposure of the site prior to offering an opportunity to purchase 150 stocks at $40,000 each to finance the ongoing excavation of what might yield $400 million, but the *Outside* article states was "worth only $47 million as of 1987."[28]

The back and forth between Kiesling and Clifford continued well into the next two decades, with McClung chiming in with an interview with the Portland, Maine, *Press Herald* that "I spent six years with Barry trying to run that project, and every time I turned round, I felt like I was being railroaded and he would ask me to say things that weren't true." The focus of the article was the exhibition "Real Pirates" at the Portland Science Center, which featured *Whydah* artifacts, and reporter Colin Woodard's asking Clifford about Kiesling and McClung's claims, and then asking them for comments. The article continued with a discussion of ongoing controversy over not only Whydah but also archaeologists' views on treasure hunting.

Criticisms over *Whydah* began in the 1980s as the project emerged in the media. Archaeologists who initially worked with Clifford were criticized, and one colleague, Ricardo Elia, in a 1995 article, stressed that what was happening, in his view, was "collaboration." The antagonism between archaeologists and treasure hunters predated Barry Clifford, and so archaeologists who worked, or tried to work, with treasure hunters for the most part did not receive a positive response from colleagues. Given that treasure hunting and shipwreck archaeology both emerged at the same time, with some cross-pollination as divers and other founders and funders of underwater archaeology also were part of treasure hunts, this ultimately resulted in what I feel was a schism that had all the trappings of a religious war. I was literally in the audience at professional conferences for more than one skirmish in that lengthy conflict.

To be clear, while I make that observation as a historian, setting my biases aside, I am also an archaeologist. I know the damage that treasure hunting has done. Like other archaeologists, I have made a number of scientific arguments against treasure hunting. I've also had to battle public perceptions of treasure hunting being the same as a focused archaeological project where no one keeps or sells anything. The moment something is assumed or asserted to have a monetary value that trumps all others, human greed gets in the way. Undersea gold fever and quickly going for the gold and destroying or discarding other artifacts and evidence for nearly all archaeologists is anathema. Being complicit in treasure hunting is even more problematic, and is akin, as some have said, to being an accredited physician who participates in the removal of healthy organs from people to be sold to rich recipients. The treasure hunters' responses have been sharply pointed, arguing that the science can be irrelevant, and that the archaeologists selfishly want it all for themselves.

The main points of the debate, as summarized by Filipe Castro of Texas A&M University's Nautical Archaeology Program, are that treasure hunting has nothing to do with archaeology. Hiring archaeologists for a treasure-hunting venture is a marketing ploy. Treasure hunting destroys cultural heritage forever, and the money from treasure hunting doesn't come from the sea but from investors' pockets. Archaeologists operate using different methods, under different rules and ethical standards that do not allow for shortcuts or ignoring a systematic, methodical approach that extracts all the data that can be gathered. As one legal expert has succinctly noted, archaeologists excavate "underwater cultural heritage...not to extract commercial benefit, but rather to study it and preserve a vital historical record."[29] When evidence is ignored, discarded, or sold, that closes the door forever on future analysis in the face of new evidence or technologies. After reviewing salvage laws with heritage laws and conventions to see if there is a legal conflict, the conclusions reached were that while salvage law seeks to return goods to the stream of commerce, with historic shipwrecks there is more intrinsic scientific value. The two bodies of law do "not conflict" because salvage law for historic and archaeologically significant wrecks "is inherently inapplicable."

Archaeologist and attorney Laura Gongaware suggests that as archaeologists grapple with treasure hunting as a consumptive use that may not yield value, they should heed a fundamental point. We archaeologists, as well as treasure hunters, cannot speak for the public, and we cannot lock things away because we're upset as archaeologists that the approach to the wreck is not what we'd do or believe in. We should not stand in the way of displays, but we should take the opportunity to make our point, share our perspective, and let the public decide. Ultimately, there will be those who see one side or the other, and some who see both points.[30] In the matter of what is best for the resource, archaeologists with decades of experience in the field have solid scientific evidence that treasure hunting is harmful to shipwrecks. It does not, as a general rule, respect scientific methods, and it is a consumptive use that cancels out other values, save the potential for profit by a few. With that said, there is also a need to be judicious in the use of the phrase "treasure hunting."

There are also strong opinions that former colonial powers, wealthy nations, and international bodies should not impose their values and make demands of other nations in regard to cultural properties. The case of *San José* is one example of where Colombia and Spain may find themselves on two different sides, not in regard to the significance of the wreck, but rather who has the right to decide what happens. I think the question boils down to what Colombia will do with 11 million coins; Spain kept all of the coins from the *Mercedes* site, and they are retained in a vault as cultural patrimony. Will Colombia do the same? They say they will. Should museums exhibit the coins and "treasure," as the Florida State Museum does with the coins it retained? Not all archaeologists agree. Museum directors interested in public attendance might argue otherwise and offer to contextualize the display in a way that shares the archaeological viewpoint. In Florida's case, these were coins from the era when treasure hunters worked under permit to recover artifacts that included gold and silver, and the state retained a percentage and had a choice in the selection of artifacts for the museum. The precedent for this was set years ago, and most recently it has been done again with the Belitung shipwreck. Whether archaeologists like it or not, the public apparently does. In a case like that, I will always argue for contextualization and sharing the archaeological point of view.

That brings us back to the Belitung shipwreck. It is known by that name, as that is the name of the island it lies closest to in Indonesia; the original name of the vessel is lost to time. The artifacts and the construction indicate, as previously noted, that it is a 9th-century AD vessel, built from wood native to Africa and the northern Arabian Peninsula. Fastened with wooden dowels, iron, and with its planks sewn together through holes bored along their edges, it may have been an older vessel repaired in Southeast Asia, which is where the plant fibers used to "sew" the planks together came from. It has features similar to later western Indian Ocean sailing craft.[31] The cargo that lay within and around the wreck totaled some 70,000 artifacts, much of it Chinese ceramics, some of them porcelain, and some of them apparently made for a Middle Eastern market. Chinese coins, bronze mirrors, star anise in jars, amber, and gold, silver, and lead ingots made it a medieval equivalent, in a way, to the Uluburun shipwreck off Turkey. Like that wreck, the Belitung ship was a cargo carrier, with purposely selected raw and manufactured goods, all of them from China's Tang dynasty. It is the earliest wreck yet found with a direct tie to maritime trade between Asia and the Middle East. International trade by sea is likely as old as seafaring craft, but direct proof with ships and cargoes is rare.

A key question was whether the Belitung wreck was a Chinese ship, or from India, or from the Arabian Peninsula or the Persian Gulf. The consensus is that the vessel had likely been built in Arabia or the Persian Gulf and then repaired in Southeast Asia. But absolute agreement on whose ship it was, and where it sailed from, is not clear. What complicates the matter are the circumstances of its discovery, excavation, and the disposition of its cargo. Like the Uluburun wreck, it was found by fishermen (in the case of Uluburun, they were sponge divers) and it was looted; artifacts from the wreck still show up for sale. Resting in Indonesian waters, the Belitung shipwreck fell under the jurisdiction of Indonesia law, which mandates commercial recovery and the private retention of artifacts. In response to an early salvage and sale of artifacts from an 18th-century Dutch trading ship, *Geldermalsen*, wrecked in Indonesia's waters, by a non-Indonesian salvor, the country had passed a law that mandated salvage with a 50 percent award to the salvager and half for the government. This is an important point. While archaeologists remain fundamentally unhappy with the fact that the excavation was done to recover artifacts for sale, it was not looting. It was done legally, and not all laws are popular.

I'm not in favor of excavating and covering the cost by selling what we find. To do so runs afoul of professional archaeological ethics, as well as those of museums. To do science with a focus on profit is viewed as a conflict of interest. That is based on examples of selective recoveries, avoiding recoveries that are expensive to preserve and study, in favor of what has been described as "the flash of gold." Physicians have the Hippocratic Oath, and archaeologists have our own ethics, guidelines, and bylaws. Over 5,000 of us in the Americas are registered professional archaeologists (RPAs). You have to have a degree, experience, and demonstrate competency through projects and publications. RPAs are bound to respect local, regional, national, and international archaeological laws, regulations, and standards. That includes not participating in the trafficking or sale of artifacts, or buying them yourself. Projects need to be planned and guided by research designs that ask what questions you seek to answer through the project, and what methods and technologies you will employ. You don't cut corners or discard any evidence that doesn't fit your theories or is "too expensive" to retain. You need to be open, transparent, and honest in all of your reporting and analysis.

You do not dig anything up without having the proper plans and funding to not only document but also to either rebury, repatriate, return, or put them in a permanent collection in a museum of archaeological repository. Museums and repositories also operate under rules and regulations and professional standards. Museums are not supposed to use their influence as a trusted public or private institution to feed the market for antiquities, art, or cultural items. Museums are supposed to only accept collections when they can properly study, curate, and protect them. Any museum will have trouble if donors perceive or know the museum is selling or giving artifacts away. What we're basically talking about is that archaeologists and museums should not have conflicts of interest, especially when it comes to lining one's pocket.

It has been argued that the artifacts of the Belitung wreck did benefit from an archaeological approach and conservation, but ran afoul of that prohibition of a conflict of interest. When the auction of the 50 percent of the finds was done to compensate the salvor, as required by law, the Sentosa Group in Singapore purchased it all and made plans for a museum. This occasioned controversy, primarily among maritime archaeologists. That controversy erupted in the United States when the Smithsonian's Freer-Sackler Gallery in Washington, D.C., announced an agreement to mount an exhibition of artifacts from the Belitung wreck. The controversy started as internal staff were upset over the exhibition of what was incorrectly seen as looted artifacts, and the fact that millions had been spent by the Sentosa Group to acquire the collection. That unrest spilled out into the media, which spread globally into one of the largest shipwreck "battles" of that decade.

A great deal of misinformation and misunderstanding ensued, with an offer from the Smithsonian and UNESCO to return to the site and re-excavate it. That offer was made without the Washington, D.C., attendees knowing that the Indonesians had already done that re-excavation. Ultimately the exhibition was canceled. This was perceived as a strong message to Indonesia that regardless of their laws and how they proceeded with this and other wrecks, a largely Euro-American and what was perceived as a colonialist viewpoint dictated what Indonesia should do with shipwrecks in its waters. Other exhibitions followed, primarily with a major ongoing exhibition in Singapore with a replica of what the vessel would have looked like when it sailed. This was a full-scale ship built in Oman, named the *Jewel of Muscat*, built under the supervision of maritime archaeologist Tom Vosmer, and sailed from the Persian Gulf to Singapore in 2010. Placed inside the Maritime Experiential Museum on Sentosa Island, with artifacts, the museum opened in 2011; the collection and the stories developed there were the basis of the planned exhibition at the Smithsonian. Meetings hosted by the Smithsonian in Washington and the new museum in Singapore quelled none of the disagreement, and the Smithsonian announced they were postponing their plans for the exhibition, and then canceled.

While the Smithsonian had canceled its exhibition, the power of the concept of a shipwreck meant that the story of the ship and its cargo was ultimately shared not by other museums. The solution, such as it was, was one of different meanings for many of the archaeologists involved. Some saw it as a "teaching moment" that explained the issues that archaeologists had with wrecks excavated for treasure, while others saw a victory in that the Smithsonian had not allowed "tainted" artifacts to be shown. Meanwhile, archaeologists from Indonesia's Jambi Office for Cultural Heritage Protection had re-surveyed the wreck site and recommended displaying the artifacts on the island—in the local community, not further away, providing legal protection for the wreck site, and undertaking rehabilitation of the marine habitat at the wreck site.

Natali Pearson, in her review of the saga of the Belitung wreck, finds both negative and positive results from the controversy and its "resolution," with the collection ultimately placed in Singapore's new Asian Civilizations Museum. Indonesian authorities stopped an illegal salvage of another wreck, Chinese authorities saw the wreck's contents as a historical justification for Chinese engagement and reopening a China-dominated modern version of the maritime Silk Road, and there is ongoing interpretation about what the wreck and its contents may inform a modern world. In addition, "as with so many shipwrecks," this specific shipwreck continues to implicate "diverse communities... bringing in communities and nations who all seek to claim a part of this story for themselves. The implications for these objects, and for other commercially salvaged underwater cultural heritage, are profound."

One aspect is, simply stated, the money. After Sweden raised, excavated, conserved (twice), and restored *Vasa*, and built a custom-designed world-class museum for it, the nation has found and celebrated other shipwrecks, but none have been raised. There has been no major shipwreck excavation and recovery in the United Kingdom since the decades of conservation, study, and museum construction for *Mary Rose*. *Monitor*'s wreck remains on the seafloor. Stripped of its major engineering components, all that remains is the hull. The engines and turret with its guns remain in conservation at the *Monitor* Center. Treatment of those artifacts will continue for decades. Only then will they be placed on display in a custom-built, $30 million addition to the Mariners'

Museum. In North Charleston, South Carolina, *H.L. Hunley*, still in conservation, awaits a permanent museum. The 17th-century wreck of the French colonial vessel *La Belle*, an epic excavation on the Texas coast, was conserved, placed in exhibition, and recently moved into storage to make way for other exhibits. No other major shipwreck excavation has taken place in the United States.

While treasure hunters might argue that their model works, for half a century, investors have financed treasure hunting on the expectation of hitting a jackpot, with the promise of untold, forgotten, or lost treasures worth millions or billions available to those who invest. Money was poured into operations that the late Peter Throckmorton cataloged as inefficient, overpriced, and in some cases fraudulent. Throckmorton analyzed a series of projects spread out over a period of years; a total of 15 projects cost over $17 million and returned an estimated $3–4 million to the investors. One project, which seemingly did better, still returned 50 cents on the dollar to investors. In the decades since, other treasure-hunting operations that have followed have seen large losses, diminishing stock prices, and considerable expenses not only in the field, but in court litigation, as previously noted, which ensued in some cases for many years.[32]

And yet investors have continued to invest, drawn by the romance of the hunt. Stephen Kiesling, in his book on the *Whydah* wreck, wrote of an interview he had in Key West with John Levin, the original financial officer of that $6 million project: "When a veteran treasure hunter gets *serious* about launching a search, he goes looking for bikinis... the flow of investment money rises inversely with the amount of material used in a bathing suit.... The sun is hot, the drinks are strong, and the bikinis are as small as the law allows. It makes men feel like kids again. Here in Key West, treasure deals are put together every day."[33] The *Whydah* project, according to journalist Alex Heard, writing in *Outside* magazine in October 1995, resulted in "no major treasure—nine gold coins, a few thousand silver coins." While the approach and appeal Kiesling described decades ago likely has not been applied by all treasure hunters, it offers an explanation as to why some people continue to invest in what Peter Throckmorton three decades ago called "the world's worse investment."

Another study more recently looked at the question of financial return from treasure hunting and documents that the treasure-hunting projects analyzed in the study lost money, reinforcing Throckmorton's earlier argument of bad investment. John Kleeberg examined the cases of the wrecks of the Spanish ships *Nuestra Señora de Atocha*, *Nuestra Señora de la Pura y Limpia Concepción*, *Whydah*, HMS *De Braak*, SS *Central America*, and SS *Brother Jonathan*, all of them notable, highly publicized treasure-hunting ventures of the 20th century. Kleeberg found that five of them had been a net loss, with *Brother Jonathan* costing "$4.9 million, versus a total of $4,828,282.22 in coins recovered, or a net loss of $71,717.78." One of the more significant losses was HMS *De Braak*. The expenses of the excavation of HMS *De Braak* were $2.5 million. The excavation recovered 26,000 artifacts, including 650 coins. The artifacts recovered were appraised by Christie's at $298,265, and the hull was appraised at $50,000. Thus, the salvage of HMS *De Braak* resulted in a loss of $2,151,735. *Atocha* may have made a slight profit, Kleeberg noted, but concluded that treasure hunts "do not produce a justified economic return to the investor."[34]

Legal and financial problems faced by treasure hunters and reported in recent times have underscored the risks of investing in treasure hunts. The most famous is perhaps the saga of Odyssey Marine Exploration (OME) and what transpired in the case of a wreck that was ultimately proved to be the Spanish naval frigate *Nuestra Señora de las Mercedes*, which had been lost in a brief battle with British ships on October 5, 1804. The wreck, lying in deep water off the coast of Portugal, was the subject of lengthy litigation between Spain and OME. OME, as a private firm, recovered artifacts including a large amount of silver coins from the site, which they identified only as the "Black Swan" wreck, and stated that it appeared to be a discarded cargo of silver coins, and not a wreck. Spanish officials thought otherwise, as OME had asked permission to find and salvage *Mercedes* and had been refused. What followed was a lengthy, expensive legal battle that stretched through years, as the case sought to prove where the site was, and what the artifacts at the site indicated in terms of identity. Not only was the identity of the wreck a warship belonging to Spain, but it was also an archaeological site that, despite the extensive recovery of artifacts (including over a half million silver coins), had not seen the release of any scientific or archaeological data. This was despite OME's assertions in its media that it was a commercial firm that adhered to archaeological standards. What happened instead was a rapid effort to recover coins from the site.

At the conclusion of the case, the court's ruling was particularly critical:

> Odyssey's protestations aside, the evidence that Spain's *Mercedes*...was, at all times pertinent to this litigation, conspicuous, plentiful, unrebutted, unmistakable, and imminently convincing beyond any reasoned doubt, especially to informed, highly motivated, experienced and smart professionals, including Odyssey and those at work in Odyssey's behalf. In sum, Odyssey's persistent denial and feigned uncertainty about the existence and identity of the wrecked vessel was a demonstrably purposeful and bad faith litigation posture effected from the beginning of this action to deflect, delay, and if possible, defeat (or, at least, compromise) Spain's rightful claim.[35]

The consequences were the loss of all of the recovered artifacts, which they had valued in the media at some $500 million, and a fine of over $1 million for "bad faith and abusive litigation."[36] OME and counsel were also found to have acted in bad faith in not recognizing Spain's ownership and sovereign immunity of the wreck. As a result, the U.S. district judge ruled that Odyssey must reimburse $1 million in Spain's attorney fees. Due "to the wariness of its investors," in the face of accumulated losses said to be $123 million, OME's stock prices fell, and in time, the company liquidated many of its assets and is effectively no longer in the treasure-hunting business.

And yet treasure hunting continues, conducted by other companies, in the waters around the world, including off Florida's "treasure coast." This troubles a number of archaeologists and cultural heritage advocates, but the public seems to enjoy it, and for many, I suspect they see no difference between what we do as archaeologists and what treasure hunters do. The lines can and have been blurred when treasure hunters use archaeological techniques and technology, or when archaeologists do a bad job on a project.[37] I am not a fan of either. A key point for me, even as an archaeologist, is that I understand that shipwrecks mean different things to different people. I accept that we archaeologists cannot control or lock down every shipwreck, but that we can and should oppose both looting and the sale of artifacts from sites. The belief that what the sea takes, and then yields, is up for any and all to take should not harm or destroy the values of a wreck to reveal more about our past, nor needlessly disturb graves, destroy marine habitat, or deny access to those who would dive or fish.

7

Shipwreck Archaeology

> As the silts and sands settled in the bottom part of the hull, they sealed the remaining cargo and lower timbers....Reduced oxygen levels preserved wood from ravages of teredo worms and decay by marine bacteria....The ship and her cargo became a time capsule from a grand—but doomed—colonial enterprise. *La Belle* now rested in a watery grave, waiting for her twentieth century rediscovery.
> —James E. Bruseth and Tony S. Turner, *From a Watery Grave: The Discovery and Excavation of La Salle's Shipwreck, La Belle*, 2005

Shipwrecks represent a special and specific focus for archaeologists. Actually, they are the subject of a number of foci, as some archaeologists study wrecks as representatives of ancient cultures, trades, or large-scale events. Others view them as "cracked" time capsules, as not everything remains in a shipwreck after it sinks, but enough can if the wreck is out of reach of human disturbance and removal—until the archaeologists arrive. Some archaeologists study shipwrecks to better understand the origins and evolution of shipbuilding, particularly as ships and other watercraft were expressions of culture, as well as engineering achievement. In the Preface, I mentioned the Polynesian voyaging canoe as an example of what is likely the most successful human sea craft in our tens of thousands of years of history.

I strongly suspect that the form and rig (sails) of those voyaging canoes date back tens of millennia and played a key role in humanity's spread out of Africa. Not everyone walked, especially on a watery planet. We only have inference—evidence in caves of offshore fishing in deep water, beyond the sight of land, for example, but not an actual seagoing canoe from 40,000 years ago. Too small—with the cargo they carried being people, food, and small tools and weapons—they would leave little evidence on the seabed. In late 2023, a "shipwreck" that survived only as a nearly 18-pound block of chiseled obsidian was discovered off the island of Capri at a depth of 100–130 feet. The site likely represents a now vanished, seagoing craft that dates back 5,000 years, during the Neolithic, or New Stone Age, when obsidian's glass-like nature made it a perfect medium for knapping flakes that could be shaped into knives, scrapers, and projectile points.

This newly found site off Capri represents two aspects of what drives archaeological interest—the craft (albeit likely gone with few or no traces, leaving only conjecture) and the cargo. Add to that a range of other finds, and what begins to emerge, not as a theory, but as a yet to be fully explored or revealed aspect of the past, is that humanity's relationship to the sea and other waters is perhaps one of the more universal experiences of most every culture. Archaeology is increasingly examining all aspects of maritime culture, and not just with shipwrecks. Shipwrecks represent one specific type of archaeological site, but shipyards, fishing weirs, docks and piers, and other sites all speak to our relationship with navigable waters.

An archaeologist studying a site sees all types of artifacts as things made or modified by humans, which range from small to larger things (including structures). They look at surviving biological evidence and human modifications to the environment. The scientific approach asks questions that start as simply: What happened? To whom did this happen? Why did it happen? An archaeological approach, especially archaeology backed by anthropology, also looks at what sites can reveal about aspects of human development, as well as whether human behavior has changed over time as different cultures developed around the world. For me, that focus is ships. Some of my colleagues specifically focus on the aspects of the individual ship—how it was built, what it was built from, and the technologies found on board ships designed specifically for use on the water. While these are important matters, they are not my focus as a maritime archaeologist. I examine the context of the how and why of a ship's voyage or voyages in its lifetime; where it went, perhaps linking it through historical research to why it went, and what happened to it. Shipwrecks, for me, speak to larger societal events and issues—in my research, that has been immigration, the slave trade, war at sea, fishing, and specifically, what started me on this path, the California Gold Rush.

Archaeology and Shipwrecks

Archaeology began as collecting things left from the past as relics.[1] Antiquarians studied ruins of earlier cultures and excavated sites in the 17th, 18th, and 19th centuries. By the late 19th and early 20th centuries, archaeologists worked to expose ancient cities, monuments, and engineering works. They excavated to find artifacts for new museums that a variety of countries were erecting and hoping to fill, such as the British Museum, the Louvre, the Neues Museum, the Hermitage, the Metropolitan Museum of Art, and the Smithsonian. Some of the most famous architectural, sculptural, religious, and funerary artifacts of antiquity and later eras reside far from their place of origin—the Parthenon marbles, the Rosetta Stone, the bust of Queen Nefertiti, the Benin bronzes, and the Ishtar Gate are just a few of examples of an extensive list.

Private collectors, acting as patrons of "archaeology," sponsored excavations in their own and other countries and were allowed to retain a portion of the finds in exchange for their patronage. A well-known example is the patronage of the Earl of Carnarvon, who sponsored Howard Carter's excavations in the Valley of the Kings, notably the tomb of Tutankhamun, which saw a number of artifacts presented to the patron, most of which are still held at his family home, Highclere Castle, or as it is known to television viewers, "Downton Abbey." The vast colonial empires of European powers became the setting for the emergence of archaeological expeditions and large excavations that added to the understanding of the past as well as the collections of museums in the colonial seats of power. Archaeology as an academic focus and as a career for scholars emerged in the 19th century. However, the foundations of archaeology as a means to acquire, collect, and hold the relics of the past have never disappeared, but gradually became, no pun intended, an underground activity that continues in the 21st century.

By the 1920s and 1930s, the era of "modern archaeology" emerged. This was the work of scholars who applied scientific methodology, consistency, and detailed documentation of every find. They were less interested in intact statues or pottery. Their focus was systematically gridding a site into units that were carefully excavated in stratigraphic layers and collecting everything. By the mid-20th century, archaeology had become a science-based discipline.[2] The archaeology of shipwrecks, like archaeology on land, began with chance discoveries as storms stripped sand from beaches, or urban and waterfront construction unearthed the buried remains of ships that had been buried by successive generations of landfill. These inspired projects by antiquarians to rescue and study, and occasionally to display, those finds. Early antiquarian projects included saving the timbers of the previously mentioned colonial-era wreck of *Sparrow-Hawk* after beach erosion exposed it at Cape Cod in 1863, as well as digging out ancient ships found in landfill in various waterfront cities. A famous example, found along the buried Roman riverfront of London, was a late third- to early fourth-century AD Roman wreck found buried at the site of London's County Hall on the south bank of the Thames in 1910. It was the first Roman vessel in the world to be "studied and published in detail." Excavated and raised in one piece in August 1911, the ship was mounted on a custom-built wooden cradle with wheels and was hauled by horses through downtown London to the London Museum for display, where it was viewed by King George V, Queen Mary, and other members of the royal family in March 1912.[3]

Not long after the County Hall discovery, workers digging a subway tunnel at the southern end of Manhattan in 1916 hit the buried remains of a ship at what is today the intersection of Greenwich and Dey Streets. The ship lay deeply buried where it had burned and sank at a site later covered by landfill. The workers cut through and recovered several feet of the bow, as well as artifacts that included a double-headed axe, trade beads, clay pipes, and a cannon ball. Based on the finds, historians identified the wreck as the Dutch ship *Tyjger*, a trading vessel that burned and sank in January of 1614 off Manhattan Island during the first Dutch voyages to the area, following Henry Hudson's 1609 voyage to the area and his discovery that the local indigenous people were eager to trade. In time, that would lead to the founding of Nieuw Amsterdam in 1624. In the 1990s, ship construction expert J. Richard Steffy of the Institute of Nautical Archaeology studied the remains of the ship, which had been preserved as an icon dating to the earliest years of New York. His studies supported the earlier conclusion that it dated to the 17th century.[4] Chance finds of buried ships continued throughout the 20th century, much to the delight of antiquarians and relic hunters as increasing demand for high-rises led to deep excavations in many waterfront cities. I'll discuss this in greater detail later.

Antiquarians and archaeologists working around the world also began recovering ships deliberately buried on land, often as tombs or as grave goods. Those finds included ancient Egyptian boats and ships buried next to tombs. Large stone-lined pits next to tombs and pyramids dating back 5,000 years from the present were observed and excavated starting in the 19th century. In some cases, at sites such as Abydos, Dashur, Lisht, and Giza, the remains of disassembled boats, several of them well-preserved, were also found in their boat pits, not just the previously mentioned solar boats of Khufu. In 1893, French archaeologist Jean-Jacques de Morgan discovered six pits with boats in them near the pyramid of Pharaoh Senwosret III. He excavated them in 1894–1895, and two were shipped to the United States, where they remain on display at the Field Museum in Chicago and the Carnegie Museum of Natural History in Pittsburgh.

Antiquarians and archaeologists also excavated Viking and Anglo-Saxon ships buried under earthen mounds. These were tombs that also contained nobles, human sacrifices, and grave goods. They included the famous finds of magnificent *drakkarskippet*, or dragon ships, at Gokstad and Oseberg in what is now Norway, and the 1939 excavation of a 7th-century AD Anglo-Saxon boat burial with magnificent grave goods at Sutton Hoo in England. The Sutton Hoo finds, most of which are in the collections of the British Museum, showed trade connections with the Byzantine Empire. Archaeologists believe that the 89-foot, lap-strake oak ship, fastened with iron rivets, was used as the tomb of an East Anglian king. The highly acidic soil had eaten away the timber, as well as the body, but the meticulous work of the archaeologists discovered the chemical traces of the corpse, and so carefully cleaned the site that the perfectly preserved outline of the ship could be cast from a plaster mold poured over the delicate traces that had survived.[5]

Early archaeological adventures with shipwrecks included chance finds dredged up from the depths. A famous 1900 discovery by sponge divers that led to the 1901 recovery of a large number of ancient bronze and marble statues from a 1st-century BC wreck off Antikythera, Greece. The bronze statues from the wreck were rare survivals from antiquity, some of them dating back centuries before the ship sank. Another famous discovery was a corroded lump of bronze that is now known as the Antikythera mechanism, the world's earliest known example of an analog computer.[6] Other antiquarian-driven projects of the early 20th century included raising the large remains of two massive "pleasure barges" belonging to the Roman Emperor Caligula from Italy's Lake Nemi, after Italian archaeologists drained it in 1929, and placing them in a custom-built museum. The museum burned during World War II in May 1944 as U.S. forces bombarded the area to drive out retreating German troops who had established positions near the museum building. Only some artifacts from the ships, photographs, and a few drawings survive.[7]

In the United States, historian and antiquarian Colonel Lorenzo Hagglund searched for and in 1935 raised the wreck of the American Revolutionary War gunboat *Philadelphia*, from Lake Champlain, where it had been sunk by British gunfire in battle in October 1776.[8] The substantially intact gunboat was a "time capsule" raised with personal effects, armament, and even the fateful cannon ball that had sunk it still in the hull. Hagglund displayed the boat as a traveling display for 25 years. After his death it was donated to the Smithsonian and in 1964 was installed in the newly built Museum of American History and Technology in Washington, D.C. It remains a popular visitor attraction as America's "oldest warship."

The focus on total recovery of famous ships continued into the 1950s and 1960s. Projects of the time included the disastrous raising of the Civil War ironclad gunboat USS *Cairo* from the Yazoo River, in the state of Mississippi and not far from Vicksburg. The first ship sunk by a "torpedo," the original term for an underwater explosive charge, *Cairo* sank in December 1862. When rediscovered in 1956, intact and exceedingly well preserved by the thick mud of the river, the sensational find sparked a multi-year project that finally raised it in October 1964. It was one of several U.S. Civil War wrecks that caught local and national attention during the centennial of the war.[9] The historic and iconic value of those wrecks, especially with the various commemorations of the Civil War, strongly drove the quest for their rediscovery and recovery. Archaeology was an afterthought. And yet, each also offered a prime example of the now-often cited concept of a shipwreck as an archaeological "time capsule." They also represented a "dead end" in maritime archaeology, as the costs of recovery, ongoing conservation to keep them from deteriorating after being raised from the water, and the vast effort of cataloging, preserving, studying, and publishing the results of what has been learned from millions of artifacts effectively drained available funding. After the initial push to raise shipwrecks, very few have been raised since as the costs are too high.

A perfect example is again that of *Vasa*. Its recovery was spurred because the wreck was an iconic find that connected "modern" Swedes to a historical era of global greatness. The warship, nearly intact, had been built as the embodiment of a warrior king, Gustavus Adolphus of the House of Vasa; it was an imposing wooden fortress. It was also a symbol of the king and of Sweden's might and its fabled ties to the heroes and gods of antiquity. The ship was, in modern terms, a giant "billboard" advertising the king and his country. Craftsmen carved over 700 wooden sculptures that were attached to the ship. Brightly painted, they depicted the king, Roman emperors, the ancient gods of mythology, angels and demons, and biblical figures such as David, the slayer of Goliath. The decorations also included snarling lions and mermaids. The symbols of power decorating the ship also included two carved figures of Polish noblemen, traditional foes of the Swedes, on their hands and knees.[10]

When found, the oak timbers of the hull were stained dark from centuries of immersion. Most of its sculptures were missing, having fallen into the mud alongside the wreck. Divers later recovered them after the wreck was lifted from its underwater grave. The sight of *Vasa* rising from the waters of Stockholm harbor captured global attention as men once again stepped on its decks—the first being King Gustavus Adolphus the Sixth. The archaeology of the warship, ranging from its construction, rigging, armament, decorations, life on board, and the stories of some of its dead, makes it one of the great maritime archaeological discoveries and excavations of the 20th century. Work to assess the massive collection of tens of thousands of artifacts found inside by archaeologists who excavated the mud-packed interior continues decades after its recovery. *Vasa* is now a historic site itself in the history of maritime archaeology. It was one of the longest, most complex, and most expensive maritime archaeological projects in the world. Part of that cost and the rationale for the expenditure was more than iconic importance. *Vasa* represents a promise that not all shipwrecks can "make"—that is, it is a time capsule. Few wrecks are as intact or packed with reminders of life and death at sea as *Vasa* is.

To the public, as well as to some colleagues, *Vasa* remains a "holy grail," and perhaps in that an unfair example of what every shipwreck should represent in its preservation and study. Much of the collection remains unstudied—with some of the work that would come with such an analysis representing a lifetime for any scholar. The costs for that work were not a high priority when the need to re-conserve was discovered. After *Vasa*'s initial, multi-million *krone* treatment and restoration, over time, study of the hull showed that the conservation had not dealt with hidden iron and sulfur concentrations. They were the legacy of centuries of sewage outfalls draining into Stockholm harbor.[11]

The remnants of the sewage, unseen but soaked into the timbers of the hull, were literally eating the modern steel fasteners used to re-bolt *Vasa* together underwater between 1958 and 1961. Those bolts remained in place when it was raised. As well, the 900-ton weight of the ship was also discovered to be too much for its weakened timbers. The hull was sagging. What this meant was a refocus on saving the ship. This included re-treatment of its hull and an upgrade of its climate-control system. It also meant the complete replacement of its 20th-century steel fasteners with new, 21st-century corrosion-resistant steel fasteners. Engineers designed a new support structure for the heavy hull. All of this was part of a decades-long war to save *Vasa*. This has been the priority. However, thanks to its curators and archaeological colleagues, including graduate students, new revelations are emerging from the unstudied collections. As they catalog and research, the artifacts like the ship itself help present the stories that *Vasa*'s vast assemblage represent.

Not all of the early iconic projects from the beginnings of shipwreck archaeology were of complete ships. A major example of one of the most significant finds of the era was the broken hulls of the collection of Viking-era ships in the shallows of the harbor at Roskilde, Denmark. The multi-year project of archaeological excavation began in the 1960s and continued well into the new millennium. That work involved surrounding the Roskilde wrecks by a cofferdam, pumping out the water, and working on the wrecks like any other dig on land. Roskilde dramatically changed archaeologists' understanding of the range and complexity of Viking ship types as a result.

What Roskilde revealed was an initial cluster of five vessels, two of them warships capable of carrying warriors and horses, two smaller merchant ships, and a fishing craft. A number of Viking-era craft have subsequently been excavated and studied throughout the Baltic region, a reminder of the fascination with these ships as icons. That fascination—or fixation—was first roused by antiquarian excavations of substantially intact Viking-era "dragon ships" in Norway in the late 19th and early 20th centuries. The early discoveries and recovery of the larger dragon ships led to their ultimate placement in a spare cathedral-style setting in

Image 7.1. One of the Viking era ships excavated, conserved, and displayed at Roskilde, Denmark.
Jakub Hakun/Wikimedia Commons.

the Viking Ship Museum in Oslo in 1929, which will be discussed in more detail later.

The finds of buried ships captivated people around the world. They were more accessible, physically and visually, and were objects of intense curiosity, especially when found in an urban context. Crowds gathered to see early 20th-century finds of Roman-era and later craft in London, including a third- to fourth-century AD vessel, the County Hall Ship, which emerged from the landfill over what had once been the Thames in 1910. Raised from its grave inside a cofferdam after excavation, the County Hall Ship was hauled through the streets of London to its new home at Stafford House, then the home of the London Museum. That journey was watched by fascinated crowds. Around the same time, the previously mentioned wreck, likely one of the first to come to rest on the shores of what is now New York City, possibly the Dutch ship *Tyjger*, emerged from a site that would later be the location of the World Trade Center. In the rebuilding at that site after the terrorist attack of 9/11, another wreck emerged—that of a British transport of the Revolutionary

War with a dark history of transporting patriot prisoners of war to prison hulks. Another New York find, which emerged from landfill during urban construction in 1982, and known as the Ronson Ship, is probably *Princess Carolina*, an 18th-century tobacco trader.[12]

Buried ships and boats are probably the most accessible "shipwrecks" in the world. You do not need to dive or go deep. I've been fascinated with finds made in a wide range of port cities around the world. They include ports on sea coasts, but also river and lake ports, some far inland. Among the finds that captured public and media attention in the past several decades are flat-bottomed river trading craft, known as bateaux. Four examples of these boats, dating from the 18th century, emerged from landfill at a dig in Quebec City in the 1980s. They were more than reminders of the once common river craft on the St. Lawrence River. Their sleek shape changed modern perceptions that these were stodgy, flat-bottomed craft built only for heavy loads. The Quebec City bateaux were sleek and likely fast, while also built to carry cargo. Now displayed in the Quebec Museum of Civilization, these urban "shipwrecks" fascinate visitors when they learn these came out of landfill. They are more than "dry land" finds.

Visitors with time between connections at Rome's Fiumicino Airport can tour a display of Roman-era wrecks that emerged as that land-filled site was excavated. Roman river wrecks buried as old waterfronts vanished to later development and landfilling have also emerged during construction in downtown Pisa, and during subway construction in Naples. Roman riverine warship wrecks revealed by dropping river levels off the German city of Mainz are a popular display, both in their skeletal remains and full-scale reconstructions of these fast, sleek, and deadly craft. A multi-year excavation of a major subway and rail hub in downtown Istanbul revealed Roman and Byzantine wrecks as well as the outlines of docks, wharves, and lost, scattered cargos of amphora. The number of finds and the scale of the dig made world news as the dig continued for years.

Later-period buried "wrecks" in downtown Stockholm, at both Helgeansholmen and Skeppsholmen islands, and a collection of Renaissance-era ships buried at Copenhagen are yet more examples of buried ships emerging from urban centers. In the land-filled, drained wetlands of Holland, the polders, draining, and archaeology have revealed nearly 500 wrecks from the 17th to the 19th centuries. Other finds include an 18th-century vessel at Buenos Aires, and San Francisco Gold Rush ships from the mid-19th century. It was those buried ships in San Francisco that sparked my passion for maritime archaeology in 1978. The unearthing of the hull of the ship *Niantic* that year was a sight I will never forget. A few years later, I was part of a dig that unearthed the bow of the intact Gold Rush ship *William Gray* at the foot of Telegraph Hill. As we pulled the mud away, we revealed the deck of the ship, and the bulwarks still held the iron rigging that supported the foremast. Much of my earliest work was on these sites in San Francisco. Every time we dug, the crowds that gathered and the television crews and newspaper reporters who regularly visited would number into over a thousand people a day. That remains with me decades later as a vivid memory of how the humblest of craft, even if burned, stripped to the bones, and reeking of mud and rot, can convey the "romance" of a lost or wrecked ship.[13]

Two finds of buried craft from urban settings brought the reality of a "shipwreck" to urban residents in an exciting way—speaking to changes in waterfronts, where water became land, and to the incongruous sight of a hull emerging from urban landfill. One was an 1849 wreck in Wellington, New Zealand, *Inconstant*, which after wrecking was hauled in close to shore and turned into a warehouse by merchant John Plimmer. Locals named it "Plimmer's Ark." Landfill and urban development overtook the hulk, as well as an 1855 earthquake that raised the land by almost a meter. The upper portions of the hull were razed, but this did not fully destroy the hulk. In 1997, renovations of the Old Bank of New Zealand building, built atop the remains in 1901 and now known as the Old Bank Arcade, revealed the lower hull of *Inconstant*. After being excavated, studied, and conserved, the wreck was replaced on the site in 2016, and visitors to the building can view the hulk through a transparent floor. Another is one that I was privileged to work on in 2001. We were surrounded by hundreds of people at the edges of the site. They peered down through chain-link fencing into the open expanse of a city block to see the intact wooden lower hull of the ship lying in the mud.

However, the discovery of wrecks underwater remains the aspect of the work that I do as an archaeologist that gets the most attention. The public is captivated with the difficulty of making a discovery and then reaching it to explore, film, or recover artifacts. The invention of SCUBA during World War II triggered a spike in interest in shipwreck diving. The premiere issue of America's first magazine dedicated to the emerging sport, *Skin Diver*, was released in December 1951. The opening of this new frontier was popularized by underwater explorers like Jacques Cousteau, with his television show, as well as the series *Sea Hunt*, starring Lloyd Bridges as diver Mike Nelson, which ran for four seasons and then remained in syndication starting in 1961 as reruns. As previously noted, *The Undersea World of Jacques Cousteau*, debuting in 1968, as well as an increased focus on diving—and shipwrecks—in motion pictures, including more than one James Bond adventure, starting with 1965's *Thunderball* and its epic undersea battle, as well as *You Only Live Twice* (1967) and *For Your Eyes Only* (1981). At this stage, the concept of shipwrecks was also popularized by the exploits of treasure hunters and relic seekers whose discoveries made headlines or were featured in magazines like *National Geographic*. The first season of *Sea Hunt* featured a dive on a wreck with a safe and sack of gold dust. With that, the advent of "archaeology" on and with shipwrecks was often explained as simply recovering artifacts, notably treasure.

In the first three decades of the emerging field of underwater, shipwreck, marine, nautical, or maritime archaeology, there was a thin line between the archaeologists, divers, salvagers, and treasure hunters. At that stage, there were no trained archaeologists specifically trained for underwater work, on a site like a shipwreck. Hence, one early book was a handbook for "skin divers" in the United Kingdom. A well-intentioned and informative book, it was an effort to enroll divers into the ranks of archaeology, not a "how to" for looters.[14] Ultimately, this approach, as will be discussed, was the basis of avocational organizations focused on shipwrecks, as well as what is now termed "citizen science." Some authors focused on "diving for pleasure and treasure."[15] Others, focused specifically on the Spanish treasure wrecks of the Florida coast and Keys, published their own accounts.[16] A few of the pioneers of shipwreck exploration at that time conducted both archaeology and treasure hunting, including Robert Stenuit, Robert F. Marx, Teddy Tucker, and Mendel Peterson, the one-time curator of ships at the Smithsonian, blurring the lines for the public who saw no difference.

Archaeologists are sensitive to the fact that our field began centuries ago as antiquarians sought ancient relics for their collections; these included statuary that emerged from renovations in Rome and other ancient cities during the Renaissance, while "gentlemen" in Europe, both notably in Britain, as well as in America, collected "curios" that ranged from artifacts to geological specimens, shells, and the skeletal remains of animals and birds. These were displayed in "cabinets of curiosities." The cabinets in time gave way to museums, but those institutions were often the beneficiaries of glorified looters who smashed open Egyptian tombs, wrested friezes from ancient ruins, or plundered other countries' heritage. Because archaeology evolved from centuries of colonial expropriation and plunder, a near religious fervor developed to separate the scientists from the grave robbers or dilettanti, and the late arrival of shipwreck archaeology to the field essentially repeated the past. Looting, collecting curiosities, and nationalism were all hallmarks of some of the earliest shipwreck "archaeology." That this level of confusion would emerge as archaeology laid "claim" to shipwrecks is not surprising.

Scientific underwater archaeological work on a wreck first took place off the Turkish coast in 1960. George F. Bass, Peter Throckmorton, and Honor Frost conducted the first complete underwater excavation of a shipwreck by archaeologists. Previously, work by the French, starting with Cousteau, but including other legendary diving pioneers like Phillipe Diolé and Frédéric Dumas, Cousteau's chief diver, had located and excavated early shipwrecks in the Mediterranean.[17] The divers were exceptional, but they were not good archaeologists, and some archaeologists were exceptional, but they were not good divers—if they dived at all. Despite the challenges of working underwater, Bass and Frost as archaeologists working underwater insisted on an excavation using the standards of archaeological excavations on land. They adapted their tools and methods to meet those standards. The excavation proved that archaeology, wet or dry, could be done to the same standards. Another noted archaeologist, John M. Goggin, who had pioneered underwater archaeology in Florida, noted that much of the work to date had focused on the "diving techniques" and artifacts recovered, and not the archaeological results. Goggin went on to firmly assert that shipwrecks and other sites underwater "are just as significant as those on land and they should be handled by trained archaeologists, not by sport or professional divers."[18]

The shipwreck that Frost and Bass turned to with Throckmorton is known as the Gelidonya Wreck, a Bronze Age ship that sank sometime around 1200 BC. While there was little trace of the ship itself, there were many artifacts, including copper and tin ingots, bronze tools (that were worn and appeared to be scrap ready for melting), and a variety of

Image 7.2. Archaeologist Joe Grinnan of SEARCH mapping a wooden shipwreck of the early 20th century on the banks of the Mobile River, Alabama. SEARCH, Inc. Photograph by Kyle Lent, Alabama Historical Commission.

stone and bronze tools used in metalworking. The finds suggested that the ship, with a cargo of ingredients for making bronze tools, might have been a traveling workshop for a metalsmith. While the prevalent archaeological theory of the time was that the ancient Greeks had dominated maritime trade in the Bronze Age Mediterranean, based on the finds and the nature of the personal artifacts, Bass argued the wreck was not Greek. Bass theorized that the ship belonged to Canaanites, early Phoenicians, or perhaps Cypriots, because of personal items and the ship's votive goddess. While controversial, Bass's point was ultimately proved correct in a series of archaeologically sound, academic articles. At the same time, he was also committed to making the projects accessible to the public through his decades-long association with the National Geographic Society, his publications, some of them cover stories, in *National Geographic Magazine*, documentary films, and books written for a popular audience.[19]

Bass knew the public fascination was with artifacts, so he forged a decades-long partnership with Donald Frey, an exceptional photographer who joined Bass's team. Frey's photographs of sites and artifacts from excavations were regularly published and became some of the more iconic images of shipwrecks and shipwreck archaeology of the 1960s, 1970s, and 1980s. While the finds by Bass's teams dominated the covers of *National Geographic Magazine* in the 1960s, the finds and projects of other archaeologists increasingly began to capture the attention of media—and the public. In the 1960s, Bass's books were joined by, and occasionally competed with, those of colleagues who published their own accounts, including Throckmorton, Frost, and Joan du Plat Taylor. Taylor specifically edited the translated accounts of a number of the pioneering French divers.[20]

Bass and his nonprofit Institute of Nautical Archaeology, and the nautical archaeology program he founded at Texas A&M University, created the Bodrum Museum of Underwater Archaeology, establishing a nearby base for their field work in Turkey.[21] Similarly, underwater and shipwreck archaeology took hold in Australia. There, pioneering archaeologists like Graeme Henderson focused on academic and popular publications, and created an iconic museum in Perth, Western Australia.[22] "Capacity building" by working with local partners, but with projects run by the foreigners, was the approach taken with these early projects. The colonial-era model of working in someone's else country, and occasionally establishing field stations abroad, had been the means by which European and American archaeologists had worked on land in the previous century and a half. However, archaeology, whether on land or underwater, was changing in an increasingly post-colonial world.

One of the changes was the technology used to find and reach shipwrecks in the deep. In addition to moving past the boundaries of diving to what lay deeper, a focus of those who sought to recover lost treasure and military secrets from Cold War naval accidents, oceanographers and other marine scientists were eager to use deep-water technology that was being declassified. Among those technologies were systems built to withstand the extreme pressure and cold, submersibles and robots that returned with images from those dark depths, and autonomous robotic vehicles that did not require being towed on a long cable to search, but were programmed to go down, survey, and return to their mother ship. While military use and deep ocean science benefited from the technological revolution in the tools for ocean exploration, those with an interest in shipwrecks—both archaeologists and salvagers—began to pay attention. One of the early books to suggest that shipwrecks beyond the reach of divers were a target worth exploring was Willard Bascom, whose 1976 book *Deep Water, Ancient Ships* theorized that organisms that ate wooden ships might not exist in the abyssal deep, meaning that even ships of antiquity might survive intact and be capable of recovery. Bascom's book captivated a number of ocean explorers' attention. What if he was right? Were there completely intact ancient ships in the abyssal depths of the world's oceans? The thought of "unreachable" shipwrecks sparked quiet projects to go deeper. For archaeologists, the focus was ancient ships; for others, it was finding *Titanic* and other "famous" shipwrecks seemingly beyond reach.

This revelation that there were more shipwrecks, at the time unreachable, sitting in a massive "vault" or undersea museum, came in the wake of Gelidonya and other projects in the 1960s and into the 1980s, when underwater archaeology evolved into an accepted sub-discipline of archaeology. Projects conducted by academic, institutional, and government archaeologists grew in number and scope through the end of the century. These projects primarily focused on "famous" or iconic shipwrecks, many of them naval craft. In the United States, a number of projects were undertaken by archaeology programs that were created by states. In Florida, as treasure hunters located and salvaged Spanish galleons, the state responded by creating the position of State Underwater Archaeologist, and the U.S. National Park Service's George Fischer pioneered the practice of underwater archaeology to work on wrecks in the various national parks off the Florida coast. In North Carolina and South Carolina, interest in Civil War shipwrecks sparked both private salvage efforts focused on recovering artifacts, and occasionally the complete remains of Union and Confederate wrecks. Both states also created state underwater archaeology programs and hired archaeologists, as did Texas. In other countries, government departments, as well as academic programs, emerged. So, too, did private organizations, some of them clubs, that worked with both governments and academia to find and document lost ships. It was an exciting time for anyone who was fascinated by lost ships. Wrecks previously found only in the pages of a history book literally emerged from the sea and lakes as artifacts and even hulls were raised. Huge cannon and personal effects from the wrecks of the Spanish Armada, an ancient Greek shipwreck's lower hull, excavated and raised off Cyprus, the Dutch East India Company's ship *Batavia*, deliberately wrecked off Australia, and the wreck of a Byzantine trader off Turkey with a massive cargo of broken and intact medieval Islamic glassware that literally resurrected not only examples of that lost art, but inspired modern appreciation, were among the many projects of the era.

There were so many discoveries, excavations, and archaeological revelations from shipwreck projects that at the end of the 1990s, a multi-year project resulted in the first encyclopedia of underwater and maritime archaeology. It was commissioned first by Facts on File, and taken over by the British Museum Press, and I was the editor. The result was, thanks to colleagues around the world, over 500 entries on sites, legislation, legal issues, methodologies and equipment, research themes and approaches, organizations, and institutions (at that time 30 listed) as well as 24 regional and national essays. As the editor, I knew there would be gaps, that the encyclopedia would be outdated by the time it went to print, and that the next volume, if it came, would have to be multi-volume, or in some other format. There is no need for a printed book now, as online databases offer far more, as does Wikipedia.

At the end of the second decade of the 21st century, underwater and maritime archaeological projects span the globe in nearly every body of water, as well as to some of the deepest depths of the ocean. There are numerous discoveries every year, at an increasing pace, thanks to increased awareness, public and private interest, government programs, the need to survey the seabed in advance of subsea industrial projects that range from oil and gas to cable-laying, and most recently the likely advent of seabed mining. Satellites detect shipwrecks in turbid near-shore waters that had not been previously seen, as well as in the shallows of Pacific atolls. Urban development continues to find buried ships in land-filled former waterfronts. The quest to completely map the seabed with accuracies not before imagined has progressed at the end of the first quarter of the 21st century to nearly 25 percent of the world's oceans—a stunning amount of the planet that is less known or mapped than the Moon or Mars. Shipwrecks and lost aircraft are being found, even far from known "established" seaways. It is both a promising time for shipwreck archaeology—and an overwhelming prospect.

Archaeology is the study of human activity. For many years, archaeologists could not access the 71 percent of the earth that is covered by water. This left a major gap in our understanding of the human past. Thanks to the past five decades of work underwater, we have evidence of humanity's constant and significant relationship with the sea. That past is one where humans were interacting with not just streams, rivers, and lakes, but also the global oceans. Whether that was when people harvested the seas for sustenance, or traveled on it, archaeological evidence gathered in the past few decades demonstrates that our interaction with the sea began tens of thousands of years ago. The oceans were the highway by which ancient peoples established and maintained trade. For them, as well as in modern times, the sea was also a highway for war. Ships in antiquity and into the modern age journeyed out on the global ocean on voyages of exploration, science, and colonial ambition. To make those voyages, ships evolved over time, both in how they were built, how they were propelled, navigated, provisioned, and equipped, and how they were armed. For many societies, the ship as a structure, and as a machine, was one of humanity's greatest achievements in engineering and architecture.

The Ship as a Human Achievement

It is one thing to build a massive monument of stone. It can be equally as challenging and as profound to build a wooden vessel that can navigate the world's oceans and bring its crew and contents back home again. Iconic shipwrecks formed the basis of initial inquiries, but as the field evolved, the study of shipwrecks shifted to the basic elements of the vessels themselves. In the beginning years of shipwreck archaeology, one of the great values associated with shipwrecks as archaeological sites was what they revealed about the development of the ship as a human artifact. Nautical archaeology specifically looks at that question, much like the study of human origins looks at the fossil remains of early human species.

Nautical archaeologists working from direct physical evidence are drawing the family tree of the ship. There are direct lines, as well as dead ends, on the road to the development of the modern ship. Paleoanthropologists study fossil evidence to determine how early species adapted to different environments, from cranial capacity to the physical differences between males and females, to the pace of childhood development. Nautical archaeologists study shipwrecks to determine how boats and ships of the past were adapted to different environments. This includes sailing near-shore, offshore, and on rivers and lakes. It includes availability of materials and methods of construction. Nautical archaeology examines the form and hence capacity: how vessels were propelled, how they were divided into areas for life on board on short- or long-term voyages, and the expected life span of a vessel.

Nautical archaeology as it developed, especially in the Mediterranean region, was once described by George Bass as finding, excavating, studying, and preserving a ship from each century. That list started, for Bass, with the oldest wreck completely excavated, a Bronze Age ship at Uluburun, Turkey, that dates to around 1350 BC, and it now continues until the advent of the industrial age. Archaeologists interested in the maritime world and its technology ultimately branched into other areas of particular study, such as shipboard weapons, the tools of navigation, or shipboard sanitation. The latter includes the focused examination of shipboard toilets. Cooking at sea, the food and the nutrition of mariners, is another focus of archaeologists.

One area of shipwreck and maritime study is the bones of drowned and buried sailors to diagnose shipboard ailments, such as scurvy, as well as injuries common to seamen. There is an entire volume on the dead sailors of the English warship *Mary Rose*, and another for the previously mentioned dead of the Swedish warship *Vasa*. An emergency excavation of the bones of 19th-century sailors drowned in two California shipwrecks found more than traces of scurvy when their bones were studied. That forensic work also showed how their bones documented the injuries from years of heavy toil: scars on bones from injuries, ruptured discs from hauling heavy loads, and calcium buildups on bone from repetitive strain injuries incurred over a lifetime. The most common site on the California bodies were their forearms and calves. Why? Sailors unfurled and furled sail, barefoot, and balanced on foot-ropes strung below the yards that the sails hung from. To "reef" or pull them up, and tuck and tie them down to reduce sail, they relied on their calf and forearm muscles—and their backs. Now forgotten, this aspect of labor at sea meant that for hundreds of years sailors had well-developed, massive calves and forearms. That's why Popeye the Sailor was drawn the way he was.

Other archaeologists have pursued the study of the "bulk containers" of the ancient world, amphorae. Yet other archaeologists focused on what was inside. An unnamed archaeologist friend who is a wine connoisseur once confessed that amphorae were his introduction to wine. While explaining his fascination with the multiple variations of amphorae and how a typology had been developed to tell where—or who—had made them, his dad simply asked, "Don't you care about what was inside?" Other amphorae have yielded olive pits, fish bones, and an amphorae from Pompeii yielded the residue of *garum*, a Roman fish-based sauce not unlike modern Asian fish sauces. If you've enjoyed Vietnamese food, then you know *nước chấm*, the savory dipping sauce of the cuisine. That's probably close to ancient *garum*. Work by archaeologist Brendan Foley and scientist Maria Hansson took seemingly empty amphorae from wreck sites, scraped the interiors, and recovered DNA from olives and oregano, while another yielded traces of mastic gum. Mastic and other resins were used in antiquity to help preserve wine. When you drink *retsina*, you are savoring an ancient taste and a vinicultural tradition that spans the millennia.

Some archaeologists study the technology of shipbuilding; that includes focused studies of how wooden ships were literally fastened together. Some of the earliest craft were lashed or "sewn" together. Centuries later, ancient ships were built with planks that butted against each other, with tenons fitting into mortises. This "shell first" style lasted for thousands of years. The remarkably well-preserved hull of an ancient Greek ship, excavated and raised from the depths off Kyrenia, Cyprus, as Bass has noted, "demonstrated that a sunken and restored hull could be every bit as important as the salvaged ancient Mediterranean cargoes that had earlier dazzled both archaeologists and the public."[23]

Ultimately, metal fasteners came into use in ancient shipbuilding, and shipwreck archaeology has shown us that this remained a constant in wooden vessel construction into the modern era. What archaeology has shown is that there was a tremendous amount of diversity and complexity in making those fasteners that changed over time. A nail wasn't just a nail, or a bolt a bolt. What evolved first with bronze and brass and then into iron and finally steel inspired a detailed study by archaeologist Michael "Mack" McCarthy, for which many of us have a special spot on our bookshelves. It's not just the concept of cleverness in making a fastener—it is using those fasteners as a tool for establishing the rough date when a vessel was built.

There are also studies of ship propulsion and the sailing efficiency of hulls from antiquity to the modern age based on their shape. No surprise, but the earliest human craft are sophisticated and show an understanding of how a hull can glide through the water. Human ingenuity in developing methods to protect those wooden hulls from being consumed by marine worms—the "termites" of the sea—is another area of study. That archaeological focus examines the shift, over the centuries, from tar and wooden sheathing to lead, copper, and then various alloys, to finally end with copper paint. There are also specific studies, drawn from the remains of lost ships, of pumps, rudders, and steering apparatus. Others have studied ships' toilets, known to sailors as heads. Other areas of study include the development of rudders to steer (ancient ships did not have them), the introduction of masts, and the changes brought about in shipbuilding when cannon were first introduced to ships. These are all aspects of nautical archaeology that have been learned through the study of shipwrecks. Artifacts that change over time, like anchors, have been thoroughly studied, documented, and cataloged, and entire treatises built on how to determine the relative age of a wreck based on the type of anchors it carried.[24]

While maritime archaeology looks at these focused details to help define the what, when, and at times the how of a shipwreck, that is not the ultimate goal of archaeology. Those particulars are part of the forensic focus of the discipline. However, understanding the wrecking process, and what may or may not have survived, helps shape the planning of an excavation and form the questions that archaeologists seek to answer by digging. What are the questions that count? When an archaeologist decides to excavate, that decision is consequential; it is like a surgeon deciding to operate. From the first incision to the first artifact lifted or sediment removed, what happens is irreversible. The ability of an excavation to answer questions, and hopefully pose additional questions based on what is found, determines if a dig will happen, and if is to happen, how much will be excavated. How old is the ship? Who built it? Who sailed it? How did they handle the ship—in both the process of sailing and in navigating? What was the purpose of the voyage? Was it a warship or trading vessel? If they were trading, what was the cargo? Did they call at more than one port, and contact different peoples and cultures? How did it wreck? From these simple "big questions," a range of other questions emerge as a dig progresses.

One example of this is how and why cargoes were handled and stowed in different ways; for example, the archaeological value of a ship's hull as an artifact, especially as finds at Gelidonya and Uluburun in Turkey, at the time they were excavated the world's oldest known shipwrecks, revealed a wide range of cargo, indicating Mediterranean-wide cross-cultural contact and trade. The artifacts also included the raw commodities of the Bronze Age—ingots of tin and copper that, when smelted together, make bronze. These heaviest parts of the cargo were stowed at the bottom of the hold inside the ship. That helped balance the load and kept the hull stable even in heavy seas, as long as the ingots did not shift. The ancient mariners who loaded them also packed them in freshly cut brush to cushion the load. That brush, known as "dunnage," was ancient "bubble wrap" of a sort. Mariners used dunnage of different sorts for millennia to avoid damage to their ships and cargoes.

For thousands of years, ships were not built with plans, but instead followed principles and practices handed down through generations. Their construction was based on practical experience and available materials. Different types of ships were built around the world. For example, Mediterranean shipbuilding and Northern European shipbuilding represented two different approaches to construction until the past several hundred years. Asian shipbuilding and European shipbuilding were also different. In the absence of written sources, or even preserved examples of early ships and their technology in museums, archaeologists have turned to shipwrecks to document, study, and interpret the details.

Shipbuilding was a craft, and it was the work of skilled laborers who worked together to create a vessel based on experience that went back generations well into the Industrial Age. That meant that while ships conformed to certain "types," like galleons, galleys, sloops, and schooners, they were produced in cookie-cutter fashion. Archaeologists studying ships of the past 500 years have learned much about regional variations in shipbuilding, and in the case of warships, how various naval powers studied and copied features from enemy ships they had captured. They have also documented trial and error in shipbuilding as new technologies arose. The 1545 wreck of the English warship *Mary Rose* is a case in point. Among the many archaeological contributions made through the excavation and study of that wreck was the realization that the ship had been constructed much like older, Viking-style ships, with overlapping hull planks, much like a clinker-built rowboat of later times. That was fine, even as a large ship, for fighting at sea when one ship came alongside another, and men fought with bow and arrow or boarded to seize the other vessel with swords and axes. Cannon on decks needed not only a stronger-built hull to carry the weight; they also needed gun ports cut into the side of the hull for the cannon to fire through. You can't cut a hull through overlapping planks without compromising its strength. Shipbuilders tore *Mary Rose* down to the waterline, and then built atop the old, clinker-fastened bottom with heavy wooden frames lined with planking, laid edge to edge. That solid construction supported gun decks and allowed for the placement of gun ports. The problem was that the changes added too much weight. Top-heavy and loaded with a large crew when it went out to fight a French fleet on July 19, 1545, *Mary Rose* rolled over and sank, taking many of the crew with it.

The lesson of imbalanced ships took a long time to learn. It happened again with *Vasa*, which capsized on its maiden voyage in Stockholm Harbor in 1622. Recent studies of the hull show that not only was it built too top-heavy, but that the king of Sweden had interfered with the ship's design halfway through the construction. As a result, *Vasa* was lopsided. The ironclad USS *Monitor*, built quickly in the early part of the U.S. Civil War, was a revolutionary new vessel that changed naval warfare. Its armored turret and low hull of iron outmatched any wooden warship afloat. But it, too, was too top-heavy, and *Monitor* capsized and sank in a storm off Cape Hatteras within its first year of service.

Unfortunately, the battle between *Monitor* and its Confederate opponent, *Virginia*, while a technical draw, was a propaganda victory for the Union, whose "little *Monitor*" had saved the U.S. Navy from a catastrophic defeat.

What followed was a series of contracts for more monitors, of different designs, but all of them with the same basic flaw in their design. With a low freeboard, monitors would capsize in heavy seas or with an underwater explosion; the U.S. Navy's USS *Tecumseh* did so in the Battle of Mobile Bay in 1864, taking most of its crew after it struck a mine (known as "torpedoes" in that age), prompting the Union commander, Admiral David Farragut, to give his famous order of "Damn the torpedoes, full speed ahead!" That mistake was also made by other navies; among the wrecks was the British ironclad HMS *Captain*, which entered service in April 1870 and sank in a gale off the coast of Spain five months later, taking most of the 500-man crew, and leaving only 18 survivors. One observation I find myself drawn to as an archaeologist is how the evidence of the past shows not only a progression of technology and innovation through the span of human existence, but also our propensity to make the same mistakes, again and again.

"Gone Missing": Solving the Cold Cases

With the Industrial Revolution, new materials and technologies dramatically changed the way ships were built. It also increased the number of ships built. The adoption of industrialization to build and equip ships is another area that archaeologists study. The transition from wooden ships to iron, and then steel, is one example. Another is the study of the development of steam technology, which ranges from the types of engines to the types of boilers that produced steam. While engineering and science played an increasing role, trial and error, as well as the all too human trait of cutting corners in the name of speed and "efficiency," factor into the study of modern shipwrecks. The price of industrialization often meant worn-out ships with multiple repairs, worked by crews who labored to keep their patched-up vessels in working order, often in trades where the margins were small and cheap ships and labor were the norm. They often ended up as wrecks. My colleague Larry Murphy referred to this as the "one more voyage" mindset, where all involved gambled on the ship and its crew to stay afloat, alive, and to scratch out one last small profit. Many of those wrecks were commonplace in bulk trades—lumber, coal, nitrate and other minerals, for example, as well as in fishing.

Modern oceanographic robotic vehicles, whether the torpedo-shaped autonomous underwater vehicles (AUVs) that can survey hundreds of square miles of deep seabed in a day, or the ship-tethered remotely operated vehicles (ROVs) that allow us to examine and document a deep wreck, are now revealing a number of shipwrecks in the deep ocean that speak to these types of losses. They may not have made the headlines, but they were and in a number of cases are still remembered by the families of the vanished who never came home from the sea. While they may not be as dramatic as Euripides's sun chariot of Helios in *Medea*, AUVs and ROVs act something like a "Deus ex machina." When an AUV, or a group of them, steadily surveying a seabed thousands of feet deep, encounters a shipwreck that was never known to have been exactly there, that discovery can solve a mystery that plagued multiple families, sometimes for more than a century.

Wrecks that we've seen and studied include late 19th- and early 20th-century wooden vessels in the deep waters of the Gulf of Mexico that were lost as dismasted, tugboat-towed barges filled with cheap bulk cargoes—coal, wood, fertilizer, and railroad iron were among the commodities shipped in an era where the older wooden fleets, especially in the U.S. merchant marine, were being pushed out of business by iron- and steel-hulled British sailing ships and by steamships built with iron and steel hulls. Wood was cheap and plentiful in the United States, so American shipbuilders had continued to build in wood, well into the 20th century, but those vessels could not compete with steamers that were larger and faster, with capacities in the thousands of tons, not hundreds. Nor did steamers rely on the wind, as did the sailing ships. No matter how sharp and fast a "clipper" hull performed at sea, a steamer could outpace them and usually arrive on schedule, and quickly unload and load with steam-driven winches and cranes.

American ships, and in time even British and other European-built iron and steel sailing ships, ended up as barges, worked by sailors who were desperate, including those who were denied opportunities on other vessels, like African Americans in the Jim Crow era. In the Gulf of Mexico, the logging of Southern yellow pine forests, coal mining in Alabama, and phosphate mining in Florida filled the hulls of sailing ships and barges, some of them working for companies, and others as individual "tramps." Two deep-water wrecks studied by archaeologists include the Vernon Basin 2109 Shipwreck and the Ewing Bank Wreck. The "names" of the shipwrecks come from the names that ocean explorers have bestowed on geological features in the depths. Thousands of feet deep, the outlines and lower hulls of these two vessels, with few artifacts, revealed details that indicated they were American-built, mid-19th-century "fast" ships known as "medium clippers," also called "downeasters" given their origins in the Northeast Coast, especially Maine. Their identities are not known, although the Vernon Basin Wreck's identity is suspected. Both appear to have been lost while in tow, and the Ewing Bank Wreck has a small amount of cheap hotel china that suggests a small crew on board to keep the lines of the tow clear and tight. Phosphate resting within the hull indicates its final trade. The Vernon Basin Wreck burned before or as it sank, but the remains of a steam boiler for towing and a powerful winch at the bow, broken and shattered by the heat, suggest that it may have been a former fast-sailing medium clipper lost in 1902 while towing a cargo of creosote-soaked railroad ties.

Another shipwreck that speaks to "one more voyage" is that of an iron-hulled sailing ship originally known only as the "Windjammer Wreck," in the waters of Dry Tortugas National Park off the Florida Keys. It was finally identified by National Park Service archaeologists as the 1875-built British ship *Killean* that lasted in a long, hard-working career. Sold to Norwegian owners and renamed *Avanti*, it sailed from Pensacola for Montevideo in January 1907 with a load of lumber. It did not make it far, blowing into the coral reefs of the Dry Tortugas, a notorious "ship trap." The loss was a footnote in the Florida newspapers, and the fate of the crew is not documented. What the wreckage reveals, as we studied it, was a desperate fight to stay off the reef; the smallest anchor the ship carried was the only one to be found, attached to a tightly stretched section of anchor chain that was only about 50 feet off the bow and dug in hard—but too short to stop *Avanti* before it hit the reef; the stern tore off, the masts fell, and the ship broke apart.

The chain locker at the bow, where the anchor chain was stored, and which passed up through the foredeck to the windlass that controlled the raising and lowering of the anchors, was empty, with the anchor chain attached to the anchor passing through a hole hastily cut into the iron bulkhead, and then wrapped around some of the bitts on the deck used to moor the ship alongside a pier. Every porthole was shut, with its cover dogged and sealed tight. An everyday, working-class ship lost in a marginal bulk trade, lost out of sight of a town, without a radio, left only a few forensic traces of a horrific event, untold heroism by a likely doomed crew, and nothing to say to families who waited in vain for someone to come home. This is an aspect of archaeological inquiry that some of us believe in sharing—how the material record can reveal the human stories of those whose fates are not often told. In this case, the shipwrecks reveal nothing that was not known about the end of sail and the bulk trades, but these are some of the first wrecks found that shine a light on a common and unpleasant reality of maritime trade.

In a recent set of studies that I worked on with colleagues, we assessed the cultural contexts of proposed high seas marine-protected areas. These are vast tracts of ocean that are not immediately offshore, although islands and submerged seamounts lie near some or beneath their waters. One of them is the area of ocean that stretches from Rapa Nui (Easter Island) to the offshore waters of Peru and Chile, and along the line of the Salas y Gomez ridge. The other is that portion of the North Pacific that begins in the Northwestern Hawaiian Islands, stretches west toward Japan, and north to the Aleutians. Resting below it are the Emperor Seamounts. Our two studies, done for Conservation International, looked at indigenous cultural connections, historical ties, including voyages, naval encounters, and the harvesting of the sea by fishing vessels and whalers, among other aspects, but it also looked at shipwrecks. In both areas, we had no definitive evidence of shipwrecks in either of these vast open areas of ocean. But the historical record suggested the potential for numerous shipwrecks in each; the lack of definitive proof was due to the fact that each area was known to mariners and was used as an ocean highway because of favorable winds and currents. Ships departed one port, bound for another, and were never seen again. Most of them never made it into the papers; their losses were often surmised, but never proved, and for years that stretched into decades, families waited for lost seafarers to somehow make it home.

A survey of the available literature found several ships engaged in the guano trade, which involved the hauling of dried bird excrement (a perfect fertilizer for crops) mined from offshore islands in Peru, that simply went missing between 1850 and 1870. The late 19th century saw the advent of the coal trade from Australia to the coast of Chile, where the coal was offloaded and nitrate was loaded. Large, three- and four-masted iron and steel sailing ships, most of them British-flagged, could carry over a thousand tons of coal or nitrate. Older, often sailing without adequate maintenance, and with smaller and often inexperienced crews—as these "tramp" trades were both entry-level as well as end-of-career jobs for mariners—these ships were vulnerable. Add to that the danger of being in a storm and having a poorly loaded cargo shift, knocking the ship onto its side, and capsizing it. Sinking from leaks, or the coal catching fire if it had been damp when stowed, meant that ships left New South Wales in Australia, bound for Valparaiso, Antofagasta, or Iquique, and were never seen again. The contemporary newspapers of the last decade of the 19th century and the first decade of the 20th offered only brief notices in contemporary newspapers:

> It is reported from Greenock that the barque *Cumbrae*, 1356 tons burden, Fisher, master, which sailed from Sydney for Valparaíso on February 9, is missing. It is feared that the vessel has been lost as she has been 80-days out.... The ship *Menai*, of 1298 tons, of Liverpool, which left Newcastle

on February 23 for Tocopilla, and has not since been heard of.... The Newcastle Marine Board held an inquiry at the offices...this afternoon, respecting the supposed loss of the iron barque *Mitredale*, which left this port on April 30 last with a cargo of coal for Callao, Peru, and has not since been reported.... Hope has been abandoned for the safety of the British ship *Patterdale*, now 128 days from Newcastle, N.S.W., for Valparaíso.... Much anxiety has been entertained for some time past for the safety of the *Clan Macpherson*—a fine British ship of 1680 tons. Sailing from the coal port on June 24 last, the vessel, in the ordinary course of events, should have put in an appearance at her destination a couple of months ago.... The overdue *Clan Macpherson* is now 130 days out, and has not been reported since she left Newcastle.

These brief accounts were common; what they do not share is the trauma for families who waited for news, in faint hope that faded through the years as their lost fathers, brothers, uncles, sons and nephews, or husbands never returned. That was the reality of these types of shipwrecks. No news, no closure, no body to bury.

In 2015–2016, an autonomous vehicle survey of the Indian Ocean to try to locate the wreckage of Malaysian Airlines flight MH370 instead found four shipwrecks resting just over 12,000 feet down on the seabed. Two were modern fishing trawlers—a reminder of the human cost of fishing on the high seas—and two were 19th-century shipwrecks. One was the scattered remains of a wooden-hulled sailing vessel. Marine organisms had eaten all of the wood, leaving only the anchors, anchor chain, an iron water tank, and the iron fasteners used to build the hull. The artifacts dated the ship's construction to the mid- to late 19th century. The location of the artifacts from the ship, scattered at a distance from each other, and a mound of anchor chain suggested that the ship had not sunk in one piece, and that this was a sudden, catastrophic loss. The cargo had been coal. Archaeologists from the Western Australian Maritime Museum analyzed the data brought back by the AUVs and suggested a number of possibilities from wooden coal carriers lost or that went missing.

The second wreck, an upright, partly broken iron-hulled sailing ship, was also a coal carrier. A large area of the seabed was littered with scattered coal. The decks had collapsed, the masts had fallen, and the hull was twisted and broken midship. The damage to the hull suggested a fire. The analysis of the site by the archaeological team from the museum suggested that it might be the 1869-built iron-hulled barque *West Ridge*, which vanished on a voyage from Liverpool to Bombay in 1883 with 28 men. A positive identification was not possible. The wreck is off the sailing route, suggesting that it may have drifted, either dismasted by a storm or burning. It may have also been leaking, and older ships of this type did not have watertight bulkheads—just an open hold—and if the pumps were clogged by coal dust, in an age of no radio, and without other vessels around, it becomes clear that no one survived this wreck. Ross Anderson, the Western Australian Museum archaeologist who conducted the analyses of the wrecks, made it a point in his media interviews to note that ships were crewed by up to 30 men, and that passengers were possibly aboard, as well as noting that captains sometimes sailed with their wives and children. "Then, as now," he said, "the disappearance of so many lives would have had a devastating impact on maritime families and communities."[25]

With this, I want to close this aspect of the discussion by returning to the subject of the Japanese craft that drifted across the Pacific in the *Kuroshio*, or "Black Current" of death. As many as a thousand or more Japanese *bezaisen*, small coastal trading ships, and their crews may have fallen victim to the current. As previously discussed, some of those craft washed ashore on the Northwest Coast, with crews dead or alive. There are many 19th-century accounts from American whaling ships that encountered drifting craft with dead or dying crews; the American whaler *James Roper* encountered the sinking *bezaisen Hojun Maru*, with seven survivors, in the open North Pacific. The crew set fire to the abandoned craft after the rescue to sink it. Whalers working in the Northwest Hawaiian Islands also reported cast-away remains of Japanese vessels on reefs and atolls, remnants of what had to have been voyages of great suffering and despair.

This aspect of the shipwreck experience affects me as both an archaeologist and as a person. In our study of the maritime history and archaeology of this vast patch of the North Pacific, and looking at various modern analyses of the number of these voyages, a pattern of probable drift and number of lost vessels suggests that approximately 3 percent of the craft caught in the current made it to the shores of America, and the experience of the crew of *Hojun Maru* was not common—most hit the beach or rocks full of corpses. Hundreds, and probably most of the thousand *bezaisen*, lie as scattered, likely faint archaeological traces in the deep ocean.[26] While an archaeological expedition focused just on finding *bezaisen* is unlikely, ongoing ocean mapping with the latest technology could find traces of those lost craft. Is there much to learn from the scant remains? Whether or not much could be learned, what archaeology could do is virtually resurrect these lost craft from their deep sea burials, and even in the absence of names of ships or lost crews, speak to a unique class of shipwrecks and the trauma of generations of Japanese families.

Shipwrecks as Part of Global Maritime Archaeology

The archaeology of shipwrecks has grown to encompass not only nautical archaeology, but also maritime archaeology. Nautical archaeology focuses on the technology of ships and how evidence from the past traces the evolution of ships through the study of hull construction, methods of propulsion, armament, navigation, and life and work on board. Archaeologists would later criticize the focus on ships and ship technology as "particularistic." Particularism essentially means the archaeologist doesn't look for evidence of common human culture based on shared behavior, a basic premise of anthropology—meaning that all societies developed technologies and philosophies at roughly the same time—but instead looks at the local environment, the history of a specific area, and local customs. For my anthropological friends, who see us humans as evolved apes (not that I am arguing against that), the idea of not tying our work together with one basic theory of human cultural development, or the particularistic approach, is a problem. Archaeologists have been arguing over theoretical perspectives for over a century, and I don't see the debate ending any time soon. What has been fascinating in my half century of watching that debate and occasionally contributing is that the idea of actually doing archaeology on shipwrecks, as opposed to collecting artifacts from them as historic sites, was not widely accepted when nautical archaeology emerged as a sub-field in the 1960s. The idea of assessing the history of humanity through ships was revolutionary. Was a wreck unique, or did it reflect an aspect of common culture from its time?

The particularists focused on individual wrecks. Early sites became celebrities in their own right as a result, starting with the first sites scientifically excavated in the Mediterranean. Being a celebrity does not mean sailing through life without criticism, and the same was true for these sites. Anthropologically focused colleagues criticized the emphasis on how a ship was built, offering a catalog of all that it carried, how it had been loaded, and perhaps why and how it was lost. They asked for answers to questions about the parameters of long-range trade by sea, cultural diffusion, and regional or broader technological evolution. For it to be archaeology, shipwreck studies had to be anthropological, focused on basic questions about human nature, and in doing so, helping "us" better understand ourselves. As this book argues, people approach shipwrecks as ideas or as places with different points of view and expectations of how to interact with them. For nautical archaeologists, that means studying shipwrecks underwater, wrecks on dry land, stranded on beaches, buried in landfill, abandoned in back waters, half submerged, but also standing and ruined.

One of the major moments in the field of archaeology was when the late Keith Muckelroy published what was then a revolutionary book, *Maritime Archaeology*, in 1978. It was an argument to link not just shipwrecks, but all aspects of the human maritime experience, to the larger study of the human past, from distant antiquity to recent events. Muckleroy stressed that archaeologists dug up people, not things. The book began to address the criticisms of particularism; moving past documenting and publishing the study of a wreck without reference to other sites, Muckelroy assessed how the ship and its artifacts reflected broader patterns of culture. In Muckelroy's framework, shipwrecks fit into a broader context as data that help archaeologists address humanity's fundamental relationship with the sea, and by extension, lakes and rivers. Muckelroy argued that maritime archaeology was a scientific study that looked beyond the craft or ship to everything associated with a site, from all the equipment on board, personal items that reflected the personal lifestyle of crew and passengers, to cargoes and other evidence that linked a wreck to the larger economic patterns—local, regional, or global.[27]

This was the first observation by a scholar working outside of a classical archaeological background (he had begun his career studying prehistoric archaeology) that shipwrecks are of particular value as archaeological sites because they represent voyages (and hence humans going about their lives) suddenly interrupted by a shipwreck event. With varying degrees of archaeological integrity (that is, the variety and degree of preservation of the ship and what it had carried), Muckelroy noted that in addition to the individual ship, a wreck had value beyond the focus of the specific vessel, its complement, cargo, purpose, or loss. It could provide a larger picture of ships as more than a vessel into which things and people were placed, with Muckelroy making the point that up to the 19th century, ships were the largest and most complex machines produced by people. They were and remain elements in military or economic systems, and as closed communities.[28]

As part of Muckelroy's argument toward a theory of maritime archaeology, he laid out the archaeology of maritime cultures as it related to broader questions about human nature, societies, and history. Muckelroy noted that the excavation of a wreck could speak beyond the individual site to address research areas focused on nautical technology, warfare, trade, and shipboard societies.

Maritime archaeology also makes incidental contributions to archaeology in general. Because shipwrecks can be "time capsules" in a sense, artifacts from communities and cultures, transported on ships, can speak to the relative date of a specific type of ceramic, for example, as a means of determining the age of the wreck. They can also speak to the distribution and spread of goods through trade and cross-cultural influences. There are valid criticisms of Muckelroy's approach, which was seen to be too focused, in some opinions, on the processes that turned a ship into a shipwreck, and for being too narrow, but nearly a half century later, Muckelroy's book continues to guide the field, and not just in the study of shipwrecks. If Keith Muckelroy had not died in a tragic diving accident two years after the publication of *Maritime Archaeology*, I have no doubt he would have revised that book in response to new finds, approaches, and perspectives.

Maritime archaeology also focuses on the "people on the shore," as colleagues Ben Ford, Jessi Halligan, and Alexis Catsambis stress in the recently published *Our Blue Planet*.[29] It reflects where the "we" as maritime archaeologists, as well as our colleagues who work on all sorts of sites that happen to be underwater, are at this stage in the history of our discipline. It both reflects and builds on earlier works, such as Muckelroy's, while looking at broader questions, such as: When did maritime societies emerge in human history? (I suspect tens of thousands of years ago) What do shipwrecks tell modern society about larger trends in history, culture, and society? What do they reveal about trends in trade, war, colonization, immigration, and for me, the role that ships and shipping played in creating the global economy that emerged in the past few centuries?

The other great book that changed the way archaeologists approach shipwrecks (and related maritime sites) was Richard Gould's *Shipwreck Anthropology*. Gould argued for shipwreck research to be tied to other aspects of archaeology and anthropology, and not as means to "add to history." What then followed was more of an emphasis on human thought, belief, and spirituality, and not just physical "tangible" artifacts and sites. That introduced the concept of maritime cultural landscapes, articulated and published by Christer Westerdahl, based on his work in Scandinavia, and which has now been adopted by archaeologists globally.[30] Colleague Peter Campbell has noted that "it has grown so broad that anything can fit under the banner," and his point is well taken.[31] For those of us who study the maritime world and culture, the linking of a shipwreck to shore is exciting. That premise is exactly why I wrote this book.

Westerdahl was arguing—and many of us have engaged happily with the point he makes—that there was, for coastal communities, no hard line between the "wet" and "dry" parts of the planet. It goes beyond ships and shipwrecks, but also includes them as major elements in a landscape of imagination, belief, culture, and physical manifestations. You cannot talk about a ship without talking about the shipyard where it was built and repaired, the church where its sailors pray, the wharf at which it docks, loads, and unloads, the lighthouse that guides it in and out of harbor, the graveyard in which its dead are interred after a lifetime of labor or accident. That gets back to the central premise of archaeology. The things we build and use reflect who we are, as humans.

The idea that shipwrecks could reorient thinking to reject old assumptions, such as an ancient world disconnected from other cultures, was upended by better methods. The archaeological excavation of the Uluburun ship, previously mentioned in this chapter, is a perfect case in point. The ship sank sometime toward the end of the 14th century BC. To date, it is the oldest shipwreck scientifically excavated, a task that took 11 seasons, from 1984 to 1994, and 22,413 dives. The wreck yielded the fragmented remains of its wooden hull, but also a vast range of artifacts that ranged from raw materials—elephant and hippopotamus ivory, rare hard woods, copper and tin ingots, and cobalt-blue-, turquoise-, and lavender-colored glass ingots, ostrich egg shells, and turtle carapaces—to gold and silver jewelry from the Canaanite and Egyptian civilizations, amber beads from the Baltic, agate, quartz, glass beads, a range of Canaanite pottery, and an ornate ceramic drinking horn, as well as surviving traces of food, including almonds, figs, olives, pomegranates, pine nuts, grapes, and spices like black cumin, coriander, and sumac. What the diversity of the cargo showed was that a complex trade existed, linking goods from different regions and at least 10–12 separate cultures.[32] Loaded into the ship, these goods represented what in modern terms would be a "worldwide" trade network for the Late Bronze Age Mediterranean. More than an exchange of goods, it indicates cross-cultural contact, not only by sea, but by land and rivers, as goods came from the Levant, equatorial Africa, and possibly other areas throughout the Mediterranean.

This is exciting stuff, especially for those who would love to believe that a shipwreck is an "underwater Pompeii" under the illusion that a wreck is like a time capsule, sealed in mud, sand, and dark, cold water. That's not quite accurate. Some wrecks are at best a "cracked time capsule." Science means looking at the various processes of transformation from ship to shipwreck. When a ship was wrecked, depending on whether it hit rocks, a beach, or foundered in the deep, or if it exploded, burned, and sank, an archaeologist also needs to study wreck sites and their environments to determine what Muckelroy called "filters" and "scrambling devices." Filters were what the process of sinking and ongoing deterioration had removed from a wreck site. These could be organic materials such as sails, food, human bodies, or even the wood of the hull. They could be things taken off as a ship sank, or which were recovered from the wreck later. Scrambling devices were factors such as the act of sinking, and the movement of the seabed that removed artifacts from their original context. These could be the physical processes of sinking, or the shifting of seabed sand, silt, or even rocks moving in the current. That is why, for archaeologists, leaving a shipwreck site untouched and undisturbed before it is carefully mapped is a key part of shipwreck science and archaeology.

Throughout the history of shipwreck investigation, that CSI element of "touch nothing until it has been mapped" has been a point of tension in regard to questions of whether to dig or to recover when the technology was insufficient. That basic premise of archaeology has progressively advanced with shipwreck discoveries, with a key moment in regard to depth being the often-contentious issue of the *Titanic* site and the salvage of artifacts from the debris field outside of the main sections of the wreck. That question was resolved when, in 2010, the team I was part of conducted the first detailed survey of the wreck site of *Titanic*. AUVs mapped the site with sonar and then with cameras, not only the large sections of the wreck, the bow and stern, but also broken-off pieces of the hull, machinery, fittings, and luggage, which at 12,436 feet down was an engineering and scientific feat. It started to answer some key questions about the nature of the wreck of *Titanic* as an archaeological site. It was only when the mapping was completed that the science team realized that as much as 90 percent, maybe more, of the artifacts that sank with *Titanic* remained inside *Titanic*. Contrary to earlier assumptions, the scatter of many artifacts around the broken wreckage did not mean the ship had emptied out as it broke apart and fell to the bottom of the sea on the early morning of April 15, 1912.

In the four decades since Keith Muckelroy published *Maritime Archaeology*, the gaps in knowledge about seafaring, and ships and humanity's ongoing interaction with the sea, have been steadily filled in; the references in this book cover some key titles but by no means all of them. The reality is that an annotated bibliography of the field of just shipwreck/maritime archaeology would be a substantial volume. Archaeologists have learned more about prehistoric and indigenous craft, and the transition from the ancient to medieval to modern ships. They've also learned more about Asian craft and maritime activities, and ships and boats on inland waters. The approach to studying shipwrecks has also proved the value of sites that are derelict, abandoned craft. These are some of the gaps that are now being addressed, as well as a shift from studies of individual ships, especially "celebrity" wrecks like *Titanic* and others, to studies in which archaeology is a tool used to find and document them, but not conduct detailed excavation. The concept of site formation processes, initially cogently argued by Muckelroy, has expanded to a wide range of sites and locations, from beaches to the deep sea. It has grown to be post-colonial, as noted, and it has also started to address shipwrecks that were never wrecked, but simply abandoned, some of them in vast ship graveyards. These types of sites are more than a collection of ship types and representatives of trends in construction, propulsion, economies, and conflicts. They are also the focus of studies that tie them to larger areas of inquiry, such as abandonment, as well as reuse, recycling, and discard.

As the hunt for individual ships continues, the field has also evolved to where wrecks are studied as they fit into larger themes. Among these are themes that speak to shipwrecks that reflect the worst in human behavior. These include wrecks associated with the slave trade and wrecks from contexts where labor was stolen or coerced from other groups. Recent work by the Slave Wrecks Project (SWP), notably the wrecks of *Sao Jose* and *Clotilda*, previously discussed in Chapter 3, are examples of this. There are also powerful examples in the wrecks of ships involved in South Seas kidnapping of indigenous islanders, and in *La Union*, a steamer used to transport captive Maya to Cuban plantations, which was lost off Mexico. There has also been a shift to a more regional approach and to the application of theoretical perspectives, moving past the historical particularism that marked the origins of shipwreck archaeology, especially with the emphasis on iconic ship types and specific "celebrity" vessels. There is more emphasis on inclusivity, in all aspects, shifting from a colonialist approach to working with colleagues in other countries and cultures as they address their sites; that also means a shift beyond the old adage of "capacity building," the old colonialist phrase for training locals in other countries. Maritime and shipwreck archaeology has been challenged to be a more active participant in the dialogue on climate change, marine pollution, social issues, and how shipwrecks fit into the archaeology of the Anthropocene, as we've reached that stage where we no longer simply react to the planet (and its oceans), but they react to us. Sara Rich has clearly articulated a call to action in the face of climate change sea level rise: "maritime and nautical archaeologists have the potential to be at the forefront of discussions surrounding the realities of the Anthropocene."[33] She also argues that "[w]recked oil tankers globally, along with the desperate flight of climate refugees resulting in more wrecked boats and ships, heightens the urgency of maritime and nautical archaeologists' involvement at the levels of interdisciplinary academic discourse and public policy." I agree. One reason I joined the National Oceanic and Atmospheric Administration (NOAA) was to focus on climate change and polluting wrecks. In addition, I wanted to draw upon humanity's fascination with the subject and connect the wider public to shipwrecks and their histories.

A wide range of practitioners, however, essentially follow the dictates of their own curiosity, or look to shipwrecks as archaeological sites that answer more than historical questions. New technologies have evolved to make the process of survey, discovery, documentation, recovery, and preservation easier. As will be seen in the concluding chapter, society is now entering a phase in which increasing numbers of shipwrecks will be found and studied, and through that process, will tell detailed stories about humanity's interaction, over many millennia, with the world's waters.

8

Why Do We Care About Shipwrecks?

> I only cut up the boats. That was my focus, on the work, not about whether there was a problem with the bones.... We worked here all the time, so we didn't pay attention to them, whether there was bones or no bones it made no difference to us.
>
> —Souudin, Indonesian welder (quoted in Lamb 2018)

It's clear that I find shipwrecks fascinating, exciting to discover, and to explore, and that I am passionate about telling their stories. Why do I care, and why do I share? It's because of the history that they can represent, especially forgotten or inconvenient history. Shipwrecks I've been privileged to help find and learn from have revealed stories of extremely inhumane conditions inside the more or less intact slave hold of the schooner *Clotilda*, the heroic but doomed efforts of the crew of the U.S. Navy tug *Conestoga*, battered by waves and sinking, just three miles from safety, long before the call went out to try to find them when their ship did not arrive at port. I previously mentioned *Avanti* in the Florida Keys. I have strong memories of my first swim through its shattered wreckage, tracing the route of a small section of anchor chain and finding mute proof of a desperate act to save a ship that was too old, with too few crew, who were sent out into rough seas and died. Why? Because the owners, with marginal returns on their investment, cut corners. Revealing stories like these is one of the reasons why I seek out shipwrecks.

In other cases, it's the attraction of seeing a famous ship, especially one thought to be forever lost at extreme depths. I suspect that's one of the main reasons people find *Titanic* fascinating, and tourists have paid to visit in submersibles. *Titanic* is a ghost town, as James Cameron powerfully made clear to a larger audience not only in his original film, but also in the brilliant way he shared the wreck in his film *Ghosts of the Abyss*. I'm not alone in finding the film literally haunting. As Cameron's camera glides over the wreck, scenes from *Titanic* provide a ghostly view of the ship and those on board. It's powerful filmmaking. It also reflects the feelings that I know I had as I drifted over those decks in a submersible. In your mind's eye, you can almost picture *Titanic* as it was. James Cameron evokes that sense in *Ghosts*.

But I also know that why I care about shipwrecks may not be why you, as the reader, care about them. I've sat down with family members who only care about a wreck because it was the place where their loved one died. Whether there are any remains that exist within that hull or not, they saw that wreck as a tomb. My interest as a historian and archaeologist mattered to them because it had been motivation for us to find and explore that wreck, or at times, because we'd been able to add details that had gone down with the ship and crew. One example was the tug *Conestoga*, where we were able to push back against unfounded, false allegations that the tug was probably lost due to their inexperience or incompetence.

The reality of the loss was an old, worn-out vessel, and a hasty repair of the ship's pumps before the final voyage. The through-hull fittings in the hull for those pumps had rusted loose. Pounding in stormy seas, the repairs likely failed as the hull plating hadn't been replaced; new pump fittings had been bolted into rusted steel. The tug started to sink; the crew, as far as we could tell, had cast off the barge they were towing and headed for the lee of a nearby island. They were getting close to saving themselves when *Conestoga* went down. Strong waves, cold water, and sharks meant that no one survived to tell the crew's story. The discovery of the wreck, with the ability to tell their story, is what mattered to the family members I met with—not the history of the tug, or that it was inside a national marine sanctuary and a fish habitat. A few families did find the thought of the wreck, covered with anemones and full of fish, as a peaceful resting place that no one would disturb.

Their perspective, as well as mine, while not unique to either, is not universally shared. This book is about the different ways in which people have responded to shipwrecks as events as well as physical entities. The reasons why people care, if they care about shipwrecks, are just like nearly every other thing we interact with on this planet. There's agreement among some, but not others, about why a shipwreck is important. In other chapters, I've explored the conflict between treasure hunters and archaeologists and salvagers. Wreck divers who collect artifacts, a community who possess incredible technical diving skills, have seen themselves as rescuers of history that is about to vanish in the decay and collapse of a shipwreck. As much as archaeologists don't like that non-archaeologists have collected artifacts, a case can be made, as Tom Layton did with the wreck of the *Frolic*. If they hadn't collected and held on to their collections, who would have?

Would it have been "better" if maritime archaeologists had dived and excavated that wreck decades earlier? Probably, if they had the same level of experience and the level of training required to dive in the cove that the wreck sits in. It is like diving in a washing machine on high cycle, and on my first dive it spit me out on the beach after what felt like multiple summersaults. I return to *Frolic* not only because of Layton's incredible project's many permutations and legacies, but also because it became a moment where wreck divers and archaeologists learned more about each other, and how we are closer to each other than each side would have liked to admit. But fundamental differences in opinion remain between the two groups—wreck divers and archaeologists—although through moments like that and the *Robert J. Walker* project, mentioned previously, we're finding common ground—or water—and where we can and should work together.

It was my tenure with the National Oceanic and Atmospheric Administration (NOAA) that opened my eyes to other perspectives, especially with wrecks that were full of oil and posed an environmental threat. That threat was the most important reason to care, not their history. There are also wrecks in sanctuaries that are valued more as habitat for rare and endangered marine life, notably coral. My biologist colleagues' focus was on the wrecks as habitat, and they were wary of any actions that we as archaeologists might take that could harm the coral and other marine life. Given the sensitivity of reef and the coral die-offs happening due to climate change, as an archaeologist, I'd be one of the first to say that my research interests likely were not as compelling as saving the coral. As well, I know from my own diving and snorkeling that it's that marine life on the wreck that many others find appealing. Decades ago, after my first dive with my wife, when I asked why she hadn't followed me into some areas of the wreck (an 1860s iron-hulled paddle steamer), she remarked that she had stayed to watch the iridescent display of clouds of fish, their scales capturing the sunlight that filtered down, and the coral—not, as she put it, "all those rusty things."

So, why we care, *if* we care about shipwrecks, not surprisingly comes back to where you're coming from. Is it a tomb or the place where a loved one died? Is it an undersea refuge for endangered marine life in an era of clear and present danger from climate change? Is it a place to visit, to experience the weightlessness of a dive, and see something that not many other people get a chance to see? Is it a chance to rescue a bit of history, even if it's a rust-stained chinaware plate from deep inside a collapsing wreck? Is it a historic site, resting beneath the water, which connects us to past events, lives, and moments in time? Is it a "ghost town," eerie, compelling, and slightly frightening to explore? Is it a probable "slicking time bomb" full of trapped oil that may go from a series of leaks to a catastrophic release and cause ecological damage? Is it an obstacle, a derelict, or a nuisance that needs to be cleared from a harbor? Is it a possibility to make money from salvaging it, or is it a repository of lost treasures?

The various reasons why people care about shipwrecks can, but don't always mesh. Like many subjects, people disagree about shipwrecks. As I have said, in the decades of my career, the 20 years spent in federal service, both with the National Park Service and the National Oceanic and

Atmospheric Administration, taught me much about different values and viewpoints. It taught me that the shipwrecks and other sites in parks, monuments, and sanctuaries were not "mine," or the agency's, but belonged to the people. My job, along with my colleagues, was to work with the public to define what was important to protect, preserve, and make accessible where and when possible. I learned that I had to balance my interests and what I thought was important with those of others. For a federal park or sanctuary, the basic rule we followed was that whatever was done needed to have the least possible impact on the resource. That resource might be a reef or a wreck. The balance was easy when it came to things like not allowing people to collect coral or arrowheads from an archaeological site. It got tougher when we were looking at who could access areas or sites, and how.

Two of the most influential experiences in that government phase of my career were a project with the nonprofit Partners for Livable Places, and being one of the two National Park Service officials assigned the task of writing and implementing guidelines for the Abandoned Shipwreck Act of 1987. The first involved working closely with Robert "Bob" McNulty, who had founded Partners, which is now known as Partners for Livable Communities, in 1975. Bob ended up being one of the more influential people in my life when it came to learning how to work with others; as their website stresses, the ethos of Partners was an organic approach to equity, respect, education, and both local initiatives and civic responsibility as core values. It was about listening, recognizing that different perspectives, values, and approaches were always going to be there, no matter what the issue or the location of a community, and that people were key—they were the "greatest resource" for change.

After a series of workshops, Bob proposed and funded an important book, *Historic Shipwrecks: Issues in Management*. That book, completed in 1988, was a loosely bound, accessible document that could easily be pulled apart and photocopied. Different authors tackled the various chapters under Joy Waldron Murphy's editorial guidance. One of the chapters assigned to me discussed the multiple values of shipwrecks. That was the genesis of my sea change in thinking about shipwrecks. As

I learned about other perspectives and aspects of wrecks, it became clear that my views, strongly felt, about the historical and archaeological importance of wrecks were not universally shared by others.

The Abandoned Shipwreck Act of 1987, signed into law as we were completing the book, came at the end of contentious debate and lobbying by various interests, including divers and treasure hunters, to change or drop the bill. As a result of the hearings held to discuss the bill, Congress directed the National Park Service to develop guidelines to assist states and federal agencies in developing legislation and regulations to meet their new responsibilities. The law asserted that the federal government owned the nation's abandoned wrecks, and transferred that title and responsibility to the various states, except for areas managed by the federal government or naval and other military vessels. The law plainly stated that shipwrecks had multiple values, and no wreck should be set aside for any one purpose or any specific group. Everyone had to work together, and the guidelines would help that process. The guidelines, like the law itself, needed to stress that wrecks were educational, economic, and recreational opportunities, for fishermen, divers, historic preservationists, and archaeologists. They were to be treated as habitats for marine life. But the law also recognized the commercial value of wrecks for tourism, "other forms of commerce," and the option of "appropriate public and state sector recovery."

With my colleague Michelle Aubry, I was assigned the task of creating those guidelines after public, nationwide consultation. We held 11 public meetings in September and October 1988; I took some and Michelle the others; one of mine was at the heart of treasure hunting in Key West, Florida. We met with other federal agencies, state officials, and a number of interest groups. Forty-seven of the states sent in details on their existing programs to manage shipwrecks, and 130 organizations and individuals wrote to express their opinions and offer recommendations. Happening at the same time as the Partner for Livable Places initiative, that year of 1988 was one where I gained more than an education; I learned to listen better, appreciate other perspectives, and accept compromise as key to getting things done.

While one value or philosophy might prevail, dialogue and compromise meant that everyone was heard. The guidelines offered advice on creating government programs, paying for projects, how to survey and how best to identify, document, and evaluate the importance of shipwrecks, including working with volunteers to encourage public participation. We argued the need to make wrecks accessible to the public with underwater dive trails, mooring buoys for dive boats, and waterproof maps for the divers. The guidelines addressed creating underwater parks and preserves, but it also gave advice on public and private-sector recovery—meaning collecting artifacts as souvenirs, salvage of shipwrecks and treasure hunting, and archaeological excavation with the finds intended for museum display. Neither archaeologists nor treasure hunters and salvors were overjoyed, but we did what Congress had told us to do. If no one was fully happy, then our (to some people) imperfect guidelines did the job. It was an important step in my lifelong journey with shipwrecks. I could agree to disagree with people. I came to appreciate their positions and their passion for what they did, even when I had chosen a different path that did not involve treasure hunting or salvage. What was important to me was setting rules for approaches that removed part or all of a wreck. That included archaeological excavation, harbor clearance, the removal of trapped oil, cargo salvage, and treasure hunting. Does that protect all shipwrecks? Absolutely not. While harbor-improvement projects, dredging, treasure hunting, and climate change all have had negative impacts on shipwreck archaeology, one global activity has done even more harm. That's commercial fishing.

Commercial Fishing and Shipwrecks

On every dive that colleagues and I have made on shipwrecks, either shallow or deep, even before we came close to one, we knew we were close. That's because there were fish all around us or following the remotely operated vehicle. Fish love wrecks because wrecks get covered over time with marine life. As these wrecks literally transform into "reefs," they became habitat for a diverse array of marine life. These include fish, large and small, that use a wreck as a refuge—a place to hide from larger predators; and yes, that's why sharks also like shipwrecks. My marine biology colleagues refer to this as the "second life" for ships, and it is an appropriate term. The number and range of marine life that reside in and on wrecks are large as well as diverse; studies by scientists working with the Bureau of Ocean Energy Research (BOEM) have discovered that microbes attracted to wrecks can radiate out in a "halo" that can reach as far as 1,000 feet away from the wreck itself. Other colleagues have found that fish and other marine life migrate in the ocean, using shipwrecks much like long-distance truckers use rest stops.[1] Those who fish in the ocean know that fish love wrecks. Fishing charters advertise "outstanding fishing," or "gamefish galore," and they're not over-selling. Some troll near and around wrecks, risking a snag. Therein lies the problem for commercial fishers, namely snagging a wreck and losing not only the catch but also the gear. That's an even worse problem for fishing trawlers with big, expensive nets.

The same aggregation of fish around wrecks has led to decades of trawling. In some cases, the level of trawling over the years was so intense that wrecks were badly damaged to the point of destroying their cultural value or as sites for hook-and-line fishing. This may not be the intent of the trawler captains; repeated hits on a wreck full of fish ultimately meant no more fishing, and hang-ups and loss of gear are costly. But the real cost is damage to the environment and marine life. In October 2022, an article by Graham Readfearn in *The Guardian* reported that enough fishing net was lost each year to completely cover Scotland, or just over 30,000 square miles—*each year*. Enough fishing line was lost to circle Earth 18 times, along with 25 million pots and traps and 14 billion hooks. The nets and gear that snag on wrecks trap and kill the marine life that congregate on them. Known globally as "ghost nets," they can continue "ghost fishing" for years. They also trap larger creatures than fish, like turtles, dolphins, and whales. Marine debris programs and volunteers work to find and destroy ghost nets, and disentangle marine life wherever they can, but the problem is too big to effectively make a major change in the world's oceans.

There are moments of success that do speak to "think globally, act locally." In 2009, the steel trawler *Patriot* of Gloucester, Massachusetts, capsized and sank off Cape Cod in Stellwagen Bank National Marine Sanctuary. The captain and his father-in-law both died in the wreck. *Patriot* not only continued to catch fish in the net that spooled out from the wreck, but was also snagged by another fishing boat's net that was hung up and lost when that boat came too close to scoop up fish that congregated around the sunken *Patriot*. In 2020, the co-owner and operator of Northern Atlantic Dive Expeditions reported that the wreck and its ghost gear were a significant problem. Among the victims of its drifting nets was a gray seal. While the wreck is deep and in dangerously cold water, volunteer divers working with the NOAA team from the sanctuary cut free over 500 pounds of nets and gear in two days of hard work. The story of *Patriot* is a reminder of two important facts about fishing shipwrecks.

Fishing has been and remains a deadly business. Fishing is a vital part of the global economy, as more than 3 billion people rely on sea harvests as their major source of protein. While statistics are difficult to track, the United Nations estimates that fishing-related fatalities in the world total some 32,000 a year. While many of these include local and indigenous fishers working from small boats, or workers who die on board or were swept overboard and lost in heavy seas, the statistics also include fishing vessels like *Patriot*. A U.S. Coast Guard survey of fishing vessel casualties between 1992 and 2007 revealed that in that 16-year period, in the United States, 1,903 fishing vessels were lost, along with 934 lives, or on average, 119 vessels a year. The wreck of *Andrea Gail*, subject of the powerful bestselling book and movie *The Perfect Storm*, is one of many fishing boat losses, and evidence of a constantly recurring tragedy that impacts fishing families and communities.

The importance of fishing as an economic necessity that places those lives at risk also leads to overfishing of certain species, with occasional fishery "collapses."[2] It destroys older shipwrecks that do not survive the impact of a trawl. My colleague Michael Brennan was the lead author on a study of bottom trawl fishing damage to ancient wrecks in the Aegean and the Black Seas based on surveys done by the science team on board the E/V *Nautilus* of Dr. Robert Ballard's Ocean Exploration Trust between 2009 and 2012. In all, they examined 45 wrecks, with return visits to one site to see if damage was repetitive, and if so, to quantify it. The wrecks, as Brennan notes, "are part of a modern submarine landscape that is heavily damaged by trawls, which also remove sediment and smooth out natural features of the seabed."[3] All of the wrecks showed varying degrees of damage, some of it extensive, resulting in the destruction of those wrecks.

The fishermen who did the trawling, at times in restricted areas (in one case in a zone with submarine cables clearly marked on the charts with a "no trawling" restriction), were not only blind to the other values of these wrecks, which they knew were down there. The loss of the wrecks and the smoothing of the bottom destroy its viability as a habitat. A comparative study by Jason Krumholz, working with Michael Brennan, found that wrecks that had been impacted by trawling and were heavily damaged had on average 55 percent less species richness, 57 percent less abundance, and 41 percent lower diversity than wrecks that had not been impacted. The problem, as quantified in this study, is widespread.[4] It is, in fact, global. It has been known for some time. As early as 2004, the Pew Charitable Trusts issued an opinion piece by Joshua Reichert that called for action to "stop the trawlers that wreck the ocean floor." How deep? Brendan Foley of Woods Hole Oceanographic Institution noted in 2012 that he'd seen sites hit in 500 meters of water, with a survey off Malta finding no wrecks, only a seabed marked by regular furrows as if it had been plowed. They also found evidence of dragging nets as deep as 1,000 meters.

The damage from trawling can be substantial, even to more modern, ruggedly built metal-hulled ships. The reason for that is a single invention that changed the face of the fisheries by mechanizing the thousands-year old technology of hauling and retrieving fishing nets. In 1953, Croatian-American fisherman Mario Puretić of San Pedro, California, patented a large pulley, coated with rubber, attached to a winch now known as the "Puretic Block." By rigging the nets, until then hauled by hand, to the block, the new mechanized system revolutionized fishing. Larger, longer nets that went deeper, with nets now made of nearly unbreakable synthetic materials, led to an explosive growth in fishing as the Puretic Block's use spread around the world. Within five years of the invention, over a thousand fishing boats were outfitted with it.[5]

The results were dramatic for the fishermen, who were able to make even more money. They also lost money, because nets got snagged on reefs and wrecks. Those of us who dive have many stories of wrecks covered with nets. In a previous chapter I talked about a trawler working at a 1,000-foot depth whose nets swept over a Japanese shipwreck, likely dating to the 1700s, whose wooden hull had deteriorated, leaving a mound of ceramic *tsuba* (jars). That mound of jars made a perfect habitat for fish, and so he kept trawling at that site, even as his nets snagged pots as well as fish, gradually removing the wreckage that had formed that deep-water "reef" of piles of pottery. It no longer exists.

There are a number of other examples of wrecks where their transformation from ship to fish habitat made them a target for fishermen. I've been told through the years that on any coast, anywhere in the world, if you wanted to find a shipwreck, ask the local fishermen. They often kept meticulous logs of snags and "hang-ups" where the fishing was good, and they could tell when it was a wreck, not a reef, when wood or other artifacts came up in the net. That's why, with few exceptions, expeditions I've been on that have "discovered" shipwrecks in relatively shallow water only hundreds of feet or at times deeper, almost always see nets on those wrecks. One of the deepest I've seen is 2,400 feet deep, off the coast of Half Moon Bay, California. There, the wreck of the carrier USS *Independence*, scuttled in 1951, just two years before the invention of the Puretic Block, is covered by thick trawl nets, with portions of the steel flight decks peeled back by nets that snagged on it before tearing free of the rest of the trawl. Another example I've seen close up was on the previously mentioned wreck of the steam freighter *Coast Trader*, sunk by a Japanese submarine attack in June 1942. Lying several hundred feet deep in the Straits of Juan de Fuca, off the Pacific coast of British Columbia and Washington, it is not far from where fishermen reported snagging another Japanese drift wreck. I wasn't surprised to see that *Coast Trader*'s superstructure was torn free by nets. Broken trawl gear and nets lie wedged in and draped around the wreck. These examples of wrecks damaged or destroyed by trawls are not isolated events. They happen all over the world in untold numbers.

Salvagers, Shipwrecks, and Impoverished Communities

The wreck of *Coast Trader* is a reminder that the two world wars of the 20th century sank over 25,000 ships, many of them merchant vessels targeted by submarine warfare. For the families of those who died in each sinking, these wrecks are tombs, and some of them, like the liner *Lusitania*, are famous because of the horrific deaths of innocent non-combatants; 1,197 people died in the sinking in May 1915. Three years after the loss of *Titanic*, a massive loss of life, families were again perishing, this time to a deliberate action the world viewed as "barbarous." It was shocking. *Lusitania* was and remains, more than a century later, a symbol of the horrific aspect of unrestricted submarine warfare and the toll of modern warfare, notably the death of non-combatants and innocents. While the wreck of *Lusitania* may be a symbol of tragedy, and a tomb, as many bodies were never found, it was also seen as a legitimate focus of salvage efforts starting in the 1930s that continued until a few years ago. Salvage of *Lusitania*, however, while upsetting to some observers, including heritage authorities in Ireland, has been legally conducted, as the British government sold the wreck to the salvagers.

This is a common practice. Years ago, I served as the archaeologist to confirm the identity of the wreck of *Carpathia*, the ship that rescued *Titanic*'s survivors. It was also sunk off Ireland, by the submarine U-55, in July 1918. Clive Cussler sponsored the successful search and discovery of the wreck in 2000. Following the discovery and our conclusive identification, the British government sold the salvage rights to the wreck at auction. The salvage that followed, as I understand it, was for selected artifacts from a famous ship. That's not what has been happening in the Pacific, however, as Chinese-sponsored salvagers have targeted the sunken warships of World War II in defiance of international law. There is another aspect of this story, though, that also speaks to the concept of the "bounty of the sea," especially for impoverished local communities.

Thousands of wartime wrecks were built of what is now known as "pre-atomic steel." That steel is valuable because modern, post-1945 manufactured steel contains traces of radioactive fallout from decades of atmospheric nuclear testing. Uncontaminated steel, as well as lead, is needed for instruments that detect ionizing radiation, known as particle detectors. Perhaps the most famous example of a particle detector is the Geiger counter. Low-particle metal is also needed for specialized medical equipment. The quest for these metals led to illicit endeavors that raised ancient Roman anchor stocks (the weights that kept a wooden anchor submerged) in violation of antiquities laws, and melting them down. But not all such uses are illicit. The National Museum of Sardinia in Cagliari transferred lead ingots from a Roman shipwreck to the Italian National Institute of Nuclear Physics to aid in particle physics experiments in 2011. This move upset a number of my archaeological colleagues. The transfer was legal, but for archaeologists the question was whether it was ethical. But was the question one of ethics or the greater good? My colleague, archaeologist Elena Perez-Alvaro, notes that the scientific use was not a "commercial use" as defined by the UNESCO Convention for the Protection of Underwater Cultural Heritage, so the use of the ancient lead in the lab falls somewhere in between; ethical for scientists, unethical for archaeologists. What is needed, she argues, is for clear protocols and dialogue to determine the better use of the lead.

That's not the issue with the warships being scrapped in the Pacific and the South China Sea by the Chinese and their proxies. There is no surgical precision in these salvages; entire wrecks of massive warships are vanishing from the seabed. Large salvage ships using large cranes grappled and lifted chunks of the warship wrecks after either blasting or cutting them apart, and dumped them onto barges. This continued until dozens of wrecks had been completely salvaged. This large-scale effort reportedly began decades ago. While the governments whose ships were salvaged have complained, because they see these as sunken warships entitled to legal protection as war graves or as underwater cultural heritage, the salvage continues. Malaysia seized the Chinese salvage vessel *Chuan Hong 68* in May 2023 for allegedly working over the wrecks of HMS *Repulse* and HMS *Prince of Wales*, sunk off Singapore in December 1941 with hundreds of lives lost. The wrecks were both full of human bones, according to divers, one of whom told me of his dive inside them. Images released by the Malaysian Coast Guard showed piles of rusted, crumpled steel and unexploded naval ammunition lying on the deck of the Chinese barge. Malaysian authorities ultimately released *Chuan Hong 68*, but boarded it once more in early July 2023 on suspicion of ongoing salvage activities, and then released it. As the end of 2024 approaches, *Chuan Hong 68* is apparently working at sea near Singapore, according to marine traffic trackers.

Image 8.1. Ceramic artifacts from the Belitung shipwreck in the Asian Civilisations Museum in Singapore, 2015.

Photograph by Jack Lee/Wikimedia Commons.

The big issue of the scrapping of military shipwrecks is not only their status as war graves, but also that most nations go to court to protect them as "sovereign" property—the same legal status as an embassy or a consulate on foreign soil. Defiance of that legal status by Chinese companies who have erased every trace of those wrecks has apparently not resulted in any litigation, or any reported diplomatic complaints to China's government that I'm aware of. Sometimes these types of communiques are discrete. However, the British Royal Navy did send survey vessels to assess the damage, and reportedly monitors wreck sites via satellite. Britain, along with the United States, Australia, and the Netherlands, has "expressed concern" and urged Indonesian and Malaysian officials to take stronger steps, which Malaysia did in 2023. Behind the headlines, what is likely happening is a pragmatic dance with formal statements, expressions of disapproval, and frankly, token actions like boarding *Chuan Hong 68*, and then letting it go.

China is a major power with a growing presence in the region. It is not in the long-term strategic interests of Indonesia, Malaysia, or other regional governments to substantively intervene in a dispute over long-dead sailors or rusting hulks. While the United States and other nations are also substantial powers, they are farther away by air and sea than China. And in regard to the British and Dutch, there is lingering unhappiness over colonialism and its legacies. Some also remember that postwar, many of the shallow-water Japanese warships that had been sunk were raised and scrapped, including those that were war graves, and there was no complaint from any government. In Indonesian culture, the disposition of human remains and the concept of death are different than those of the Western world. There is also the fact that for impoverished people living in coastal villages, the business of scrapping the warships represents a bounty from the sea. Families in these villages see a chance to earn more than what they can through subsistence fishing. The systematic reduction of chunks of warships, even when teeth and personal effects are found wedged in mud-filled dents and cracks or collapsed sections of deck, do not involve their ancestors. The work they get from the Chinese scrappers makes a positive difference in their daily lives.

A similar case with a far older find comes from Vietnam, and a village far up the Mekong that I visited my late friend George Belcher as we followed up on a tale of an amazing discovery in the river. Working from small, open boats, villagers work as sand dredgers, using small pumps to lift sand into a second boat. Once full, they sell that load of sand to a broker who shifts the cumulative boatloads of sand onto a small barge. He then takes his barge to the local concrete plant and sells it. These details are important. The people of that village live hand to mouth. When their dredging found a submerged boat-shaped coffin dating back more than 2,000 years, they raised it, finding a variety of stone and bronze artifacts. They knew that these had value to relic sellers. The artifacts were bought by a local man, with a connection to an antiquities seller in Saigon, who paid the sand dredgers US$5–20 for various artifacts, which was equal to months of income for them. The dealer in Saigon paid him several hundred dollars for the artifacts. She then sold "the best" to an antiques house in Hong Kong for a few thousand dollars. They auctioned them off in Hong Kong for far more than that. As for the boat coffin, the villagers did not waste the wood, cutting it into strips to form a pen for pigs. The value of the find for the sand dredgers was utilitarian, as well as a rare, maybe once in a lifetime, jackpot—not an archaeological discovery.

A Case Study in Conflicting Values—*Sub Marine Explorer*

A different take on differing values comes from the Islas Perlas (the Pearl Islands) in Panamá and the small island known as Isla San Telmo, where a strange craft appeared with the daily tide fall (which in the Bay of Panamá averages 10 feet, or 3 meters). This strange craft and its story entered my life decades ago, and it remains one of the most fascinating wreck projects I have ever worked on. It was said to be a Japanese World War II midget submarine, scuttled after an aborted attack on the Panamá Canal at the end of the war, but archaeological study revealed it to be a

19th-century submersible, *Sub Marine Explorer*. Designed in 1864 and constructed in 1865–1866, it was a complex cast and wrought iron craft designed by German American engineer Julius H. Kroehl and built at the Brooklyn shipyard of Ariel Patterson. Essentially an "auto-mobile diving bell," *Explorer* was a multi-chambered craft with a complex system of water ballast tanks, a reinforced chamber for pressurized air, and a working or crew compartment. Valves allowed the ballast chamber to flood; pressurized air from the main air chamber would expel ballast water to allow the craft to rise. The pressurized air was also used to equalize the pressure inside the working chamber to match that of the ambient pressure of the water at *Explorer*'s operating depth. This allowed the crew to open large hatches on the bottom of the craft to work on the seabed.[6]

Kroehl designed the craft for military use, but the end of the Civil War led the U.S. Navy not to buy *Explorer*. Kroehl's backers, a group of businessmen mainly from New York, incorporated as the Pacific Pearl Company, sent the craft and Kroehl to Panamá. There, in the Bay of Panamá, *Explorer* was to be put to work harvesting pearls from the seabed. The Panamá pearl fishery, known and exploited since prehistoric times, had been heavily fished by enslaved divers since colonial times. By the mid-19th century, the pearl fishery was barely productive. Kroehl's backers were convinced that Yankee ingenuity and an industrial approach would reap benefits. *Explorer* was truly revolutionary and an engineering landmark. It also was a failure. Julius Kroehl died not long after arriving in Panamá, reassembling *Explorer*, and taking it on test dives that were also public demonstrations. His death from fever left the submersible stranded on a Panamanian beach, with no one else knowledgeable enough to operate its complex mechanisms. When a new engineer arrived in 1869, he nearly lost the craft in a dangerous deep dive, and then, with a crew of locals, went deep and exhaustively harvested oysters. They reached beyond the limits of the breath-holding free divers who had worked those waters for decades.

The 1869–1870 season saw *Explorer* effectively wipe out a generation of oysters, leaving an even more depleted pearl fishery. It also appears to have crippled and possibly killed some of its crew. Taking the craft down to depths, pressurizing it, and then working at that pressure for hours, and then surfacing without depressurization, exposed the crew to decompression sickness, or the "bends." This can be painful, crippling, and even fatal. Newspaper accounts of the dives refer to the crew suffering from "fever," which may mean they were experiencing some of the symptoms of a disease only then being discovered by workers laboring in pressurized caissons building the Eads Bridge in St. Louis and the Brooklyn Bridge.

Explorer was essentially abandoned on the beach, where the locals warned any passing visitor with an interest to stay outside, explaining that those who entered would die. Others had salvaged from the wreck; a wire rope wrapped around the conning tower showed someone had tried to tow it off the beach. Damage at the stern revealed that at one time the craft had been blasted open to salvage its internal machinery, which included a huge bronze flywheel and brass pumps. Rust and floating logs hitting it at high tide had started to peel open its compressed air chamber. Embedded in the sand, *Explorer* was now more a reef and a refuge for marine life than a machine. It was also a missing link in the family tree of early submarines. As an "auto-mobile," or human-propelled diving bell, *Explorer* was the world's first successful deep-diving submersible. Its form and technology were more suggestive of submarines built at the end of the 19th and the start of the early 20th century than during the Civil War. Its only flaw was the result of Kroehl's lack of understanding of the effects of prolonged exposure to pressure on the human body. It was not until 1907 that the nature of decompression sickness was fully understood and the process of slow decompression to prevent it was published. News of the identification of *Explorer* made international headlines and led to a decade of expeditions to partially excavate, thoroughly document, and reconstruct *Explorer* on paper. The work we did on the wreck in the early 2000s resurrected the intricacies and engineering of the craft, working from scant traces, broken pieces, and a few written accounts left by an inventor who was paranoid that his invention would be copied and his ideas stolen. It was accomplished through creating three-dimensional scans and detailed engineering drawings, the latter now preserved in the Historic American Engineering Record in the Library of Congress. It has been the subject of blogs, online stories, and an online paper model that anyone can download, print, cut out, and tape together.

Explorer is also one of those shipwrecks that reflects the many values associated with wrecks. It has been the subject of a number of artistically arranged photographs and paintings, and it inspired two separate television documentaries. One was for National Geographic, and the other, originally in German for *Der Spiegel*, was also produced in English for the Smithsonian Channel. It has inspired a German-language semi-fictional account of the life of Julius Kroehl, who thanks to the discovery is now revered as a favorite son of Klaipeda, formerly Memel, in Lithuania, where he was born in 1820.

Explorer's role as a muse continued with a Chicago indie folk-rock band formed by Steve Hendershot and his wife, Clare. As Steve explained in a band blog, the story of *Explorer* inspired not only their first song, "Pacific Pearl Company 1869," on their debut album *Behold the Bitter Monument*, but also the name of the band, "The Diving Bell":

> The song itself is largely faithful to the historical narrative, not because I set out to write a journalistic song—I get enough of that elsewhere—but because the actual story of Julius Kroehl and his craft are fascinating on their own and don't need embellishment. Here you have a technological marvel, the masterwork of a desperate inventor in search of a defining moment. And you have a surprise twist: that even though Kroehl's submarine represents a crucial innovation, it exists for a commercial purpose—pearl fishing—for which it is pretty much a bust.[7]

While the story of the sub resonated, the next to final lyrics are powerful: "The craft is a failure, and the crew disperse. Just the captain remains, greeting the wreck each day as the tide falls."

The legacy of *Sub Marine Explorer* is also reflected in its importance to the community that lies a few miles away, across the Bahia San Telmo that separates Isla San Telmo from Isla del Rey. La Esmeralda is a small, isolated community, reached only by water, with a population of roughly 500 people. It was the pearl divers of La Esmeralda who told visitors that all who entered the sub died. Their ancestors may have been hired to work in the craft in 1869 and suffered. As word of the craft's true identity made international news, the sub took on new meaning for the community. That was underscored by increasing visitors, all eager to be taken to see *Explorer* when the tide fell. *Explorer* was a relic that they could take visitors to and tell its story from their perspective. Even that, in the end, failed. *Explorer* is now falling apart, likely from both the fallen trees that drift in and strike its corroding shell, from well-meaning tourists who now clamber atop it, and the ongoing corrosion that eats away the metal. But the story of the submarine, now known around the world, also inspires visits to the community where the pearl divers show their skill and sell the pearls they harvest. The machine built to replace them wiped out the pearl beds, and it now crumbles.

There has been renewed interest in "saving" *Explorer* and taking it away from the islands. I long ago made the decision to stop pursuing funds to recover it. The goal to conserve it and place it in a museum either in Panamá or back in the United States made no sense to me. It had been extensively documented. However, historic, archaeological, and cultural values notwithstanding, *Explorer*'s most relevant value was as a beacon for tourism. *Explorer* was left to the tides to rust in peace and provide extra income to La Esmerelda's people. While it is starting to fall apart, it remains of value to La Esmeralda until it is no more. This did not compromise the historical and archaeological values of *Explorer*. It has been studied extensively, documented, and shared with the world in other ways, without having to be taken away from the setting of its brief use and abandonment, and it is now, I believe, inexorably a part of that landscape. I agree with Steve when he says, "Behold the Bitter Monument."

Treasure Hunting and Commercial Treasure Salvage

Having addressed a situation in which archaeological and historical values might have been in conflict with tourism values, and one in which the "compromise" was not going to an extreme, it's time to focus on another conflict in values where there has been decades of intense debate: treasure hunting. Finding a lost treasure is a common dream, a recurrent theme in fiction, and something romantically portrayed in popular culture. One of the most common questions maritime archaeologists are asked, when they explain what they do, is "Have you ever found any treasure?" Indiana Jones, Lara Croft, Long John Silver, Jack Sparrow, and a host of other characters have helped reinforce that perception.

As the modern era dawned and technology allowed easier access underwater, the birth of deep-water recovery through the use of "submarine armor" and diving bells also gave rise to treasure fever. Nineteenth-century accounts in the press included tales of expeditions and partnerships being mounted. "Captain" William H. Taylor, America's first successful hard-hat diver, promoted his newly patented "submarine armor" in an 1837 treatise, *New and Alluring Sources of Enterprise in the Treasures of the Sea, and the Means of Gathering Them*, offering his services and describing himself as "most particularly familiar with the Venezuelan coast, where both pearls and rich wrecks abound."[8]

Two decades later, Brutus de Villeroi, a French inventor who immigrated to the United States in 1856, announced his intent to take his newly constructed submarine to salvage. The targets were the steamer *Central America*, which foundered off the coast of the Carolinas in a hurricane in September 1857, and HMS *De Braak*, a British sloop-of-war, said to have carried treasure, that was lost in a storm off Lewes, Delaware, in 1798.[9] Many of these early endeavors were more or less contemporary marine salvage instead of treasure hunting. To return to an earlier point, modern treasure hunting is not maritime salvage. The lines can be blurred, especially in media and marketing campaigns, but salvage is a means to return goods or commodities—or a ship—back into the stream of commerce from which they were associated. A marine salvor traditionally returns a vessel to service, or raises a cargo of ore, ingots, or oil, or specie to the government or banking system which minted or coined it. Specie or valuables made centuries or millennia ago, if recovered, can only be returned to one form of commerce, the antiquities market.

Treasure hunting that focused on older wrecks came into being in the post–World War II era as scuba diving opened the ocean to increasing numbers of people. Some were enthralled with not having to be a professional hard-hat diver or marine salvor to find riches beneath the sea. The late Peter Throckmorton, one of the pioneers of underwater archaeology, traced the "modern" treasure-hunting boom to Florida in the 1960s as beachcombing revealed gold coins from a Spanish fleet lost in a major hurricane in 1715. Romanticized and heralded in *National Geographic* and on television, the thought of instant riches appealed to the American vision of no barriers to fortune if you had a willingness to work hard and a touch of luck. In time, treasure hunting morphed into a larger industry, backed by investors and lawyers who fought to establish their clients' rights to wrecks. By the 1980s, Throckmorton reported that about 25 companies were promoting their ventures and garnering a total of some $100 million. From Florida, the shipwreck treasure-hunting industry spread to other parts of the United States. From there, it spread globally, especially to the Caribbean, the Pacific and Southeast Asian waters, and then to the high seas.

Treasure hunting was especially destructive, particularly in its earlier days. Rather than focus on the slow, meticulous scientific approach of archaeology, treasure hunters would smash through a wreck, seeking a quick profit from gold, silver, jewels, and collectable objects. In addition to the recovery of specie, bullion, or jewelry, artifacts of archaeological value were given away, or sold at auction without conserving archaeological information. These might be a rusted ship's fastening, a corroded ship's bell, navigational instruments, or ceramics. The sale of these artifacts, abetted by major auction houses, only encouraged the creation of companies and partnerships that sought to profit from shipwreck recovery.

What confounded and angered the archaeological community was that the introduction of shipwreck materials into the global commercial market under salvage law had created a double standard. There were laws protecting archaeological sites on land from illicit trafficking. The double standard now existed because both the law and public belief treated a shipwreck site differently from an archaeological site on land because of the application of salvage law and the law of finds. That ancient law sought to return cargoes to the flow of commerce, and to rescue and return ships to service. It continues to focus in that fashion, as discussed earlier. I personally do not have an ethical problem in salvagers recovering lost rare metals, or gold and silver, from 20th-century wrecks if it is done under the terms of the law, with the owners or a court's approval, is sensitive in regard to human remains and the feelings of families, and it isn't called archaeology.

But the antiquities market offers artifacts for sale; some if it is legal, representing items from the past recovered either before or in the early days of archaeology, or in accord with the laws of different nations and the international community. Some of it is illicit, taken through theft from museums or other collectors, looting archaeological sites, or by bribing officials. It is an international problem, and it also includes both national and international bodies of water. It is also a growing problem that some, such as the United Nations and international heritage organizations, as well as professional archaeological organizations, are working hard to combat in the face of intensifying pressure within and outside of the archaeological community to rationalize or accept the loss of sites. In this, it is important to note that no matter where one's views fall on the spectrum of what should happen to sites, including shipwrecks, the consensus is that there is no consensus.

There are a variety of reasons for this. Archaeology focuses on obtaining the maximum amount of information from the traces of the past, using scientific methods, and recovering all available information. However, total excavation of a site is uncommon. This may be a pragmatic decision, as in available time and resources, but it can also be a professional decision to wait for as yet undiscovered techniques or technologies to be introduced. A few cases in support of the latter are the more recent development of highly accurate underwater mapping by both acoustics and lasers, which replaced earlier hand measurement by stretching waterproof measuring tapes across wreck sites. Another was the realization, previously noted, that whatever lay preserved inside ancient amphorae was also archaeological evidence, and the subsequent realization that even if an amphora was found "empty," ancient DNA fragments could be recovered that revealed the original contents.[10] These and other developments in the methods, techniques, and technology of underwater archaeology are part of the argument for leaving sites alone, or simply testing them through partial excavation.

What archaeologists have observed over the years is that when the motive is profit, archaeology takes a back seat. This isn't a simple assertion, but an observation based on fact; as archaeologist Peter Campbell has noted, "if you are able to sell silver coins, would you spend an equal amount of time recording wooden timbers?"[11] Most would not, and the history of many shipwreck treasure-hunting operations is one in which the quest to make money from a shipwreck through treasure hunting has irreparably destroyed any other value associated with that wreck.

In conclusion, conflicting needs and values have always swirled around shipwrecks. They mean different things to different people, and in a commercial sense, an opportunity to make money often assumes paramount importance. That comes whether it is for a family seeking to put food on the table, for a village to prosper with a chance "jackpot" find, for a commercial fisherman to keep shaving close to a wreck to get as many fish as possible, or for a treasure salvager to seek bullion, coins, or antiquities that will reward shareholders, company officers, and those who work for them. Confronted by a flash of gold, many people will overlook other values, the perceptions or needs of others, and simply focus on the treasure and profit.

Conclusion

Shipwrecks in the 21st Century

The deep liquid void is still a great enigma.
—Clive Cussler, 2002

After five decades of my ongoing interaction with maritime history and archaeology, I've seen incredible technological progress, increased public interest, and projects that now span the global ocean. The projects now include wrecks at depths that, when I started, were as accessible as a voyage into deep space. And yet, humanity does not know as much as we could, or should, about the deep, even in the high-tech world of the 21st century. The planet's final frontier, the oceans, are largely unexplored, while we have highly accurate maps of the surfaces of the Moon and Mars. Even in areas where the ocean floor has been mapped, the data in a number of cases are old, have low resolution, or are "spotty." One example is found in the cumulative online database of archived sonar data for the Canadian Arctic. Not long ago, in going through that data, I discovered that they were limited to a few areas. Much of what is in the database are single track lines laid down as sonar-equipped vessels transited the Northwest Passage. The depths of the Arctic Ocean are not alone in being uncharted, or charted with older systems that mean the data are less accurate. It's like trying to make out details in an old photograph taken with a shaky camera. Many people are probably not aware of Seabed 2030. Co-sponsored by the Nippon Foundation and GEBCO (General Bathymetric Chart of the Ocean), it is a global, cooperative initiative to complete the high-resolution mapping of the seabed for the benefit of all humankind. The biggest benefit would be gaining a complete understanding of the planet, as much of it, below the water, remains unknown. Seabed 2030 began in 2017, with the goal of completing the mapping by 2030. That digital map will be freely available to all. In June 2024, Seabed 2030 completed mapping an area of the seabed equal to the size of the entire European Union. That brought the total amount of the seabed that has been mapped to modern high-resolution to just over 26 percent. Are they finding shipwrecks? Yes.

Work on shipwrecks, especially those in deep water, is increasingly part of dedicated science missions that employ the latest technology to reach into the depths. That technology provides instant public access to sites during the process of discovery, examination, and analysis through telepresence via satellite connection. It also provides for highly accurate documentation to virtually raise and make wrecks accessible without the costs of recovery. The pace of shipwreck discovery is rapidly growing, so that by mid-2024, it seems only a few days pass before the media announce another find. Scanning, documenting, and leaving alone those shipwrecks that we can—with the ability to reassess if or when intervention, such as detailed archaeology and recovery, is merited or needed—may be the path forward for archaeologists.

Any work that we do as archaeologists or marine scientists with shipwrecks, however, needs to be publicly accessible and relevant. What makes it relevant is open and transparent study, and for scientists to freely share what they are seeing and learning in plain language. Technical reports, articles, and books are the stuff of which scientific careers are made, and peer-reviewed science informs and advances the exchange of knowledge. But to simply leave it to an article or a book that a few hundred—or a few dozen—colleagues might read is not enough. Working with educators, journalists, using methods like telepresence and live-streamed exploration, has and will continue to engage the public. If a social scientist doesn't bring the interested public along with them on the journey toward knowledge, sharing both the excitement of discovery and of learning something new, then they have failed to meet a key goal in terms of social responsibility.

Shipwrecks open a door to a place where questions are posed and answered, inspiring curiosity for not only the imagination, but also the determination to explore. It was curiosity and other human desires that have taken humanity to sea and left the record of our history, some of it forgotten, that now lies written in lost ships. So much of our past is tied to our connections to the ocean and the waters of Earth. As humanity faces new challenges, learning from the past, through the study of shipwrecks, is key to helping place current struggles in context as we face the future.

Extending the Range: The Rise of Deep-Water Research

By comparison to the unmapped ocean floor elsewhere in the world, there are more detailed data and mapping of the seabed of the Gulf of Mexico and the North Sea because of industry-led surveys for subsea oil and gas. However, much of that data is proprietary, but because of U.S. federal law protecting cultural resources, the industry provides the nation's stewards, the Bureau of Ocean Energy Management (BOEM) and its regulatory compliance sister agency, the Bureau of Safety and Environmental Enforcement (BSEE), with the data for each known or suspected shipwreck or natural features. But many of these sites are "uncharacterized." They are provocative ship-shaped sonar targets, or blurry shapes that *might* be a wreck. In some cases, features found in these surveys are analyzed by contractors working for the industry. As part of their work, BOEM and BSEE also fund shipwreck studies and work cooperatively with other partners to characterize targets. This has led to over a hundred deep-sea shipwreck discoveries in the Gulf of Mexico alone.

The requirements of federal law and the diligence of the two federal agencies, combined with the cooperation of the offshore oil and gas industry and the work of contractors in the Gulf of Mexico, can be seen as a model. Industry avoids costly negative interactions with important shipwrecks or significant natural features, the public interest is upheld at low cost to the taxpayer, and the ocean floor and that which it holds is being explored. The Gulf is an energy frontier, representing 17% of U.S. offshore oil production and 5% of offshore natural gas. There are over 1,880 facilities and just over 17,500 miles of undersea pipeline. In addition to the hundred some discoveries, hundreds of other suspected and likely shipwreck targets have been avoided by the deep-sea work of the industry. The work in the Gulf also highlights a growing trend in ocean exploration and interaction with shipwrecks. Since the last decade of the 20th century, BOEM-funded, telepresence-assisted multidisciplinary research, often using "rides of convenience" with NOAA's ocean exploration-funded cruises, have seen scientists conduct deep-sea research projects that treat archaeology, biology, and geochemistry as equal with regard to project goals. By integrating research efforts, new insights and discoveries have been made. These endeavors and the discoveries could only have been achieved through this type of integrated multidisciplinary research. These missions are the true integration of approaches and perspectives that work with multiple values represented by looking at wrecks as more than undersea "time capsules."

Shipwrecks are not time capsules, nor are they completely perfect underwater versions of Pompeii. A new branch of study is defining a better sense of how a ship transitions from being a floating vessel to a wreck. Keith Muckelroy, as I've noted, was one of the first to address this in the 1970s. His approach to defining the landscape and environment of a wreck site was a key step in taking shipwreck investigation in a new direction. Rather than assigning a greater value to a site based on "intactness," or as a pristine, sealed time capsule, archaeologists came to realize that sites could yield detailed information even if scattered. This work started with shallower wrecks, like the Spanish Armada wrecks broken up on rocks, ships cast up on beaches, or violently disassembled by a storm or a battle at sea. The opening of the deep-water shipwreck frontier in the 1980s after the discovery of *Titanic* demonstrated what lay down there could at times be a "time capsule," and discoveries since of more modern vessels, especially warships from World War II, have yielded images of lost ships and aircraft, still painted, their names even spelled out. This has fed excitement over these "ghost towns" in the dark. Repeated visits to *Titanic*, in particular, have documented change, some of it dramatic deterioration.

What is also becoming apparent is that the natural processes of the underwater environment represent a progression of change. Some of it is biological (*Titanic*'s steel is being consumed by bacteria), while some of it comes from chemical and mechanical processes. Metal corrodes and weakens in current until a hull collapses. In shallower water, ships drag their anchors through a wreck site, tearing it apart. Some of it is also directly attributable to human impact, as repeated expeditions disturb the wreck and as trash from the surface can drift down to the seabed. Shipwreck work in the deep is increasingly focusing on these processes. New technologies can extract DNA from wreck sites to reveal types of wood or perishable cargoes, as well as assess what was present based on what came to colonize or ingest it. This means that archaeological integrity is not confined to how "intact" a wreck might seem. New technologies go deep, take accurate measurements, and document sites in three-dimensional detail. Robotic tools excavate and sample where no human can reach. This has changed not only how we work on wrecks, but also how we work underwater.

As ongoing missions in the deep progress, one hope among many maritime archaeologists is the ability to find and work on faintly tangible sites of greater age and push back the study of ships and seafaring beyond the three millennia limit we currently sit at. "What if" in the next decades highly sensitive, autonomous robotic surveyors find the faint traces of deeply fallen remains of vessels of even greater antiquity? We are beginning to see finds of older craft in the Black Sea, which have yielded well-preserved wooden ships of antiquity, some with the bones of their lost crews. But coming back to the earlier point of shedding a bias toward "intact" hulls, as exciting as they may be, work on a recent project thousands of feet down off the Carolinas at Blake Ridge shows the potential of a wreck that was more the ghost of the vessel, as only traces of its hull survived. Despite this, as we documented those traces, we documented the form, layout, and nature of the wreck as an early to mid-19th-century small fishing craft that may have been worked by African-American fishermen from nearby Charleston.

The Blake Ridge Shipwreck was an accidental find made in 2015 during a non-archaeological oceanographic research project led by Dr. Cindy Van Dover of Duke University with the Woods Hole Oceanographic Institution. The submersible *Alvin* was cruising along the seabed in over 3,000 feet of water, searching for a missing instrumentation package. A slight line on the sonar that looked like it might be the mooring chain for the package was instead a rusted run of anchor chain that led to a faintly visible ghost of a shipwreck in the sediment. The science team in *Alvin* spotted a small pile of bricks, a few dark glass wine bottles, and a ship's navigational octant. It was a tantalizing discovery, and one that some scientists thought could be a wooden wreck from the period of the American Revolutionary War. This made headlines, as did the image of the octant. On shore, analysis of the footage from the dive revealed enough details to see that while the wooden hull appeared "gone," the fittings and ceramics all suggested a 19th-century date, perhaps no later than 1840 to 1850. The wreck would never have been found by conventional, hull-mounted sonar systems used to map the seabed; there was no relief that would make it stick out or show on a sonar, and the faint line of the anchor chain could have easily been passed up as a natural feature if not for the thought that it might be the chain from the missing instrument package.

This wreck fascinated me; it was nothing more than a "ghost" ship in a way, with much of its wooden hull consumed by marine organisms. The artifacts were few—and while the octant had attracted the attention of the media, I suspected that there were other artifacts and clues to what this vessel had been, and what it was likely doing so far from shore. What was needed was another chance to examine the wreck. I also strongly believed that documenting this particular wreck was important. A chance to go back and document it would better define the potential

Image C.1. Archaeological team on board the E/V *Nautilus* on a deep-dive telepresence mission to the wreck of USS *Independence*.
Photograph by Julye Newlin, Ocean Exploration Trust/National Oceanic and Atmospheric Administration.

of a wreck, even one as minimally preserved as this, to yield answers about its type and trade, and maybe, at some future time, its identity.

It took years before the opportunity to do that dive was available. When plans for a cruise through the area by the NOAA exploration ship *Okeanos Explorer* with its remotely operated vehicles (ROVs) led to a call for proposals for dives, a collaborative group of archaeologists from NOAA, the Bureau of Ocean Energy Management, and other organizations proposed the "Blake Ridge Wreck," and were granted a dive. The dive in 2018 focused on slowly and systematically mapping the wreck site in high resolution. The goal was to pick up every aspect, including the faintest traces of a ship that had fallen into the dark almost 200 years ago. What made that a challenge was that the wooden hull has been consumed by marine organisms. The faint traces of the hull, however, were enhanced and became understandable data through three-dimensional mapping. This was made by possible by exceptionally talented ROV pilots and the crew of *Okeanos Explorer* who held the ship motionless in the water as the ROV systematically and slowly "mowed the lawn" suspended just above the wreck site.

The final mosaic map, after the data were processed, is essentially a high-resolution, 100 percent representation of the entire exposed area of the wreck. With that on all of our screens as we watched from locations across the country, but in constant, immediate communication with each other, archaeologists and scientists ashore have since investigated and cataloged numerous wreck sites in the comfort of an office, meticulously making notes. We can virtually re-dive any site any time, without sending a ship back out and incurring the cost of another mission. There is no need to go back unless it would be to conduct other studies, or an archaeological excavation.

The Blake Ridge dive revealed traces of the wooden hull in the sediment, as outlines of what were once heavy beams, frames, and planks. It is the lower hold of the ship, and their form reveals it was a 40-foot long, two-masted schooner. The iron rigging for the masts, while heavily corroded and broken, suggest that rig, which was the most common type of American merchant craft of the 18th and 19th centuries. It was built with

Image C.2. Orthomosaic of the Blake Ridge Wreck.
National Oceanic and Atmospheric Administration, Office of Ocean Exploration and Research, and the Bureau of Ocean Energy Management.

iron fasteners, and it was not sheathed with copper, something used by vessels engaged in open ocean trade, and an expensive thing to do. The artifacts we see confirm the sense that this is a ship built no earlier than 1835 and lost no later than 1850. It was probably a work-a-day, humble schooner or sloop worked by fishermen. The mapping clearly delineates an open area in the middle of the wreck that was a "wet well" or flooded portion of the hull that held fish for sale ashore as fresh food before the advent of ice on fishing boats. The ceramic containers for food, the wine bottles, and other artifacts not only help date the wreck, but also suggest a crew of three to five. The bricks and the remains of an iron kettle buried in the sediment mark the location of the galley where meals were prepared, but there is no stove here, only the bricks. This again is evidence of a small, humble craft. In the area of the wet well, a pile of queen conch shells (not native to these waters and depths) was evidence of a stop in the Bahamas or Florida, where these were gathered as fresh food.

What also shows up are a few small items, in addition to the octant seen in 2015, that speak to the people on board. There is a slate, a small clay tobacco pipe, a comb, and a sewing kit known as a "sailor's wife" that lies with a pile of brass buttons. The presence of all of these items of personal value means that the crew left the ship in a hurry or went down with it. The wreck, located well offshore and at the edges of the Gulf Stream, may have gone down in a storm. It may have left no survivors, and families ashore who wondered and waited for years for closure that never came. In more contemporary terms, this was likely a vessel lost in a "perfect storm," like the modern and famous *Andrea Gail*.

Beyond the aspects of what archaeology suggests, the significance of this wreck and the work done is that deep-sea technologies and techniques are opening up the deep frontier to new discoveries that would have never been found unless by accident in a vast, still mostly unexplored ocean. The frontier is going to continue to open up, especially with autonomous underwater survey craft working long range, and at depth, to map. The techniques deployed to map wrecks are virtually raising them for further study. The range of exploration and discovery of wrecks in the deep has reached new depths, going as far as over three and a half miles down. This was demonstrated by the May 2019 discovery of the battle-lost destroyer USS *Johnston*, which sank in the Battle of Samar in Leyte Gulf, off the Philippines in October 1944. At 20,400 feet down, the find and the ROV documentation of it by a team led by Rob Kraft on the R/V *Petrel* pushed "the limit of their underwater search equipment."[1] It's that pushing that means the next decade is going to be an exciting one for all with an interest in shipwrecks. The range of the shipwreck frontier is not confined to great depth, however; increasing interest and new discoveries are happening as we also focus on the other rapidly emerging area of finds. That aspect of the frontier includes wrecks that appear on beaches, as well as shipwrecks that emerge from the landfilled former waterfronts of the world's port cities.

Canaries in a Coal Mine? Shipwrecks and Climate Change

Climate change is nothing new in human history, and those of us who work underwater, even if we have not worked on submerged Paleolithic sites, know that much of what is now the shallow coastal margin of the world—as deep as nearly 400 feet down—was dry land during the last Ice Age. When the Ice Age ended as a result of global warming, the melting of glacial ice during that 20,000-year thaw flooded the coastal plains of Asia, Europe, Africa, and the Americas. As carbon dioxide levels rise, the melting of glacial ice at both poles is now causing the fastest rise in the sea level of the past 6,000 years, according to scientific studies around the world. While it will be centuries and perhaps millennia before Earth experiences the type of global melting and flooding that followed the Ice Age, the effects of climate change are already being felt on a planetary scale. By the end of this century, the sea level is forecast to be some four feet higher than it was in the past century. Meanwhile, droughts are resulting in low river levels, followed by extreme floods. The scale of these floods is massive and devastates lower-lying areas on their banks. As the weather warms and more storms take place, especially hurricanes, flooding will follow. The flooding of New Orleans by Hurricane Katrina is a powerful example of that flooding, while Hurricane Helene is yet another demonstration of the power of storms to flood vast areas, turning streams and rivers into raging torrents. The pace and intensity of storms are only going to increase.

Where do shipwrecks fit into this picture? They are canaries in the coal mine. Coastal erosion from storms has revealed the buried remains of shipwrecks for centuries, but the pace of these exposures has intensified. Higher sea levels, even an inch more, mean more beach erosion. Three months of winter storms in 2024 offer a brief, focused look; in January 2024 these included the periodic re-emergence of a 18th-century wreck, *Defiance*, at York, Maine. A large piece of another wooden wreck emerged on the beach at Cape Ray, Newfoundland, while a section of the hull of the schooner *William H. Sumner*, wrecked on North Carolina's Outer Banks in 1919, was also exposed by erosion. January storms also resulted in the first exposure in decades of the scattered wreckage of the Canadian schooner *Tay*, which wrecked in 1911 in what is now Acadia National Park in Maine. It had last been exposed in 1985.

Two back-to-back storms at the start of the year stripped the sand dunes off the beach and smashed the hull of the wreck on the rocks. A subsequent storm in March swept the remaining timbers off the beach. That same March, storms that hit Massachusetts's North Shore revealed the broken hull of the schooner *Ada K. Damon* where it wrecked in 1909 on Crane Beach, near Ipswich. While periodically exposed by storms, the March 2024 event revealed a previously unknown portion of the wreck that had remained buried during past exposures for over a century. Across the Atlantic, a storm that stripped sand off the beach and intertidal zone washed out a section of a centuries-old wooden hull in Orkney, while other wrecks re-emerged from the sands of the German North Sea island of Sylt.

Archaeologist Daniel Zwick is leading a survey of Sylt's wrecks. He and a team study them as they continue to be exposed and break up in the intertidal zone as a result of dramatic coastal erosion made worse by sea level rise. In 2016, Daniel and colleagues documented a late 17th-century wreck, which they named the Hörnum Odde wreck, which had emerged for the first time in 300 years from a sand dune. The Hörnum Odde wreck's remains were thoroughly documented in extremely difficult conditions as the sea tore away sand and battered the remains of the hull. That project was followed by others, as Dr. Zwick and his colleagues see the spit and sands of Sylt as a site where the effects of climate change and sea level rise on shipwrecks can be documented, while also working in an equivalent of battlefield triage to rescue what they can. While assessing the impacts of storms on shipwrecks on beaches, less work has been done with submerged shipwrecks subjected to storm surges and undersea erosion. Archaeologists have used marine geophysical techniques to assess seabed changes around sunken shipwrecks, seeking to determine which are natural seabed dynamics as opposed to any that are caused by climate change–related forces.[2] I expect more of this work will be done and it will add to our understanding of what happens out of human sight as the oceans respond to climate change.

What is not happening out of human sight is fluctuating river levels, which are occuring more frequently because of droughts. The falling water reveals shipwrecks—and they make the news, sometimes internationally. The Mississippi River is arguably the best-known river in the United States. It is also a vital part of the overall American economy, as millions of tons of cargo are moved on the river, generating billions of dollars in economic benefits. Ninety-two percent of American agricultural products move on the river. When severe droughts caused by climate change drop the river level to record lows, this halts river traffic. A multiyear study by several U.S. government agencies, known as the National Integrated Drought Information System, documented a century of severe drought events, starting with the first year of official measurement of rain in 1895. These included the 1930s droughts that are still remembered as the Dust Bowl, as well as a drought in 1988, and one in 2012, which eclipsed the Dust Bowl and cost the American economy $35 billion.

The droughts of late 2022, which continued into 2024, have made the river fall to near-record lows, and river shipwrecks are again "canaries in the coal mine" as news stories share images of wrecks that people can walk on, not dive. These include the October 2022 exposure of a late 19th-century wreck, the wooden-hulled *Brookhill Ferry*, which sank in 1915 near Baton Rouge, Louisiana. The drought was not confined to one river; the Missouri River also dropped. Near St. Charles, the drought revealed the wreck of the massive wooden steamboat *Montana*, which wrecked in 1884. Previous droughts had exposed the wreck, in 2002–2003, and again in 2012, when archaeologists from East Carolina University conducted a major archaeological survey of that "skeleton in the sand."[3] Another wreck exposed by drought when a tributary of the Missouri River fell was the steamboat *South Dakota*, which wrecked in 1870. When water levels dropped on the Vermillion River in 2021, the steamboat *North Alabama* re-emerged for the first time since 2004; it had previously been exposed in 1906, during the Dust Bowl in the 1930s. Falling river levels re-exposed the wreck in 2022. In August 2023, as river levels dropped on Texas's Neches River, it revealed five large wooden wrecks.

The shipwrecks in the American heartland are not the only examples of shipwrecks as climate change "canaries." On the Danube, near Prahovo, Serbia, a well-known ghost fleet is increasingly creating problems for barges and river cruise boats as water levels keep dropping. They are all that remain of the World War II German Black Sea Fleet and Danube Flotilla. As the war in the east began to turn against the Nazis, the pro-German government of Romania turned on the Germans, forging an alliance with the Allies on August 23, 1944. German naval forces, now effectively trapped in enemy territory, began a retreat up the Danube; in all, between 170 and 250 vessels, including smaller craft like torpedo boats, minesweepers, as well as barges, fled, fired on by Romanian forces on the river banks. With no chance to retreat, the Germans began scuttling the ships in the river. As many as 200 were scuttled between September 7 and 20, 1944. Local lore suggests that ships with dead and wounded, including the hospital ship *Bamberg*, were sunk and hold human remains. They also are filled with unexploded ordnance, including sea mines. A Romanian ship hit one of the wrecks in 1984, and it exploded, killing several of the crew.

At least 40 of the German wrecks lie in the Danube near Prahovo; I am one of many who have sailed past them. The Germans scuttled the ships in a zig-zag pattern to block the channel. Our ship proceeded slowly, hugging the opposite bank as we passed the wrecks, which take up as much as half the channel when the water is low. The first major modern exposure of the wrecks came with low water levels in 2003. Those levels were the lowest reached since the river's previously lowest level in 1840. The dramatic exposure of the German wrecks, stretching along 26 miles of river, in 2022, 2023, and again in 2024, made global news. The Danube wrecks are now iconic symbols of climate change. They are also the focus of efforts to remove them. The Danube is part of the Pan-European Corridor and critical to the economy of the European Union.[4] The scuttled patrol boats, S-boats (fast attack boats—*schnellboote*), R-boats (minesweepers—*minenräumboote*), barges, landing craft, and tankers near Prahovo were the focus of a comprehensive survey in 2020. The results of the survey were dramatically unveiled by the low river levels, and the coverage as well as the risks—any ships navigating past them need a special insurance rider—has led to action. Serbia and neighboring countries have begun to plan for the $30 million cost to remove the wrecks. A more recent risk analysis for removing 23 of the wrecks was completed in 2024.[5]

Less visible are wrecks that are beginning to feel the effects of climate change underwater. Ocean temperatures are rising. Corrosion of iron and steel increases as temperatures rise. The higher temperatures change the dynamics of bacterial growth, as well as higher levels of chlorides (salts), electrical conductivity, pH, and how much oxygen and carbon dioxide there is in the water. The ocean's acidity is increasing through the absorption of carbon dioxide. Ocean acidification dissolves the shells of bivalves that cover wrecks, protecting them, and accelerates corrosion. But marine life is adapting where it is not dying. Coral, as noted, is growing on wrecks in unlikely circumstances, such as at Bikini. Increased levels of salinity and warmer water have introduced marine organisms that eat wooden shipwrecks where they did not previously exist.

We are now seeing these worms in the Baltic, fabled for its intact wooden wrecks dating back centuries. In the South Atlantic, where these worms did not live, they are advancing. The Falkland Islands were decades ago promoted as the home of the "Ghosts of Cape Horn," namely abandoned and derelict, nearly intact wooden ships of the early to mid-19th century that put in to port, never to leave after seeking passage around the storm-tossed tip of South America. They included the above-water wrecks of an immigrant packet ship, the last American clipper ship, and the last ship left above the water that had sailed into San Francisco Bay during the Gold Rush year of 1849. I once joked that the Falklands were to maritime archaeologists what Disneyland is to kids. Not anymore; I went with a team of colleagues several years ago to "autopsy" the collapsed, now largely sunk remains of that Gold Rush ship, the barque *Vicar of Bray*—a ship that was so intact there were plans (never realized) to put it on a barge and return it to San Francisco in the 1960s. Storms tore the worm-infested hull apart before we arrived. There are now serious worries, with global warming, that the Arctic, as it heats and the ice retreats, will lose the intact wooden ships of 19th-century exploration that have been found. I have already written about the ships of the ill-fated Franklin expedition of 1845, which sought to find the last unmapped portion of the Northwest Passage. HMS *Erebus* and *Terror* are at risk, and not only if worms arrive and eat them. Increasingly violent storms, caused by climate change, and less ice protecting it in the winters, have battered *Erebus*, lifting off part of the deck and collapsing portions of it. Archaeologists from Parks Canada warned in early 2024 that time was running out for archaeological work.

The Golden Age of Shipwreck Discoveries

In March 2024, a *New York Times* reporter called to interview me, along with other colleagues, about shipwrecks.[6] His question, which became the headline, was "It's a Golden Age for Shipwreck Discoveries. Why?" The answer is more than the new technologies that are revolutionizing human access and our understanding of Earth's final frontier that rests below the surface of oceans and lakes. It's in part a result of climate change. It's the attention paid to the oceans by wealthy individuals, like the late Paul Allen, and others, but it is also the "democratization" of underwater exploration. Wreck divers, dive clubs, and nonprofit organizations are also making major discoveries. There are also the incidental finds being made as the seabed is increasingly the focus of industrial and commercial interests. Technology is playing a powerful role, but let's not forget that tech is a tool. Human interest, curiosity, and desire are the hand that deploys that tech. It is also important to remember that not every shipwreck find was deliberate. Some of them result from large-scale surveys done in advance of oil and gas development, in advance of anticipated deep seabed mining, or laying communications cables.

Let's start with climate change. I've already discussed a number of finds that emerged from eroding beaches or drought-induced falling river and lake levels. A project I worked on in late 2023 was an indirect result of climate change. The low-lying historic city of St. Augustine, Florida, is a floodplain that 90 percent of the city's residents live atop of. Every storm, with tidal surges, even heavy rains that coincide with peak tides, and an aging infrastructure cause flooding downtown and occasionally in other neighborhoods. St. Augustine's city website records 11 floods between 1994 and 2017, including major events like Tropical Storm Gabrielle in 2001, Tropical Storm Fay in 2008, Hurricane Matthew in 2016, and Hurricane Irma in 2017. The pace of hurricanes and tropical storms has intensified since then. In 2023, the Florida Department of Transportation began work on a new, larger storm drain system on the alignment of one of the city's oldest thoroughfares, King Street.

The wide, deep trench, excavated along the alignment of King Street, had yielded a wide range of artifacts in the landfill and former city front when an alert archaeological monitor stopped the next scrape of the backhoe when he spotted a curved plank in the dark mud. It was the bottom of a small, single-masted vessel of the mid- to late 19th century. What followed was a quick, systematic excavation that I co-directed with my colleagues from SEARCH. We are a national leader in archaeology and cultural preservation in the United States. With the construction crew's assistance, the team completely exposed the craft, pilings from the old waterfront still covered with clusters of long dead oysters, and artifacts, some possibly associated with the vessel, and other items either thrown into the water or lost as people stepped on and off vessels tied at the dock that once stood there.

The boat was made of local soft wood, primarily pine, with iron nails. It was small, with the surviving bottom of the hull only 19 feet long and just under 7 feet wide at its broadest dimension. The bottom of the vessel, with some of the frames that reinforced the hull, retained only one plank that marked the edge of the hull on all sides, the "trunk" in which the remains of the centerboard—a large plank that pivoted down to give the flat-bottomed craft more stability when sailing—and a curved "knee" that supported the bow. Two cut-out "steps" indicated the position that the boat's operator would have placed a single mast, close to the bow, as they sailed. Marine organisms had consumed the upper works before the vessel was filled over with sand, likely in the early 20th century as the waterfront underwent another wave of development.

Coins found lying on it included the dates 1869 and 1883, and the pilings that pierced the hull are from a wharf that appears in an 1885 photograph of the area. The craft is vernacular, likely locally built and similar in form to shallow draft, small craft engaged in local fishing and oyster harvesting. It also may have been used to transport goods to waterfront markets. Its simple form and construction indicate it was built by someone who knew how to build a boat, but who likely was not employed in a boat- or shipbuilding yard. These types of craft were typically built by their owners. The postbellum era coast and waterways of the Southeastern United States that stretched from Charleston to Jacksonville—including St. Augustine—were the home waters of a large number of craft just like this, locally known as the "mosquito fleet," that worked the tidal marshes, creeks, rivers, estuaries, and sounds of the coast, as well as ranging in craft like this as far as 32 kilometers offshore in search of fish. These fisheries were predominately worked by African Americans, some of whose families had worked the waters as enslaved fishers. Side by side with the construction team and volunteers from the local Lighthouse Archaeological Maritime Program (LAMP), we carefully excavated the extremely fragile, water-soaked wooden craft, and systematically dismantled it after using photogrammetry to three-dimensionally document it. The dismantled craft now rests in freshwater storage at LAMP's St. Augustine facility as analysis continues. This humble craft, first noted in local news, also became a national and then an international news story.

Other finds over the two-year spread included Roman wrecks off the Italian mainland near Rome, an ancient Greek wreck off Sicily, and another wreck off the coast of Mallorca, but the major find that inspired multiple stories in the international media was the "world's oldest wreck" off Israel. The wreck, which archaeologists suggest dates back 3,200 years based on the artifacts found on it, rests nearly 6,000 feet deep. Discovered in 2023 during surveys of Israel's offshore gas fields, it dates to the Bronze Age, a time of international trade that spanned not only the Mediterranean world, but beyond, into Africa, the Far East, and the Baltic. The presence of amphorae that are Canaanite, the antecedents of the Phoenicians and other Middle Eastern peoples and cultures, ties the wreck to that dynamic time in human history. It also is proof that ancient navigators were competent and unafraid to navigate in open waters well beyond sight of shore, and did not hug the coastline.[7] The wreck discovery came as part of a larger survey done by Energean, a London-based company working to develop energy resources in the Mediterranean. Surveys like these are common as relatively unmapped seabeds need to be carefully mapped to better understand what lies below with focus and detail, avoiding environmentally and culturally sensitive areas, and also ensuring careful placement of undersea infrastructure. Announcement of the Energean find came after a cooperative project with Israeli archaeologists from the Israel Antiquities Authority. The recovery of Canaanite amphorae came after careful mapping of the site and helped provide a date for the wreck.

The nature of the find was a pleasant surprise, but that it happened was not. As said, pre-development surveys by and for industry take place, often not publicly, around the world. The public usually hears about them when a consequential discovery is made. In the United States, the U.S. government agency BOEM, which I've discussed previously, keeps a database of wrecks as part of their oversight of offshore oil, gas, and now wind-farm energy projects. Those surveys are required by U.S. environmental and historic preservation law and have been ongoing since the 1970s.[8] That database includes thousands of targets, hundreds of which are known to be shipwrecks. Some of the wrecks in the BOEM database are several thousand feet deep. As drilling technology evolved to seek oil and gas in deeper waters, surveys kept pace and evolved. Outside of military systems, industrial technological development has been the main driver for deep-sea survey and exploration technology.

I'm excited by the increased pace of shipwreck discoveries being made around the world as a result of industrial focus. That excitement is tempered by a strong belief that with finds that are made, the responsible parties behave as the American oil and gas energy companies have and as Energean has also demonstrated off Israel. I know they are not alone and that other global industrial interests pay attention to cultural sites and community beliefs. To help inform them and the public, a number of colleagues and I, working with environmental groups, have authored scholarly overviews of the cultural contexts, including known and suspected shipwrecks and other submerged cultural sites, for deep-sea areas. The first was for the seabed off the west coast of Africa and the sea routes from Africa to Europe, the Caribbean, and North and South America. This was the marine highway for the transatlantic slave trade, the "Middle Passage." We referenced the more than 40,000 voyages, the transport of more than 12.5 million Africans against their will, the large number of deaths and the ruthless disposal of dead and dying Africans into the ocean, as well as yet undiscovered shipwrecks as we appealed the International Seabed Authority and industry to consider ways to respect and memorialize those who came to rest on the seabed in advance of mineral exploitation.[9]

The next overviews, as previously mentioned, were for the Salas y Gomez Ridge in the South Pacific and the Emperor Seamounts and Aleutians in the North Pacific. We recently completed the fourth for the

Blake Plateau and adjacent Blake Ridge off the southeastern coast of the United States. The plateau is noted for deep-sea minerals, but our latest study notes its cultural significance to the Gullah-Geechee people of the region, who are the descendants of enslaved Africans. We stress the fact that the plateau is the terminus of the Middle Passage's route, with its attendant horrors and callous disposal of the dead and dying. We noted that it rests beneath an ocean highway for colonial exploration, commerce, war, and the economic development of the United States and neighboring countries. The legacy of these activities includes shipwrecks historically documented, yet undiscovered, and those which have been found, such as the Blake Ridge Wreck.

In October 2024, I co-led the archaeological documentation of a largely forgotten warship, USS *Stewart*. Ocean Infinity, one of the global leaders in deep-sea mapping and exploration, was conducting a series of dives to synchronize and fine-tune systems with their HUGIN 6000 autonomous underwater vehicles from the vessel *Island Pride*. Andy Sherrell, their director of Marine Operations, reached out to Russ Matthews, who has been a friend and partner on numerous expeditions, including those with his nonprofit Air/Sea Heritage Foundation. *Island Pride* was operating out of San Francisco. Were there any "targets" we'd be interested in finding? Russ and I have a pocketful of targets around the world. *Stewart* was obvious; it had been scuttled in 1946 at the end of World War II after a fascinating career that included pre–World War II service in the Far East and fierce naval battles against overwhelming odds against invading Japanese forces at the start of the war. It was scuttled with explosive charges as it awaited repairs in a floating dry dock that quickly fell behind enemy lines.

Japanese naval forces raised the wreck, repaired and rearmed it, and as Patrol Boat No. 102 it served in antisubmarine war patrols as a Japanese warship through the rest of the war. As Allied forces fought their way back across the Pacific, reports of a strange ship that resembled an American warship led to the realization that it was the former *Stewart*. Now known as the "Ghost ship of the Pacific," *Stewart* was recaptured and returned to the U.S. Navy at the end of the war. Towed to San

Francisco, it was quickly scuttled in what was essentially a ceremonial burial at sea. I've wanted to find that wreck for a long time, as it lies within the waters of NOAA's Cordell Banks National Marine Sanctuary, whose depths had not been accurately mapped. Russ and I advanced finding the wreck as a priority for Pacific Ocean exploration in meetings and workshops that were setting policies and priorities for government agencies and their industry and nonprofit partners. Years ago, thanks to Ocean Infinity's testing and practice runs, we worked together to discover the famous battleship USS *Nevada*, deep off Hawaii. Like that find, *Stewart*'s story made global news when we announced the discovery with Ocean Infinity, SEARCH, NOAA, and the Navy History and Heritage Command.

However, it does not take big ships or highly sophisticated and expensive vehicles like a HUGIN to make the news in the "Golden Age of Shipwreck Discoveries." What I've seen through the years is that it takes people and passion. There are wreck divers, dive clubs, avocational archaeological groups and societies, as well as dedicated archaeologists and volunteers who work in government agencies and ministries around the world who devote their time, resources, and money to seeking out lost ships. It's their research, their boats, their gear, and their dive equipment that they commit to the cause of finding lost ships. I've been privileged and proud to work with some of them, notably my friends and colleagues in Canada with the Underwater Archaeological Society of British Columbia.

Among the finds made in 2023–2024 by groups made up of these special individuals, a forgotten tragedy, the 1856 sinking of the transatlantic passenger steamer *Le Lyonnais*, was remembered when the wreck was discovered hundreds of miles away from where previous searchers had looked. A tragic World War I loss was remembered when divers found the wreck of HMS *Hawke*, torpedoed by a German U-boat in 1914, killing most of the crew. Another one of the most consequential discoveries came in 2023 when the nonprofit Silentworld Foundation, which focuses on supporting and promoting Australasian maritime archaeology, history, culture, and heritage, working with deep-sea survey company

Fugro, discovered the wreck of the transport *Montevideo Maru* off the coast of the Philippines in 13,000 feet of water. A U.S. submarine, when its crew sank *Montevideo Maru* on July 1, 1942, fired without knowing that it was carrying prisoners of war and civilians captured by the Japanese. It was the worse maritime disaster in Australian history, with 979 Australian dead, among the 1,060 lost from 14 different countries. The discovery, noted Australia's prime minister, spoke "for the enduring truth of Australia's solemn national promise to always remember and honour those who served our country."[10] Their families now know where those lost loved ones rest.

In late 2024, the U.S. Navy announced that the Australian Royal Navy discovered the wreck of the destroyer USS *Edsall*, which had been sunk on March 1, 1942, in 18,000 feet of water in the Indian Ocean after a hard-fought and valiant engagement with Japanese ships and aircraft. No one from the ship survived the war, and the discovery of the wreck brought closure to families. It sits intact and upright on the seabed. It is the tomb for more than 200 of its crew and U.S. Army Air Force pilots whom *Edsall* had rescued after their ship had been sunk. The discovery is also a reminder of what Admiral Samuel Cox of the Naval History and Heritage Command termed "one of the most gallant and glamour actions in the history of the U.S. Navy" as they faced an overwhelming onslaught and fought with no chance of victory or escape.

In American and Canadian waters of the Great Lakes, individuals and dive groups discovered lost schooners, wooden steamers, freighters, and a steam tug whose wrecks span the last half of the 19th century and the first decade of the 20th. The Great Lakes have long been a model for individual researchers, wreck hunters, and historians who have made many discoveries, using their research and resources to find the lost ships of the inland seas. Their commitment is like that of divers who work in the Baltic, and whose discoveries are also monumental in meaning, even when the wreck may not be a famous or notorious loss. Rarely are these efforts supported by governments, although in the Great Lakes, state archaeology programs and NOAA contribute where they can, as do others. Ultimately, though, it is individuals. One of my favorite shipwreck discovery stories of 2023 is that of a father and his four-year-old daughter who went fishing together in Lake Michigan and discovered a long-lost schooner that the Wisconsin Historical Society has identified as the *George I. Newman*, which wrecked in October 1871.

Shipwrecks and their stories transcend generations. I began this book noting that shipwrecks are among our oldest tales and have inspired religious thought, philosophy, culture, and an ongoing quest to find them. We are now indeed in the "Golden Age of Shipwreck Discoveries," and after nearly five decades in search of history, and often finding it in lost ships, I'm excited about what the future holds. I love boldly going out onto and under the water, and I am fascinated by each wreck found or explored, as its story unfolds during those dives or through research. My enthusiasm and passion have never ebbed. Why? Because shipwrecks speak to us, as human beings, and for me, what matters most is people. Years ago, working with Clive Cussler as we shared our adventures on television through the *Sea Hunters* program, I loved how he closed each episode: "Now it's your turn, to get up off that couch, and go into the deserts, go into the mountains, go into the rivers, the lakes and the sea, and search for history. You'll never find a more rewarding adventure." Amen, Clive, Amen.

Notes

CHAPTER 1

1. On shipwrecks as the muse, see Riding 2013 and Blumenberg 1997.
2. Twain 1917, p. 372.
3. Thucydides, *Peloponnesian War*, 4.24.5.
4. Virgil, *Aeneid*, 3.429ff.
5. Strabo, *Geography*, 1.2.36.
6. Veyrat 2017, p. 171.
7. Souza 1998, p. 42.
8. See Woodman 1992; Delgado 1999; Hutchinson 2017; and Cohen 2013.
9. Anonymous 1878, p. 296.
10. The wreck of *El Faro* and the human stories are powerfully related by Slade 2018; there are numerous news stories about the loss of the ship and the subsequent investigations; I drew the quotes from the crew as they called and emailed, *in extremis*, from them.
11. Huffman (2009) does an excellent job in sharing the story of *Sultana*.
12. The coal ship statistics come from Clark 2007, p. 3.
13. Mrs. Bates told her story in her 1857 book.
14. The accounts of the loss of *Morro Castle* come from Hicks 2006 and Coyle and Whitcraft 2012.
15. See Delgado 1996 and 2016.
16. See Weisgall 1990.
17. The best book on the subject is McCartney 2018.
18. https://www.statista.com/statistics/236250/looses-of-ships-worldwide/.

CHAPTER 2

1. Hendel 1995 and Pederson 2004.
2. See Mentz 2015.
3. Berthelot 2013.
4. The quote from Burke is from the 1998 edition, p. 102.
5. Landow 1982, p. 4.
6. Huntress 1974, p. xvii.
7. Watson 1893, p. 54.
8. Huntress 1974, p. xiii.
9. On Longfellow, see Jackson 1998, p. 471.
10. The text of Longfellow's "Wreck of the *Hesperus*" is from Longfellow 1888.
11. On the winter of 1839 wrecks and *Hesperus*, see Clark 1909, pp. 5–6; and Hugenin 1960, p. 48.
12. Longfellow's comments on the Wreck of the *Hesperus* are from Longfellow 1888, p. 1.
13. On the wrecks on Cape Cod, see Thoreau 1864, p. 137.
14. See Dickens 1869, p. 4; Palmer 1989; also see Kerr 2022, p. 143.
15. Palmer 1989, p. 52.

16. This is from Twain's original account of the wreck in the Sacramento *Daily Union* of July 19, 1866.
17. On the wreck of *Hornet* and Mark Twain, see Stone 1961; Scharnhorst 2015; and Krause 2016.
18. This is also from Mark Twain's account of the wreck in the Sacramento *Daily Union* of July 19, 1866.
19. "my fat envelope was thrown by a strong hand"; see Scharnhorst 2015. Also see Zmijewski 1999, p. 57.
20. On the wreck of *Hornet* being well known, see Brown 1974; Jackson 2010; and Krause 2016.
21. "If death did not come, the ordeal itself was transcendent, offering life-changing transformation"; see Morrison 2014, p. 4.
22. Crane 1898, p. 1.
23. Gerstenberger 1972, p. 557; and Thompson 2013, p. 1
24. Tomlinson 1930, p. 331.
25. See Morrison 2014, p. 9. As a song, presented in a public performance, see Heiden 1997, p. 221. I summarize the role of songs in Delgado 1984, p. 32.
26. Reid 2013, p. 139.
27. The "Wreck of the *Central America*" was first published in Stone 1858, p. 7. I discussed the song and its context in Delgado 1984, p. 42.
28. MacKay and Russell 1834.
29. Russell and Crawford 1846.
30. See Mentz 2015.
31. Varney 1911, p. 138.
32. Biel 1998, pp. 64–71; and on "Nearer My God, to Thee," Biel 1998, pp. 85–86.
33. As cited in Foster 1999, pp. 22–23. Also see Biel 2012.
34. Stan Rogers, "Mary Ellen Carter" (© Fogarty Cove Music).
35. See Miles 2007.
36. Riding 2004, p. 1.
37. Miles 2007, p. 181.
38. See Costello 2017, p. 103.
39. See Costello 2017, pp. 101–102, and 223.
40. Erickson and Hulse 2000, p. 316.
41. Wood's 2004 analysis is brilliant.
42. Dahm and Douglas, *Ghost Ships*, p. 11.
43. Dahm and Douglas 2021, p. 123.
44. See Rich 2021, and my review of this brilliant book in Delgado 2022. I drew upon that review in my discussion of *Shipwreck Hauntography* for this book.
45. See Character et al. 2021.
46. On ocean color satellite imagery, see Baeye et al. 2016.
47. Biel reproduces Hardy's poem in Biel 1998, pp. 25–26.
48. Small in size and rich in detail, "Heroic Age of Diving" by Kuntz 2016 is a must-read.
49. One of my all-time favorite archaeologists and big thinkers is Pete Capelotti, his observations of and on the "wreck" of *Orca* II are from Capelotti 2018, pp. 3–24.
50. Clive Cussler summarized some of the dives and finds that made it into the series in Cussler 1996, 2002, and I did so in Delgado 2004.
51. To "solve the mysteries behind the dark underwater graves of ships, planes and submarines" is from the online International Movie Database entry for the show (ImDb).

NOTES

CHAPTER 3

1. Green 1859, p. 18.
2. See Lipke 1984.
3. See Delgado 1988; Broadwater 2012; Holloway and White 2017.
4. Delgado 1997.
5. Durkin 2024, pp. 56–57.
6. Robertson 2008, p. 143.
7. See Hurston 2018.
8. See Robertson 2008; Diouf 2007; Delgado et al. 2021; Tabor 2023; Durkin 2024.
9. Revelations 20:13.
10. Stewart 2011, p. 4.
11. The number of fatalities is from Stewart 2011, p. 7.
12. Stewart 2011, p. 129.
13. Stewart 2011, p. 131.
14. Elena Perez Alvaro 2022, p. 2.1.a.
15. Wilfred Gilberry's memorial is described in Stewart 2011, pp. 2–3.
16. Stewart 2011, p. 133.
17. The *Estonia* Treaty is online at https://treaties.un.org/doc/Publication/UNTS/Volume%201890/volume-1890-I-32189-English.pdf.
18. Stewart 2011, p. 129.
19. Green 1859, p. 19.
20. The harrowing ordeal of recovering the body is recounted in O'Keefe and Macdonald 1998, pp. 104–106.
21. The recovery of and the number of *Titanic* dead comes primarily from Beed 2012.
22. Pellegrino recounted this in *Ghosts of the Titanic* (2000) on p. 113.
23. USS *Arizona*'s loss, salvage, and transition to a memorial and icon are recounted in Delgado, "Recovering the Past of USS *Arizona*: Symbolism, Myth and Reality" (1992).
24. Jasper et al. 2001, p. 176.
25. The saga of the after-loss memorialization of the Libyan immigrant wreck is found in Olivieri et al. 2018.
26. https://www.theartnewspaper.com/news/christoph-buechel.
27. https://www.theguardian.com/artanddesign/2019/may/07/boat-in-which-hundreds-of-migrants-died-displayed-at-venice-biennale.
28. The condition of the bodies is from Introna, Di Vella, and Campobasso 2013, p. 871.
29. Varotsos's project is described in Giaracuni and De Luca 2017.
30. Varotsos's quotes are from Hecht 2016, p. 40.

CHAPTER 4

1. Mallefet et al. 2008, p. 7.
2. See Gambi et al. 2011.
3. See Lengkeek et al. 2013.
4. See Asner 2019.
5. See Smith 2014.
6. See Scott-Ireton 2014.
7. The language on the Shipwreck Coast sanctuary proposal is from Ertel 2017, p. 17.
8. The history and significance of Mallows Bay are described by Shomette 1996.

9. Franke's artwork is discussed in https://www.cnn.com/2013/03/07/world/americas/underwater-gallery-vandenberg-key-west/index.html.
10. See Otis 1864.
11. Macaulay 1966, p. xv.
12. See Franzen 1960.

CHAPTER 5

1. Cressy 2022, p. 1. Also see Bathurst 2005.
2. See Grover 2002, pp. 51–62; also see Belyk 2001, pp. 121–152; and Rogers 1974, pp. 134–142.
3. Cressy 2022, p. 2.
4. Stevenson 1912, p. 39.
5. See Byram 2013; Panich et al. 2018; Panich et al. 2021; and Delgado et al. 2020.
6. Endicott and Jenkins 1923, p. 38.
7. See Chandler's (2023) excellent article.
8. Korsgaard 2010 was a helpful source in helping me frame this discussion.
9. Marden 1957.

CHAPTER 6

1. Hugill 1993, p. 151.
2. On marine insurance, see Martin 1876.
3. See Coll 2018.
4. See Langewiesche 2014.
5. See Peterson 2016.
6. See Martin and Craigie-Halkett 2007.
7. On the reported recovery of over 51,000 tons of "non-ferrous cargoes" from wartime wrecks, see Martin and Craigie-Halkett 2007.
8. Wharton 2000, p. 81.
9. On the gold bars recovered, see Wharton 2000, pp. 107 and 147.
10. Blagg 2014, p. 8.
11. On the recovery of the bell, see Wharton 2000, pp. 97–98, 147–148.
12. Blagg 2014, p. 13.
13. On the potential amount of silver in the wreck, see Pickford 1999, p. 159.
14. On the "Grab 3000 System" and the recovery of the coins, see Mearns and Hudson 2000, and Pickford 1999, pp. 161–162.
15. I drew much of my insight into *Islander* from Delano 2011. I am also familiar with the ship and the shipwreck from my time as director of the Vancouver Maritime Museum.
16. Philips 2007; Philips et al. 2019, pp. 176–177.
17. Zenkiewicz and Wasilewski 2019, p. 320.
18. Zenkiewicz and Wasilewski 2019, p. 328.
19. Zenkiewicz and Wasilewski 2019, pp. 335 and 336.
20. Zenkiewicz and Wasilewski 2019, p. 342.
21. Martín, Díaz, and Pretel 2021, p. 457.
22. *The Independent*, February 25, 2024.
23. Masters 1924, p. 12.
24. See Tigner 2019.
25. See Gately and Benjamin 2018.
26. Kiesling 1994, pp. 193–194.

27. Kiesling 1994, pp. 207–208.
28. Heard 1995.
29. Juvelier 2018, pp. 1025, 1036, and 1045.
30. Gongaware 2013, p. 88.
31. Pearson 2023, p. 20.
32. Throckmorton 1990, p. 8.
33. Kiesling 1994, pp. 193–194.
34. Kleeberg 2013, pp. 23, 26; and Powers 2006, p. 360.
35. On the ruling over the wreck of *Mercedes*, see Delgado and Goold 2022.
36. Temiño 2017, pp. 196 and 200.
37. Among the titles that I believe have blurred the lines between archaeology and treasure hunting are Stenuit 1972; Marx 1967, 1978, 1990; and Peterson 1973.

CHAPTER 7

1. See Brodie et al. 2000; Brodie et al. 2001; Brodie et al. 2006; Muscarella 2008.
2. See Bahn 2012; Stiebing 1993; and Trigger 1989.
3. Marsden 1994, pp. 111 and 115.
4. See Steffy 1994; and Cantwell and Wall 2001.
5. See Bruce-Mitford 1975.
6. See Kaltsas, Vlachogianni, and Bouyia 2012.
7. See Muckelroy 1978, pp. 148–149; and McManamon 2023.
8. See Bratten 2002.
9. See Bearss 1980.
10. On *Vasa* as a giant "billboard" advertising the king and his country, see Soop 1992; Cederlund 1997.
11. On the reconservation, the issues with sulfur and additional work, see Hocker 2006; Hocker et al. 2012.
12. See Riess and Smith 2015; and Riess 2023.
13. On the various buried and rediscovered hulls, see Boetto 2000; D'Oriano and Riccardi 1999; Bruni and Abbado 2000; Kocabas 2008; Delgado 2009; also see Delgado 2011, pp. 196–197; Smith 2023; Bruni and Abbado 2000; Cantwell and Wall 2001; D'Oriano and Riccardi 1999; Delgado 2009; Lemee 2006, 1994; Pomey 1994, 2003; Pulak et al. 2015; and Van der Heide and Varenius 1985.
14. The book is St. John Wilkes 1971; I have it in my library as one of the earliest titles I bought.
15. Among the "diving for pleasure and treasure" titles are Blair 1960 and Crile and Crile 1954.
16. One of the best-known titles is Wagner 1966.
17. See Diolé 1954 and Dumas 1976.
18. Goggin 1960, pp. 348, 350.
19. Bass 1967; Throckmorton 1964; and Bass 1975, pp. 1–59.
20. Among the books published by Bass's contemporaries are Throckmorton 1964, 1969, 1987; Frost 1963; and du Plat Taylor 1965.
21. On Bass's legacies with Texas A&M and the Institute of Nautical Archaeology, see Bass 1966, 1972, 1975, 1988, and 2005.
22. See Henderson 1986.
23. Bass 2005, p. 5.

24. Among the more noteworthy specialized nautical archaeological studies are McCarthy 2005; Oertling 1996; and Simmons 1997.
25. See Anderson 2018; his comment was noted in a story by Bridget Katz in *Smithsonian Magazine* in May 2018.
26. I've drawn from multiple sources; Davis 1872; Brooks 1876; Callaghan 2003; Plummer 1991; and Webber 1984.
27. Harpster 2009.
28. Muckelroy 1978, p. 216.
29. Ford, Halligan, and Catsambis 2020, p. 10.
30. On maritime cultural landscapes, Westerdahl 1992, p. 6.
31. Campbell 2020, p. 19.
32. See Pulak, Ingraham, and Jones 2015.
33. Rich and Campbell 2023, p. 51.

CHAPTER 8

1. Paxton et al. 2024.
2. See Zeller et al. 2016 and Zeller et al. 2018.
3. Brennan et al. 2016, p. 82.
4. Krumholz and Brennan 2015, p. 127.
5. On the Puretic Block, see Schmidt 1959, p. 401.
6. I have written extensively about *Explorer* in Delgado 2006 and Delgado 2012.
7. Steve Hendershot shared the story in Hendershot 2014.
8. Delgado 2006, p. 17.
9. On the plans to use the submarine to salvage the wrecks, see Delgado 2011, pp. 45–46; also see Shomette 1993.
10. On ancient DNA fragments that could be recovered from amphorae, see Hansson and Foley 2008.
11. See Campbell 2021.

CONCLUSION

1. https://news.usni.org/2019/10/30/wreck-of-famed-wwii-destroyer-uss-johnston-may-have-been-found.
2. Gregory et al. 2022, p. 6.
3. Corbin 2008.
4. Karović 2018.
5. Marinković et al. 2024.
6. Levenson 2024.
7. Schuster 2024.
8. Jones 2023.
9. Turner et al. 2020.
10. Prime Minister Albanese's remarks were quoted in the Australian Broadcast Corporation's online story of April 21, 2023.

References and Further Reading

Acheson, Steven, and James P. Delgado. 2004. "Ships for the Taking: Culture Contact and the Maritime Fur Trade on the Northwest Coast of America," in Tim Murray, ed., *The Archaeology of Contact in Settler Societies*. Cambridge; New York; Port Melbourne; Madrid; Cape Town: Cambridge University Press, pp. 48–78.

Acti, Andrea. 2019. "Navigating the 'Southern Seas,' Miraculously: Avoidance of Shipwreck in Buddhist Narratives of Maritime Crossings," in Marina Berthet, Fernando Rosa, and Shaun Viljoen, eds., *Moving Spaces: Creolisation and Mobility in Africa, the Atlantic and Indian Ocean*. Leiden: Brill, pp. 50–77.

Adams, Jon. 2013. *A Maritime Archaeology of Ships*. Oxford: Oxbow Books.

Adams, Jon, and Johann Rönnby, eds. 2013. *Interpreting Shipwrecks: Maritime Archaeological Approaches*. Southampton: Highfield Press.

Ahlstrom, Christian. 1997. *Looking for Leads: Shipwrecks of the Past Revealed by Contemporary Documents and the Archaeological Record*. Helsinki: The Finnish Academy of Science and Letters.

Anderson, Ross. 2018. *Marine Archaeological Analysis of Two Historic Shipwrecks Located During the MH370 Aircraft Search*. Report No. 322, Department of Maritime Archaeology, Western Australian Museum.

Anonymous. 1878. *Great Shipwrecks: A Record of Perils and Disasters at Sea, 1544 to 1877*. London: Thomas Nelson and Sons.

ARKA. 2012. Informe de Peritaje Arqueológico Subacuático Monumento Histórico Corbeta Esmeralda. Valparaíso: ARKA Arqueología Marítima.

Asner, Greg. 2019. *Guns, Coral and Steel: Are Nuclear Shipwrecks a Biodiversity Hotspot?* Mongabay, online at https://mongabayimages.s3.amazonaws.com/documents/Are%20Nuclear%20Shipwrecks%20a%20Biodiversity%20Hotspot.pdf (accessed June 23, 2019).

Aznar, Mariano J. 2021. *Maritime Claims and Underwater Archaeology: When History Meets Politics*. Leiden; Boston: Brill.

Baeye, Mathias, Rory Quinn, S. Deleu, and Michael Fettweis. 2016. "Detection of Shipwrecks in Ocean Colour Satellite Imagery." *Journal of Archaeological Science* 66: 1–6, https://doi.org/10.1016/j.jas.2015.11.006.

Babits, Larry, and Hans K. Van Tilburg, eds. 1998. *Maritime Archaeology: A Reader of Substantive and Theoretical Contributions*. New York: Plenum.

Bahn, Paul. 2012. *Archaeology: A Very Short Introduction*. New York; Oxford: Oxford University Press.

Ballard, Robert D., ed. 2008. *Archaeological Oceanography*. Princeton, NJ; Oxford: Princeton University Press.

Barker, Alex W. 2018. "Looting, the Antiquities Trade, and Competing Valuations of the Past." *Annual Review of Archaeology* 47 (October): 455–474.

Barr, Bradley W. 2013. "Understanding and Managing Marine Protected Areas Through Integrating Ecosystem-Based Management Within Maritime Cultural Landscapes:

Moving from Theory to Practice." *Ocean & Coastal Management* 84 (November): 184–192.

Bascom, Willard. 1976. *Deep Water, Ancient Ships: The Treasure Vault of the Mediterranean.* Garden City, NY: Doubleday.

Bass, George F. 1966. *Archaeology Under Water.* New York; London: Thames & Hudson.

Bass, George F. 1967. *Cape Gelidonya: A Bronze Age Shipwreck, Transactions of the American Philosophical Society* 57 (part 8).

Bass, George F. 1972. *A History of Seafaring Based on Underwater Archaeology.* New York; London: Thames & Hudson.

Bass, George F. 1975. *Archaeology Beneath the Sea.* New York; London: Thames & Hudson.

Bass, George F. 1988. *Ships and Shipwrecks of the Americas.* New York; London: Thames & Hudson.

Bass, George F. 2005. *Beneath the Seven Seas: Adventures with the Institute of Nautical Archaeology.* New York; London: Thames & Hudson.

Bates, Mrs. D. B. 1857. *Incidents on Land and Water: Or, Four Years on the Pacific Coast. Being a Narrative of the Burning of the Ships Nonantum, Humayoon and Fanchon, Together with Many Startling and Interesting Adventures on Sea and Land.* Boston: James French and Company.

Bathurst, Bella. 2005. *The Wreckers: A Story of Killing Seas and Plundered Shipwrecks, From the 16th Century to the Present Day.* Boston; New York: Houghton Mifflin.

Bearss, Edwin C. 1980. *Hardluck Ironclad: The Sinking and the Salvage of the Cairo.* Baton Rouge: Louisiana State University Press.

Beasant, John. 1996. *Stalin's Silver.* London: Bloomsburg.

Beed, Blair. 2012. *Titanic Victims in Halifax Graveyards.* Halifax: Nimbus.

Belyk, Robert C. 2001. *Great Shipwrecks of the Pacific Coast.* New York: John Wiley.

Berrocal, Maria Cruz, and Chen-hwa Tsang. 2017a. *Historical Archaeology of Early Modern Colonialism in Asia Pacific: The Southwest Pacific and Oceanian Regions.* Gainesville: University Press of Florida.

Berrocal, Maria Cruz, and Chen-hwa Tsang. 2017b. *Historical Archaeology of Early Modern Colonialism in Asia Pacific: The Asia-Pacific Region.* Gainesville: University Press of Florida.

Berthelot, Kate. 2013. "A Classical Ethical Problem in Ancient Philosophy and Rabbinic Thought: The Case of the Shipwrecked." *The Harvard Theological Review* 106(2): 171–199.

Biel, Steven. 1998. *Titanica: The Disaster of the Century in Poetry, Song and Prose.* New York; London: W. W. Norton.

Biel, Steven. 2012. *Down with the Old Canoe: A Cultural History of the Titanic Disaster* (updated edition). New York; London: W. W. Norton.

Blagg, Michele. 2014. Let Her Rest in Peace: HMS *Edinburgh* and Her Cargo of Gold, pp. 1–12, http://public.bacs.daisy.websds.net/PDFFiles/Articles/108001.pdf (accessed October 12, 2019).

Blair, Clay. 1960. *Diving for Pleasure and Treasure.* Cleveland: World Publishing.

Blow, Michael. 1992. *A Ship to Remember: The Maine and the Spanish-American War.* New York: William Morrow.

Blue, Lucy. 2019. *In the Footsteps of Honor Frost: The Life and Legacy of a Pioneer in Maritime Archaeology.* Leiden: Sidestone Press.

Blumenberg, Hans. 1997. *Shipwreck with Spectator: Paradigm of a Metaphor for Existence*, trans. Steven Rendall. Cambridge, MA: The MIT Press.

Boetto, G. 2000. "The Lake Roman Fiumicino 1 Wreck: Reconstructing the Hull," in Carlo Beltrame, ed., *Down the River to the Sea: Proceedings of the Eight International Symposium on Boat and Ship Archaeology.* Oxford: Oxbow, pp. 66–70.

Bratten, John R. 2002. *The Gondola Philadelphia and the Battle of Lake Champlain.* College Station: Texas A&M University Press.

Brennan, Michael L., Frank Cantelas, Kelley Elliott, James P. Delgado, Katherine L. C. Bell, Dwight Coleman, Allison Fundis, Jack Irion, Hans K. Van Tilburg, and Robert D. Ballard. 2018. "Telepresence-Enabled Maritime Archaeological Exploration in the Deep." *Journal of Maritime Archaeology* 13(2): 97–121.

Brennan, Michael, Dan Davis, Robert D. Ballard, Arthur C. Trembanis, Ian Vaughn, Jason S. Krumholz, James P. Delgado, Christopher N. Roman, Clara Smart, Katherine L. C. Bell, Muhammet Duman, and Carter DuVal. 2016. "Quantification of Bottom Trawl Fishing Damage to Ancient Shipwreck Sites." *Marine Geology* 371 (January): 82–88.

Broadwater, John D. 2010. "Naval Battlefields as Cultural Landscapes: The Siege of Yorktown," in Clarence R. Geier, Lawrence E. Babits, Douglas D. Scott, and David G. Orr, eds., *Historical Archaeology of Military Sites: Method and Topic.* College Station: Texas A&M University Press, pp. 177–187.

Broadwater, John D. 2012. *USS Monitor: A Historic Ship Completes Its Final Voyage.* College Station: Texas A&M University Press..

Brodie, N., J. Doole, P. Watson. 2000. *Stealing History: The Illicit Trade in Cultural Material.* Cambridge: Cambridge University Press.

Brodie, Neal, Jenny Doole, Colin Renfrew. 2001. *Trade in Illicit Antiquities: The Destruction of the World's Archaeological Heritage.* Cambridge: Cambridge University Press.

Brodie, Neal, Morag M. Kersel, Christina Luke, and Kathyrn Walker Tubb. 2006. *Archaeology, Cultural Heritage and the Antiquities Trade.* Gainesville: University Press of Florida.

Brogger, A. W., and Haakon Shetelig. 1971. *The Viking Ships.* Oslo: Dreyers Forlag.

Brooks, Charles Wolcott. 1876. *Japanese Wrecks Stranded and Picked Up Adrift in the North Pacific Ocean.* San Francisco: California Academy of Sciences.

Brown, Alexander Crosby. 1974. *Longboat to Hawaii: An Account of the Voyage of the Clipper Ship Hornet of New York, Bound for San Francisco in 1886, as Recorded in the Journals of Captain Josiah A. Mitchell, Master, Henry Ferguson, Passenger, Samuel Ferguson, Passenger: Together with Observations on the Burning of the Vessel.* Centreville, MD: Cornell Maritime Press.

Bruce-Mitford, Rupert. 1975. *The Sutton Hoo Ship-Burial*, Volume 1: *Excavations, Background, the Ship, Dating and Inventory.* London: British Museum Publications.

Bruni, S., and M. Abbado. 2000. *Le Navi Antiche di Pisa: Ad Un Anno Dall'inizio delle Richerche.* Firenze: Poolistampa.

Bruseth, James E., Amy Borgens, Bradford D. Jones, and Eric D. Ray. 2017. *LaBelle: The Archaeology of a Seventeenth Century Ship of New World Colonization.* College Station: Texas A&M University Press.

Bullen, Ripley P., and Harold K. Brooks. 1967. "Two Ancient Florida Dugout Canoes." *Quarterly Journal of the Florida Academy of Sciences* XXX(2) (June): 97–107.

Burke, Edmund. 1998. *Philosophical Enquiry into the Sublime and Beautiful and Other Pre-Revolutionary Writings*, ed. David Womersley. New York: Penguin Books.

Burström, Mats. 2017. *Ballast: Laden with History.* Lund: Nordic Academic Press.

Byram, R. Scott. 2013. *Triangulating Archaeological Landscapes: The U.S. Coast Survey in California, 1850–1895.* Contributions of the Archaeological Research Facility, University of California, Vol. 65. University of California, Berkeley.

Cain, Emily. 1983. *Ghost Ships: Hamilton and Scourge, Historical Treasures from the War of 1812*. New York; Toronto: Olympic Marketing Company.
Callaghan, R. T. 2003. "The Use of Simulation Models to Estimate Frequency and Location of Japanese Edo Period Wrecks Along the Canadian Pacific Coast." *Canadian Journal of Archaeology/Journal Canadien d'Archéologie* 27: 74–94.
Campbell, Peter B. 2020. "The Sea as a Hyperobject: Moving Beyond Maritime Cultural Landscapes." *Journal of Eastern Mediterranean Archaeology Heritage Studies* 8(3): 1–22.
Campbell, Peter B. 2021. "The Anthropocene, Hyperobjects and the Archaeology of the Future Past." *Antiquity* 95(383): 1315–1330.
Cantwell, Anne-Marie, and Diana diZerega Wall. 2001. *Unearthing Gotham: The Archaeology of New York City*. New Haven, CT: Yale University Press.
Capelotti, P. S. 2018. *Adventures in Archaeology: The Wreck of the Orca II and Other Explorations*. Gainesville: University Press of Florida.
Caporaso, Alicia, Daniel J. Warren, and Steven R. Gittings. 2018. "The Evolution of Recent Multidisciplinary Deep-Water Archaeological and Biological Research on the Gulf of Mexico Outer Continental Shelf," in M. Souza and D. Costa, eds., *Historical Archaeology and Environment*. Champlain: Springer, pp. 207–228.
Casson, Lionel, and Richard D. Steffy. 1991. *The Athlit Ram*. College Station: Texas A&M University Press.
Castro, Filipe. 2019. "Treasure Hunting," online at https://nautarch.tamu.edu/index_treasurehunters.htm (accessed September 23, 2019).
Catsambis, Alexis, Ben Ford, and Donny L. Hamilton, eds. 2014. *The Oxford Handbook of Maritime Archaeology*. New York: Oxford University Press.
Cattaneo, C., M. Tidball Binz, L. Penados, J. Prieto, O. Finegan, and M. Grandi. 2015. "The Forgotten Tragedy of Unidentified Dead in the Mediterranean." *Forensic Science International* 250: e1–e2, https://doi.org/10.1016/j.forsciint.2015.02.007.
Cederlund, Carl Olaf. 1997. *Nationalism eller vetenskap? Svensk marinarkeologi i ideolisk belysning*. Stockholm: Carlsson.
Cederlund, Carl Olaf, and Fred Hocker, eds. 2006. *Vasa 1: The Archaeology of a Swedish Warship of 1628*. Stockholm: National Maritime Museums of Sweden.
Chandler, Lisa. 2023. "The Rescue of William D'Oyly: Colonial Castaway Encounters and the Imperial Gaze." *Australian and New Zealand Journal of Art* 23(1): 96–110.
Character, Leila, Agustin Ortiz, Jr., Tim Beach, and Sheryl Luzzader-Beach. 2021. "Archaeologic Machine Learning for Shipwreck Detection Using Lidar and Sonar." *Remote Sensing* 13(9): 1–15, http://dx.doi.org/10.3390/rs13091759.
Chiu, Chung-Shen, Chung-Ping Liu, Ki-Yin Chang, Wen-Jui Tseng, and Yung-Wei Chen. 2017. "Cost of Salvage—A Comparative Form Approach." *Journal of Marine Science and Technology* 25(6): 742–751.
Chong, Alan, and Stephen Murphy, eds. 2017. *The Tang Shipwreck: Art and Exchange in the 9th Century*. Singapore: Asian Civilizations Museum.
Clark, Helen Archibald. 1909. *Longfellow's Country*. New York: Baker & Taylor.
Clark, Michael. 2007. "'Bound Out for Callao!' The Pacific Coal Trade, 1876–1896: Selling Coal or Selling Lives? Part 2." *The Great Circle* 29(1): 3–21.
Cohen, Andrew. 2013. *Lost Beneath the Ice: The Story of HMS Investigator*. Toronto: Dundurn.
Coll, Charo. 2018. "An Assessment of the Current State of the Marine Salvage Industry," ITS 2018, Marseilles, June 27, online at http://www.marine-salvage.com/media-information/conference-papers/an-assessment-of-the-current-state-of-the-marine-salvage-industry/.

Conlin, David L., and Matthew A. Russell. 2006. "Archaeology of a Naval Battlefield: H.L. *Hunley* and USS *Housatonic*." *The International Journal of Nautical Archaeology* 35(1) (April): 20–40.

Corbin, Annalies. 2008. *The Steamboat* Montana *and the Opening of the West: History, Excavation, and Architecture.* Gainesville: University Press of Florida.

Costello, Leo. 2017. *J.M.W. Turner and the Subject of History.* Burlington, VT: Ashgate.

Coyle, Gretchen F., and Deborah C. Whitcraft. 2012. *Inferno at Sea: Stories of Death and Survival Aboard the Morro Castle.* West Creek, NJ: Down the Shore.

Crane, Stephen. 1898. *The Open Boat and Other Stories.* London: W. Heinemann.

Cressy, David. 2022. *Shipwrecks and the Bounty of the Sea.* Oxford; New York: Oxford University Press.

Crile, Jane, and Barney Crile. 1954. *Treasure-Diving Holidays.* New York: Viking Press.

Crisman, Kevin, ed. 2016. *Coffins of the Brave: Lake Shipwrecks of the War of 1812.* College Station: Texas A&M University Press.

Crumlin Pederson, Ole, and Olaf Olsen. 2002. *The Skuldelev Ships I: Topography, Archaeology, History, Conservation and Display.* Roskilde: The Viking Ship Museum.

Cussler, Clive, and Craig Dirgo. 1996. *The Sea Hunters: True Adventures with Famous Shipwrecks.* New York: Simon & Schuster.

Cussler, Clive, and Craig Dirgo. 2002. *The Sea Hunters II: More True Adventures with Famous Shipwrecks.* New York: G. P. Putnam's Sons.

Dahm, Jonas, and Carl Douglas. 2021. *Ghost Ships of the Baltic Sea.* Stockholm: Bokforlaget Max Ström.

Davis, H. 1872. *Record of Japanese Vessels Driven Upon the North-West Coast of America and Its Outlying Islands.* Worcester, MA: Charles Hamilton.

Delano, Leonard H. 2011. *Sunken Klondike Gold: How a Lost Fortune Inspired an Ambitious Effort to Raise the S.S. Islander.* Chicago: Delano.

Delgado, James P., ed. 1997. *The British Museum Encyclopaedia of Underwater and Maritime Archaeology.* London: British Museum Press.

Delgado, James P. 1983. "Murder Most Foul: San Francisco Reacts to the Loss of the S.S. *Central America*." *The Log of Mystic Seaport* XXXV(1) (Spring): 3–15.

Delgado, James P. 1984. "'Their Bones Should Be Left in the Ocean to Rot': Notes on an Unusual Shipwreck Song." *The Book Club of California Quarterly News-Letter* XLIX(2): 31–43.

Delgado, James P. 1988. *A Symbol of American Ingenuity: Assessing the Significance of USS* Monitor. Washington, DC: National Park Service.

Delgado, James P. 1992. "Recovering the Past of USS *Arizona*: Symbolism, Myth and Reality." *Historical Archaeology* 26(4): 69–80.

Delgado, James P. 1996. *Ghost Fleet: The Sunken Ships of Bikini Atoll.* Honolulu: University of Hawaii Press.

Delgado, James P. 1997. "'Til Isen er du Bygget': Rapport om vraket av Hudson's Bay Company Ship *Baymaud*, ex-polarskipet *Maud*." *Norsk Sjøfartsmuseum Årbok* 1997: 11–47.

Delgado, James P. 1999. *Across the Top of the World: The Quest for the Northwest Passage.* Vancouver; Toronto: Douglas & McIntyre.

Delgado, James P. 2000. "Underwater Archaeology at the Dawn of the 21st Century." *Historical Archaeology* XXXIV(4): 9–13.

Delgado, James P. 2004. *Adventures of a Sea Hunter: In Search of Famous Shipwrecks.* Vancouver; Toronto: Douglas & McIntyre.

Delgado, James P. 2006. "Archaeological Reconnaissance of the 1865 American-Built *Sub Marine Explorer* at Isla San Telmo, Archipielago de las Perlas, Panama." *International Journal of Nautical Archaeology* 35(2) (October): 230–252.

Delgado, James P. 2007. "*Titanic*, Hollywood, and Shipwrecks," in Julie M. Schlabitsky, ed., *Box Office Archaeology: Refining Hollywood's Portrayals of the Past*. Walnut Creek, CA: Left Coast Press.

Delgado, James P. 2009. "Survey of the Steam Yacht *Fox* at Qeqertarsuaq (Disko Island, Greenland, 20th Century)." *Journal of Field Archaeology* XXXIV(1) (Spring): 25–36.

Delgado, James P. 2011. *Silent Killers: Submarines and Underwater Warfare*. Oxford: Osprey.

Delgado, James P. 2012. *Misadventures of a Civil War Submarine: Iron, Guns, and Pearls*. College Station: Texas A&M University Press.

Delgado, James P. 2016. "After Crossroads: The Fate of the Atomic Bomb Target Fleet." *Journal of Maritime Archaeology* 11: 25–31.

Delgado, James P. 2019. *War at Sea: A Shipwrecked History from Antiquity to the Twentieth Century*. Oxford; New York: Oxford University Press.

Delgado, James P. 2022. *The Curse of the Somers: The Secret History of the Navy's Most Notorious Mutiny*. New York: Oxford University Press.

Delgado, James P. 2022a. "Review of Sara A. Rich: Shipwreck Hauntography: Underwater Ruins and the Uncanny." *Journal of Maritime Archaeology* 17(4): 639–641, https://doi.org/10.1007/s11457-022-09341-4.

Delgado, James P. 2024. "Maritime Archaeology of the Post-Ancient World (1400–1946)," in Mark Aldenderfer, ed., *Oxford Research Encyclopedia of Anthropology*. New York: Oxford University Press, https://doi.org/10.1093/acrefore/9780190854584.013.626.

Delgado, James P. 2024a. "Shipwrecks, The Middle Passage and Jim Crow: The Signatures of Systemic Racism and Injustice at Two Maritime Archaeological Sites," in Christopher Fennell, ed., *Grappling with Monuments of Oppression*. New York: Routledge, pp. 123–136.

Delgado, James P. 2024b. "Skeletons in the Sand: National Park Service Work on Intertidal Shipwrecks, 1980–1990," in Jennifer Jones, Daniel Zwick, and Calvin S. Mires, eds., *The Intertidal Shipwreck: Management of a Historic Resource in an Unmanageable Environment*. Gainesville: University Press of Florida.

Delgado, James P., Bradley W. Barr, Matthew S. Lawrence, and Hans K. Van Tilburg. 2017. "The Search for the 1871 Whaling Fleet of the Western Arctic: Writing the Final Chapter." *International Journal of Nautical Archaeology* XLVI(1): 149–163, https://doi.org/10.1111/1095-9270.12205.

Delgado, James P., Amy Borgens, Deborah Marx, Matthew Lawrence, and David Eynon. 2021. "Archaeological Survey and Contextualization of the Barque *Vicar of Bray* (1841, Modified 1858–1859), Goose Green, Falkland Islands/Islas Malvinas." *Journal of Maritime Archaeology* XVI(3) (August): 223–251, https://doi.org/10.1007/s11457-021-09298-w.

Delgado, James P., and Michael L. Brennan. 2018. "Special Issue: Maritime Archaeology on the Final Frontier: Telepresence-enabled Robotic Missions into the Deep." *Journal of Maritime Archaeology* 13(2) (August).

Delgado, James P., and Michael L. Brennan. 2023b. "Wreck 15563: An Early Nineteenth Century Merchant Vessel in the Gulf of Mexico." *Journal of Maritime Archaeology* 18(3): 477–520, http://dx.doi.org/10.1007/s11457-023-09370-7.

Delgado, James P., Michael L. Brennan, Robert A. Church, and Daniel J. Warren. 2023a. "Late Nineteenth Century Bulk Trade and Barges: An Historical Overview and the Likely Context of Two Deep-Water Shipwrecks in the Gulf of Mexico." *Journal of Maritime Archaeology* 18(3) (September): 591–645, https://doi.org/10.1007/s11457-023-09369-0.

Delgado, James P., Michael Brennan, Larrie Ferreiro, Josh Broussard, and Michael Arbuthnot. 2022. "Discovery and Initial Documentation of USS *Nevada* (BB-36): An Artifact of Two World Wars and the Advent of the Cold War." *Journal of Maritime Archaeology* 17: 93–129, https://doi.org/10.1007/s11457-022-09324-5.

Delgado, James P., M. L. Brennan, Sergio A. Rapu Haoa, Julianna H. Rapu Leong, Carlos F. Gaymer, Diego Carabias, Emily Stokes, and Daniel Wagner. 2022. "The Hidden Landscape: Maritime Cultural Heritage of the Salas y Gómez and Nazca Ridges with Implications for Conservation on the High Seas." *Marine Policy* 136: 104877, https://doi.org/10.1016/j.marpol.2021.104877.

Delgado, James P., Michael L. Brennan, Jan Roletto, Frank Cantelas, Russell Mathews, Kelly Elliott, Kai Vetter, Christopher Figueroa, Megan Lickliter-Mundon, and Robert V. Schwemmer. 2017. "Exploration and Mapping of USS *Independence*." *Oceanography* 30(1): 34–35.

Delgado, James P., Ben L. Ford, and Michael L. Brennan. 2023c. "Nineteenth Century Shipwrecks and the Maritime Cultural Landscape of the Gulf of Mexico." *Journal of Maritime Archaeology* 18(3): 371–403, http://dx.doi.org/10.1007/s11457-023-09375-2.

Delgado, James P., and James A. Goold. 2022. "Background to the 'Black Swan' Case: The Identification as *Nuestra Señora de las Mercedes*." *International Journal of Nautical Archaeology* 50(2): 352–360, https://doi.org/10.1080/10572414.2021.2020595.

Delgado, James P., Nicole Bucchino Grinnan, and Michael L. Brennan. 2023d. "Fishing in the Gulf of Mexico in the Nineteenth Century: An Historical Overview and the Likely Context of Three Deep-Water Shipwrecks." *Journal of Maritime Archaeology* 18(3): 553–589, https://doi.org/10.1007/s11457-023-09367-2.

Delgado, James P., Jack Irion, and Michael L. Brennan. 2023f. "Wreck 15377: A Probable Immigrant and Cargo Packet of the Mid-Nineteenth Century in the Gulf of Mexico." *Journal of Maritime Archaeology* 18(3): 521–552, https://doi.org/10.1007/s11457-023-09373-4.

Delgado, James P., Terry Kerby, Hans K. Van Tilburg, Steven Price, Ole Varmer, Maximilian D. Cremer, and Russell Matthews. 2016. *The Lost Submarines of Pearl Harbor: The Rediscovery and Archaeology of Japan's Top-Secret Midget Submarines of World War II*. College Station: Texas A&M University Press.

Delgado, James P., Deborah Marx, Kyle Lent, Joseph Grinnan, and Alex De. 2023. *Clotilda: The History and Archaeology of the Last Slave Ship*. Huntsville: University of Alabama Press.

Delgado, James P., William Gomez Pretel, and Juan Guillermo Martin. 2023e. "Shipwrecks in the Western Caribbean (Archipelago of San Andres, Old Providence and Santa Catalina): Between Narratives and Hurricanes." *Journal of Maritime Archaeology* 18(3): 405–446, https://doi.org/10.1007/s11457-023-09372-5.

Delgado, James P., Robert V. Schwemmer, and Michael L. Brennan. 2020. "Shipwrecks and the Maritime Cultural Landscape of the Gulf of the Farallones." *Journal of Maritime Archaeology* 15(2): 131–163, https://doi.org/10.1007/s11457-020-09254-0.

Delgado, James P., Hans K. Tilburg, Bruce G. Terrell, Deborah Marx, Catherine Marzin, Stephen Gittings, William Kiene, Valerie Grussing, and Pamela Orlando. 2016. "How NOAA's Office of National Marine Sanctuaries Engages the Public in the Ocean Through the Science and Management of Maritime Heritage." *Aquatic Conservation: Marine and Freshwater Ecosystems* XXVI(Supp. 2): 200–212.

Dickens, Charles [writing as S. Eyetinge, Jr.]. 1869. *The Uncommercial Traveler, and Additional Christmas Stories*. London: Chapman and Hall.

Diolé, Philippe. 1954. *4,000 years Under the Sea: Excursions in Undersea Archaeology*. London: Sidgwick and Jackson.

Diouf, Sylviane A. 2007. *Dreams of Africa in Alabama*. Oxford: Oxford University Press.
Donne, John. 1855. *The Poetical Works of Dr. John Donne, With a Memoir*. Boston: Little Brown and Company.
D'Oriano, R., and E. Riccardi. 1999. "A Lost Fleet of Ships in the Port of Olbia," in S. Kingsley, ed., *Encyclopedia of Underwater Archaeology, Barbarian Seas, Late Rome to Islam*. London: Periplus, pp. 89–85.
Dromgoole, Sarah. 2013. *Underwater Cultural Heritage and International Law*. Cambridge: Cambridge University Press.
Dumas, Frédérick. 1976. *30 Centuries Under the Sea*. New York: Crown.
Duncan, Brad, and Martin Gibbs. 2015. *Please God Send Me a Wreck: Responses to Shipwreck in a 19th Century Australian Community*. New York: Springer.
Du Plat Taylor, Joan, ed. 1965. *Marine Archaeology*. New York: Thomas Y. Crowell.
Durkin, Hannah. 2024. *The Survivors of the Clotilda: The Lost Stories of the Last Captives of the American Save Trade*. New York: HarperCollins.
Ellingham, Sarah Theresa Dorothea, Pierre Perich, and Morris Tidball-Binz. 2017. "The Fate of Human Remains in a Maritime Context and Feasibility for Forensic Humanitarian Action to Assist in Their Recovery and Identification." *Forensic Science International* 279: 229–234, https://doi.org/10.1016/j.forsciint.2017.07.039.
Endicott, William, and Lawrence Waters Jenkins. 1923. *Wrecked Among Cannibals in the Fijis: A Narrative of Shipwreck & Adventure in the South Sea*. Salem, MA: Marine Research Society.
Erickson, Peter, and Clark Hulse. 2000. *Early Modern Visual Culture: Representation, Race and Empire in Renaissance England*. Philadelphia: University of Pennsylvania Press.
Eriksson, Niklas, and Johan Rönnby. 2017. "*Mars* (1564): The Initial Archaeological Investigations of a Great 16th-Century Swedish Warship." *International Journal of Nautical Archaeology* 46(1): 92–107.
Ertel, Darryl. 2017. Shipwreck Coast National Marine Sanctuary Nomination, Lake Superior, MI, online at https://nmsnominate.blob.core.windows.net/nominate-prod/media/documents/shipwreck-coast-nmsn-lake-superior-mi.pdf (accessed September 24, 2019).
Firth, Antony. 2015. "East Coast War Channels: A Landscape Approach to Battlefield Archaeology in the North Sea." *International Journal of Nautical Archaeology* 44(2): 438–446.
Flatman, Joe. 2003. "Cultural Biographies, Cognitive Landscapes and Dirty Old Bits of Boat: 'Theory' in Maritime Archeology." *The International Journal of Nautical Archaeology* 32(2): 143–157.
Flatman, Joe. 2007. "The Origins and Ethics of Maritime Archaeology." *Public Archaeology* 6(2): 77–97.
Flecker, Michael. 2000. "A Ninth-Century AD Arab or Indian Shipwreck in Indonesian Waters." *International Journal of Nautical Archaeology* 29(2): 199–217.
Flecker, Michael. 2001. "A Ninth-Century AD Arab or Indian Shipwreck in Indonesia: First Evidence for Direct Trade with China." *World Archaeology* 32(3): 335–354.
Flecker, Michael. 2002. "The Ethics, Politics and Realities of Maritime Archaeology in Southeast Asia." *International Journal of Nautical Archaeology* 31(1): 12–24.
Flecker, Michael. 2008. A Ninth-Century AD Arab or Indian Shipwreck in Indonesian Waters: Addendum." *International Journal of Nautical Archaeology* 37(2); 384–386.
Flecker, Michael. 2011. "Wrecked Twice: Shipwrecks as a Cultural Resource in Southeast Asia," in John Miksic, Geok Yian Goh, and Sue O'Connor, eds., *Re-thinking Cultural Resource Management in Southeast Asia: Preservation, Development and Neglect*. London; New York: Anthem Press, pp. 15–35.

Flecker, Michael. 2017. "The Origin of the Tang Shipwreck: A Look at Its Archaeology and History, in Alan Chong and Stephen A. Murphy." *The Tang Shipwreck: Art and Exchange in the 9th Century*, Singapore, Asian Civilsations Museum, pp. 22–39.

Foley, Brendan. 2007. "Archaeology in Deep Water: Impact of Fishing on Shipwrecks," https://www.whoi.edu/sbl/liteSite.do?litesiteid=2740&articleId=4965 (accessed September 26, 2019).

Ford, Ben, ed. 2011. *The Archaeology of Maritime Landscapes*. New York: Springer.

Ford, Ben, Jessi Halligan, and Alexis Catsambis. 2020. *Our Blue Planet: An Introduction to Maritime and Underwater Archaeology*. New York; Oxford: Oxford University Press.

Foster, John Wilson, ed. *Titanic*. New York and London: Penguin Books.

Franzen, Anders. 1960. *The Warship Vasa: Deep Diving and Marine Archaeology in Stockholm*. Stockholm: Norstedt and Bonnier.

Frost, Honor. 1963. *Under the Mediterranean: Marine Antiquities*. London: Routledge and Kegan Paul.

Gambi, M., A. Schulze, and E. Amato. 2011. "Record of Lamellibrachia sp. (Annelida: Siboglinidae: Vestimentifera) from a Deep Shipwreck in the Western Mediterranean Sea (Italy)." *Marine Biodiversity Records* 4: E24.

Garzke, William H., Jr., Robert O. Dulin, Jr., James Cameron, and William J. Jurens. 2019. *Battleship Bismarck: A Design and Operational History*. Annapolis: Naval Institute Press.

Gately, Iain, and Jonathan Benjamin. 2018. "Archaeology Hijacked: Addressing the Historical Misappropriations of Maritime and Underwater Archaeology." *The Journal of Maritime Archaeology* 13(1) (April): 15–35.

Gerstenberger, Donna. 1972. "The Open Boat: Additional Perspective." *Modern Fiction Studies* 17(4) (Winter): 557–561.

Gesner, Peter. 1991. *Pandora: An Archaeological Perspective*. Queensland, South Brisbane: Queensland Museum.

Giaracuni, G., and L. De Luca, eds. 2017. *Costas Varotsos: L'Approdo*. Maglie: Opera all'Umanità Migrante, Carlo Toma Edizioni.

Goggin, John M. 1960. "Underwater Archaeology: Its Nature and Limitations." *American Antiquity* 25(3): 348–354.

Gongaware, Laura Lynn. 2012. "To Exhibit or Not to Exhibit? Establishing a Middle Ground for Commercially Exploited Underwater Cultural Heritage under the 2001 UNESCO Convention." *Tulane Maritime Law Journal* 37(1): 203–229.

Gongaware, Laura Lynn. 2013. "Finding a Middle Ground in the Protection of Underwater Cultural Heritage," thesis, Texas A&M University, College Station, Texas. Online at http://oaktrust.library.tamu.edu/bitstream/handle/1969.1/151631/GONGAWARE-THESIS-2013.pdf;sequence=1.

Gould, Richard. 1983. *Shipwreck Anthropology*. Albuquerque: University of New Mexico Press.

Gould, Richard. 2011. *Archaeology and the Social History of Ships*. Cambridge; New York: Cambridge University Press.

Govier, Katherine. 2005. *Three Views of Crystal Water: Of Pearls and Passion, of Belonging and Betrayal*. London; New York: Fourth Estate.

Green, Elizabeth S., and Justin Leidwanger. 2017. "Damien Hirst's Tale of Shipwreck and Salvaged Treasure." *American Journal of Archaeology* CXXII(1), online museum review, https://www.ajaonline.org/online-museum-review/3581.

Green, J. B. 1859. *Diving With & Without Armor: Containing the Submarine Exploits of J.B. Green, the Celebrated Submarine Diver*. Buffalo, NY: Faxon's Steam Power Press.

Greenhill, Basil, and John Morrison. 1995. *The Archaeology of Boats and Ships: An Introduction*. London: Conway Maritime Press.

Gregory, David, Tom Dawson, Dolores Elkin, Hans Van Tilburg, Chris Underwood, Vicki Richards, Andrew Viduka, Kieran Westley, Jeneva Wright, and Jorgen Holleson. 2022. "Of Time and Tide: The Complex Impacts of Climate Change on Coastal and Underwater Heritage." *Antiquity* 96(390): 1396–1411.

Grover, David H. 2002. *The Unforgiving Coast: Maritime Disasters of the Pacific Northwest*. Corvallis: Oregon State University Press.

Hansson, Maria C., and Brendan P. Foley. 2008. "Ancient DNA Fragments Inside Classical Greek Amphoras Reveal Cargo of 2400-Year Old Shipwreck." *Journal of Archaeological Science* 35(5): 1169–1176.

Harpster, Matthew. 2009. "Keith Muckelroy: Methods, Ideas and Maritime Archaeology." *Journal of Maritime Archaeology* 4: 67–82, https://doi.org/10.1007/s11457-009-9045-2.

Harpster, Matthew. 2013. "Shipwreck Identity, Methodology and Nautical Archaeology." *Journal of Archaeological Method and Theory* 20(4): 588–622.

Heard, Alex. 1995. "To Cut a Deal with the Pirate Prince." *Outside Magazine* (Outsideonline), October 1, https://www.outsideonline.com/1922576/cut-deal-pirate-prince.

Hecht, Randy B. 2016. "The Natural." *Glass Quarterly* 142 (Spring): 36–43.

Heiden, Bruce. 1997. "The Iliad and Its Contexts." *Arethusa* 30(2) (Spring): 221–240.

Heizer, Robert F. 1941. "Archaeological Evidence of Sebastian Rodriquez Cermeño's California Visit in 1595." *California Historical Society Quarterly* 20(4): 315–328.

Hendel, Ronald S. 1995. "The Shape of Utnapishtim's Ark." *Zeitschrift für die Alestamentliche Wissenschaft* 107(1): 128–129.

Hendershot, Steve. 2014. "Behind the Song: Pacific Pearl Co. 1869," blog, October 30, https://divingbellmusic.tumblr.com/post/101392386488/behind-the-song-pacific-pearl-co-1869 (accessed October 1, 2019).

Henderson, Graeme. 1986. *Maritime Archaeology in Australia*. Nedlands: University of Western Australia Press.

Hicks, Brian. 2006. *When the Dancing Stopped: The Real Story of the Morro Castle Disaster and Its Deadly Wake*. New York; London; Toronto; Sydney: Free Press.

Hocker, Emma. 2006. "From the Micro- to the Macro-: Managing the Conservation of the Warship, Vasa." *Macromolecular Symposia* 238(1): 16–21, https://doi.org/10.1002/masy.200650603.

Hocker, Emma, G. Almkvist, and M. Sahlstedt. 2012. "The Vasa Experience with Polyethylene Glycol: A Conservator's Perspective." *Journal of Cultural Heritage* 13(3): S175–S182, https://doi.org/10.1016/j.culher.2012.01.017.

Hocker, Fred. 2004. "Shipbuilding, Philosophy, Practice, and Research," in Fred Hocker and Cheryl Wards, eds., *The Philosophy of Shipbuilding: Conceptual Approaches to the Study of Wooden Ships*. College Station: Texas A&M University Press.

Hocker, Fred. 2011. *Vasa: A Swedish Warship*. Stockholm: Medströms.

Huffman, Alan. 2009. *Sultana: Surviving Civil War, Prison and the Worst Maritime Disaster in American History*. New York: Collins.

Hugenin, Charles A. 1960. "The Truth About the Schooner *Hesperus*." *New York Folklore Quarterly* 16(1): 48–53.

Huggins, Michael. 1995. "Saudi Treasure Fails to Find Buyer." *UPI*, November 16, https://www.upi.com/Archives/1995/11/16/Saudi-treasure-fails-to-find-buyer/4576816498000/.

Hugill, Peter. 1993. *World Trade Since 1431*. Baltimore, MD: Johns Hopkins University Press.

Huntress, Keith, ed. 1974. *Narratives of Shipwreck and Disasters, 1586–1860*. Ames: Iowa State University Press.

Hurston, Zora Neale. 2018. *Barracoon: The Story of the Last "Black Cargo."* New York: HarperCollins/Amistad.

Hutchinson, Gillian. 2017. *Sir John Franklin's Erebus and Terror Expedition: Lost and Found.* London: Bloomsbury.

Introna, F., G. Di Vella, and C. P. Campobasso. 2013. "Migrant Deaths and the Kater Radez I Wreck: From Recovery of the Relict to Marine Taphonomic Findings and Identification of the Victims." *International Journal of Legal Medicine* 127: 871–879, https://doi.org/10.1007/s00414-012-0807-2.

Ireland, John. 1845. *The Shipwrecked Orphans: A True Narrative of the Shipwreck and Sufferings of John Ireland and William Doyley, Who Were Wrecked in the Ship Charles Eaton, on an Island in the South Seas.* New Haven: S. Babcock.

Isto, Raino. 2021. "Otranto—A Time-Based Monument to Albania's 1997 Migration: A Conversation with Latent Community." *ArtMargins Online*, https://artmargins.com/otranto-a-time-based-monument-to-albanias-1997-migration-a-conversation-with-latent-community/.

Jackson, Joe. 2010. *A Furnace Afloat: The Wreck of the Hornet and the Harrowing 4,300-Mile Voyage of Its Survivors.* New York: Free Press.

Jackson, Virginia. 1998. "Longfellow's Tradition, or, Picture-Writing a Nation." *Modern Language Quarterly* 59(4): 471–496.

Jasper, Joy Waldron, James P. Delgado, and Jim Adams. 2001. *The USS Arizona: The Ship, the Men, the Pearl Harbor Attack, and the Symbol That Aroused America.* New York: St. Martin's Press.

Jewitt, John R. 1815. *Narrative of the Adventures and Sufferings of John R. Jewitt: Sole Survivor of the Crew of the Ship Boston, During a Captivity of Nearly Three Years Among the Savages of Nootka Sound; With an Account of the Manners, Mode of Living, and Religious Opinions of the Natives.* Middleton, CT: Seth Richards.

Johnson, Peter. 1999. *Glyphs and Gallows: The Rock Art of Clo-ose and the Wreck of the John Bright.* Surrey, BC: Heritage House.

Johnston, Paul Forsythe. 1993. "Treasure Salvage, Archaeological Ethics and Maritime Museums." *International Journal of Nautical Archaeology* 22(1): 53–60.

Jones, Douglas. 2023. "The Offshore Oil Exploration Industry and Archaeology in the Gulf of Mexico." *Journal of Maritime Archaeology* 18(3): 351–370.

Jourdan, David W. 2015. *The Search for the Japanese Fleet: USS Nautilus and the Battle of Midway.* Lincoln, NE: Potomac Books.

Juvelier, Ben. 2018. "'Salvaging' History: Underwater Cultural Heritage and Commercial Salvage." *American University International Law Review* 32(5): 1023–1036.

Kaltsas, Nikolaos, Elena Vlachogianni, and Polyxeni Bouyia, eds. 2012. *The Antikythera Shipwreck: The Ship, the Treasures, the Mechanism. National Archaeological Museum, April 2012–April 2013.* Kapon; Athens: Hellenic Ministry of Culture and Tourism; National Archaeological Museum.

Karović, Gordana. 2018. "Remains of the German Fleet Sunken Near Prahovo," in Jelena Jovanović Simić and Zorica Civrić, eds., *The Danube in Serbia—A Journey Through Technical Museums.* Belgrade: Museum of Science and Technology, pp. 185–193.

Keddie, Grant. 2004. "Japanese Shipwrecks in British Columbia—Myths and Facts: The Question of Cultural Exchanges with the Northwest Coast of America." *The Midden* XLIX(3): 15–27.

Keddie, Grant. 2006. "The Early Introduction of Iron Among the First Nations of British Columbia." http://royalbcmuseum.bc.ca/staffprofiles/files/2013/08/An-Early-Introduction-to-Iron-inB.C.-Grant-Keddie.pdf.

Keith, Matthew, ed. 2016. *Site Formation Processes of Submerged Shipwrecks.* Gainesville: University Press of Florida.

Kennedy, Greg. 1997. "Maritime Strength and the British Economy, 1840–1850." *The Northern Mariner/Le Marin du Nord* VII(2) (April): 51–69.

Kerr, Matthew P. M. 2022. *The Victorian Novel and the Problems of Marine Language: All at Sea.* Oxford: Oxford University Press.

Kimura, Jun. 2016. *Archaeology of East Asian Shipbuilding.* Gainesville: University Press of Florida.

Kimura, Jun, Mark Staniforth, Lê Thi Lien, and Randall Sasaki. 2013. "Naval Battlefield Archaeology of the Lost Kublai Khan Fleets." *International Journal of Nautical Archaeology* 43(1): 76–86.

King, T. F., and W. F. Upson. 1970. "Protohistory on Limantour Sandspit: Archaeological Investigations at 4-Mrn-216 and 4-Mrn-298," in R. E. Schenk, ed., *Contributions to the Archaeology of Point Reyes National Seashore: A Compendium in Honor of Adan E. Treganza*, pp. 114–194. Treganza Museum Papers No. 6, San Francisco State College.

Kleeberg, John M. 2013. "A Critique of the Fundamentals of the 'Commercial Salvage' Model of the Excavation of Historic Shipwrecks: An Examination of the Profitability of Six Commercial Salvage Ventures." *Technical Briefs in Historical Archaeology* 7: 19–30.

Kocabaş, Ufuk, ed. 2008. *Yenikapı Shipwrecks: The "Old Ships" of the "New Gate."* Istanbul: Yenikapı Batıkları, Yenikapı'nın Eski Gemileri.

Kolay, Selçuk, Okan Taktak, and Savas Karakas. 2013. *Echoes from the Deep: Wrecks of the Dardanelles Campaign.* Istanbul: Vehbu Koc Foundation, Ayhan Sahenk Foundation.

Korsgaard, Annika. 2010. *Shipwrecks and Seafaring in the Solomon Islands, 1788–1942.* Honours dissertation, Department of Archaeology, University of Sydney.

Kozik, Jennifer. 2020. *Shipwrecks of the Pacific Northwest: Tragedies and Legacies of a Perilous Coast.* Guilford, CT: Globe/Pequot.

Krahl, Regina, John Guy, J. Keith Wilson, and Julian Raby. 2010. *Shipwrecked: Tang Treasures and Monsoon Winds.* Washington, DC; Singapore: Arthur M. Sackler Gallery, Smithsonian Institution, and the National Heritage Board and the Singapore Tourism Board.

Krause, Kristin. 2016. The *Last Voyage of the Hornet: The Story That Made Mark Twain Famous.* Unionville, NY: Royal Fireworks Press.

Krumholz, Jason S., and Michael L. Brennan. 2015. "Fishing for Common Ground: Investigations of the Impact of Trawling on Ancient Shipwreck Sites Uncovers a Potential for Management Synergy." *Marine Policy* 61(c): 127–133.

Kuntz, Jerry. 2016. *The Heroic Age of Diving: America's Underwater Pioneers and the Great Wrecks of Lake Erie.* Albany: State University of New York Press.

Lamb, Kate. 2018. "Lost Bones, a Mass Grave and War Wrecks Plundered off Indonesia." *The Guardian*, February 27, 2018, online at https://www.theguardian.com/world/20.18/feb/28/bones-mass-grave-british-war-wrecks-java-indonesia.

Landow, George P. 1982. *Images of Crisis: Literary Iconology, 1750 to the Present.* Boston; London; Henley: Routledge and Kegan Paul.

Langewiesche, William. 2014. "Salvage Beast." *Vanity Fair*, December 2014, online at https://www.vanityfair.com/news/2014/12/nick-sloane-costa-concordia-salvage.

Layton, Thomas N. 1990. *Western Pomo Prehistory.* University of California, Los Angeles, Institute of Archaeology, Monograph 32.

Layton, Thomas N. 1995. "The Journey of the *Frolic.*" *Society for California Archaeology Newsletter* 29(1): 1, 3–5.

Layton, Thomas N. 1997. *The Voyage of the* Frolic: *New England Merchants and the Opium Trade.* Stanford, CA: Stanford University Press.

Layton, Thomas N. 2002. *Gifts from the Celestial Kingdom: A Shipwrecked Cargo for Gold Rush California.* Stanford, CA: Stanford University Press.

Layton, Thomas N. 2021. *The "Other" Dixwells: Commerce and Conscience in an American Family.* Germantown, MD: Society for Historical Archaeology.

Lemée, Christian P. P. 2006. *Renaissance Shipwrecks from Christianshaven: An Archaeological and Architectural Study of Large Cargo Vessels in Danish Waters, 1580–1640.* Roskilde: Viking Ship Museum, in collaboration with the National Museum of Denmark.

Lengkeek, W., J. W. P. Coolen, A. Gittenberger, and N. Shrieken. 2013. "Ecological Relevance of Shipwrecks in the North Sea." *Nederlandse Faunistische Mededelingen* 41: 49–57.

Lenihan, Daniel J., ed. 1987. *Submerged Cultural Resource Study, Isle Royale National Park.* Santa Fe, NM: National Park Service.

Lenihan, Daniel J. 1989. *USS Arizona Memorial and Pearl Harbor National Historic Landmark: Submerged Cultural Resources Assessment.* Santa Fe, NM: National Park Service.

Lenihan, Daniel J. 2002. *Submerged: Adventures of America's Most Elite Underwater Archeology Team.* New York: Newmarket Press.

Levenson, Michael. 2024. "It's a Golden Age for Ship Discoveries. Why?" *New York Times*, March 23, 2024, https://www.nytimes.com/2024/03/23/science/shipwreck-sinking-sea-why.html.

Lightfoot, Kent G. 2005. *Indians, Missionaries, and Merchants: The Legacy of Colonial Encounters on the California Frontiers.* Berkeley: University of California Press.

Lightfoot, Kent G., and W. S. Simmons. 1998. "Culture Contact in Protohistoric California: Social Contexts of Native and European Encounter." *Journal of California and Great Basin Anthropology* 20(2): 138–170.

Limburg, Peter R. 2005. *Deep-Sea Detectives: Maritime Mysteries and Forensic Science.* New York; Lincoln; Shanghai: ASIA Press.

Linenthal, Edward T. 1991. *Sacred Ground: Americans and Their Battlefields.* Champaign: University of Illinois Press.

Lipke, Paul. 1984. *The Royal Ship of Cheops: A Retrospective Account of the Discovery, Restoration and Reconstruction. Based on Interviews with Hag Ahmed Youssef Moustafa.* Oxford: British Archaeological Reports.

Longfellow, Henry. 1888. *The Wreck of the Hesperus, Illustrated.* New York: E. P. Dutton.

Maarleveld, Thijs. 2011. "Ethics, Underwater Cultural Heritage, and International Law," in Alexis Catsambis, Benjamin Ford, and Donny L. Hamilton, eds., *The Oxford Handbook of Maritime Archaeology.* Oxford: Oxford University Press, pp. 917–941.

Macauley, Rose. 1966. *Pleasure of Ruins.* New York: Walker.

MacKay, Charles, and Henry Russell. 1834. *The Ship on Fire. A Narrative Scene.* Boston: Oliver Ditson.

Macleod, Ian. 2008. "Shipwreck Graves and Their Conservation Management 1." *AICCM Bulletin* 31: 5–14, 10.1179/bac.2008.31.1.001 (accessed October 19, 2019).

Mallefet, J., V. Zintzen, C. Massin, A. Norro, M. Vincx, V. DeMaersschalck, M. Steyaert, S. Degraer, and A. Cattrijsse. 2008. *Belgian Shipwrecks: Hotspots for Marine Biodiversity (BEWREMABI).* Final Scientific Report. Belgian Science Policy, online at http://www.

vliz.be/nl/open-marien-archief?module=ref&refid=126030&printversion=1&drop IMIStitle=1.

Manders, Martijn. 2008. "In-Situ Preservation: The Preferred Option." *Museum International* 60(4): 31–41.

Marc, Jacques. 1997. *The Underwater Heritage of Friendly Cove*. Vancouver: Underwater Archaeological Society of British Columbia.

Marden, Luis. 1957. "I Found the Bones of the Bounty." *National Geographic Magazine*, CXII(6): 725–790.

Marinković, Dijana, Bojan Kuzmanović, and Dejan Đorđević. 2024. "Risk Management During the Removal of Sunken Ships on the Waterway—Base Study for the Danube—Prahovo Region." *International Journal of Economics and Law* 14(41): 43–62.

Mariners' Almanac. 1877. *A Shipwreck*. Philadelphia: Morwitz & Co.

Marsden, Peter. 1994. *Ships of the Port of London: First to Eleventh Centuries AD*. Swindon: English Heritage.

Martin, Colin. 1975. *Full Fathom Five: The Wrecks of the Spanish Armada*. New York: Viking Press.

Martin, Frederick. 1876. *The History of Lloyd's and of Marine Insurance in Great Britain*. London: Macmillan.

Martín, Juan, Juan Díaz, and William Gomez Pretel. 2022. "Underwater Archaeology in Colombia: Between Commercial Salvage and Science." *International Journal of Historical Archaeology* 26: 457–473, 10.1007/s10761-021-00610-x.

Martin, Roy, and Lyle Craigie-Halkett. 2007. *Risdon Beazley, Marine Salvor*. Southampton: Martin & Craigie-Halkett.

Marx, Robert F. 1967. *Always Another Adventure*. New York: World Publishing.

Marx, Robert F. 1978. *The History of Underwater Exploration*. New York: Dover Books.

Marx, Robert F. 1990. *The Underwater Dig: Introduction to Marine Archaeology*. Houston: Gulf Publishing.

Marx, Robert F., and Jenifer Marx. 1993. *The Search for Sunken Treasure: Exploring the World's Greatest Shipwrecks*. Toronto: Key-Porter Books.

Masters, David. 1924. *The Wonders of Salvage*. New York: Dodd, Mead.

Maupassant, Guy de. 1889. *The Odd Number: Thirteen Tales*. Trans. Jonathan Sturges. New York: Harper & Brothers.

McCarthy, Michael. 2001. *Iron and Steamship Archaeology: The Success and Failure in the SS Xantho*. New York: Springer.

McCarthy, Michael. 2005. *Ships' Fastenings: From Sewn Boat to Steamship*. College Station: Texas A&M University Press.

McCarthy, Michael. 2010. *HMAS Sydney II*. Welshpool: Western Australian Museum Press.

McCarthy, Michael. 2011. "Archaeology and the HMAS *Sydney*." *The Journal of the Australasian Institute for Maritime Archaeology* 35: 18–27.

McCarthy, Michael. 2011a. "Museums and Maritime Archaeology," in Alexis Catsambis, Benjamin Ford, and Donny L. Hamilton, eds., *The Oxford Handbook of Maritime Archaeology*. Oxford: Oxford University Press, pp. 1032–1054.

McCartney, Innes. 2015. *The Maritime Archaeology of a Modern Conflict: Comparing the Archaeology of German Submarine Wrecks to Historical Text*. New York; London: Routledge.

McCartney, Innes. 2018. *Jutland 1916: The Archaeology of a Naval Battlefield*. London; New York: Conway.

McCartney, Innes. 2019. *Scapa 1919: The Archaeology of a Scuttled Fleet*. London; New York: Bloomsbury.

McCarty, Jennifer Hooper, and Tim Foecke. 2009. *What Really Sank the Titanic: New Forensic Discoveries*. New York: Citadel Press.

McGee, Frederick L. 1997. "Toward a Postcolonial Nautical Archaeology." *Assemblage* 3(1), https://assemblagejournal.wordpress.com/wp-content/uploads/2017/05/mcghee-towards-a-postcolonial-nautical-archaeology.pdf.

McGrath, H. Thomas Jr. 1981. "The Eventual Preservation and Stabilization of the USS *Cairo*." *The International Journal of Nautical Archaeology and Underwater Exploration* 10(2): 79–94.

McGrail, Seán. 2001. *Boats of the World: From the Stone Age to Medieval Times*. Oxford; New York: Oxford University Press.

McManamon, John. 2023. *From Caligula to the Nazis: The Nemi Ships in Diana's Sanctuary*. College Station: Texas A&M University Press.

Mearns, David L. 2009. *The Search for the Sydney*. Pymble, New South Wales: HarperCollins.

Mearns, David L. 2017. *Shipwreck Hunter: A Lifetime of Extraordinary Discoveries on the Ocean Floor*. Crows Nest, Australia: Allen & Unwin.

Mearns, David L., and A. R. Hudson. 2000. *Development of a Controllable Grab System for Deep Water Recovery*, https://diving-rov-specialists.com/index_htm_files/rov_22-devellopment-grab-system-deep-water.pdf (accessed March 7, 2025).

Meide, Chuck. 2013. *The Development of Maritime Archaeology as a Discipline and the Evolving Use of Theory by Maritime Archaeologists*. PhD dissertation, College of William and Mary, Department of Anthropology, Williamsburg, VA.

Meighan, Clement W. 1950. *Excavations in Sixteenth Century Shellmounds at Drake's Bay, Marin County*. University of California Archaeological Survey Report No. 9, Papers on California Archaeology No. 9. Department of Anthropology, University of California, Berkeley.

Meighan, Clement W. 2002. "The Stoneware Site: A 16th Century Site on Drakes Bay," in W. J. Wallace and F. A. Riddell (eds.), *Essays in California Archaeology: A Memorial to Franklin Fenenga*, pp. 62–87. Contributions of the University of California Archaeological Research Facility No. 60. University of California, Berkeley.

Meighan, Clement W., and Robert F. Heizer. 1952. "Archaeological Exploration of Sixteenth-Century Indian Mounds at Drake's Bay." *California Historical Society Quarterly* 31(2): 99–108.

Mentz, Steve. 2015. *Ship Modernity: Ecologies of Globalization, 1550–1719*. Minneapolis: University of Minnesota Press.

Mentz, Steve. 2020. *Ocean*. London: Bloomsbury.

Miles, Jonathan. 2007. *The Wreck of the Medusa*. New York: Grove/Atlantic, Inc.

Milne, Gustav, Colin McKewan, and Damian Goodburn. 1998. *Nautical Archaeology on the Foreshore: Hulk Recording on the Medway*. Swindon: Royal Commission on the Historical Monuments of England.

Morrison, James V. 2014. *Shipwrecked: Disaster and Transformation in Homer, Shakespeare, Defoe, and the Modern World*. Ann Arbor: University of Michigan Press.

Moseley, Brandon. 2019. "Alabama Historical Commission Files Admiralty Claim on the *Clotilda*." *Alabama Political Reporter*, July 30, online at https://www.alreporter.com/2019/07/30/alabama-historical-commission-files-admiralty-claim-on-the-clotilda/.

Muckelroy, Keith. 1978. *Maritime Archaeology*. London; New York; Melbourne: Cambridge University Press.

Murphy, Joy Waldron, ed. 1988. *Historic Shipwrecks: Issues in Management.* Washington, DC: National Trust for Historic Preservation and Partners for Livable Places.

Muscarella, Oscar White. 2008. "Archaeology and the Plunder Culture." *International Journal of the Classical Tradition* 14(3–4): 602–618.

Nesmeyanov, Eugene. 2018. *Titanic Expeditions: Diving to the Queen of the Deep, 1985–2010.* Cheltenham: History Press.

Oertling, Thomas J. 1996. *Ship's Bilge Pumps: A History of Their Development, 1500–1900.* College Station: Texas A&M University Press.

O'Keefe, Betty, and Ian Macdonald 1998. *The Final Voyage of the Princess Sophia: Did They All Have to Die?* Surrey, BC: Heritage House.

Olivieri, Lara, Debora Mazzarelli, Barbara Bertoglio, Danilo De Angelis, Carlo Previderè, Pierangela Grignani, Annalisa Cappella, Silvano Presciuttini, Caterina Bertuglia, Paola Di Simone, Nicolò Polizzi, Agata Iadicicco, Vittorio Piscitelli, and Cristina Cattaneo. 2018. "Challenges in the Identification of Dead Migrants in the Mediterranean: The Case Study of the Lampedusa Shipwreck of October 3rd, 2013." *Forensic Science International* 285: 121–128, https://doi.org/10.1016/j.forsciint.2018.01.029.

Otis, Amos. 1864. *An Account of the Discovery of an Ancient Ship on the Eastern Shore of Cape Cod.* Albany: J. Munsell.

Palmer, William J. 1989. "Dickins and Shipwreck." *Dickens Studies Annual* 18: 56–59.

Panich, Lee M., Tsim D. Schneider, and R. Scott Byram. 2018. "Finding Mid-Nineteenth Century Native Settlements: Cartographic and Archaeological Evidence from Central California." *Journal of Field Archaeology* 43(2): 152–165.

Panich, Lee M., GeorgeAnn DeAntoni, and Tsim D. Schneider. 2021. "'By the Aid of His Indians': Native Negotiations of Settler Colonialism in Marin County, California, 1840–70." *International Journal of Historical Archaeology* 25: 92–115.

Paxton, Avery B., Christopher McGonigle, Melanie Damour, Georgia Holly, Alicia Caporaso, Peter B. Campbell, Kirstin S. Meyer-Kaier, Leila J. Hamdan, Calvin H. Mires, and J. Christopher Taylor. 2024. "Shipwreck Ecology: Understanding the Function and Processes from Microbes to Megafauna." *BioScience* 74(1): 12–24.

Pearson, Natali. 2023. *Belitung: The Afterlives of a Shipwreck.* Honolulu: University of Hawaii Press.

Pederson, Ralph K. 2004. "Traditional Arabian Watercraft and the Ark of the Gilgamesh Epic: Interpretations and Realizations." *Seminar for Arabian Studies* (34), Papers from the thirty-seventh meeting of the Seminar for Arabian Studies held in London, 17–19 July 2003: 231–238.

Pellegrino, Charles. 2000. *Ghosts of the Titanic.* New York: William Morrow.

Penrose, Barrie. 1982. *Stalin's Gold: The Story of HMS Edinburgh and Its Treasure.* Frogmore, St. Albans, Herts: Granada Publishing Company.

Perez-Alvaro, Elena. 2019. *Underwater Cultural Heritage: Ethical Concepts and Practical Challenges.* London; New York: Routledge.

Perez-Alvaro, Elena. 2022. "Shipwrecks and Graves: Their Treatment." *International Journal of Intangible Heritage* 17: 184–195.

Peterson, Mendel. 1973. *History Under the Sea: A Handbook for Underwater Exploration.* Alexandria, VA: Published by the author.

Peterson, Oliver. 2019. "Coimbra Solution Offers Big Payoff for Vintage Oil Collectors." *Dan's Papers*, May 26. www.danspapers.com/2019/05/coimbra-solution-vintage-oil-collectors (accessed August 25, 2019).

Philbrick, Nathaniel. 2000. *In the Heart of the Sea: The Tragedy of the Whaleship Essex*. New York: Penguin Books.

Philips, Carla Rahn. 2007. *The Treasure of the San José: Death at Sea in the War of the Spanish Succession*. Baltimore, MD: Johns Hopkins University Press.

Philips, Carla Rahn, John B. Hattendorf, and Tom Beall. 2008. "The Sinking of the Galleon San José on 8 June 1708: An Exercise in Nautical Detective Work." *The Mariner's Mirror* 94(2): 175–186.

Pickford, Nigel. 1999. *Lost Treasure Ships of the Twentieth Century*. Washington, DC: National Geographic.

Plimsoll, Samuel. 1873. *Our Seamen: An Appeal*. London: Virtue & Co..

Plummer, Katherine. 1991. *The Shogun's Reluctant Ambassadors: Japanese Sea Drifters in the North Pacific*. Portland: Oregon Historical Society Press.

Pomey, Patrice. 1994. "Les épaves Greques et Romaines de la Place Jules-Verne Marseille," in *Comptes redues des sieclés de l'anne 1995 (avril–juin)*, 445–484. Paris: Academie des Inscription & Belles Lettres.

Pomey, Patrice. 2003. "Reconstruction of Marseilles 6th Century BCE Greek Ships," in Carlo Beltrame, ed., *Proceedings of the Ninth International Symposium on Boat and Ship Archaeology*. Oxford: Oxbow, pp. 57–65.

Pond, Captain B. F. 1858. *Narrative of the Wreck of the Barque "Julia Ann," in the South Pacific Ocean*. New York: Francis & Loutrel.

Powers, Dennis M. 2006. *Treasure Ship: The Legend and Legacy of the S.S. Brother Jonathan*. New York: Kensington.

Pulak, Cemal, Rebecca Ingram, and Michael Jones. 2015. "Eight Byzantine Shipwrecks from the Theodosian Harbour Excavations at Yenikapi in Istanbul, Turkey: An Introduction." *The International Journal of Nautical Archaeology* 44(1): 39–73.

Quimby, George I. 1985. "Japanese Wrecks, Iron Tools, and Prehistoric Indians of the Northwest Coast." *Arctic Anthropology* 22(2): 7–15.

Raoul, Bénédicte Hénon, ed. 2014. *Vestiges of War: The Archaeology of the Battle of Normandy, 6 June–25 August 1944*. Normandy: INRAP and Regional Cultural Affairs Department.

Redknap, Mark, ed. 1997. *Artefacts from Wrecks: Dated Assemblages from the Late Middle Ages to the Industrial Revolution*. Oxford: Oxbow Books.

Reid, Kirsty. 2013. "Shipwrecks on the Streets: Maritime Disaster and the Broadside Ballad Tradition in Nineteenth-Century Britain and Ireland," in Carl Thompson, ed., *Shipwreck in Art and Literature: Images and Interpretations from Antiquity to the Present Day*. New York; London: Routledge.

Rich, Sara A. 2021. *Shipwreck Hauntography: Underwater Ruins and the Uncanny*. Amsterdam: Amsterdam University Press.

Rich, Sara A., and Peter B. Campbell, eds. 2023. *Contemporary Philosophy for Maritime Archaeology: Flat Ontologies, Oceanic Thought, and the Anthropocene*. Leiden: Sidestone Press.

Richards, Nathan. 2008. *Ships Graveyards: Abandoned Watercraft and the Archaeological Site Formation Process*. Gainesville: University Press of Florida.

Richards, Nathan, and Sami L. Seeb, eds. 2013. *The Archaeology of Watercraft Abandonment*. New York: Springer.

Rickard, Thomas A. 1939. "The Use of Iron and Copper by the Indians of British Columbia." *The British Columbia Historical Quarterly* 3(1): 25–50.

Riding, Christine. 2004. "Staging The Raft of the Medusa." *Visual Culture in Britain* 5(2) (Winter): 1–26.

Riding, Christine. 2013. "Shipwreck, Self-Preservation and the Sublime," in Nigel Llewellen and Christine Riding, eds., *The Art of the Sublime*. Tate Research Publication, January 2013, https://www.tate.org.uk/art/research-publications/the-sublime/christine-riding-shipwreck-self-preservation-and-the-sublime-r1133015 (accessed February 18, 2024).

Riess, Warren. 2023. *Studying the Princess Carolina: Anatomy of the Ship That Held Up Wall Street*. College Station: Texas A&M University Press.

Riess, Warren, and Sheli O. Smith. 2015. *The Ship That Held Up Wall Street*. College Station: Texas A&M University Press.

Robertson, Natalie G. 2008. *The Slave Ship Clotilda and the Making of AfricaTown, USA: Spirit of Our Ancestors*. Westport, CT; London: Praeger.

Rodgers, Bradley A., Wendy M. Coble, and Hans K. Van Tilburg. 1998. "The Lost Flying Boat of Kaneohe Bay: Archaeology of the First U.S. Casualties of Pearl Harbor." *Historical Archaeology* 32(4): 8–18.

Rodley, Edward. 2012. "The Ethics of Exhibiting Salvaged Shipwrecks." *Curator* 55(4): 383–391.

Rogers, Fred. 1973. *Shipwrecks of British Columbia*. Vancouver; Toronto: Douglas and McIntyre.

Rule, Margaret. 1982. *The Mary Rose: The Excavation and Raising of Henry VIII's Flagship*. Annapolis: Naval Institute Press.

Ruppe, Carol, and Jan A. Barstad, eds. 2002. *The Handbook of Underwater Archaeology*. New York: Kluwer Academic/Plenum.

Russell, Henry, and Mrs. Crawford. 1846. *Man the Life Boat! A Descriptive Song*. New York: William Hall and Son.

Russell, Matthew A. 2011. *Encounters at tamál-húye: An Archaeology of Intercultural Engagement in Sixteenth-Century Northern California*. Dissertation, University of California, Berkeley, https://escholarship.org/uc/item/40x2d7w2.

Sanchez, J. P. 2001. "From the Philippines to the California Coast in 1595: The Last Voyage of San Agustin Under Sebastian Rodriquez Cermeño." *Colonial Latin American Historical Review* 10(2): 223–251.

Sands, John O. 1983. *Yorktown's Captive Fleet*. Charlottesville: University of Virginia Press.

Scharnhorst, Gary. 2015. "Notes and Documents: Mark Twain Reports the Hornet Disaster." *American Literary Realism* 47(3) (Spring): 272–276.

Schenk, Hilbert, Jr., and Henry Kendall. 1950. *Shallow Water Diving for Pleasure and Profit*. Cambridge, MD: Cornell Maritime Press.

Schmidt, Peter G., Jr. 1959. "The Puretic Power Block and Its Effect on Modern Purse Seining," in Hilmar Kristjonssen, ed., *Modern Fishing Gear of the World*. London: Fishing News (Books), pp. 400–413.

Schneider, Tsim. 2018. "Making and Unmaking Native Communities in Mission and Post Mission Era Marin County, California," in Kathleen L. Hull and John G. Douglas, eds., *Forging Communities in Colonial Alta California*. Tucson: University of Arizona Press, pp. 88–110.

Schneider, Tsim. 2019. "Heritage In-Between: Seeing Native Histories in Colonial California." *The Public Historian* 41(1): 51–63.

Schuster, Ruth. 2024. "Energy Company Finds Earliest Deep-Sea Shipwreck in the World, and It's Canaanite." *Hareetz*, June 20.

Scott-Ireton, Della, ed. 2014. *Between the Devil and the Deep: Meeting Challenges in the Public Interpretation of Maritime Cultural Heritage*. New York: Springer.

Scott-Ireton, Della A., Jennifer E. Jones, and Jason T. Raupp, eds. 2023. *Citizen Science in Maritime Archaeology*. Gainesville: University Press of Florida.

Shangraw, Clarence, and Edward P. Von der Porten. 1981. *The Drake and Cermeño Expeditions' Chinese Porcelains*. Santa Rosa; Palo Alto: Santa Rosa Junior College and the Drake Navigators Guild.

Shomette, Donald. 1993. *The Hunt for HMS De Braak: Legend and Legacy*. Durham: Carolina University Press.

Shomette, Donald. 1996. *The Ghost Fleet of Mallows Bay and Other Tales of the Lost Chesapeake*. Centreville: Tidewater.

Simmons, Joe J., III. 1997. *Those Vulgar Tubes: External Sanitary Accommodations Aboard European Ships of the Fifteenth through Seventeenth Centuries*. College Station: Texas A&M University Press.

Skowronek, Russell K., and George R. Fischer. 2009. *HMS Fowey Lost and Found: Being the Discovery, Excavation and Identification of a British Man-of-War Lost off the Cape of Florida in 1748*. Gainesville: University Press of Florida.

Slade, Rachel. 2018. *Into the Raging Sea: Thirty-Three Mariners, One Megastorm, and the Sinking of El Faro*. New York: Ecco Press.

Smith, Lindsay S. 2014. "The Florida Panhandle Shipwreck Trail: Promoting Heritage Tourism in the Digital Age," in Della Scott-Ireton, ed., *Between the Devil and the Deep: Meeting Challenges in the Public Interpretation of Maritime Cultural Heritage*. New York: Springer, pp. 109–118.

Smith, Sheli O. 1990. "Fair Wind, Fair Gender, Fair Due," in Toni L. Carrell, ed., *Underwater Archaeology Proceedings from the Society for Historical Archaeology, Society for Historical Archaeology*, Rockville, MD.

Smith, Sheli O. 2023. "Repurposing and Reusing Ships," in Marco Meniketti, ed., *The Long Shore: Archaeologies and Social Histories of California's Maritime Cultural Landscapes*. New York; Oxford: Berghahn, pp. 163–181.

Soop, Hans. 1992. *The Power and the Glory: The Sculptures of the Warship Vasa*. Stockholm: Kungliga Vittterhets.

Souza, Donna J. 1998. *The Persistence of Sail in the Age of Steam: Underwater Archaeological Evidence from the Dry Tortugas*. New York: Plenum.

St. John Wilkes, Bill. 1971. *Nautical Archaeology: A Handbook for Skin Divers*. New York: Stein and Day.

Staniforth, Mark. 2003. "Annales-Informed Approaches to the Archaeology of Colonial Australia." *Historical Archaeology* 37(1): 102–113.

Staniforth, Mark, and Michael Nash. 2008. *Maritime Archaeology: Australian Approaches*. New York: Springer.

Steffy, J. Richard. 1994. *Wooden Ship Building and the Interpretation of Shipwrecks*. College Station: Texas A&M University Press.

Stenuit, Robert. 1972. *Treasures of the Armada*. Devon: Newton Abbot.

Stevenson, Robert Louis. 1912. *The Works of Robert Louis Stevenson: Records of a Family of Engineers, Additional Memories and Portraits, Later Essays, Lay Morals, Prayers Written for Family Use at Vailima*. London: Chatto and Windus.

Stewart, David J. 2011. *The Sea Their Graves: An Archaeology of Death and Remembrance in Maritime Culture*. Gainesville: University Press of Florida.

Stiebing, William., Jr. 1993. *Uncovering the Past: A History of Archaeology*. New York; Oxford: Oxford University Press.

Stone, Albert E., Jr. 1961. "Mark Twain and the Story of the Hornet." *The Yale University Library Gazette* 35(4) (April): 141–157.

Stone, John A. 1858. *Put's Golden Songster; Containing the Largest and Most Popular Collection of California Songs Ever Published*. San Francisco: D. E. Appleton.

Suman, Daniel, Mano Shivlani, and J. Walter Milon. 1999. "Perceptions and Attitudes Regarding Marine Reserves: A Comparison of Stakeholder Groups in the Florida Keys National Marine Sanctuary." *Ocean and Coastal Management* 42: 1019–1040.

Taub, Ben. 2015. "The Real Value of the ISIS Antiquities Trade." *The New Yorker*, December 4, online at www.newyorker.com/news/news-desk/the-real-value-of-the-isis-antiquities (accessed August 22, 2019).

Taylor, Kate. 2011. "Treasures Pose Ethics Issues for Smithsonian." *New York Times*, April 24, online at https://www.nytimes.com/2011/04/25/arts/design/smithsonian-sunken-treasure-show-poses-ethics-questions.html.

Temiño, Ignacio Rodríguez. 2017. "The Odyssey Case: Press, Public Opinion and Future Policy." *The International Journal of Nautical Archaeology* 46(1): 192–201.

Thompson, Carl. 2007. *The Suffering Traveler and the Romantic Imagination*. Oxford; New York: Oxford University Press.

Thompson, Carl, ed. 2013. *Shipwreck in Art and Literature: Images and Interpretations from Antiquity to the Present Day*. New York; London: Routledge.

Thoreau, Henry David. 1864. *Cape Cod*. Boston: Ticknor and Fields.

Throckmorton, Peter. 1964. *The Lost Ships: An Adventure in Underwater Archaeology*. Boston: Little, Brown.

Throckmorton, Peter. 1969. *Shipwrecks and Archeology: The Unharvested Sea*. Boston: Little, Brown.

Throckmorton, Peter. 1987. *The Sea Remembers: Shipwrecks and Archaeology from Homer's Greece to the Rediscovery of the Titanic*. New York: Weidenfeld & Nicolson.

Throckmorton, Peter. 1990. "The World's Worst Investment: The Economics of Treasure Hunting with Real Life Comparisons," in Toni Carrell, ed., *Underwater Archaeology Proceedings from the Society for Historical Archaeology Conference*, Pleasant Hill, CA, pp. 6–10.

Tigner, Brooks. 2019. "Europe Moves to Curb ISIS Antiquity Trafficking," *The Atlantic Council*, Friday, September 13, online at www.atlanticcouncil.org/blogs/new-atlanticist/europe-moves-to-curb-isis-antiquties-trafficking (accessed October 5, 2019).

Tomlinson, H. L., ed. 1930. *Great Sea Stories of All Nations*. Garden City, NY: Doubleday, Doran & Company.

Treganza, Adan E. 1959. *The Examination of Indian Shellmounds in the Tomales and Drake's Bay Areas with Reference to Sixteenth Century Historic Contacts*. Archaeological Archives Manuscript No. 283, Phoebe A. Hearst Museum of Anthropology, University of California, Berkeley.

Treganza, Adan E., and Thomas F. King, eds. 1968. *Archaeological Studies in Point Reyes National Seashore*. San Francisco State College Archaeological Survey and Santa Rosa Junior College.

Trigger, Bruce, 1989. *A History of Archaeological Thought*. Cambridge: Cambridge University Press.

Tucker, Teddy. 1966. *Treasure Diving with Teddy Tucker*. Bermuda: Published by the author.

Turner, Philip J., Sophie Cannon, Sarah DeLand, James P. Delgado, David Eltis, Patrick N. Halpin, Michael I. Kanu, Charlotte S. Sussman, Ole Varmer, and Cindy L. Van Dover. 2020. "Memorializing the Middle Passage on the Atlantic Seabed in Areas Beyond National Jurisdiction," *Marine Policy* CXXII (December), https://doi.org/10.1016/j.marpol.2020.104254.

Twain, Mark. 1917. *Life on the Mississippi*. New York; London: Harper & Brothers.

Van Der Heide, G. D. 1955. *Archaeological Investigations on New Land*. The Hague: W. A. Ruysch.

Van Tilburg, Hans. 2007. *Chinese Junks on the Pacific: Views from a Different Deck*. Gainesville: University Press of Florida.

Van Tilburg, Hans. 2010. *A Civil War Gunboat in Pacific Waters: Life on Board USS Saginaw*. Gainesville: University Press of Florida.

Varenius, Björn. 1985. "Medieval Ships from the Centre of Stockholm," in Carl Olaf Cederlund, ed., *Post Medieval Boat and Ship Archaeology*. Stockholm: Swedish National Maritime Museum, pp. 437–440.

Varmer, Ole, and Caroline M. Blanco. 2018. "The Case for Using the Law of Salvage to Preserve Underwater Cultural Heritage: The Integrated Marriage of the Law of Salvage and Historic Preservation." *Journal of Maritime Law & Commerce* 49(3): 401–424.

Varney, George Leon. 1911. "Songs Inspired by Sorrow." *The National Magazine* 34(1): 135–138.

Veronico, Nicholas A. 2015. *Hidden Warships: Finding World War II's Abandoned, Sunk, and Preserved Warships*. Minneapolis: Zenith/Quarto.

Veyrat, Élisabeth. 2017. "The Two Shipwrecks of La Natière, Saint-Malo, France: An Archaeological Contribution to the Atlantic Maritime Landscape of the First Half of the 18th Century," in Jerzy Gawronski, André van Holk, and Joost Schokkenbroek, eds., *Ships and Maritime Landscapes: Proceedings of the 13th International Symposium on Boat and Ship Archaeology (Amsterdam, 2012)*. Eelde: Barkhuis, pp. 171–178.

Von der Porten, Edward P. 1968. *The Porcelains and Terra Cottas of Drakes Bay*. Point Reyes, CA: Drake Navigators Guild.

Von der Porten, Edward P. 1972. "Drake and Cermeño in California: Sixteenth Century Chinese Ceramics." *Historical Archaeology* 6: 1–22.

Wagner, H. R. 1924. "The Voyage to California of Sebastian Rodriguez Cermeño in 1595." *California Historical Society Quarterly* 3(1): 3–24.

Wagner, Kip (as told to L. B. Taylor, Jr.). 1966. *Pieces of Eight: Recovering the Riches of the Lost Spanish Treasure Fleet*. New York: E. P. Dutton.

Watson, Rev. John Selby, Trans. 1893. *Lucretius on the Nature of Things*. London; New York: George Bell & Sons.

Watts, Gordon P. 1975. "The Location and Identification of the Ironclad USS *Monitor*." *International Journal of Nautical Archaeology* 4(2): 301–329.

Watts, Gordon P. 2014. *Shipwrecked: Bermuda's Maritime Heritage*. Hamilton: National Museum of Bermuda Press.

Webber, Bert. 1984. *Wrecked Japanese Junks Adrift in the North Pacific Ocean*. Fairfield, WA: Ye GalleonPress.

Westerdahl, Christer. 1992. "The Maritime Cultural Landscape." *The International Journal of Nautical Archaeology* 21(2): 5–14.

Wharton, Ric. 2000. *The Salvage of the Century*. North Palm Beach, FL: Best Publishing.

Wickler, Stephen. 2019. "Iconic Arctic Shipwrecks, Archaeology and Museum Narratives." *International Journal of Nautical Archaeology* 48(2): 427–438.

Wolf, Norbert. 2003. *Caspar David Friedrich, 1774–1840: The Painter of Stillness*. Cologne: Taschen.

Wood, Peter H. 2004. *Weathering the Storm: Inside Winslow Homer's Gulf Stream*. Athens: University of Georgia Press.

Woodman, David C. 1992. *Unraveling the Franklin Mystery: Inuit Testimony*. Montreal; Kingston: McGill-Queen's University Press.

Yoshimura, Akira. 1982. *Shipwrecks*. San Diego; New York; London: Harvest Books/Harcourt.

Zeller, D., T. Cashion, M. L. D. Palomares, and D. Pauly. 2018. "Global Marine Fisheries Discards: A Synthesis of Reconstructed Data." *Fish & Fisheries* 19(1): 30–39.

Zeller, D., M. L. D. Palomares, A. Tavakolie, M. Ang, D. Belhabib, W. W. L. Cheung, and D. Pauly. 2016. "Still Catching Attention: *Sea Around Us* Reconstructed Global Catch Data, Their Spatial Expression and Public Accessibility." *Marine Policy* 70: 145–152.

Zenkiewicz, Maciej, and Tadeusz Wasilewski. 2019. "The Galleon 'San Jose': Almost Four Decades of Legal Struggles on the National and International Plane." *Comparative Law Review* 25: 319–342, 10.12775/CLR.2019.012.

Zmijewski, David. 1999. "The *Hornet*: Mark Twain's Interpretations of a Perilous Journey." *The Hawaiian Journal of History* 33: 55–67.

Zwick, Daniel. 2013. "Conceptual Evolution in Ancient Shipbuilding: An Attempt to Reinvigorate a Shunned Theoretical Perspective," in Jon Adams and Johann Rönnby, eds., *Interpreting Shipwrecks: Maritime Archaeological Approaches*. Southampton: Highfield Press, pp. 46–71.

Index

Note: Figures are indicated by an italic "*f*" following the page number.

For the benefit of digital users, indexed terms that span two pages (e.g., 52–53) may, on occasion, appear on only one of those pages.

A

Abandoned Shipwreck Act of 1987 219–221
accident investigations 3–6
Acts of God 34–37
Ada K. Damon (ship) 249
Adieu (Guillou) 49
Aeneid (Virgil) 7
aesthetic value of shipwrecks 111–113
Africatown, Alabama 73–74
After the Hurricane (Homer) 50
airplane crashes 28–29
Aivzovsky, Ivan 49
A.J. Goddard (ship) 55
Albania, shipwrecks in xvi
Alberg, David 117–118
Alexander Macomb (ship) 149
Algerine (ship) 87
Allan, Jim 136–137
allegorical meaning of shipwrecks 36
Alvin (submersible) 244
Ambassador (ship) 66–67
Amoco Cadiz (ship) 76–77
amphorae, study of 194–195
Anderson, Ross 204–205
Andrea Doria (ship) 9, 51–52
Andrea Gail (ship) 13–14, 57, 223
And the Sea Gave Up the Dead Which Were in It (Leighton) 77
Anglo-Saxon ships 178–179
Antarctic shipwrecks 10
Anthropocene, archaeology of 213–214
Antikythera (Greece), artifacts from wreck near 179

Apurímac (ship) xiii
archaeological study of shipwrecks
  archaeological significance of wrecks x–xi
  buried ships 177–179, 183–185
  "cold cases," shipwrecks as 199–206
  in early 20th century 179–180
  Gelidonya wreck 187–190
  global maritime archaeology 206–214
  history of archaeology 176–177
  modern archaeology 177
  overview 3, 174–176
  partial recovery of famous ships 182–183
  ships as human achievements 193–206
    "big questions" in archaeology 196–197
    family tree of the ship 193–194
    handling of cargoes 197
    particular areas of archaeological study 194–196
    shipbuilding 195–199
    study of amphorae 194–195
    study of bones 194
  shipwrecks salvaged by Indigenous tribes 134–137
  technological developments and growth of field 190–193, 237–238
  total recovery of famous ships 179–182
  treasure hunting versus 164–169
  underwater archaeology, emergence of 186–187
Arctic shipwrecks 11–12, 50, 67–72
"Ariel's Song" (*The Tempest*) xi

INDEX

Arlington National Cemetery (Washington)
  USS *Maine* memorial in 81
  USS *Monitor* memorial in 117–119
artificial intelligence (AI) 55
artificial reefs 26–27, 97–100
Artificial Reef Society of British Columbia 26
artistic responses to shipwrecks 48–56
Asner, Greg 98–99
Atlantis submarines 106
atomic bomb testing 18–19, 22–23
Aubry, Michelle 220
Austria (ship) 14–15
autonomous underwater vehicles (AUVs) xv–xvi, 200
Avanti (ship) 201–202, 215–216

B

Back, George 67–68
Ballard, Robert 22–23, 87–88, 223–224
Barca Nostra (Our Ship) Project 91–92
barratry 20
Bascom, Willard 190
Bass, George F. 187–190, 194–195
Basta, Daniel 117–118
Batavia (ship) 116
bateaux 184
Bates, D. B. 15–16
Battle of Midway xv
beach erosion 248–250
"Beeswax Wreck," Oregon 129–131
Belcher, Edward 68–70
Belcher, George 230
Belfast (Ireland), memorials to *Titanic* in 81–82
Belitung shipwreck 165–169, 228f
Benchley, Peter 58–59
Bermuda, shipwrecks in 7–8
Bermuda 100 Project 55–56
Bertrand (ship) 119–121
bezaisen 205–206
Biblical references to shipwrecks 34–35
"big questions" in archaeology 196–197
Bikini Atoll xvi, 18–19, 98–99
biodiversity on shipwrecks 97–99, 122–123, 221–222
"Black Current" (*kuroshio*) 131–132, 205–206
Blagg, Michele 152

Blake Plateau 257–258
Blake Ridge Shipwreck 244–248, 246f, 257–258
Bligh, William 139–140
BlueView® 55
Bluewater Recoveries 185–187
bodies, recovery of
  from *Kateri i Radës* 92–94
  from *Princess Sophia* 84
  from *Titanic* 86–89
  from USS *Maine* 84–85
  from USS *Monitor* 90, 117–119
Bodrum Museum of Underwater Archaeology 189–190
BOEM (Bureau of Ocean Energy Management) 221–222, 241–242, 256–257
boiler explosions 4–5, 15
bones found in shipwrecks, study of 194
books, shipwrecks in 38–43, 57–60
Boston (ship) 133–134
Bounty (ship) 139–141
"bounty of the sea"
  coastal communities and 125, 127–128
  impoverished communities and 226–230
  Indigenous peoples and 129–131
  looting and 159–160
Breadalbane (ship) 69–70
Brennan, Michael 223–224
Brookhill Ferry (ship) 250–251
Brother Jonathan (ship) 171
Bruseth, James E. 174
BSEE (Bureau of Safety and Environmental Enforcement) 241–242
Büchel, Christophe 91–92
Bugara (submarine) xvi
bullion and specie, salvage of
  Belitung shipwreck 165–169
  from *Central America* 158–159
  from *Edinburgh* 149–152
  funding for treasure hunting 169–173
  global antiquities trade 160
  international disputes over 156–158, 165–169
  from *Islander* 154–155
  from *John Barry* 152–154
  litigation and 158–159
  prop wash deflection 162–163
  from *San José* 156–158
  shipwreck archaeology 167

versus treasure hunting 149–150
treasure hunting versus
    archaeology 163–169
from *Whydah* 162–163
Bureau of Ocean Energy Management
    (BOEM) 221–222, 241–242,
    256–257
Bureau of Safety and Environmental
    Enforcement (BSEE) 241–242
burial at sea (of people) 77–79, 86–87
burial at sea (of ships) 20. *See also*
    scuttling
buried shipwrecks
    accessibility of 183–185
    Bertrand 119–121
    climate change and 248–253
    early discoveries of 177–179
    in St. Augustine, Florida 255–256
Burke, Edmund 35
B.W. Blanchard (ship) 101*f*

C
Cairo (ship) 117, 180
California, United States
    California Gold Rush xii,
        134–137, 184–185
    1873 chart of shipwrecks in and around
        San Francisco 37–38
    Indigenous peoples and
        shipwrecks 134–135
    Manila galleon shipwrecks 129–130
    pollution from shipwrecks 22–23
    scuttled ships off coast of 22–23
Cameron, James 56–57, 104–106,
    110, 215–216
Campbell, Peter 209–210, 238
"Camp Castaway," Oregon 135
Canadian Pacific Railroad (CPR) 84
cannibalism 30, 48, 68, 138
capacity building 189–190
Capelotti, Pete 58–59
Captain Lincoln (ship) 135–136
Carabias, Diego 86
cargoes of ships 197
Carnarvon, Earl of 176–177
Carpathia (ship) 226–227
Case, W. K. 51–52, 51*f*
Casilli, Remo 51–52
Castro, Fidel 63
Castro, Filipe 164

Catsambis, Alexis 209
celebrity shipwreck 111
cenotaphs 79–81
Central America (ship) 43–44, 158–159, 235
Challenger Deep exploration 105–106
Chapin, Harry 46–47
Charles Eaton (ship) 138
Charles W. Morgan (ship) 65–66
Charybdis 6–7
Chattahoochee (ship) 117
Chatterton, John 59–60
Chernaiev, Genya 103*f*, 104
Chile, shipwrecks off of 202–204
Chinese-sponsored salvagers 227–229
Christian, Fletcher 139–141
Chuan Hong 68 (ship) 227–229
Church, Frederick 50
Chuuk Lagoon 98–99
citizen science 186–187
City of Chester (ship) 9
Clifford, Barry 162–163
climate change 213–214, 248–255
Clotilda (ship) xiii–xiv, 72–76
coal, spontaneous combustion of 15–16
coal trade 202–205
coastal erosion 248–250
Coast Trader (ship) xv, 24–25, 225–226
coffin ships 5–6
Coimbra (ship) 24–25, 146–147
"cold cases," shipwrecks as 199–206
Cold War shipwrecks xvi, 21
collections of ancient relics 187
collision, shipwrecks caused by 9
Colombian claims on *San José*
    156–158, 165
Colossi of Memnon, in Egypt 53–54
Columbus America Discovery Group
    158–159
commercial fishing, impact on
    shipwrecks 221–226
commercial treasure salvage 234–238
Commodore (ship) 41–43
composite-built ships 66–67
Conestoga (ship) 216–217
conservation and preservation of shipwrecks
    Cairo 180
    costs of 180
    Mary Rose 116–117
    USS *Monitor* 117
    Vasa 62, 114–116, 180–182, 198–199

Constellation (ship) 99–100
"Convergence of the Twain, The" (Hardy) 57
coral growth on shipwrecks 98–99
Corbino, Sam 120
Cormoran (ship) xiv–xv
Correa, Juan David 158
Costa Concordia (ship) 144–146, 145f
County Hall Ship, England 177, 183–184
Cousteau, Jacques 58, 186
Cox, Samuel 260
Crane, Stephen 41–43
Cressy, David 125, 127
Cristobal Colon (ship) xiv
CSI, shipwreck xii–xiii
CSS *Virginia* (ship) 64–65
cultural significance of shipwrecks
  accounts of undersea explorers 57–60
  aesthetic and romantic values 111–113
  artistic responses 48–56
  films 56–57
  musical responses 43–47
  religious responses 34–35
  shipwrecks in literature 38–43
  tales of shipwrecks 36–38
  underwater photography and film 51–56
Curtis, Frank 154–155
Curtis-Wiley Marine Salvors 154–155
Cussler, Clive 20–21, 59, 226–227, 239, 261
Cutty Sark (ship) 66–67

D

Dahm, Jonas 52–53
"Dance Band on the *Titanic*" (Chapin) 46–47
Danube river wrecks 251–252
D-Day 17–18
dead, recovery of
  from *Kateri i Radës* 92–94
  from *Princess Sophia* 84
  from *Titanic* 86–89
  from USS *Maine* 84–85
  from USS *Monitor* 90, 117–119
Death Ship, The (Traven) 5–6
death ships 5–6
De Braak (ship) 171
Deep, The (Benchley) 58–59
deep ocean survey and discovery 192, 239–240, 256–257
Deep Sea Detectives (TV show) 59–60

Deep Sea Expeditions 102–103
Deep Water, Ancient Ships (Bascom) 190
deep-water research 241–248
Defiance (ship) 249
Demont-Breton, Virginie 49
Denmark
  buried shipwrecks found in urban areas 184–185
  Roskilde ships 113–114, 182, 183f
"Derelict, The" (Tomlinson) 43
De Soto Wildlife Refuge 120–121
Dickens, Charles 3–4, 39–40
Die Gescheiterte Hoffnung (The Polar Sea) (Friedrich) 50
digital imagery 54–56
Dion, Celine 46–47
Disaster at Sea, or The Wreck of the Amphritite (Turner) 49
Diving Bell, The (band) 233
diving to shipwrecks
  aesthetic and romantic values of wrecks 111–113
  biodiversity on shipwrecks 97–99
  emergence of underwater archaeology 186
  growth in number of divers 123
  international dive destinations 107–108
  in parks and marine sanctuaries 106–110
  scuba diving and snorkeling 97–99
  scuttled ships 26–27
  submersibles 102–106
  technology of 54–55, 102–103, 123, 190–193, 237–238
  undersea museums 106–110
DNA, shipwrecks and 194–195, 243
Doris (ship) 12–14
Dorothea (ship) 18
Douglas, Carl 52–53
D'Oyley, William 138–139
dragon ships 182–183
Drain the Oceans (TV show) 59–60
Drake, Francis 62
Drakes Bay, California 129–131
Dresden (ship) xiv–xv
"drift junks" (Japanese) 131–132, 205–206
droughts 250–251
Dry Tortugas, Florida 7–8, 201–202
dunnage 197

INDEX

E

Eadie, Tom 58
economic benefits from shipwrecks. *See also* salvage; treasure hunting
   insurance fraud 20–21
   salvaging by locals 125, 127–128
economy, importance of ships in x–xi
Edinburgh (ship) 149–152
Edmund Fitzgerald (ship) 13, 47
Effie M. Morrissey (ship) 69
Egyptian ships 63, 178
El Faro (ship) 13–14
Elia, Ricardo 163
Empress of Ireland (ship) 121
encyclopedia of underwater and maritime archaeology 191–192
Endicott, William 137–138
Endurance (ship) 10–12, 51–52, 55–56, 71
Energean 256
England
   County Hall Ship 177, 183–184
   Cutty Sark 66–67
   Franklin's expedition 11, 67–71, 79, 253
   Mary Rose 62, 116–117, 197–198
   Mary Rose Museum in 116–117
   memorial in St. James's cemetery (Liverpool) 79
   quest for a Northwest Passage 67–69
   Sutton Hoo boat excavation 178–179
environmental threats from scuttled ships 20–25
Epic of Gilgamesh 33–34
Erebus (ship) 11–12, 68–71, 253
Erickson, Peter 50
Ericsson, John 64–65
Esmeralda (ship) 85–86
Essex (ship) 30–31, 56
Estonia (ship) 82–83
Everett, Richard 135
Ewing, Walter C. 79
Ewing Bank Wreck 201
Explorer (ship) 9–10
Exxon Valdez (ship) 76–77
Ezekiel 27:34 34

F

Falkland Islands 253
family tree of the ship 193–194
Fanchon (ship) 15–16
Fernstream (ship) 24–25
filming underwater 51–56
films about shipwrecks 56–59, 140, 186
filters 210–211
financial returns from shipwreck salvage 234–238
fires, as cause of shipwrecks 14–17
Fitzsimmons, Scott 102–103, 103*f*
Florida, United States
   Dry Tortugas 7–8, 201–202
   Oriskany 27
   "treasure coast" of 161–162, 171–172
   underwater archaeology in 190–191
   underwater art gallery in 110
   "Windjammer Wreck" 201–202
   wreck found in St. Augustine 254–256
Florida Keys National Marine Sanctuary 110
Florida Panhandle Shipwreck Trail 106–107
Foley, Brendan 194–195, 224
Ford, Ben 209
forensics 75, 94, 115, 117–118, 194
Foster, John 135
Fox (ship) xiii
Fram (ship) 69
Franke, Andreas 110
Frankfurt (ship) 18
Franklin, John 11, 67–71, 79, 253
Franzen, Anders 114–115
Frey, Donald 52, 189
Friedrich, Caspar David 50
Frolic (ship) 134–135, 217
From a Watery Grave: The Discovery and Excavation of La Salle's Shipwreck, La Belle (Bruseth & Turner) 174
Frost, Honor 187–190
Fulton, Robert 18
funding for treasure hunting 169–173

G

Gallo, Dave 55
G.B. Church (ship) 26
Gelidonya shipwreck 187–190, 197
George I. Newman (ship) 260–261
Géricault, Théodore 48–49
ghost fleets 18–20, 251–252
ghost nets 222–223
ghost ships 52

Ghost Ships of the Baltic Sea (Dahm & Douglas) 52
Ghosts of Cape Horn 253
Ghosts of the Abyss (Cameron) 56–57, 110, 215–216
ghost towns 110
gifts from the sea, shipwrecks as 129–131
Gilberry, Wilfred 79
Gjoa (ship) 63, 69
Glide (ship) 137–138
global antiquities trade 159–161, 230, 236–237
global maritime archaeology. *See* maritime archaeology
Goggin, John M. 187–188
Gokstad ship replica 62
gold, recovery of. *See* bullion and specie, salvage of
"Golden Age of Shipwreck Discoveries" 253–261
Golden Hinde (ship) 62
Gongaware, Laura 164–165
"Gooseberry" 17–18
Gould, Richard 209–210
Grab 3000 System 185–187
Granma (ship) 63
Grau Seminario, Miguel 85–86
graves, shipwrecks as 77–79
"Graveyard of the Atlantic" 7–8
"Graveyard of the Pacific" 7–8, 112–113
Greater Farallones National Marine Sanctuary 136–137
Great Lakes, shipwrecks in 107–109, 260–261
Green, John 58
Greene, John 61
grief after shipwrecks 31–32
Grinnan, Joe 188*f*
Guerra del Pacifico 85–86
Guillou, Alfred 49
Gulf of Mexico, seabed mapping in 241–242
Gulf of the Farallones, California 22–23
Gulf Stream, The (Homer) 50

H

Hagglund, Lorenzo 179–180
Haida people 131–132
Halligan, Jessi 209

Hans Hedtoft (ship) 9–10
Hansson, Maria 194–195
harbors, shipwrecks in 8–9
Hardy, Thomas 57
Hauntography 54
Hawaii, scuttled ships off coast of 25–26
Hays, Charles Melville 87
Heard, Alex 162–163, 170
Hendel, Ronald 33–34
Hendershot, Claire 233
Hendershot, Steve 233
"Heroic Age of Diving" 58
heroic ships 62
high-resolution sonar 54–56
high seas marine-protected areas 202–204
historical significance of shipwrecks
  Clotilda 72–76
  contributing factors 76–77
  National Historic Landmarks 63–65
  Northwest Passage exploration 67–72
  participation in trade 65–67
Historic Shipwrecks: Issues in Management (McNulty) 219–220
History of the Peloponnesian War (Thucydides) 7
HMAS *Sydney* (ship) 89
HMC *Annapolis* (ship) 27
HMS *Breadalbane* (ship) 11
HMS *Captain* (ship) 199
HMS *Doterel* (ship) xiii–xiv
HMS *Erebus* (ship) 11–12, 68–71, 253
HMS *Fury* (ship) 67–68
HMS *Goliath* (ship) xiv–xv
HMS *Hawke* (ship) 259–260
HMS *Hood* (ship) 89
HMS *Investigator* (ship) 11, 68–70
HMS *Terror* (ship) 11–12, 68–71, 253
HMS *Triumph* (ship) xiv–xv
HMS *Volage* (ship) xvi
Hojun-Maru (ship) 131–132
Holland, buried shipwrecks in 184–185
"holy grail" of shipwrecks 156–158
Homer 7
Homer, Winslow 50
Hornet (ship) 40–41
Hörnum Odde wreck 249–250
Huáscar (ship) 85–86
Hudson's Bay Company 67–68
Hugill, Peter 142–143

Humaitá (submarine) xvi
human error, as cause of shipwreck 6–7
Humayoon (ship) 15–16
Hunters Point Naval Shipyard, San Francisco 22
Huntress, Keith 36–37
Hurley, Frank 51–52
hurricanes, as cause of shipwrecks 13–14
hymns about shipwrecks 45

I
ice, as cause of shipwrecks 9–12
Iceberg (Church) 50
iconic shipwrecks 61–63, 190–191. See also *Titanic* (ship); *Vasa* (ship)
IFREMER 185
impoverished communities, salvaging by 226–230
Inconstant (ship) 185
Independence (ship) 4, 5f, 126
Indigenous peoples and shipwrecks
  attacks on ships 131–134
  "Beeswax Wreck" 129–131
  Boston 133–134
  Bounty 139–141
  Captain Lincoln 135–136
  Frolic 134–135
  Japanese "drift junks" 131–132
  Manila galleon shipwrecks 129–131
  Oxford 136–137
  petroglyphs of wrecks 132–133
  salvaging 134–137
  shipwrecks as gifts from the sea 129–131
  in South Seas 137–141
  Susan Sturgis 132
  Tonquin 133–134
  in United States and Canada 127–137
  Vancouver 132
industrialization of shipbuilding 199–200
Ingraham (ship) 25–26
in irons 7–8
insurance, marine 20–21, 142–143
intelligent grab 185–187
International Convention for the Safety of Life at Sea (SOLAS) 6
international dive destinations 107–108
International Ice Patrol 6

International Salvage Union (ISU) 143–144
In the Heart of the Sea (film) 30–31, 56
Ireland, John 138–139
Isaacman, Jared 105–106
Islander (ship) 154–155
Island Pride (ship) 258
Israel, "world's oldest wreck" in 256

J
Jackson (ship) 117
Jacobsen, Selmer 84
James Caird (boat) 10
Januszczak, Waldemar 91–92
Japan, volcanic eruption in 29–30
Japanese "drift junks" 131–132, 205–206
Jaws (Benchley) 58–59
Jenny Lind (ship) 4, 5f
Jessop, Keith 150–152
Jessop Marine Recoveries, Ltd 150–152
Jeune fille contemplate un n crâne près d'un bateau naufragé au bord de la mer (Young Woman Contemplating a Skull by a Shipwreck on the Beach) (Renan) 49–50
Jewel of Muscat (ship) 168
Job 1:21, 31
John Barry (ship) 152–154
John Barry Group 184–187
John Bright (ship) 132–133
Jones, Leslie 51–52
Julia Ann (ship) 1–2
Junger, Sebastian 13–14, 57, 223

K
Kaaparen (ship) 149
Kaiyo Maru No. 5 (ship) 29–30
Kateri i Radës (ship) 92–94
Katzev, Michael 116
Keck, Charles 85
Khufu's solar ship 63, 178
Kiesling, Stephen 162–163, 170
Killean (ship) 201–202
Kleeberg, John 171
Klondike Gold Rush xiii, 55, 154–155
Kohler, Richie 59–60
Kovacs, Evan 55
Kraft, Rob 247–248
Kroehl, Julius H. 230–231, 233
Krumholz, Jason 224
Kuester, Falko 55–56

INDEX

Kulamanu (ship) 25
kuroshio ("Black Current") 131–132, 205–206
Kyrenia ship 116

L
Lady Hobart (ship) 9–10
Lake Huron, shipwrecks in 100–101, 101f, 108
LAMP (Lighthouse Archaeological Maritime Program) 255–256
La Natière 7–8
Landseer, Edwin 50
Langewiesche, William 144–145
L'Approdo. Opera all'Umanità Migrante (The Landing. Work Dedicated to Migrating Humanity) 94
lawsuits, shipwrecks and 157–159, 171–172
Layton, Tom 134–135, 217
lead ingots 227
Leighton, Frederic 77
Le Lyonnais (ship) 259–260
Lenihan, Daniel 160–161
Le Radeau de la Méduse (Raft of the Medusa) (Géricault) 48–49
Levin, John 170
Lewis, Cudjo 75
LIDAR (Light Detection and Ranging) 54–56
lifeboat regulations 6
Life of Pi, The (film) 57
Life on the Mississippi (Dickens) 4
Lightfoot, Gordon 47
Lighthouse Archaeological Maritime Program (LAMP) 255–256
literature, shipwrecks in 33–34, 38–43, 57–60
litigation, shipwrecks and 157–159, 171–172
Longfellow, Henry Wadsworth 38–39
looting of shipwrecks 159–161, 187
"Loss of the *Central America*, The" (song) 43–44
Lusitania (ship) 226

M
Mabus, Roy 118–119
Macaulay, Rose 111–112
MacKay-Bennett (ship) 86–87
Malaysia Airlines Flight 370 28–29
Mallakh, Kamal el- 63
Mallows Bay National Marine Sanctuary 109
Manhattan, shipwrecks found in 177–178, 183–184
Manila galleon shipwrecks 129–131
Man Proposes, God Disposes (Landseer) 50
mapping of seabed 239–240, 256–257
Marden, Luis 140
marine insurance 20–21, 142–143
marine life near shipwrecks 97–99, 221–222
marine painting 48–56
marine protected areas 202–204
Marine Protection, Research and Sanctuaries Act (MPRSA) of 1972 25
Mariner's Chronicle, The 36
Mariners' Museum in Newport News, Virginia 117–119
marine sanctuaries, shipwrecks in 106–110
maritime archaeology 206–214
    accessibility of future discoveries 240–241
    deep-water research 241–248
    discoveries in 210–214
    emergence of 206–210
    maritime cultural landscapes 209–210
    seabed mapping 239–240
    technological developments and growth of field 237–238
Maritime Archaeology (Muckelroy) 207–209
maritime cultural landscapes 209–210
Maritime Museum 26–27
Marschall, Ken 55
Martinique, volcanic eruption on 29–30
Mary Celeste (ship) 20–21
Mary Celestia (ship) xiii
"Mary Ellen Carter, The" (Rogers) 47
Mary Rose (ship) 62, 116–117, 197–198
Mary Rose Museum, England 116–117
Masset people 132
Masters, David 142, 159
Mather, Rod 18
Matthews, Russ 258–259
Maud (ship) 69–72
McCallum, Rob 102–103
McCarthy, Michael "Mack" 195–196
McCartney, Innes 20
McClung, Rob 162–163

McGinnis, Joe 69–70
McNulty, Robert "Bob" 219–220
Melville, Herman 30–31
memento mori, shipwrecks as 53–54
memorials, to shipwrecks 13, 83
   Barca Nostra (Our Ship) Project 92
   in cemeteries 78–95
   cenotaphs 79–81
   classes of 80
   to *Estonia* 82–83
   placing plaques on shipwrecks 89
   Russalka Memorial in Estonia 80–81
   Titanic memorials 81–82
   "Tragedy of Otranto" 92–94
   USS *Arizona* 80, 80f, 90–91
   USS *Maine* 81, 85
   for World Wars 81
merchant ships 5–6
metal fasteners, used in shipbuilding 195–196
metals, salvage of 147–149
"Middle Passage" 257–258
Minia (ship) 87
Mir submersibles 102–105, 103f
Mississippi River shipwrecks 250–251
Missouri River shipwrecks 250–251
Mitchell, Josiah 40–41
Mitchell, William L. "Billy" 18
Moby Dick (film) 56
Moby-Dick (Melville) 30–31
modern archaeology 177
monetary value of shipwrecks. *See* salvage
Monohansett (ship) 100–101
Monsarrat, Nicholas 31, 41–42
Montana (ship) 250–251
Montevideo Maru (ship) 259–260
Montmagny (ship) 87
Moonlit Seascape with Shipwreck
   (Aivzovsky) 49
Morgan, Jean-Jacques de 178
Morro Castle (ship) 16–17
mosquito fleet 255–256
Mossap, Wilfred 79
Mount Pelée eruption, Martinique 29–30
movies, shipwrecks in 56–59, 140, 186
MPRSA (Marine Protection, Research and
   Sanctuaries Act) of 1972 25
Muckelroy, Keith 207–211, 242–243
Munger T. Ball (ship) 24–25
Murphy, Larry 199–200

Museum für antike Schifffahrt in Mainz,
   Germany 116
Museum of Underwater Archaeology in
   Bodrum, Turkey 122
museums, shipwrecks and artifacts in 113–124
museums, shipwrecks as 106–110
musical responses to shipwrecks 43–47, 233
"My Heart Will Go On" (Dion) 46–47
mythology, shipwrecks and 6–7

N

Nanhai #1 wreck 121
Narratives of Shipwrecks and Disasters,
   1588–1860 (Huntress) 36–37
National Historic Landmarks, United
   States 62–65, 90–91
National Historic Sites, Canada 70–71
nationalistic pride in ships 61–63
National Marine Sanctuaries, United States
   Cordell Banks 258–259
   Florida Keys 110
   Greater Farallones 136–137
   in Great Lakes 107–109
   Gulf of the Farallones 22–23
   Mallows Bay 109
   Shipwreck Coast 108–109
   Stellwagen Bank 223
   Thunder Bay 100–101, 108
National Museum of Sardinia in
   Cagliari 227
National Oceanic and Atmospheric
   Administration (NOAA) 23–25,
   88, 136–137, 245–246, 245f
National Parks 90–91, 190–191, 201–202
National Register of Historic Places,
   United States
   Clotilda 72–76
   Coimbra 146–147
   Frolic 135
   Mallows Bay wrecks 109
nautical archaeology 193–206
   "big questions" in digs 196–197
   family tree of the ship 193–194
   handling of cargoes 197
   particular areas of study 194–196
   particularism 206–208
   shipbuilding 195–199
   study of amphorae 194–195
   study of bones 194

Nautilus (exploration vessel) 21–22, 223–224, 245f
"Nearer, My God to Thee" (song) 45–46
Nehalem Bay, Oregon 129–131
Nehalem-Tillamook peoples 129–131
"Neptune's Raging Fury" (song) 43–44
New Bedford (Massachusetts), cenotaph in Rural Cemetery of 79
New York, shipwrecks found in 177–178, 183–184
Niantic (ship) 184–185
Ninth Wave, The (Aivzovsky) 49
NOAA (National Oceanic and Atmospheric Administration) 23–25, 88, 136–137, 245–246, 245f
Nonantum (ship) 15–17
North Alabama (ship) 250–251
Northwest Passage exploration 11, 63, 67–72
Nuestra Señora de las Mercedes (ship) 171–172

O
OceanGate 105–106
Oceanic (ship) 9
Ocean Infinity 258–259
ocean temperature and acidification 252
Odyssey (Homer) 7
Odyssey Marine Exploration (OME) 171–172
Offshore Services Association (OSA) 150–152
oil leaks from shipwrecks 23–25
oil recovery from shipwrecks 146–147
oil tankers, shipwrecks of 76–77, 146–147
Okeanos Explorer (ship) 245–246
OME (Odyssey Marine Exploration) 171–172
O'Neill, Hugh 153
"one more voyage" mindset 199–206
"Open Boat, The" (Crane) 41–43
"Operation Crossroads" 18–19
Oquendo (ship) xiv
OSA (Offshore Services Association) 150–152
Ostfriesland (ship) 18
Our Blue Planet (Ford, Halligan, & Catsambis) 209
"Our Sea Heroes" (Thibault) 45–46

Our Seamen: An Appeal (Plimsoll) 5–6
Oxford (ship) 136–137

P
Pacificateur (ship) 18
Pacific Missile Range Facility 25–26
Pacific Northwest coast, shipwrecks in 129–134
"Pacific Pearl Company 1869" (song) 233
paintings of shipwrecks 48–56
Paixhans, Henri-Joseph 18
Palo Alto (ship) 27
Panagiotis (ship) 111–112
Panamá pearl fishery 231–234
Parker, Gilman C. 20–21
parks, shipwrecks in 106–110
Parry, William Edward 67–70
particle detectors 227
particularism 206–208
Partners for Livable Communities 219
Patriot (ship) 223
patrons of archaeology 176–177
Pearl Harbor xv
Pearson, Natali 169
Pederson, Ralph K. 33–34
Pellegrino, Charles 87–88
Perez-Alvaro, Elena 78–79, 227
Perfect Storm, The (film) 57, 223
Perfect Storm, The (Junger) 13–14, 57, 223
Peru, shipwrecks off coast of 202–204
Peter Iredale (ship) 112–113
petroglyphs of wrecks 132–133
Philadelphia (ship) 179–180
Philosophical Enquiry into Our Ideas of the Sublime and Beautiful (Burke) 35
photography, shipwreck 51–56
photomosaics of shipwrecks 54–56, 246–247
Piccard, Jacques 105–106
Pier 21 in Halifax, Canada 121
plaques, placing on shipwrecks 89
pleasure barges 179
Pleasure of Ruins (Macaulay) 111–112
Plimmer, John 185
Plimsoll, Samuel 5–6
Plimsoll line 5–6
poetry, about shipwrecks 34–35, 38–39, 57
polar exploration 11, 63, 67–72
Pollard, George 30–31

pollution from shipwrecks 18–19, 22–25, 213–214
Polynesian voyaging canoe x, 174–175
Pomo people 134–135
Pond, B. F. 1
popular culture, shipwrecks in
  accounts of undersea explorers 57–60
  in art 48–56
  in films 56–57
  in literature 38–43
  in music and songs 43–47
  in religion 34–35
  tales of shipwrecks 36–38
  underwater photography and film 51–56
ports, shipwrecks in 8–9
power of sea, as cause of shipwrecks 12–14
Prat, Arturo 85–86
pre-atomic steel 227
Princess May (ship) 51–52, 51*f*
Princess Sophia (ship) 84
Prinz Eugen (ship) 24–25
prop wash deflection 160–161
Purcell, Jesse 120
Puretić, Mario 224–225
Puretic Block 224–226

Q
Quebec City bateaux 184

R
Rabbi Akiva 34–35
Racal-Decca 150–152
radioactive waste 18–19, 22–23
Rae, John 68
Raise the Titanic (Cussler) 59
raising of wrecks
  Cairo 180
  County Hall Ship 177, 183–184
  displaying in museums 113–124
  Kateri i Radës 92–94
  Mary Rose 62, 116–117, 197–198
  Maud 71–72
  Nanhai #1 wreck 121
  Philadelphia 179–180
  Vasa 180–182
Randolph, D. 13
Readfearn, Graham 222

rebreathers 101
recovery of dead from shipwrecks 83–87
refugee shipwrecks 91–94
refugia 97–98, 122–123
registered professional archaeologists (RPAs) 167
regulations for ships 3–6
Reichert, Joshua 224
religious responses to shipwrecks 34–35, 45
remotely operated vehicles (ROVs) 22–23, 184–187, 200, 245–246
REMUS 6000 autonomous vehicles 156–157
Renan, Ary 49–50
replicas of ships 62, 168
Resolve Marine 24–25, 146–147
Rich, Sara A. 53–54, 95, 213–214
Riding, Christine 48
Riley, H. McGuire 153
Risdon Beazley 147–149
Rissolo, Dominique 55–56
river shipwrecks, climate change and 250–252
RMS *Titanic* Memorial Act of 1985 89
Roche, Emma 75
Rogers, Stan 47
Roman-era wrecks 184, 256
romantic value of shipwrecks 111–113
Ronson Ship 183–184
Roraima (ship) 29–30
Roskilde ships, Denmark 113–114, 182, 183*f*
Ross, John 67–70
Rouja, Philippe 55–56
ROVs (remotely operated vehicles) 22–23, 184–187, 200, 245–246
Royal Charter (ship) 39–40
RPAs (registered professional archaeologists) 167
Rush, Stockton 105
Russalka (ship) xiii
Russalka Memorial in Estonia 80–81
Russian *Mir* submersibles 102–105

S
sailboats, causes of shipwrecks in 6–8
Saint-Malo, France 7–8
Saint Paul 34–35

salvage
　of bullion and specie
　　Belitung shipwreck 165–169
　　from *Central America* 158–159
　　from Edinburgh 149–152
　　funding for treasure hunting 169–173
　　global antiquities trade 160
　　international disputes over
　　　156–158, 165–169
　　from Islander 154–155
　　from *John Barry* 152–154
　　litigation and 158–159
　　prop wash deflection 162–163
　　from *San José* 156–158
　　shipwreck archaeology 167
　　versus treasure hunting 149–150
　　treasure hunting versus
　　　archaeology 163–169
　　from *Whydah* 162–163
　of *Costa Concordia* 144–146, 145f
　impoverished communities and
　　226–230
　of oil from *Coimbra* 146–147
　overview 142–144
　revenues from 143–145
　Risdon Beazley 147–149
　scrapping of military
　　shipwrecks 226–229
Salvage Association of London 155
salvaging from shipwrecks
　by coastal communities 125, 127–128
　by Indigenous peoples 129–131
Samuel S. Lewis (ship) 4, 5f
San Agustin (ship) 129–131
San Francisco Xavier (ship) 129
San José (ship) 156–158, 165
Santo Cristo de Burgos (ship) 129–131
saturation diving 102, 151
Scandinavian museums 113–116
Scandinavism 61–62
Schneider, Tsim 136–137
Schwemmer, Robert 135
Scott Byram 135
scrambling devices 210–211
scrapping of military shipwrecks 226–229
scuba diving to shipwrecks 99–102, 102f,
　　123. See also diving to shipwrecks
scuttling 17–27
　artificial reefs 26–27
　barratry 20

burial at sea 20
environmental consequences 20–25
ghost fleets 18–20, 251–252
SINKEXs 21–22, 25–26
in wars 17–18, 20
weapons testing 18–19
Scylla 6–7
Sea Beast, The (film) 56
Seabed 2030 239–240
seabed mapping 239–240, 256–257
Sea Hunt (TV series) 186
Sea Hunters, The (TV series) 59, 261
sea ice, ships trapped in 10
sea mines 18
SEARCH, Inc. 188f, 254–255
Sea Search Armada (SSA) 156–158
2 Corinthians 11:25 34–35
Shackleton, Ernest 10, 71
shallow submersible diving 106
Sherrell, Andy 258
shipbuilding, study of 195–200
ship collision shipwrecks 9
ships as human achievements 193–206,
　"big questions" in archaeology ·
　　196–197
　family tree of the ship 193–194
　handling of cargoes 197
　particular areas of archaeological
　　study 194–196
　shipbuilding 195–199
　study of amphorae 194–195
　study of bones 194
ship traps 7–8, 201–202
Shipwreck Alley 108
Shipwreck Anthropology (Gould)
　209–210
shipwreck biodiversity 97–99
shipwreck CSI xii–xiii
Shipwreck Hauntography (Rich) 54
shipwrecking, as deliberate action
　127–128
shipwrecks
　defined 2
　disasters and regulations 3–6
　fires as cause of 14–17
　grief after 31–32
　human error as cause of 6–9
　ice as cause of 9–12
　nature of 2–3
　power of sea as cause of 12–14

scuttling 17–27
   unusual losses 28–32
   war as cause of 28
Shipwrecks (Yoshimura) 125
Shipwrecks and the Bounty of the Sea
      (Cressy) 125, 127
shipwreck trail 106–107
Shoemaker, Brian 153
Sibilia (ship) 92–94
silver, recovery of. *See* bullion and specie,
      salvage of
SINKEXs 21–22, 25–26
site formation processes 212–213
slave ships 72–76, 213–214, 257
Slave Wrecks Project (SWP) 213–214
Sloane, Nick 144–146
snorkeling, shipwrecks and 99–101
Somers (ship) xiii
songs about shipwrecks 43–47
South Dakota (ship) 250–251
Southey, Robert 36
South Seas, shipwrecks in 137–141
Spanish-American War xiv
Spanish shipwrecks
   emergence of underwater archaeology
      and 190–191
   looting of 161–162
   Manila galleon shipwrecks 129–131
   Nuestra Señora de las Mercedes
      171–172
   San José 156–158
   treasure hunting in 236
Sparrow-Hawk (ship) 111–112, 112*f*, 177
St. Augustine (Florida), wreck found
      in 254–256
Steamboat Act of 1838 3–4
Steamboat Inspection Service 4–5
steamboats, accidents and regulation
      of 3–5, 5*f*
Steffy, J. Richard 177–178
Stella Maris (Demont-Breton) 49
Stephaniturm (ship) 150–152
Stevenson, Robert Louis 127–128
St. James's cemetery (Liverpool),
      memorial in 79
Stockholm (ship) 9
Stone Fleet 17
storms, as cause of shipwrecks 12–14
straits, shipwrecks in 6–7
Straits of Messina 6–7

stranding, as cause of shipwreck 6–7
Straus, Isidor and Ida 81–82
St. Roch (ship) 63, 69
sublime nature of shipwrecks 35
submarine armor 235
Sub Marine Explorer (submarine)
      xiii, 230–234
submarines xvi
submersibles 102–103, 190
Sullenberger, Chesley "Sully" 28–29
Sultana (ship) 4–5, 15
superstitions of sailors 77–78
Susan Sturgis (ship) 132
Sutton Hoo (England), boat excavation
      in 178–179
SWP (Slave Wrecks Project) 213–214
Sylt island wrecks 249–250
symbols, shipwrecks as 36, 61–64, 93
Syrian civil war, wrecks with
      refugees from 91

T

tales of shipwrecks 36–38
Tay (ship) 249
Taylor, Joan du Plat 189
Taylor, William 58, 235
tea clippers 65–67
technical diving 101–102
telepresence 240–242, 245*f*
television series about shipwrecks 58–60,
      186, 261
Tempest, The (Shakespeare) xi, 95
Tenerife airport disaster 28–29
Tennessee (ship) 4, 5*f*
Tennyson, Alfred 79
Terror (ship) 11–12, 68–71, 253
Thibault, E. J. 45–46
Thompson, Tommy G. 159
Thoreau, Henry David 39
three-dimensional digital
      imagery 54–56, 245–246
Throckmorton, Peter 170–171,
      187–190, 236
"Throw Out the Lifeline" (Ufford) 45
Thucydides 7
Thunder Bay National Marine
      Sanctuary 100–101, 101*f*, 108
"time capsules," concept of shipwrecks
      as 119–121, 180, 208–211,
      242–243

Titanic (ship)
  accident investigation 3
  discovery of 87–88
  films about 56–57
  first detailed survey of 211
  Ghosts of the Abyss 110, 215–216
  as gravesite 87–89
  high-resolution images of 55
  international standards set after sinking of 6
  memorial to dead 81–82
  Mir submersible dives to 102–106, 103*f*
  museums 122
  news of shipwreck 31
  photographs of dead and personal effects xii
  poem about 57
  recovery of bodies from 86–87
  songs about 45–47
  as well-known wreck ix
Titanic Belfast museum 122
Titanic Museum in Pigeon Forge, Tennessee 122
Titan submersible 105–106
tombs, shipwrecks as 83
tombs, shipwrecks buried in 178
Tomlinson, H. M. 43
Toms Point, California 136–137
Tonquin (ship) 133–134
torpedo testing 18
Torres Strait islanders 138–139
tourism, on and at shipwreck sites 99–106,
  aesthetic and romantic values of wrecks 111–113
  biodiversity on shipwrecks 97–99
  in parks and marine sanctuaries 106–110
  scuba diving and snorkeling 99–102
  shipwrecks in museums 113–124
  Sub Marine Explorer (submarine) 233–234
  submersibles 102–106
  undersea museums 106–110
trading ships, shipwrecks of 65–67, 202–204
tragedies of shipwrecks 31–32
"Tragedy of Otranto" 92–94
Trapani, Maria Chiara Di 92
Trask, Harry 51–52
Traven, B. 5–6
trawling, damage to shipwrecks from 221–226
"treasure coast" of Florida 161–162, 171–172

treasure hunting
  commercial treasure salvage and 234–238
  financing of 169–173
  legal and financial problems 171–172
  looting 159–161
  prop wash deflection 162–163
  salvaging versus 149–150
  versus shipwreck archaeology 163–169, 186–187
tube worms 97, 253
Turner, J. M. W. 49
Turner, Tony S. 174
Tveskov, Mark 135
Twain, Mark 40–41
two-dimensional digital imagery 54–56
Tyjger (ship) 177–178, 183–184

U

U-215 (submarine) 149
U-701 (submarine) 102*f*
Ufford, Edward S. 45
Uluburun ship, Turkey 194, 197, 210
undersea explorers, accounts of 57–60
undersea museums 106–110
Undersea World of Jacques Cousteau, The (TV series) 58, 186
underwater archaeology
  emergence of 186–187
  Gelidonya wreck as first project 187–190
  technological developments and growth of field 190–193, 237–238
underwater photography and film 51–56
Unseaworthy Ships Bill 5–6
US Airways Flight 1549 28–29
U.S. Civil War shipwrecks xiii
  emergence of underwater archaeology and 190–191
  in museums 117
  scuttled ships 17
  USS *Monitor* 64–65
USNS *General Hoyt S. Vandenberg* (ship) 110
USS *Arizona* (ship) 80, 80*f*, 90–91
USS *Baltimore* (ship) xiv
USS *Edsall* (ship) 260
USS *Hatteras* (ship) 55
USS *Independence* (ship) 22–23, 225–226, 245*f*
USS *Johnston* (ship) 247–248
USS *Kailua* (ship) xv–xvi

INDEX

USS *Maine* (ship) 81, 84–85
USS *Merrimac* (ship) xiv
USS *Mississinewa* (ship) 23
USS *Monitor* (ship) 64–65, 65f, 117–119, 198–199
USS *Nevada* (ship) 19f
USS *Oriskany* (ship) 27
USS *Peterson* (ship) 21–22
USS *Stewart* (ship) xv–xvi, 258–259
USS *Tecumseh* (ship) 199
USS *Utah* (ship) 90

V

Valencia (ship) 126–127
Vancouver (ship) 132
Vancouver Maritime Museum 131
Vandenberg (ship) 110
Van Dover, Cindy 244
Varotsos, Costas 94
Vasa (ship) 62, 114–116, 180–182, 198–199
Vasa Museum, Sweden 114–116
Verne, Jules 96
Vernet, Claude-Joseph 48
Vernon Basin 2109 Shipwreck 201
Vescovo, Victor 105–106
Vestris (ship) 51–52
Vicar of Bray (ship) 253
Victory (ship) 62
Vietnam, salvaging in 230
Viking (ship) 62
Viking Ship Museum at Roskilde, Denmark 113–114
Viking Ship Museum in Oslo, Norway 182–183
Viking ships 61–62, 113–116, 178–179, 182, 183f
Villeroi, Brutus de 235
Virgil 7
Vizcaya (ship) xiv
volcanic eruptions, as cause of shipwrecks 29–30

W

Walsh, Don 105–106
war, as cause of shipwrecks 28
Waterworld (film) 76–77
weapons testing 18–19, 19f, 21–22, 25–26
Wellington (New Zealand), discovery of *Inconstant* in 185

Westerdahl, Christer 209–210
whaling ships 30–31, 65–66
Wharton, Ric 150–152
Wharton & Williams 150–152
"When That Great Ship Went Down" (song) 46–47
Whydah (ship) 162–163, 170
William C. Ralston (ship) 23
William Gray (ship) 184–185
William H. Sumner (ship) 249
Winchell, Al 84
Winchell, Ilene 84
wind, as cause of shipwrecks 12–14
"Windjammer Wreck" 201–202
Wonders of Salvage (Masters) 142
Wood, George Thomas "Tom" 136–137
Wood, Peter 50
"world's oldest wreck" 256
World War I xiv–xv, 20
World War II
    author's exploration of warships from xv–xvi
    D-Day 17–18
    ghost fleet in Serbia 251–252
    memorials to dead in shipwrecks 81
    recent discoveries of shipwrecks from 259–260
    recovery of oil from sunken ships 24–25
    salvage of bullion and specie from shipwrecks 149–154
    salvage of ships after 147–149
    scuttling in 17–18, 23
    shipwrecks in 28
worms 97, 253
wreck diving. *See* diving to shipwrecks
Wrecked Among Cannibals in the Fijis (Endicott) 137–138
wrecking ships 127–128
"Wreck of the *Edmund Fitzgerald*, The" (Lightfoot) 47
"Wreck of the *Hesperus*, The" (Longfellow) 38–39

Y

Yoshimura, Akira 125

Z

Zegrahm Expeditions 102–103
Zwick, Daniel 249–250